Integrating NetWare Into The Enterprise Network

Mark

I really appreciate your support in making networking a reality

INTEGRATING NETWARE INTO THE ENTERPRISE NETWORK

Kurt Ziegler, Jr.

A Wiley-Interscience Publication

JOHN WILEY & SONS, INC.

New York   •   Chichester   •   Brisbane   •   Toronto   •   Singapore

Copyright © 1994 by John Wiley & Sons, Inc.

Library of Congress Cataloging in Publication Data:

Integrating netWare into the enterprise nework/
Kurt Ziegler, Jr.
  p. cm.
"A Wiley-Interscience publication."
Includes index.
ISBN 0-471-01584-9 (paper: acid-free paper)

Printed in the United States of America

10 9 8 7 6 5 4 3 2 1

Printed and bound by Malloy Lithographing, Inc.

Contents

Preface

This book describes how enterprises are integrating NetWare and NetWare-related products into their enterprise network. The emphasis is on identifying the enterprise network issues and how NetWare can help the enterprise to meet its business goals.

Novell's NetWare is one of the core software products that has and continues to receive significant visibility as one of the major keys to high productivity and organizational responsive to business needs at a departmental and interdepartmental level. NetWare has provided a technical basis for network computing and client-server solutions. The next evolutionary step is to apply the NetWare-based technologies to the enterprise network. This step is probably more of an organizational, philosophical, and communications challenge than a technical challenge, although there are many technical considerations.

Most NetWare users use the term NetWare LAN (local area network) to refer to an environment that has a NetWare network operating system and numerous other NetWare-based and NetWare complementary applications. As a result a simple one liner:"We used NetWare to downsize," is not very informative to someone trying to find a solution to their integration challenge.

The first step to moving NetWare into the enterprise network context is to understand that the term *NetWare* has come to mean much more than a network operating system piece of software.

In this book I put some meat around the term NetWare in the broader view. After reading this book you should be more aware of the options and considerations associated with integrating NetWare into your company and more confident in the technical flexibility inherent in the implementation.

I was motivated to write this book by a number of business and technical professional colleagues who have been frustrated in their attempts to find any management-level information that ties NetWare network computing capabilities and implementations with their existing mainframe or midrange systems. These

Changing Environment
- **Workstations**
- **LANs**
- **Network integration**

Book describes:
- **Network computing**
- **Client-server**
- **NetWare integration with existing**

Book discusses NetWare in the broader context

New terms but no magic
- Downsizing
- Rightsizing
- Object-oriented
- Reengineering
- Open

friends have identified a huge experiential, objectives, and communications gap between the professionals selling, designing, installing, and managing departmental solutions using network computing and those professionals who have spent the last two decades implementing what is frequently referred to as legacy systems. The material includes analysis of some popular approaches to responding to technology change. These approaches include techniques associated with downsizing, rightsizing, and reengineering in an enterprise network context.

This book is intended to bridge the information gap for those with enterprises that have or are planning to support mixed workstation environments that include DOS, Windows, OS/2, Macs, and UNIX; one or more network operating system, including NetWare; one or more mainframe and midrange system; and have various wide area network connections including an SNA network.

Overview of what works today

The information is intended to help those trying to visualize the integrated network computing and client-server environment, those planning on integrating such a network and those trying to manage the resulting integrated environment. This is done by discussing the business, organizational, cultural, and technical aspects of integrating NetWare into the existing enterprise network. The topics are presented at various levels of detail ranging from the conceptual and practical applications right down to some very detailed examples as warranted.

This book is not a substitute for how-to-use or reference books. There are already many very good books regarding NetWare, mainframes, midrange systems, TCP/IP, and SNA already available. I have identified several in the bibliography. Instead this book addresses the areas that these books usually don't cover - how the various pieces work together and how they can be managed.

Why should I read this book?

This is the only book available that comprehensively describes implementation and management considerations associated with integrating Novell NetWare network computing and client-server into an enterprise with IBM midrange and mainframe systems.

This book provides insights on how your company can economically and responsively introduce the newer information technologies required to meet your business needs without having to start-from-scratch. It also discusses how the newer technologies can yield an immediate and long-term return on your technology investment (ROTI). The discussions include exploring functions and technologies, and approaches that can help in the management of the inherent complexity introduced when integrating function and support capabilities across an enterprise network. Armed with this information you will be able to chart your course to providing the required services while reducing the effort and time required to sort through the large number of decisions and trade-offs associated with selecting a technology or product to compete in a constantly changing business environment.

Information Technology
● **Important to compete**
● **How to assure ROTI**

Integration from terminal emulation to interoperability

The discussions and explanations in this book can save you and your company considerable hours of analysis, false starts, and rework as your enterprise network evolves.

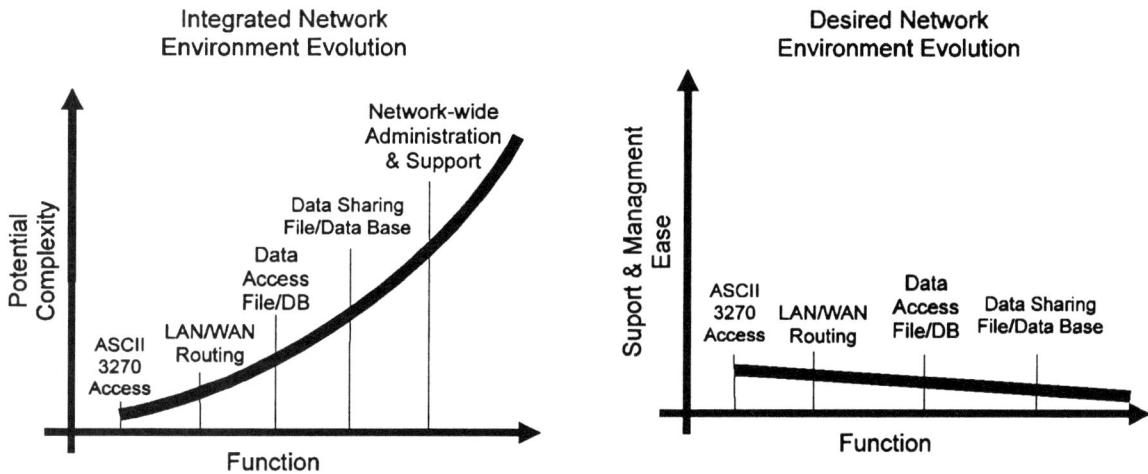

Integrated Network Environment Evolution

Desired Network Environment Evolution

Who should read this book?

This book is directed at those brave business and technical professionals who have accepted the challenge of trying to posi-

Audience.
- CIO
- IS Executive
- LAN administrator
- Network supervisor
- Integrator
- Consultant

tion and manage information technology for their business in the 1990s. Specifically, those individuals responsible for leveraging current information systems investments with the ever-changing information technologies in response to the very dynamic business environment.

If you are looking at this book you are probably:

- A chief information officer (CIO), IS, or MIS executive

- An information systems (IS) professional in a traditional IS organization

- A LAN administrator, LAN manager, Network manager, or professional responsible for a specific business organization (e.g., department)

- An integrator or consultant who is interested in the integration of NetWare LANs with their company's or client's company traditional information systems

Each of you come from different backgrounds and have both common and sometimes conflicting, motivations and objectives, concerns, scope of responsibilities, and business measurements. However, you all share the need to understand these differences since you recognize that this understanding is fundamental to a successful integration.

You also probably already understand that to maximize the benefits of the newer information technology capabilities at an enterprise level, the personnel responsible for the integration of the technologies must understand the attributes and considerations of both the existing and the new.

To help you in this regard this book discusses solutions ranging from terminal emulation to seamless interoperability with total systems (network) management using cost-effective approaches to opening up SNA networks and IBM mainframes with NetWare and NetWare-based applications.

Business and technical considerations

The NetWare integration considerations are presented in terms of the business, organizational, funding, control approaches, connectivity, information sharing, tools, network management, service-level management, security, adaptability, and cost aspects being experienced by representative 1000 companies.

After reading this book you should be more aware of the options and considerations associated with integrating NetWare into your company and more confident in your technical flexibility.

How should I read this book?

It is unrealistic to discuss NetWare as a piece of code or an operating system that supports LANs, since even though that might have been how it was described in the beginning, it has significantly expanded its scope and has been augmented and complemented with literally thousands of applications and management tools. As such, this book discusses this broader view since that is really what integrating into the enterprise network is all about.

The topics include such management considerations as why companies are changing the way they provide IS services, what client-server technology is and how it is being applied, what client-server applications are and how they can be applied. The book also delves into mainframe and midrange connectivity options and flexibility as well as the management of a potentially different network.

Discusses NetWare in the broader enterprise context

Several chapters describe how NetWare and NetWare-associated tools and facilities can be used to improve the service controls and improve the overall productivity of the user. Additionally, there are several chapters that describe NetWare services and structure. These chapters answer many of the pertinent system management questions that must be answered for any industrial strength-operating system environment, including such items as how various workstation operating systems are supported, security, data backup/recovery, accounting, print services, and remote access.

NetWare discussions include:
- *network*
- *server support*
- *client support*
- *network management*

Because of the breadth of the pertinent aspects of integrating NetWare into the enterprise it is expected that readers will come from a very diverse background of experience and terminology. Some readers who have been charged with integrating NetWare into the enterprise will never have even seen a mainframe, AS/400 or VAX system or its attached terminals much less the management infrastructure around it. Other readers will never have seen or used a server, much less a NetWare server. To both of these example groups the other environment is often alien from a terminology, technology, and management philosophy standpoint.

This book tries to speak to both types of audience. The book is structured with the expectation that you are interested in only some very specific aspects of the integration. Graphics are used to reinforce concepts and allow you to visualize many of those considerations that are difficult to describe with the current vocabulary.

Because of the various backgrounds and the merging of multiple technology solutions, it has become almost impossible to pragmatically discuss business and technical information technology solutions without resorting to terminology that has either lost its traditional meaning or may in fact have several very diverse meanings. I recommend that as you scan this book you also scan those items that you are intimately familiar with since the way these technologies and terminology apply in the new enterprise network context may be different.

Kurt Ziegler, Jr.

San Jose, California

Acknowledgments

I would like express my appreciation to my wife, Dianne, for her long hours of text entry, editing, and patience, to Novell and the numerous folks who took the time to provide me with information and feedback, to the many other vendors and consultants who provided me with information, demonstrations and insights, and last but not least, to the many business and technical folks who helped me tell their story.

Trademark Acknowledgments

Every effort has been made to supply trademarks about company names, products, and services mentioned in this book. Listed below are the trademarks that I was able to compile. Images used in this document include some protected by copyright. Sources include CorelDRAW, New Vision Technologies, Inc.'s Presentations Task Force, and Software Publishing Corp.'s Harvard Draw.

80386™ of Intel Corp.
80486™ of Intel Corp.
3Com™ of 3Com Corp.
Acer® of Acer America Corp.
ACF/VTAM™ of International Busines Machines Corp.
AIX® of International Business Machines Corp.
ALR® of Advanced Logic Research, Inc.
Anthem® of Anthem Electronics, Inc.
Apple® of Apple Computer, Inc.
AppleShare™ of Apple Computer, Inc.

AppleTalk®of Apple Computer Inc.

Archive® of Archive Corp.

ArCNet® of Datapoint Corp.

AS/400™ of International Business Machines Corp.

ASCII is a designation of the American National Standard Code of Information
    Interchange

ASCOM IV® of Dynamic Microprocessor Associates

Ashton-Tate® of Ashton-Tate Corp.

AST® of AST Research, Inc.

AT® of International Business Machines Corp.

AT&T® American Telephone & Telegraph

ATerm™ of Dynamic Microprocessor Associates

Btrieve™ of Novell, Inc.

Certified NetWare Engineer is a collective mark of Novell, Inc.

Certified NetWare Instructor is a collective mark of Novell, Inc.

Codex® of Codex Corp.

Compaq® of Compaq Computer Corp.

CompuServe® of CompuServe, Inc.

Connecting/Room™ of Helix

Corvus Omninent™ of Corvus Systems

CP/M™ of Digital Research, Inc., a wholly owned subsidiary of Novell, Inc.

Crosstalk® of Persoft, Inc.

Da Vinci Systems ® of Da Vinci Systems Corp.

DB2™ of IBM Database 2

dBase™ of Ashton-Tate Corp.

DCA® of Digital Communications Associates, Inc.

DEC®of Digital Equipment Corp.

DECnet™of Digital Equipment Corp.

DFSMS™ of International Business Machines Corp.

DIGITAL™ of Digital Equipment Corp.

DrawPerfect™ of WordPerfect Corp.

DR DOS® of Novell, Inc.

DR DOS LANPack™ of Digital Research, Inc.,a wholly owned subsidiary of Novell,
Inc.

DR Multiuser DOS™ of Digital Research, Inc., a wholly owned subsidiary of Novell,
Inc.

DynaComm® of Future Soft Engineering, Inc.

Dynamic M design® of Memorex Telex N.V.

Emerald Systems™ of Emerald Systems Corp.

Enterprise System/9000™ of International Business Machines Corp.

Enterprise System Connection Architecture™ of International Business Machines Corp.

ES/9000™ of International Business Machines Corp.

ESCON™ of International Business Machines Corp.

EtherLink™ of 3Com Corp.

EtherLink II™ of 3Com Corp.

EtherLink Plus™ of 3Com Corp.

EtherTalk®of Apple Computer, Inc.

Everex® of Everex Systems, Inc.

Excel™ of Microsoft Corp.

EXOS 205™ of Novell, Inc.

EXOS 215™ of Novell, Inc.

FastPath™ of Novell, Inc.

File Express™ of Novell, Inc.

FlexNET™ of Digital Research, Inc., a wholly owned subsidiary of Novell, Inc.

FlexOS™ of Digital Research, Inc., a wholly owned subsidiary of Novell, Inc.

Framework™ of Ashton-Tate Corp.

Gigatrend® of Gigatrend, Inc.

Gupta™ of Gupta Technologies, Inc.

Harvard Graphics® of Software Publishing   Corp.

Hayes® of Hayes Microcomputer Products, Inc.

Hewlett-Packard® of Hewlett-Packard   Company

HP® of of HewlettPackard Company

Host Presenter™ of Novell, Inc.

Hot Fix™ of Novell, Inc.

HyperCard™ of Apple Computer, Inc.

IBM® of International Business Machines Corp.

IBM-AT™ of International Business Machines Corp.

ImageWriter® of Apple Computer, Inc.

Intel® of Intel Corp.

InterConnections™ of InterConnections, Inc., an Emulex Company

Internetwork Packet Exchange™ of Novell, Inc.

IPX™ of Novell, Inc.

IRMA™ of Digital Communications Associates

LANalyzer™ of Novell, Inc.

LAN Manager™ of Microsoft Corp.

LANtern™ of Novell, Inc.

LAN WorkPlace™ of Novell, Inc.

LaserWriter®of Apple Computer, Inc.

LAT™ of Digital Equipment Corp.

LattisNet™ of SynOptic Communications, Inc.

LC™ of Novell, Inc.

LocalTalk® of Apple Computer, Inc.

Lotus® of Lotus Development Corp.

Lotus 1-2-3® of Lotus Development Corp.

Macintosh®of Apple Computer, Inc.

MacTCP®of Apple Computer, Inc.

Maynard™ of Maynard Electronics, Inc.
MC68000™ of Motorola Corp.
Memorex Telex® of Memorex Telex N.V.
MICOM™ of MICOM Systems, Inc.
Micro Channel® of International Business Machines Corp.
Microcom® of Microcom Systems, Inc.
Microsoft® of Microsoft Corp.
MicroVAX™of Digital Equipment Corp.
Motorola® of Motorola Corp.
Mountain® of Mountain Network Solutions, Inc.
MS-DOS® of Microsoft Corp.
Multimodem™ of Multi-Tech Systems, Inc.
MVS™ of International Business Machines Corp.
MVS/ESA™ of International Business Machines Corp.
NASI™ of Novell, Inc.
NCR® of NCR Corp.
N-Design® of Novell, Inc.
NEC® of NEC Corp.
NetExplorer™ of Novell, Inc.
NetView® of International Business Machines Corp.
NetWare®of Novell, Inc.
NetWare 3270 LAN Workstation™ of Novell, Inc.
NetWare 3270 LAN Workstation for Macintosh™ of Novell, Inc.
NetWare Access Server™ of Novell, Inc.
NetWare Asynchronous Communication Services™ of Novell, Inc.
NetWare Asynchronous Services Interface™ of Novell, Inc.
NetWare Btrieve™ of Novell, Inc.
NetWare ElectroText™ of Novell, Inc.
NetWare Expert™ of Novell, Inc.
NetWare Express™ of Novell, Inc.
NetWare FleX/IP™ of Novell, Inc.
NetWare Global Messaging™ of Novell, Inc.
NetWare HUB Services™ of Novell, Inc.
NetWare Loadable Module™ of Novell, Inc.
NetWare Logotype (teeth)™ of Novell, Inc.
NetWare Management System™ of Novell, Inc.
NetWare Messaging CONNECT™ of Novell, Inc.
NetWare MultiProtocol Router™ of Novell, Inc.
NetWare Name Service™ of Novell, Inc.
NetWare NFS™ of Novell, Inc.
NetWare Print Server™ of Novell, Inc.
NetWare Runtime™ of Novell, Inc.
NetWare for SAA™ of Novell, Inc.

NetWare SQL™ of Novell, Inc.
Netwires a registered service mark of Novell, Inc.
Netwise™ of Netwise, Inc.
Network File System® of Sun Microsystems, Inc.
Network Support Encyclopedia™ of Novell, Inc.
Newport Systems Solutions™ of Newport Systems Solutions,
NFS™ of Sun Microsystems, Inc.
NSE® of Sun Microsystems, Inc.
Novell® of Novell, Inc.
Novell Authorized Education Center is a collective mark of Novell, Inc.
Novell Labs™ of Novell, Inc.
Office Vision™ of International Business Machines Corp.
Okidata® of Oki America, Inc.
One Slot™ of Star Gate Technologies, Inc.
OnLAN/MAC™ of Novell, Inc.
OnLAN/PC™ of Novell, Inc.
Operating System/2 ® of International Business Machines Corp.
Operating System/400® of International   Business Machines Corp.
Oracle® of Oracle Corp.
OS/2® of International Business Machines Corp.
OS/400® of International Business Machines Corp.
PageMaker® of Aldus Corp.
Paradox® of Borland International, Inc.
PC/AT® of International Business Machines Corp.
PC-DOS™ of International Business Machines Corp.
PC XT™ of International Business Machines Corp.
PD1508™ of Pure Data Ltd.
Persoft® of Persoft, Inc.
Personal Computer XT™ of International Business Machines Corp.
Personal Systems/2® of International Business Machines Corp.
Persuasion® of Aldus Corp.
PLUS™ of Western Digital Corp.
PostScript® of Adobe Systems, Inc.
Practical Peripherals® of Practical Peripherals, Inc.
PROFS® of International Business Machines Corp.
ProNET-10™ of Proteon, Inc.
Proprinter® of International Business Machines Corp.
Proteon™ of Proteon, Inc.
PROFS® of International Business Machines   Corp.
PS/2® of International Business Machines Corp.
Pure Data™ of Pure Data Ltd.
Q&A™ of Symantec Corp.
Quattro® of Borland International, Inc.

RISC System/6000™ of International Business Machines Corp.
RPC™ of Sun Microsystems, Inc.
S/370™ of International Business Machines Corp.
S/390™ of International Business Machines Corp.
SAA™ of International Business Machines Corp.
SCO™ of Santa Cruz Operations, Inc.
SFT™ of Novell, Inc.
SideKick® of Borland International, Inc.
Smartcom® of Hayes Microcomputer Products, Inc.
Smartmodem™ of Hayes Microcomputer Products, Inc.
Smartmodem 1200™ of Hayes Microcomputer Products, Inc.
Smartmodem 2400™ of Hayes Microcomputer Products, Inc.
Smartmodem 9600™ of Hayes Microcomputer Products, Inc.
SmarTerm® of Persoft, Inc.
SMC® of Standard Microsystems Corp.
SNA® of International Business Machines Corp.
Sony® of Sony Computer Peripheral Products Company
SQL/DS™ for IBM Structured Query Language/Data System
Standard Microsystems® of Standard Microsystems Corp.
StarLAN™ of American Telephone & Telegraph
Sun™ Of Sun Microsystems, Inc.
Sun Microsystems® of Sun Microsystems, Inc.
Sybase™ of Sybase, Inc.
Symantec™ of Symantec Corp.
System/370™ of International Business Machines Corp.
System/390™ of International Business Machines Corp.
System Application Architecture™ of International Business Machines Corp.
Syzygy Communications® of Syzygy Communications, Inc.
Syzygy Communications is a service mark of Syzygy Communications, Inc.
Tektronix™ of Tektronix, Inc.
Telebit® of Telebit
Telenet® of Telenet Communications Corp.
TeleVideo® of Televideo Systems, Inc.
Trailblazer® of Telebit Corp.
Trailblazer Plus™ of Telebit Corp.
Transactional Tracking System™ of Novell, Inc.
TTS™ of Novell, Inc.
ULTRIX™ of Digital Equipment Corp.
Unisys® of Unisys Corp.
UNIX® of UNIX Systems Laboratories, a subsidiary of American Telephone & Telegraph
USRobotics® of U.S. Robotics, Inc.
V-series™ of Hayes Microcomputer Products, Inc.

VAX™ of Digital Equipment Corp.

VAX/VMS Mail™ of Digital Equipment Corp.

ViewMAX™ of Digital Research, Inc., a wholly owned subsidiary of Novell, Inc.

VINES® of Banyan Systems, Inc.

Virtual Machine/Extended Architecture™ of International Business Machines Corp.

Visual Basic™ of Microsoft Corp.

VMS™of Digital Equipment Corp.

VM/XA™ of International Business Machines Corp.

VTAM™ of International Business Machines Corp.

Wang® of Wang Laboratories, Inc.

Western Digital®of Western Digital Corp.

WNIM® of Gateway Communications

WordPerfect® of WordPerfect Corp.

WORLDPORT™ of Touchbase Systems, Inc.

Wyse® of Wyse Technology

Xerox® of Xerox Corp.

X/GEM™ of Digital Research, Inc., a wholly owned subsidiary of Novell, Inc.

XQL™ of Novell, Inc.

XT™ of International Business Machines Corp.

Xtrieve® of Novell, Inc.

Xtrieve PLUS™ of Novell, Inc.

X-window System™ of Massachusetts Institute of Technology

Windows™ of Microsoft Corp.

Acronyms

AARP	AppleTalk Address Resolution Protocol
ABI	Application Binary Interface
ADSP	AppleTalk Data Stream Protocol
AEP	AppleTalk Echo Protocol
AFP	AppleTalk Filing Protocol
AIO	Asynchronous Input/Output
ALM	AppWare Loadable Module
ANSI	American National Standards Institute
API	Application Programming Interface
APPC	Advanced Program-to-Program Communications
APPN	Advanced Peer-to-Peer Networking
APT	Application Programmer's Toolkit
ARP	Address Resolution Protocol
ASCII	American Standard Code for Information Interchange
ATM	Asynchronous Transfer Mode
ATP	AppleTalk Transaction Protocol
ATPS	AppleTalk Print Services
ATXRP	AppleTalk Extended Remote Printer
BIOS	Basic Input/Output System

BOOTP	Bootstrap Protocol
BSD	Berkeley Software Distribution
CAD/CAM	Computer-aided Design/Computer-aided Manufacturing
CBT	Computer-based Training
CCITT	Consultative Committee on International Telegraph and Telephone
CD-ROM	Compact Disc Read-Only Memory
CGA	Color Graphic Adapter
CICS	IBM's Customer Information Control Systems
CIO	Chief Information Officer
CLIB	C-Library
CNA	Certified NetWare Administrator
CNE	Certified NetWare Engineer
CNI	Certified NetWare Instructor
COBOL	Common Business Oriented Language
CPI-C	Common Programming Interface-Communications
CPU	Central Processing Unit
CRT	Cathode ray Tube
CSL	Call Support Layer
CSMA	Carrier Sense Multiple Access
CSMA/CD	Carrier Sense Multiple Access with Collision Detection
CSU	Channel Service Unit
CSV	Comma-Separated Variable
DAL	Data Access Language
DATC	Drake Authorized Testing Centers
DBMS	Database Management System
DDE	Dynamic Data Exchange (Microsoft Windows)
DDS	Direct Digital Service
DEC	Digital Equipment Corporation
DES	Data Encryption Standard
DISOSS	Distributed Information Service Office Support System
DLL	Dynamic Link Library
DNS	Domain Name Service
DOS	Disk Operating System
DP	Dual Processor

DSM	Dedicated Server Module
DSU	Digital Service Unit
ECNE	Enterprise Certified NetWare Engineer
EDDP	Extended Datagram Delivery Protocol
EDP	Electronic Data Processing
EGA	Enhanced Graphic Adapter
EHLLAPI	Emulator High-level Language Application Programming Interface
EISA	Extended Industry Standard Architecture
ELAP	Ethernet Link Access Protocol
EMM	Expanded Memory Manager
EMS	Extended Memory Specifications
EOI	End of Interrupts
ESD	Electronic Software Distribution
ESDI	Enhanced Small Disk Interface
FAT	File Allocation Table
FDDI	Fiber Distributed Data Interface
FIPS	Federal Information Processing Standards
FSP	File Service Process
FTAM	File Telecommunications Access Method
FTP	File Transfer Protocol
GB	Gigabyte
GMHS	Global Message Handling Service
GOSIP	Government OSI Protocols
GUI	Graphical User Interface
HCSS	High-capacity Storage System
HLLAPI	High-Level Language/Application Program Interface
HMI	Hub Management Interface
I/O	Input/Output
IBM	International Business Machines
ICCCM	Interclient Communications Conventions
ICMP	Internet Control Message Protocol
IEEE	Institute of Electrical and Electronics Engineers
IETF	Internet Engineering Task Force
IMSP	Independent Manufacturer Support Program
IP	Internet Protocol
IPC	Interprocess Communications
IPX	Internetwork Packet Exchange

IS	Information Systems
ISA	Industry Standard Architecture
ISDN	Integrated Services Digital Network
ISO	International Standards Organization
IS-IS	Intermediate System to Intermediate System
ISV	Independent Software Vendors
KB	Kilobyte
Kbit	Kilobit
Kbps	Kilobits per second
LAN	Local Area Network
LAT	Local Area Transport
LIP	Large Internal Packets
LPD	Line Printer daemon
LPDCWY	Line Printer Gateway
LSL	Link Support Layer
LU	Logical Unit
MB	Megabyte
MCA	Microchannel Architecture
MHS	Message-handling Service
MIB	Management Information Base
MIS	Management Information Systems
MLID	Multiple Link Interface Driver
MSL	Mirrored Server Link
MVS	Multiple Virtual Storage
NACS	NetWare Asynchronous Communication Services
NAEC	Novell Authorized Education Center
NAS	Network Application Support
NASC	Novell Authorized Service Center
NASI	NetWare Asynchronous Services Interface
NBP	Name Binding Protocol
NCP	NetWare Core Protocol
NCS	Novell Consulting Services
NDIS	Network Device Interface Specification
NDS	NetWare Directory Services
NEAPs	Novell Education Academic Partners
NETUCONs	NetWare Users' Conferences
NFS	Network File System
NLM	NetWare Loadable Module

NLP	NetWare Lite Protocol
NMA	NetWare Management Agent
NMS	NetWare Management System
NNS	NetWare Name Service
NOS	Network Operating System
NPSI	Network Packet-Switching Interface
NSE	Network Support Encyclopedia
NSM	NetWare Services Manager
NSP	NetWare Lite Sideband Protocol
NTS	Novell Technical Support
NUC	NetWare UNIX Client
NUI	NetWare Users International
NVT	Novell Virtual Terminal
OA&M	Operations, Administrations, and Management
ODI	Open Data-link Interface
OEM	Original Equipment Manufacturer
OS	Operating System
OSF	Open Software Foundation
OSI	Open Systems Interconnection
OSPF	Open Shortest Path First Routing Protocol
PAP	Printer Access Protocol
PBX	Private Branch Exchange
PC	Personal Computer
PCS	IBM's Personal Computer Support Program
PDD	Physical Device Driver
PDP	Professional Developer's Program
POSIX	Portable Operating System Interface for UNIX
PPP	Point-to-Point Protocol
PROM	Program Read-Only Memory
PU	Physical Unit
QLLC	Qualified Logical-link Control
RAID	Redundant Array of Inexpensive Drives
RAM	Random Access Memory
RARP	Reverse Address Resolution Protocol
RCS	Resource Construction Set
RIP	Routing Information Protocol
RMCC	Ronald McDonald Children's Charities
RMF	Remote Management Facility

RMHS	Remote Message Handling Service
ROM	Read-Only Memory
RPC	Remote Procedure Call
SAA	System Application Architecture
SAP	Service Advertising Protocol
SBK	System Builder's Kit
SCO	Santa Cruz Operations, Inc.
SCSI	Small Computer System Interface
SDK	Software Developer's Kits
SDLC	Synchronous Data-link Control
SES	Strategic Engineering Support
SFT	System Fault Tolerance
SLIP	Serial Line Internet Protocol
SMB	Server Message Block
SMF	Standard Message Format
SMS	Storage Management System
SMTP	Simple Mail Transfer Protocol
SNA	System Network Architecture
SNADS	System Network Architecture Distribution Services
SNMP	Simple Network Management Protocol
SPX	Sequenced Packet Exchange
SQL	Structured Query Language
SVID	System V Interface Definition
SVGA	Super Video Graphics Array
SVR	UNIX System V Release
TB	Terabyte
TCP/IP	Transmission Control Protocol/Internet Protocol
TLI	Transport-level Interface
TSA	Technical Support Alliance
TSR	Terminate-and-Stay Resident
TTS	Transaction Tracking System
UDP	User Datagram Protocol
UPS	Uninterruptible Power Supply
USE	UnixWare Support Encyclopedia
UTP	Unshielded Twisted-pair Wiring
VAP	Value-added Process
VAR	Value-Added Reseller
VAX	Virtual Address Extender

VDD	Virtual Device Driver
VGA	Video Graphics Array
VLM	Virtual Loadable Module
VMS	Virtual Memory System
VTAM	Virtual Telecommunications Access Method
WAN	Wide-area Network
WKSH	Windowing Korn Shell
WNIM	Wide area Network Interface Module
WORM	Write Once, Read Many
WSUPDATE	Automated Workstation Software Update Utility
XDR	External Data Representation Protocol
ZIP	Zone Information Protocol

Integrating NetWare Into The Enterprise Network

Section 1

NetWare and the Enterprise Network

This section puts some structure around the term, enterprise network. It does this by defining some of the various boundaries that can be used to delimit the enterprise. The section goes on to describe how NetWare and Novell are positioned to play an important role as the enterprise network operating system.

The important ideas that should be gleaned from this section are:

- There are various boundaries that a company can set for the enterprise network. The boundary that most meets the business need usually ends within the users workstation or mobile computer.

- The ability to provide the user this desired boundary is a function of control and risk.

- The appropriate enterprise network technologies minimize the risk, provide maximum flexibility, and evolve with a company's needs.

- Novell's NetWare family of products is well positioned to provide the necessary network, internetwork, and workstation support required for the enterprise network of the 1990s. This family of products can provide maximum flexibility with minimum risk.

Chapter 1

The Enterprise Network

1.1 What is an Enterprise Network?

Enterprise network is usually the label for the centrally managed corporate wide communications network that connects and supports multiple organizations in multiple locations. The enterprise network may be used by users who depend entirely on the informations systems (IS) organization for information technology solutions and support, semiautonomous or fully autonomous organizations that can make their own information technology and application decisions but need to share a communications bandwidth, communications support, and access to their own department and IS-managed data. University environments are a good example of the latter.

Enterprise network provides centrally managed:
- **Connectivity**
- **Support**
- **Services**

The term *enterprise network* has also come to imply interconnection and user services that include information access, security, information protection, user workstation support, and even procurement and installation assistance. The enterprise network infrastructure is usually provided by the IS organization. The enterprise network IS organization usually has the responsibility of providing contracted levels of service that include such items as response time, availability, responsiveness and protection of the corporate information assets for the corporation. As such the enterprise network typically conveys the image of a *controlled* and *managed* environment that is comprised of a collection of diverse applications, different physical and logical connections, a variety of operating systems, and a diverse set of users who have different expectations and requirements.

Enterprise Network means:
- **Controlled**
- **Managed**
- **Service levels**

Enterprise Network
- **Interconnection**
- **Security**
- **Information protection**
- **User workstation support**
- **Procurement**
- **Installation help**

3

> **The enterprise network**
>
> - **Supports a variety of workstations**
> - **Supports a variety of interconnections**
> - **Delivers implied service level**
>
> *The enterprise network is the glue between the workstation and the services*

1.2 The Enterprise Network Boundaries

Multiple views of what an enterprise network is

If you were to do a survey today and ask what an enterprise network is, you would invariably get multiple and diverse answers. It seems as if any time people connect several workstations together using any kind of media, including wireless, they have an enterprise network. Figure 1-1 portrays this situation.

Since this book is focused on the enterprise network I must put more framework around the label. My model of the enterprise

NETWORK

Figure 1-1 Multiple Views of Network Boundaries

network extends from inside the workstation across all media and to the target resources, workstations, or mainframe as portrayed in Figure 1-2.

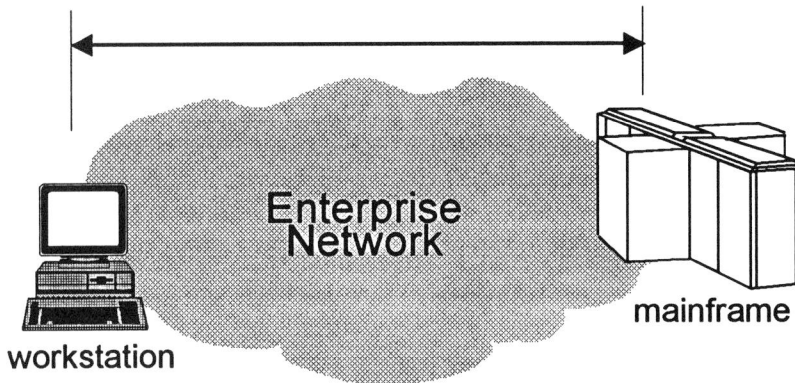

Figure 1-2 End-to-End Enterprise Network Boundary

By inside the workstation I mean that there are responsibilities that are associated with the enterprise network that tie to the usage and support of the workstation. I am not suggesting, nor precluding, that the workstation is owned and managed by the enterprise network. However, I am suggesting that independent of the ownership, there are enterprise network infrastructure responsibilities for the workstation. For example, a point-of-sale workstation is a clear candidate for being owned and managed by the enterprise network infrastructure. On the other hand, a departmental end user's workstation might more readily be owned and managed by the users or the local departmental administrator, while the enterprise network infrastructure would be responsible only for the workstation software and controls associated with accessing enterprise network resources.

Enterprise network extends from inside the workstations

With this definition I am explicitly describing a network with more inter-node management attributes than provided by a public "internet." By public *internet* I mean a physical network service that provides port-to-port connectivity. In this context, internets include networks such as are provided by Advantis, MCI, and Sprint. These networks can be viewed part of a company's enterprise network, but more often than not, only in the context of reliable communications. Therefore, if present, these internets can be viewed as a subset (*rented or leased portions*) of the enterprise network.

For general discussions this broad definition provides an outer boundary of the enterprise network. For practical application, however, it is appropriate to identify the specific lines of demarcation for the various services that the enterprise network organization(s) provides. It is also important to know why the demarcation boundary is important because they increase or decrease workload and support risk. When selecting these boundaries, security, value add, technical ability and costs dominate. Ironically, the extended boundaries may reduce the complexity rather than increase it. However, the simplification may require flexibility and control trade-offs by the workstation user.

The demarcation boundaries determine the quality of service and the demand for management technology

For example, how does your company treat interenterprise network connection and access? The demarcation boundary is ideally a port (or ports) that provide the access to network "A". (See Fig. 1-3.) Who is responsible for this port in terms of security, availability, and charges?

Each company will define their own boundaries

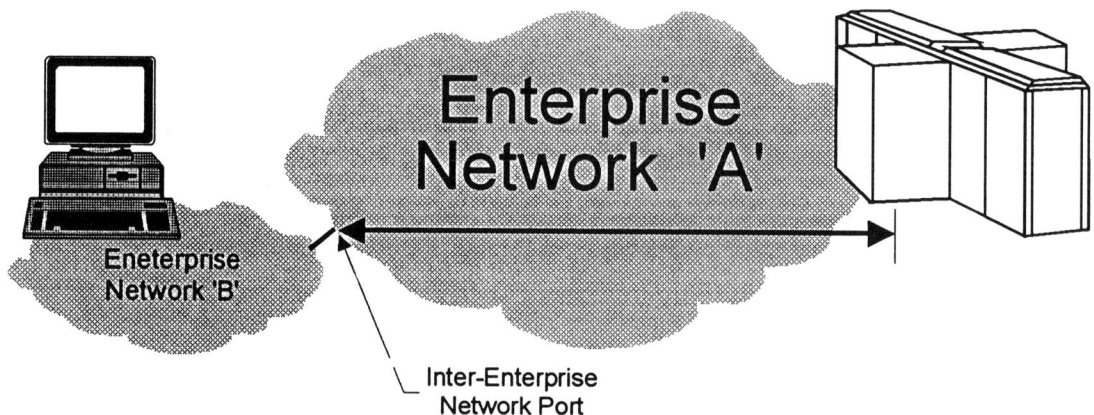

Inter-Enterprise
Network Port

Figure 1-3   Inter-Enterprise Port

The responsibility may reside at different points in your company when compared to another company, but the intent is usually the same. The objective is to minimize the expose of unauthorized access to corporate assets. In some cases, the controls vary within a company. In those cases where the risk or control is inadequate to meet the corporate standard, the access is limited to a local network with no paths into the enterprise network.

Individual workstations can be outside of the enterprise

Similarly, if a department has their own local area network and wants to connect to the enterprise network, the connection to the enterprise network could be managed or administered by the someone accountable to the enterprise network. (See Fig. 1-4.)

Department network can be outside of enterprise network

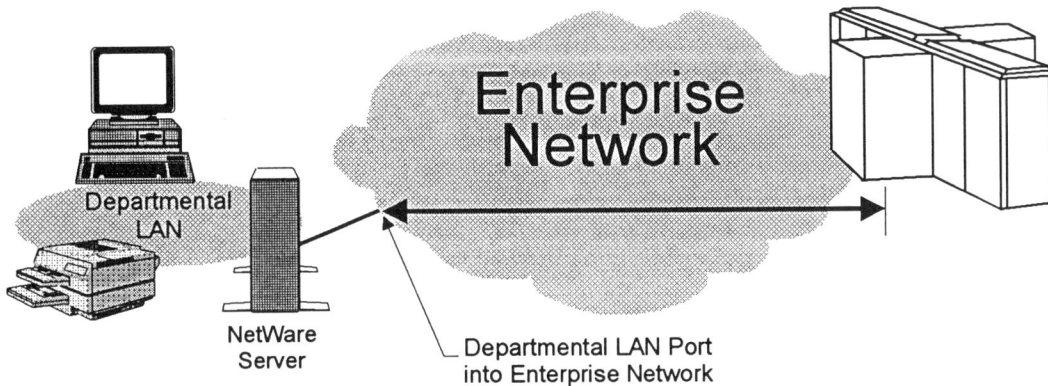

Figure 1-4 Enterprise Network Departmental Port

Figure 1-5 Workstation Network Boundary Example

A single workstation user wanting enterprise network connectivity can be treated similarly. In this case the boundary would be at the workstation port. (See Fig. 1-5.)

1.2.1 Two Approaches to Interconnection

However, there are two very different approaches to enterprise network interconnection that a user workstation might see: user controlled or enterprise network controlled. (See Fig. 1-6 and Fig. 1-7.)

The easiest network interconnection technique is using terminal emulation. (See Fig. 1-6.) The workstation user uses terminal emulation to access the enterprise resource as if the connection were via a terminal. This assures the network backbone supports the connection and demands minimum coordination between the

A connection port demarcation example

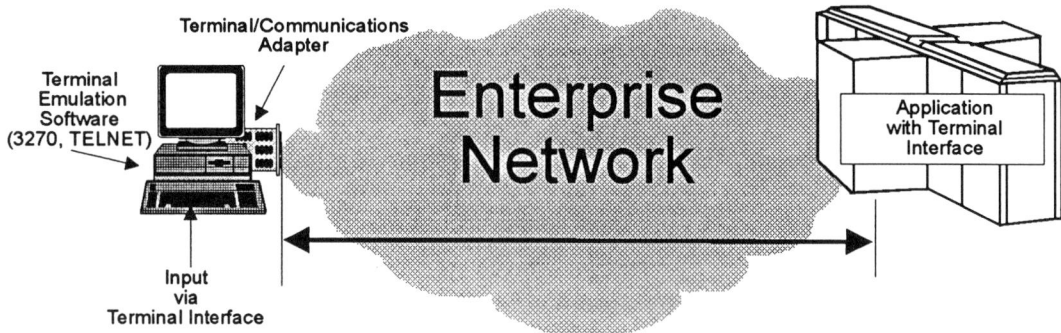

Figure 1-6 Emulation Software in Workstation Boundary

application and the user's workstation.

Examples of this terminal emulation connection are workstations with connection software such as IBM 3270 emulation software (Figure 1-6) or TCP/IP TELNET software that connects to the physical network and provides connectivity to existing applications.

The primary coordination required in supporting this boundary (the terminal emulation software boundary) is that: the terminal emulation software appears as a terminal type supported by the network, the appropriate addressing is set up, and the appropriate user authentication interfaces are available. This approach allows the enterprise network demarcation to end at the connection to the enterprise network (a network port). The primary corporate asset protection consideration is that as the user's access authority increases, the user is provided with increasingly more rigorous mechanisms for controlling unauthorized network access from the user's workstation. (These will be discussed in more detail later in this book.)

Some companies dictate which terminal emulators can be used with the network

The second enterprise network interconnection approach uses what I refer to as the *matched software* approach. The *matched software* resides at both ends of the connection. (See Fig. 1-7.) Applications using the matched software approach can provide more comprehensive interoperability and performance controls, but application development can be significantly more complex and the software requires rigorous coordination.

Figure 1-7   Matched Software Boundary

With the terminal emulation boundary, the target application only sees (or thinks it sees) a terminal on the other end of the network. With matched software, both ends of the connection are aware of the other.

There are various implementations of the matched software approach being used today. These implementations are identified with labels such as *distributed processing, peer-to-peer* and *client-server* applications. While these labels are often considered synonyms by many, others have identified subtle and important differences that directly affect the development and management complexity. Independent of their subtitles matched software implementations and terminal emulation come under the umbrella of distributed processing. Terminal emulation and client-server implementations can be among the least complex of these implementations. We will discuss how NetWare and client-server fits shortly. For now the focus will be on the enterprise network demarcation and coordination of two pieces of software.

Distributed processing applications require the enterprise network to extend into the worksta-

For the matched software approach both workstation and host software must be coordinated in order to interoperate. This usually implies workstation operating systems, software levels and hardware capacity sensitivity. As a result, the enterprise network demarcation must include a minimum workstation configuration and the actual software and applications on the workstation. These must be coordinated every time a program change that affects both pieces is made. As a direct consequence, software change management tools are fundamental to distributed or client-server implementations.

A comprehensive change management system is a prerequisite to distributed processing

1.2.2 Enterprise Network Boundaries Summary

In summary the enterprise network boundaries need to be drawn in relationship to the responsibilities of the enterprise network organization. These responsibilities tend to be focused on providing quality service and security. The exposures range from its ability to responsively and economically identify and resolve service-related problems, deal with unexpected network traffic and unexpected network load, and protect the users of the network from user workstation, server, or host penetration and associated information theft, information compromise or other destructive act. The enterprise network boundaries will therefore align with the level of control or exposure a connection introduces when the enterprise network allows external access.

Boundary based on ability to:
● **Provide service**
● **Protect**

The boundaries are usually a function of the technology and risk management

As a result the enterprise network organization focuses on the robustness of the technologies it has available to ensure the quality of service it is contracted to provide. NetWare and Net-Ware associated products play multiple roles in moving the boundaries while meeting this criterion.

> **Enterprise network boundaries are based on the organization's ability to support or management's willingness to take risk.**

1.3 Picking the Right Technology

We are told that *workstation, client-server,* and *network computing* technologies are at the apex of computing in the 1990s. Proponents of these technologies emphasize the benefits of using newer and less expensive hardware and software with reduced user skill requirements.

Pieces of the puzzle:
- **Workstations**
- **Client-server**
- **Network computing**

The proponents of these technologies predict that a company that does not embrace these new technologies could quickly move from the competitive driver's seat to a passenger seat. The primary challenge is to integrate these technologies without incurring the costs typically associated with providing service in complex environments or being forced to make strategic decisions before being ready.

Competitiveness is tied to effective exploitation of new technologies

It has become apparent that the specific use of these technologies can become the bridge or the moat that integrates or separates the company's information assets. Additionally, the ways to apply these technologies without significant unexpected expense, mismanaged expectations, and turmoil is often far from clear.

Technology can be :
- **Bridge**
- **Moat**

The results depend on the integrator's grasp of the technologies and the company's approach to implementing these technologies.

Given the current dynamics of solutions and technologies in the industry, an appropriate approach is to identify common denominator technologies that allows a response with a solution today, that doesn't preclude change and provides the necessary longer range flexibility. When it comes to enterprise networks one major common denominator is the network operating system. Selecting the right network operating system is significantly

Common denominator is the networking operating system

NOSs
- **NetWare**
- **Vines**
- **LAN Server**
- **Windows for Workgroups**

easier than selecting the applications for the enterprise network. Once the network operating system has been selected, one is in a good position to select the services and applications that the enterprise can support.

If you were to do a networking operating system survey for an enterprise network today, you would probably come away with brand names such as Novell's NetWare, Banyan's Vines, Microsoft's LAN Manager, and IBM's LAN Server. For comparison purposes once you get past the common label, networking operating system (NOS), these systems have very few services in common. These products came from different design points and objectives and as a result they don't line up nicely for comparison.

For example, while IBM's LAN Server, which runs on IBM's OS/2 operating system, is often evaluated as a NOS, it would be more appropriate to evaluate it as a server technology consistent with its name. (See Fig. 1-8.) When combined with some other software components, such as IBM's Communication Manager/2, IBM's LAN/NetView, or other service, application, management, and support products, the result would more closely fit into a NOS evaluation.

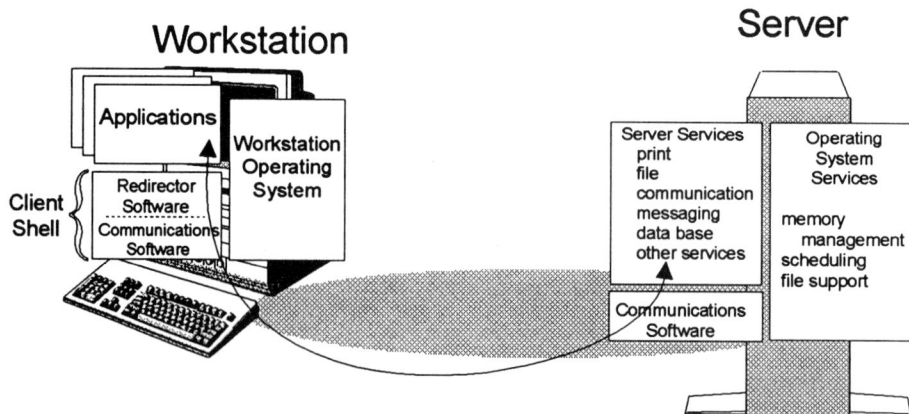

Figure 1-8 A Server and Workstation Configuration

Another technology that often ends up in the NOS evaluation is peer-to-peer networking, also known as peer networking or workgroup networking. Implementations include Novell's Personal NetWare and Microsoft's Windows for Workgroups. (See Fig. 1-9.)

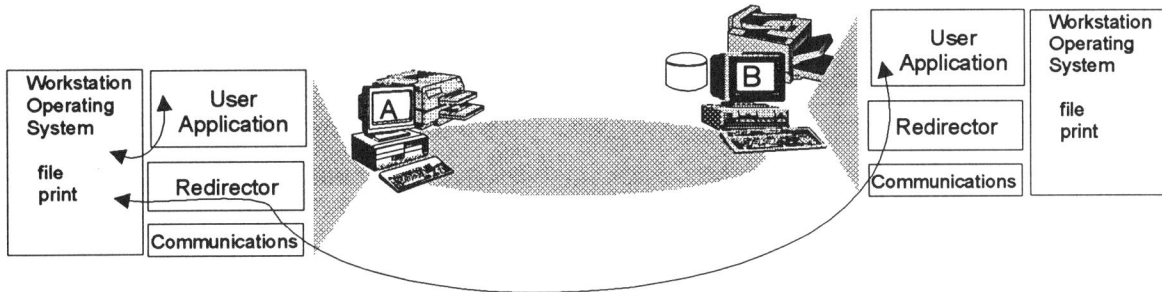

Figure 1-9 A Peer-to-Peer Network

These peer networks are comprised of workstations, no server is required. Typically, peer networking software supports the sharing of resources among workstations running the same operating system software, such as DOS or DOS and Windows. Microsoft's Windows for Workgroups extends the resource sharing to application participation for group activities including electronic mail exchange and workgroup scheduling. Windows for Workgroups also works in conjunction with Microsoft's LAN Manager (a server product) or NetWare. Novell's Personal NetWare also works in conjunction with NetWare servers and networking.

While both these IBM and Microsoft products enhance the capabilities and functionality at the workstation, the necessary NOS management capabilities must be provided by other products. It appears that both of these networking solutions originate from specific workstation operating systems and extend out. This has provided extensive workstation productivity and robustness for the user, but significantly less emphasis has been placed on

Microsoft and IBM NOS products originate from workstation operating system and evolved out

the other networking aspects, especially in the actual physical network and internetworking areas.

Novell NetWare has different roots and has come at the networking opportunity from a different angle, as Figure 1-10 characterizes. Novell has packaged NetWare as some core technology and optional services under the same family name, **NetWare**, to identify it as part of the network operating system.

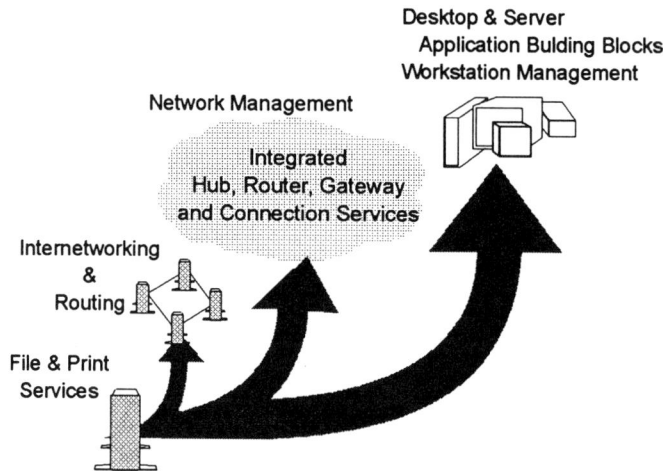

NetWare packaged as a comprehensive NOS

Desktop & Server
Application Bulding Blocks
Workstation Management

Network Management

Integrated
Hub, Router, Gateway
and Connection Services

Internetworking
&
Routing

File & Print
Services

Figure 1-10 Novell NetWare Approach to Networking

From a network standpoint, rather than coming from the workstation, NetWare comes to the workstations. As such NetWare extends the workstation services (file serving, print serving, data base serving, application enabling, and desktop system support), provides interconnection (LAN, WAN, routing and gateway services) to diverse services and applications independent of their architecture, and provides the tools necessary to support the physical connection and the overall management of the components. For example, there are more than 1,500,000 routers carrying IPX traffic.

Novell has also focused on the organizational and budget control changes associated with departmental computing. Early on, Novell recognized that departments often had the final say and the budget to purchase networking equipment and software.

This emphasis is now expanding to the larger enterprise infra-structure.

Novell, also, continues to dramatically influence the network computing marketplace as a whole by increasing the number of consumers involved. This is being accomplished by significantly reducing the perceived difficulty and complexity traditionally associated with networks and network solutions.

Figure 1-11 depicts some of the elements and roles of the NetWare networking operating system. We will look at each of these elements and their interrelationships throughout this book.

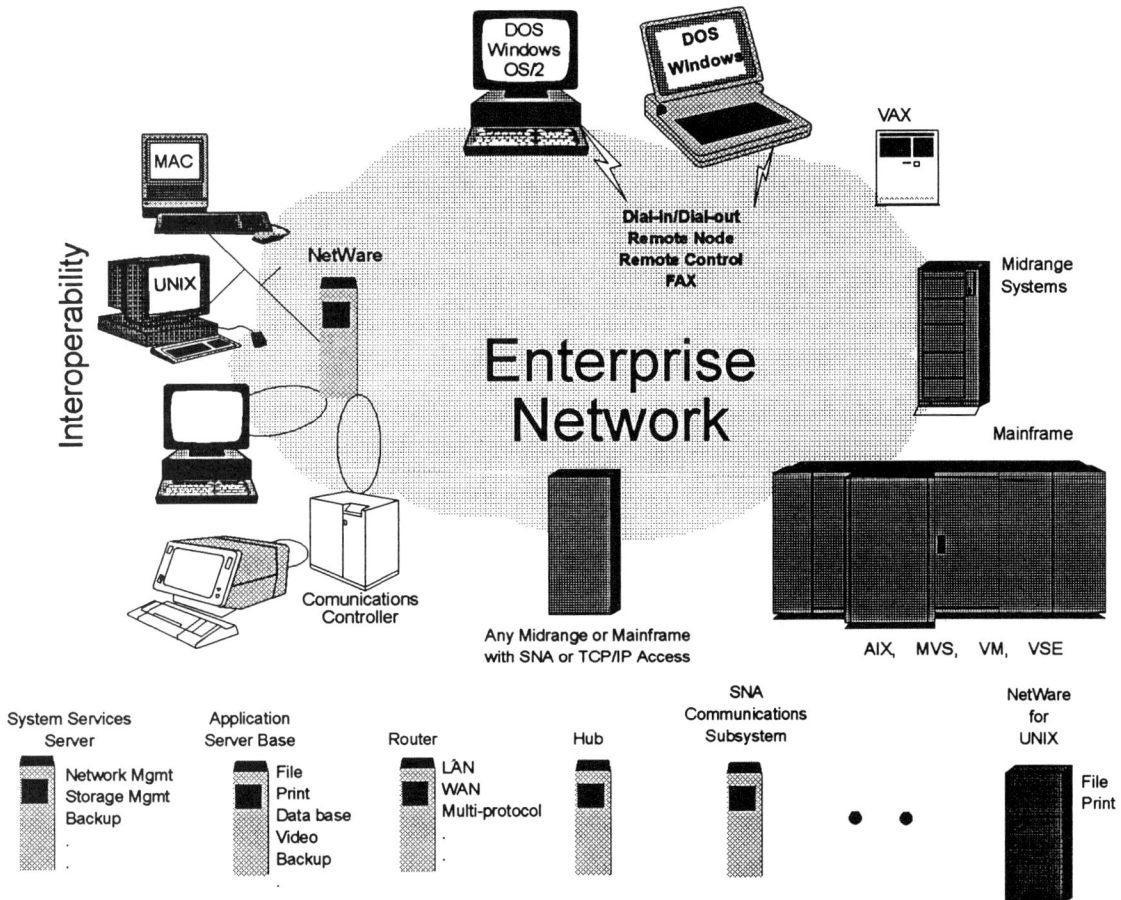

Figure 1-11 NetWare as part of the Enterprise Network

Select your NOS(s)
based on your enterrise
network boundary

services, these services can be combined into one or more servers as workload, system capacity, performance, and economies dictate. (See Fig. 1-12.) Additionally, NetWare provides workstation shells for DOS and Windows. These workstations can access NetWare server services while sharing peer resources with Personal NetWare.

1.4 Summary

In recap, the easiest network boundary is at the backbone network

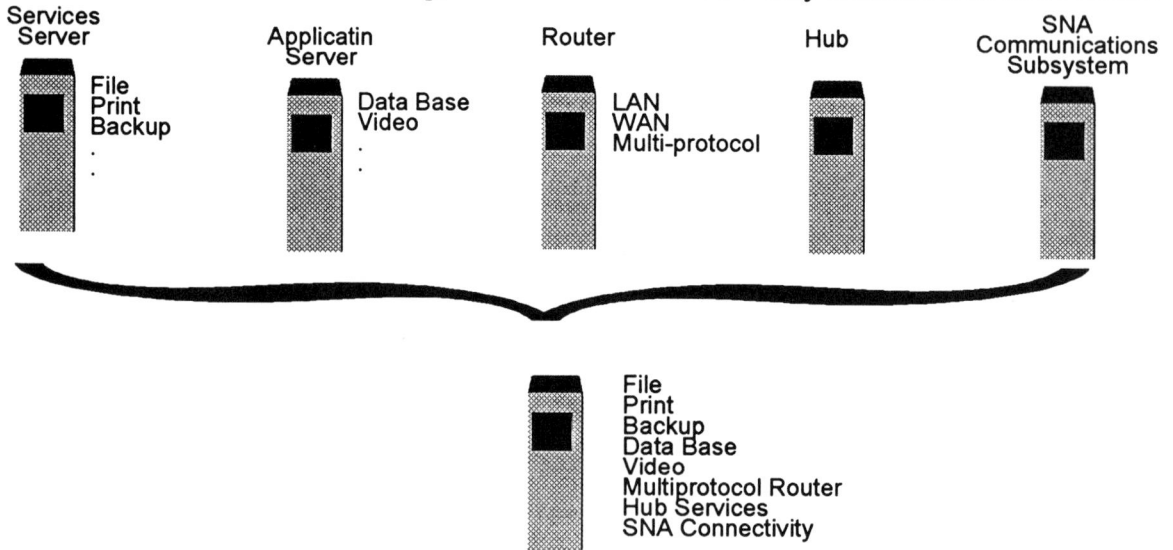

Services
Server
    File
    Print
    Backup
    .
    .

Applicatin
Server
    Data Base
    Video
    .
    .

Router
    LAN
    WAN
    Multi-protocol

Hub

SNA
Communications
Subsystem

File
Print
Backup
Data Base
Video
Multiprotocol Router
Hub Services
SNA Connectivity

Figure 1-12 A Multifunction NetWare Server

Make sure your
evaluation criteria
is for what you need

port. The network management tools to support these types of networks are well established. The next logical boundary includes the physical LAN which requires more remote network management tools and capabilities. The next enterprise boundary includes the physical LAN and the servers on that that LAN. This requires additional network management tools, controls, and invariably additional skills. The next logical step is to extend the enterprise network boundary to include some portions of the workstation such as operating system maintenance level, software licensing, client software and data backup. This last layer is the most complex of all the boundary options because it not only stretches the traditional network management infrastructure, it also crosses departmental and organizational management philosophies and approaches.

For discussion purposes we use an enterprise network management boundary that extends into the workstation. This will allow us to explore the various considerations associated with this and the less complex models and how they relate to your enterprises network operating system.

The role of your NOS will change as the network boundary expands.

Now let's look at NetWare in this context.

As the enterprise network boundary expands so must the capabilities of your network operating systems (NOS) and associated support infrastructure.

NetWare appears to be well positioned to respond to the expanding role of the NOS.

We will explore the various considerations and requirements and discuss how NetWare addresses them.

Chapter 2

NetWare:
An Enterprise Network NOS

2.1 Meeting a Need

Most seasoned enterprise network information systems (IS) executives, when given a choice, will select an enterprise network networking operating system (NOS) that:

- Meets their current business needs
- Meets their technical needs
- Moves them forward toward their strategic goals

This means that acceptable *quick fix* solutions (short term and short life solutions) must be containable, migratable, or disposable. Additionally, because of the continued pressure on funding and the movement of funding from IS to the business units, IS organizations are less focused on large-scale projects using leading-edge technology and more focused on meeting the demand for new applications while responding to needs with technologies that conform to the budget pressures.

These IS professionals recognize that although many of the values (considerations) in their computing models have changed significantly over the last five years, the original parameters (e.g., business responsiveness, service reliability, user support, response time, security, data integrity, data protection, backup, recovery, disaster backup, etc.) are fundamental to a durable and

Timelines parameters
- Responsiveness
- Reliability
- User support
- response time
- Recurity
- Data integrity
- Data protection
- Disaster backup

18

scalable enterprise network, even when the technologies applied to the solutions might be dramatically less expensive.

Technologies and applications that demonstrate the required attributes are referred to as *industrial strength*. Those that don't are often referred to as *erector kits* or *toys*.

While this may seem somewhat arrogant to some, it is important to remember that many of the current enterprise-mission-critical applications have been effective for upward of 25 years. These applications have migrated through multiple models of hardware, multiple versions of operating systems, and potentially even more versions of network connectivity without significant disruption to the business or the users. The infrastructure associated with these *legacy systems* include such predictable items as level of security, data integrity, protection of investment, user education, procedures, skills, staffing, and sensitivity to the profit and loss statement.

It is very probable that those who have abandoned the basic parameters have already or will shortly experience the consequences. I liken this to the television ad of a mechanic inducing us to buy automobile motor oil: "You can pay me now or can pay me later!" Since selecting "the" internetworking solution is substantially more complex than selecting oil for your car, it is best to opt for a solution that demonstrates the flexibility to correct direction or add function.

The ability to know the options and the industrial strength before applying the technology is an extremely valuable attribute of durable information solutions. Unfortunately this predictability aspect is often missed in the zeal focused on the high price of operating and maintaining *legacy systems* in downsizing and reengineering articles. Once the predictability attributes are put into play, the primary considerations tend to be the organization's ability to smoothly migrate or cut-in the solution and cost of buying their way out of a problem should maximum correction be required. If this assessment is positive, the risk is acceptable. If not, the proposal is not ready for a prime-time enterprise network.

Industrial strength applications have withstood the test of time - 25 years

Legacy not a bad word

Options:
- **Will play**
- **Won't play**
- **Might play with backout**
- **Cost effective**

Predictability is probably the most important attribute

Section Criteria
- **Meets needs**
- **Protects investment**
- **Easy to introduce**
- **Easy to remove**
- **Affordable**

2.2 NetWare Fits the Business Model

Initial investment may have already been made

NetWare plays well to this IS theme because of Novell's approach to marketing, which fosters significant industry participation. This high participation reduces the risk and increases the investment protection. NetWare can easily be introduced and easily removed, although the alternative non-NetWare solutions that provide comparable services and performance may be quite costly.

In other words, the NetWare solution can be introduced without major strategic considerations and the costs of a contingency plan are readily definable from the onset. To make matters easier the initial investments may already have been incurred by the individual departments or business units.

I like to think of NetWare in the same vane as the term PC compatible. That is, there are very few products that the typical IS organization or end-user department uses that are not NetWare compatible. Additionally, because Netware runs on PC compatible hardware it can easily be reused for workstations or other servers.

NetWare provides a high-impact, minimum-risk NOS solution

2.3 Keeping Your Eye on the Ball

Since 1983, when Novell declared it was going to accelerate the growth of network computing, it has focused on just that. This focus has remained paramount despite some rather bizarre attempts to divert Novell's attention by an increasing number of trade press and trade journal articles, the most bizarre being the specter of a *battle for the LAN* between Novell and Microsoft. This type of press coverage really misses the mark by confusing the IS organization, which can ill afford to take sides, and it confuses the end user, who often doesn't understand the issues. Novell's approach to growth and acceptance has been to *cooperate* and *collaborate*. Novell believes that this is how to develop the opportunity. Any analysis shows that as Microsoft increases its market, Novell benefits since there are a larger number of workstations accompanied by greater internetworking opportunities. Are there business practice differences between these companies? Yes. Should these differences impact the IS decision process? No.

Novell's business approach is cooperation and collaboration

Selection of a NOS for your enterprise network is not a simple task given the number of considerations, but very little time should be spent on artificial battles. If you are concerned with choosing NetWare as your NOS you might use the "what is the worst thing that could happen?" scenario. If NetWare doesn't grow with your business needs, then you and thousands of other companies must move to a NOS that meets your requirements. Would this be very difficult? No. Why not? Because any vendor that has a better solution must provide an easy migration path for you and the other thousands of companies.

If you are wrong about Netware you will have lots of company and lots of alternatives

This makes NetWare a low-risk decision, but you should also be confident that NetWare will meet and keep up with your company's business needs. So let's look at Novell's track record.

Novell focuses on expanding the industry with cooperation not competition

2.4 The Track Record

NetWare has evolved and developed since 1903

In 1983 Novell saw a growing customer need to economically extend their workstations and provide interoperability among these workstations. Novell saw that the only viable solution to fulfill the envisioned requirements was to provide a network operating system that supports heterogeneous environments. The Novell solution was introduced as NetWare, which has evolved from a simple file server and printer server into a comprehensive and extensive network operating system that has the potential of removing the walls between mainframes/midrange systems and workstations.

Novell saw a huge marketplace that IS preferred to ignore

Novell's initial thrust was at what I will refer to as departmental or workgroup computing, a marketplace that in 1983 was a major challenge and major opportunity. The challenge was the lack of IS interest and a huge marketplace of relatively inexperienced departmental personnel that, given the right price tag and support, could become a major catalyst in the network computing arena.

Given this environment Novell evolved a marketing strategy that focused on:

Novell focuses on expanding and supporting the market

- Growing a large customer base (now in excess of 20,000,000 users)
- A price that is within the discretionary range of departmental management
- Continuous end-user advertising with easy-to-understand messages highlighting quick-fix solutions
- Emphasis on easy-to-use and self-managing systems
- Objective-oriented education programs and seminars
- The ready availability of qualified support
- Continuous addition of applications for NetWare
- Marketing and sales channels (more than 22,000 reseller partners worldwide have fully qualified support staffs)

- Developing development partnerships (now in excess of 1000 such partners)
- The provision of system and application development tools
- Third party programs to foster application growth
- Rapid response to requirements with in-house development, acquisition, or third-party partners solutions

Novell has also developed an everexpanding third-party and ancillary marketing thrust that attracted a large number of companies to augment and complement NetWare. These efforts have resulted in more than 10,000 applications that either run on NetWare networks or exploit specific NetWare services and capabilities.

Novell focuses on reducing the time from sale to installation. Novell makes it very easy to install the basic and most valuable network services (file and print serving) within a department by using objective- oriented cook book-type instructions and identifying professionals (certified) who can help implement the network, if necessary. Once the momentum started, more customers and partners joined the parade. Novell provides constant market visibility that focuses on customer successes and the business partners and distribution channels.

Focus on problem identification and solution

Novell also fostered a technical certification program that now ranges from an entry-level Certified NetWare Administrators program to an Enterprise Certified NetWare Engineers program whose graduates are qualified to service complex, enterprisewide network computing environments. More than 24,000 people have attained Certified NetWare Engineer status.

As a network vendor Novell also focuses on minimizing the exposures associated with mixing software, hardware, and applications from multiple vendors, different architectures, and design points. Novell has implemented several compatibility-assurance programs to help customers and vendors.

yes

It runs with
NetWare®

yes

NetWare®
Tested and
Approved

Enterprise network
NOS:
● **Perform**
● **Remotely managed**
● **Maintain service
   levels**

One such program is the "Yes, It Runs with NetWare" label. This program is usually a self-certification program in which each vendor qualifies their software or hardware.

A second program qualifies a product for the "Tested and Approved" label. This label identifies products that have gone through a rigorous certification process in Novell's Labs.

> **Novell focuses on removing the inhibitors and improving the ease of using the network to solve business problems**

2.5 Enterprise Network Focus

But succeeding as the enterprise network NOS is much more difficult that succeeding as a departmental NOS. There are primarily three criteria that Netware has to meet in order to succeed as the enterprise network NOS. They are: to perform when using the enterprise network backbone network, to be able to remotely manage the servers and workstations on the LANs, and to maintain the current service levels and security.

So let's see how NetWare has evolved with regard to the IS infrastructure.

2.5.1 An Ambivalent Environment

By the late 1980s NetWare had become an industry standard for departmental solutions, and Novell looked to extend its value by adding onto the enterprise network. The steps included providing access to the mainframe with more extensive interconnect technologies, such as Systems Network Architecture (SNA) gateway software in 1987 and Transmission Control Protocol/Internet Protocol (TCP/IP) technology in 1989.

To additionally improve the industrial strength of the network server, Novell introduced a high availability implementation of

NetWare, NetWare System Fault Tolerant (SFT) in 1988. Beginning with keeping two copies of the files, SFT III now includes two separate systems which run with the data synchronized such that the secondary automatically takes overrunning the application without data loss or interruption of network service if the primary server fails.

The NetWare solutions, however, were not graciously accepted by most traditional IS organizations. The IS organizations viewed the PC-based local area network (LAN) software and the applications using it the same way they viewed *code-and-go* programs. *Code-and-go* implied minimal planning accompanied usually accompanied by future support, scalability, and flexibility problems. The IS community saw relatively inexpensive physical LANs such as Ethernet, ARCnet and LocalTalk LANs being connected to the NetWare server as depicted in Figure 2 -1. The IS community was far more comfortable with Token Ring LANs predictability and OS/2 reliability on the workstations.

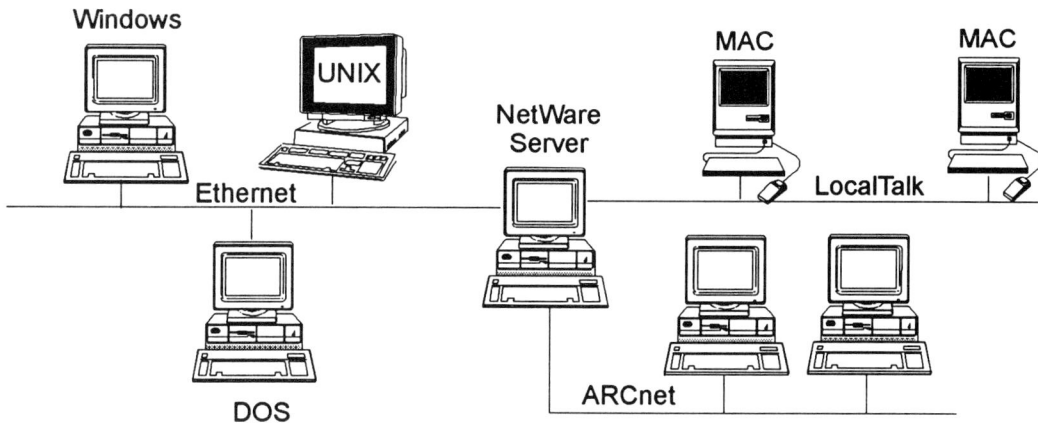

Figure 2-1 Typical NetWare Configurations

2.5.2 Awareness and IS Confusion

In 1990 Novell continued to enhance the capabilities of the departmental network, as well as begin working more closely with the Fortune 1000 companies to provide a better solution for the enterprise network.

This period saw the emergence of departmental wide area networks (WANs) using NetWare and bridges and routers and an increase in the number of NetWare SNA gateways to connect to the mainframe. (See Fig. 2- 2.) The WAN activity caused the IS organization to pay more serious attention to NetWare. (Note that dedicated systems were used as SNA gateways for enterprise network access to the mainframe.)

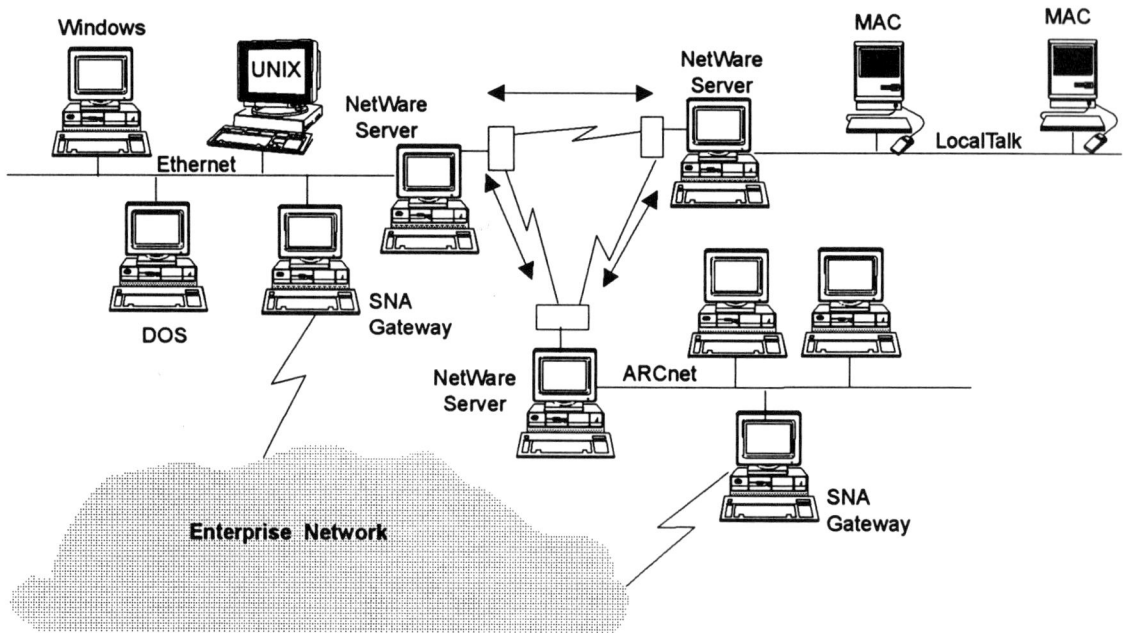

Figure 2-2 Departmental Wide Area Networks

The IS staffs began to study what NetWare was. However, they found themselves faced with a major communication problem.

The Novell marketing channels and the companies' own Net-Ware users didn't speak the same technical language and looked at desktop computing and network management in an entirely different context. They couldn't understand the IS terminology nor the IS perspective when being questioned. The LAN-oriented trade press didn't help to bridge the communications gap with their articles that declared the death of the mainframe and its expensive infrastructure by the installation of inexpensive solutions installed and managed by office workers.

The answers that the IS organization heard didn't make sense. It was unclear to them what problem was being solved and where the controls were. It was also very difficult for the IS professionals to learn about NetWare from the documentation. The manuals were cookbooklike, written with very easy to follow *how to install and how to operate* instructions. The in-depth concepts and facilities and planning guides that the IS organization normally studied were nowhere to be found. Additionally the documents available focused on the LAN side of the equation.

Overall the initial results of trying to bring NetWare into the enterprise network were not very fruitful since there were now essentially two camps that did not appreciate the other's point of view and couldn't communicate. (At this time in the evolution, I was meeting with many departments in Fortune 500 companies to better understand their perspective and enterprise network requirements. There overall findings were that many NetWare users wanted to have the IS organization provide the enterprise network connectivity management and manage the data backup.)

2.5.3 Meeting Requirements

By 1991 the communication problem was recognized by Novell and most large companies. To overcome this problem Novell began working closely with major enterprise network vendors such as IBM and selected IS organizations around the world. This resulted in a much better appreciation of NetWare and the enterprise networking issues for all involved.

As a quick fix to solve the knowledge gap between the IS organizations and the departmental LAN owners many compa-

Step 1
● Bring LAN
 administrators inside
 infrastructure

Step 2
● Focus on the effective
 management of the
 network

**Hardware independent
network connection
services**

nies restructured their IS organization to include departmental LAN administrators. This brought some of the necessary NetWare skill into the IS infrastructure and cleared the path to addressing the control issues. This organizational restructuring effectively extended the enterprise network organization boundary to the LAN and sometimes into the workstation, plus it also provided a career path and a support infrastructure for the LAN administrator within the enterprise network.

Having addressed the organizational issue the next step was to provide the support more effectively. To move inside the enterprise network management boundary NetWare had to meet the network interconnectivity, network management, network security, and data-integrity prerequisites. Additionally these have to fit within a scalable management infrastructure.

Probably the biggest single NetWare enhancement for the enterprise network environment came with NetWare 3.1x. NetWare 3.1x significantly improved the ability to develop and run service and applications on the NetWare servers. This provided the option of running services, such as SNA gateways, on the NetWare file resulting in significantly more configuration flexibility and potential cost reductions.

Using NetWare server resident services and applications, the customer had the option to eliminate one or more personal computer systems and a network interface adapters. Running services on the server also significantly improved the ease of managing these services since they were now under NetWare server control. (Prior to NetWare 3.1x most of the network-based services were on dedicated systems using a DOS base. Each such server used NetWare connectivity but there were no common ways of managing these servers.) (See Fig. 2-3 and note that the SNA gateway capability resides on the NetWare server.)

By 1993 Novell and its business partners including IBM had implemented extensive interconnection, internetworking, and network management software that was designed to address the needs of the enterprise network. These include being able to

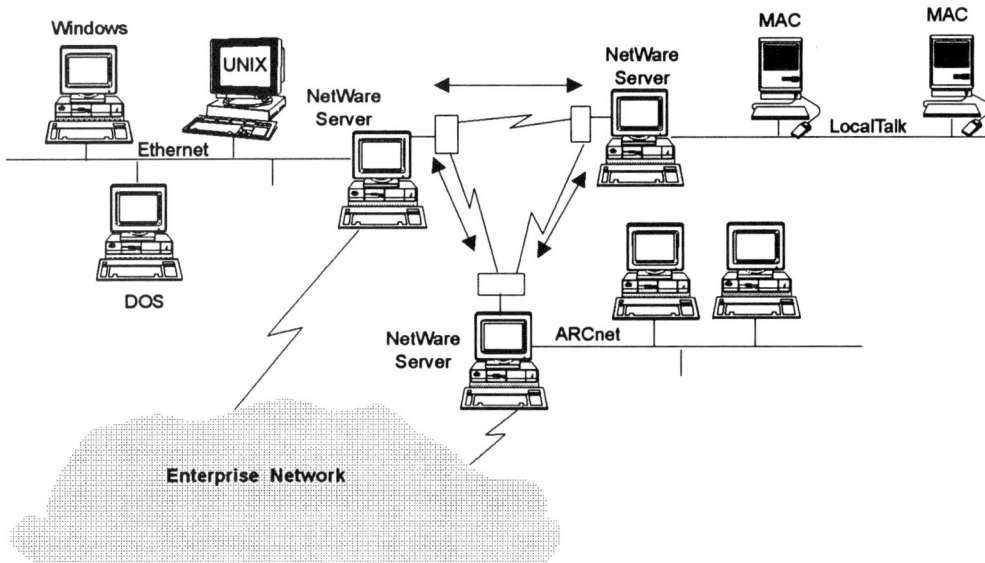

Figure 2-3   A NetWare Network Environment

integrate NetWare server management under the IBM NetView or Simple Network Management Protocol (SNMP) umbrella.

1993:
- **The year of the enterprise network**

That same year Novell introduced NetWare 4.0 software the tenth generation of its base networking operation system. NetWare 4.0 introduced global directory services, enhanced security, and focused on simplifying the use and management of complex networks. The NetWare network now includes the necessary security features that most IS organizations require to protect the users of the enterprise network. These include capabilities such as definable user rights, password encryption, data signatures, remote dial-back and extensive audit trails.

Robust security

There have also been significant functional enhancements for managing the communication network and interconnectivity. These enhancements include remote problem alerts, remote problem determination, enhanced internetworking options such as server-based hub servers and multiprotocol routers, and robust SNA connectivity to mainframes and midrange systems. A Net-

NetWare-based server and network managomont

Ware-based subsystem lets system administrators monitor network activity, optimize performance and fix potential problems before they become critical, plus offers the flexibility to centralize and distribute network management. It also integrates other Novell facilities that provide network connection, optimization, and troubleshooting details, as well as monitoring and managing all the NetWare to IBM host connections.

Additionally, extensive network management tools have been introduced by Novell and vendors that support the NetWare environment to more effectively manage other aspects of the NetWare network in terms of workstation inventory, software distribution, network security, and software metering, as well as providing a global directory to administer the user access controls. One key aspect of these management tools is that they can be applied locally, remotely and centrally using IBM's NetView.

NetWare-based workstation management

Overall the focus on the support tools and capabilities have made significant strides toward the effective and efficient integration of NetWare into the enterprise.

2.6 Extending the LAN

2.6.1 A Communications Server

NetWare provides software to interconnect remote LANs using dial-up, leased-line, and switched networks using X.25, Frame Relay, and asynchronous transfer mode (ATM) services. NetWare can also be used as a platform for hub management or be housed in hubs, as well as can be configured as a multiprotocol router for network traffic among LAN-and-wide-area network(WAN) connected routers. (See Figure 2-4 .)

NetWare can be configured on a PC with the appropriate hub hardware, LAN and communications adapters, and digital service unit (DSU/CSU) cards to provide an inexpensive and flexible system that is managed with the familiar NetWare tools. For example DSU/CSU units can be integrated into a server or NetWare Router using Novell's Integrated Communications Interface and the appropriate intelligent adapter (see Figure 2-5).

This approach consolidates the CSU functions into the communications adapter eliminates the need for serializing the data and the intelligent adapter off-loads some of the host PC communications preparation workload.

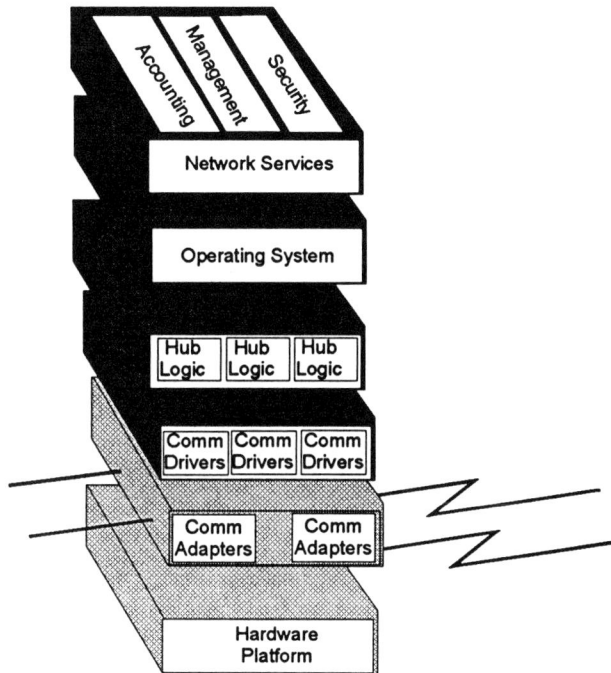

Figure 2-4 A Software-based Communication Server

DSU-Digital (Data)
Service Unit
• Interfaces with your server or router WAN synchronous adapter
• Converts signal for CSU to understand

CSU - Channel Service Unit
• Interfaces to telephone connection
• Provides error detection and keeps link up

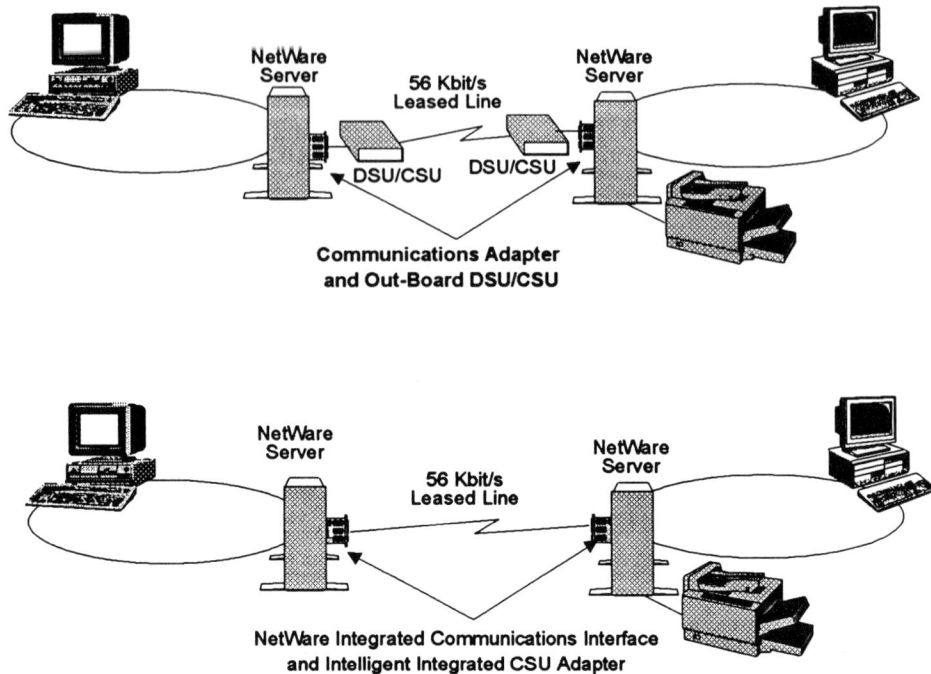

Figure 2-5   Integrated Communications Interface

2.6.2 Extending LAN Protocols for the WAN

NetWare protocols
initially optimized for
LANs

NetWare's communication protocols were designed to provide
the users with the maximum flexibility and highperformance.
NetWare dynamically configures the network and provides extremely high performance on ARCnet, Ethernet, and Token Ring
LANs. These attributes served the LAN environment well, however, the four protocols: Internet Packet Exchange (IPX), NCP
(Netware Core Protocol), Routing Information Protocol (RIP),
and Service Advertising Protocol (SAP) that were so effective for
the LAN do not scale well when the traffic must travel over a
WAN that is many times slower than the LAN and as the number
of interconnected nodes increases.

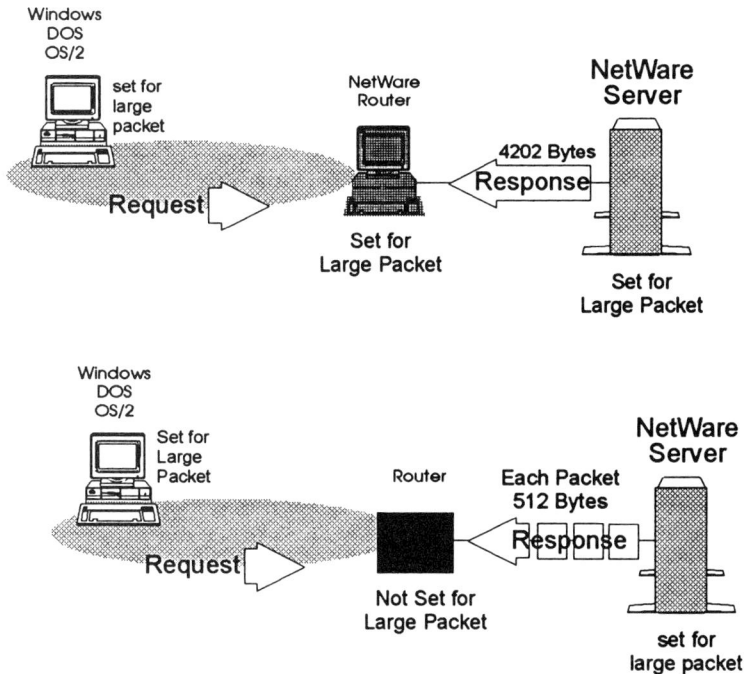

Figure 2-6 Large Internet Packet Support

To meet the requirements of the WAN connections Novell has made several extension to the original protocols. Two such efforts included the ability to send larger packets (referred to as *large internet packet*, LIP or *Large Packet*) and to send multiple packets before waiting for an acknowledgment (referred to as *Packet Burst* or Pburst).

Large internet packets focus on increasing the efficiency of the transmission through the router. Prior to Large Internet Packet the maximum packet size was set to 576 bytes (512 bytes of data and 64 bytes of header information). With the Large Internet Packet NetWare loadable module (NLM) the client can negotiate a packet size of up to 4202 bytes. This enhances the throughput over bridges and routers (assuming that they support the packet size increase). To take advantage of the Large Packet capability

Large Packet enhance throughput

Packet size must be optimized to match your workload profile

all servers and routers in the path must also be set to support the large packet size. The negotiated size is determined by the smallest packet size supported as depicted in Figure 2 -6). In the example scenarios the top router is prepared to handle the increase packet size and in the second scenario the router does not support the larger packets.

For the most part LAN-WAN performance discussions focus on data transfer. Data transfer is usually discussed in terms of throughput. This throughput is reported in terms of number of bytes per second. This is an appropriate measure when the applications are transferring files and response time is not a primary performance criteria. A short form mechanism to discuss both throughput and response time is packets per second. The

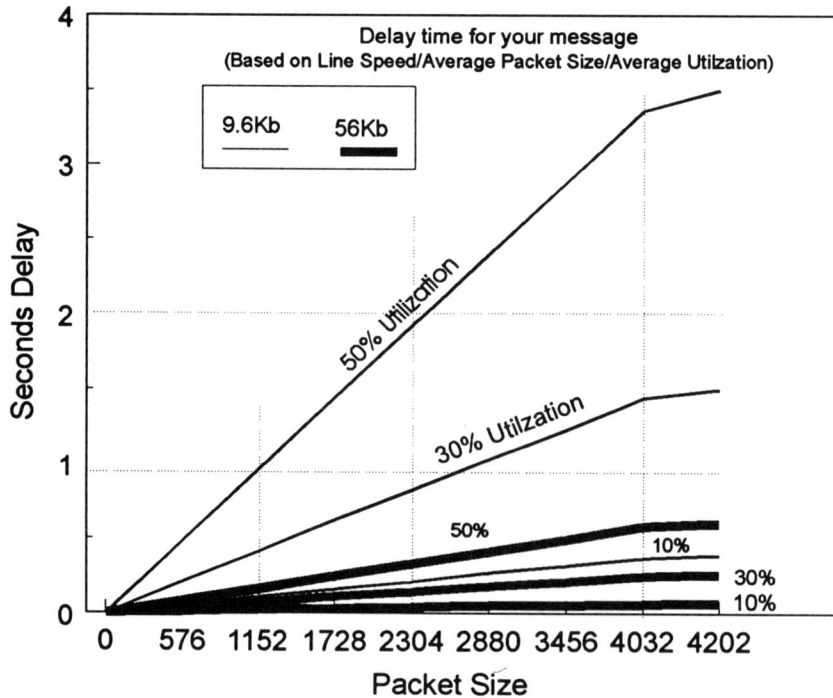

Figure 2-7 Packet Size - Transmission Duration

under lying assumption to using this short hand approach is that the packet sizes are the same for all transmissions. This will not be the case when some applications are using large packets and more care must be taken when planning performance. This is especially true for network traffic that involves small packets such as key strokes or data base requests mixed in behind large packets.

The tuning challenge is to balance the delay caused by waiting for larger packets versus the number of packets that can be transferred per second. On low-speed lines the application mix will dictate the performance objectives. When conceptualizing the design it is important to remember that a 9600-bits-per-second line equates to 1200 bytes per second, which means that the line can mathematically, at best, handle two 576-byte packets per second. A 4042-byte packet will take almost 4 seconds. This means that a message in the queue behind this packet could easily wait 4 seconds and more depending on who will be serviced next and what their packet size is. Figure 2 -7 depicts the expected delays that a given message might encounter on a 9.6-Kbit per second line and a 56-Kbit per second line. The obvious answer is to use a high-speed line such as T1 whenever possible and use data compression for the lower speed lines.

There is no substitute for high speed lines - like T1

Another way to improve performance is to minimize the time lost waiting for acknowledgment of packets sent. Packet Burst is intended to speed up the transfer of multiple packet NCP file reads and writes (see Fig. 2 -8). This technique helps performance in two ways: (1) it allows multiple packets to be sent without having to wait for acknowledgment, and (2) there are fewer acknowledgments, resulting in less traffic.

Packet Burst sends many packets before acknowledgment

Packet Burst has been implemented such that the client can negotiate the transfer of up to 64-KBytes without an acknowledgment. The actual number of packets sent are a function of a dynamic rate control mechanism based on a complex transmission- rate algorithm. (Without Packet Burst the client requests are limited to 4-KBytes per acknowledgment.) Missing or dropped packets are requested separately.

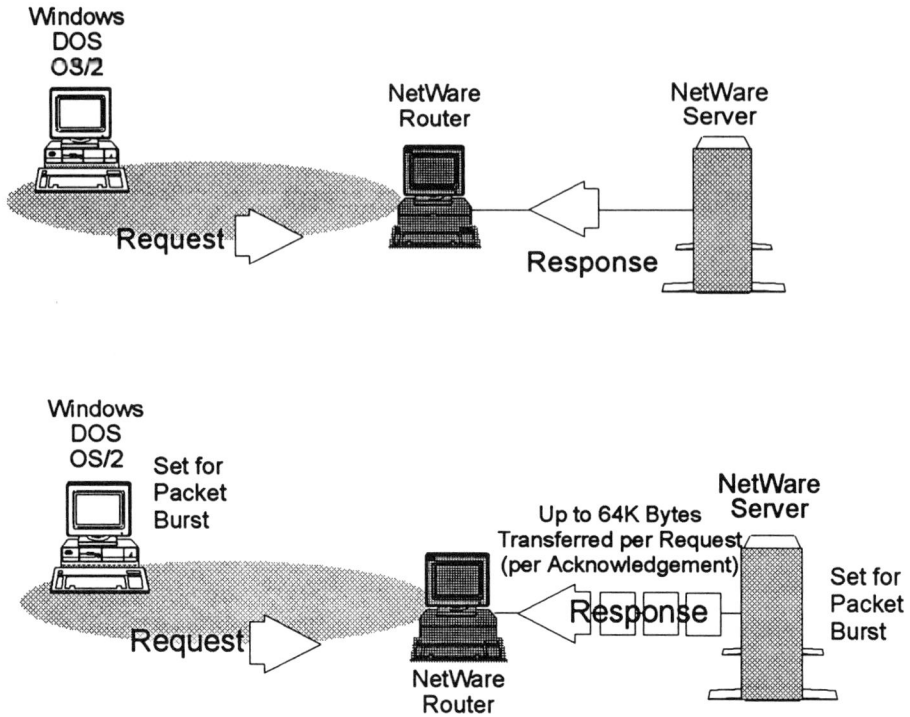

Figure 2-8   Packet Burst Scenarios

In general the best results are achieved for traffic over high-speed links such as 56-Kbit/s or greater. Independent of the network traffic both the workstation and server workload are reduced because of the reduction in the number of requests being handled. In order to activate Packet Burst, both the sending and receiving nodes must be enabled for Packet Burst otherwise the transfer will revert to one for-one mode.

The applications must also help to meet performance over WANs

Additionally, independent of the connection type, packet size, and deferral of acknowledgment, other performance techniques are usually required. These techniques must often be provided by the applications themselves. For example, data base systems that are designed to cross WANs separate their client server logic to minimize network traffic. Similarly, we also look at remote control and remote-node service interfaces, which are typically used for dialup connections, but are equally applicable for leased-line connections.

Another area that Novell and router vendors can affect directly is the services advertising protocol frequency. Netware normally broadcasts SAPs every 60 seconds. This works very effectively in high-speed networks, but can cause congestion on low-speed networks (9.6-Kbit/s or less) and can generate billable traffic across public or unit-of-traffic billable networks, such as X.25 and frame relay. The quick fix is to alter the period of broadcast to several minutes. Some routers offer SAP filtering, and only broadcast when there is a change in state.

SAPs generate traffic and can increase your bills

As part of the focus on WAN support Novell has introduced two new protocols: IPXWAN and NLSP (NetWare Link Services Protocol).

IPXWAN, an extension to IPX, was designed to operate over multiple WAN technologies, including PPP, X.25, Frame Relay, and ISDN. IPXWAN focuses on providing the quick identification and resolution of interconnection problems that connection-oriented protocols provide without compromising the connectionless IPX protocol. The IPXWAN specifications have been published and Novell is working with the major router vendors to assure that the enterprise network has the flexibility to mix and match Novell routers and servers with other vendors' routers.

IPXWAN improves responsiveness in resolving connection problems

NetWare Link Services Protocol (NLSP) is a link-state routing protocol designed to enhance performance, scalability, and manageability of internetworked environments. Netware Link Services Protocol will replace the RIP and SAP protocols with a link-state algorithm closely related to Internet's open shortest path first (OSPF) and the intermediate system-to-intermediate system (IS-IS) routing algorithm standards. (OSPF was developed by the Internet Engineering Task Force and designed to support large networks in the efficient propagation of changes in topology information and fast convergence to improve availability.)

NSLP provides less broadcast oriented network dynamics

Enhanced protocols:
- **Large packet**
- **Packet burst**
- **IPXWAN**
- **NLSP**

NetWare Protocols

IPX - The IPX protocol is the network-layer protocol that guides every NetWare packet from its point of origin to its destination. NCP, RIP and SAP protocols use IPX.

NCP - The NCP protocol carries service requests and data between the workstations and the NetWare. The NCP handles all DOS, Windows, and OS/2 services.

SAP - Each NetWare server regularly broadcasts SAPs to announce the availability of the services it has available to the other network nodes.

RIP - Each NetWare server regularly exchanges routing tables to inform all the other servers (or routers) about the network paths.

IPXWAN - An extension to IP that was designed to operate over multiple WAN technologies, including PPP, X.25, Frame Relay, and ISDN.

NLSP - A link-state routing protocol designed to enhance performance, scalability, and manageability of internetworked environments. NLSP will replace the RIP and SAP protocols.

Network Identifier Note

Assure that every NetWare server within your enterprise has a unique network identifier. This will avoid subsequent interconnectivity problems. NetWare requires that all NetWare servers (routers) have unique network identifiers within a network. Consider establishing an enterprise network service that provides unique network identifiers. Novell also offers a similar service that is ideal for organizations planning inter-enterprise connections - Novell Network Registry.

Vendors such as 3Com, Cisco, Proteon, Inc., and Wellfleet Communications, Inc. are planning to support Novell's NLSP and IPXWAN routing protocols. For example, users of 3Com's NETBuilder bridge/router family routers can reliably communicate with Novell's MultiProtocol Router over a wide area. Similar LAN/WAN interoperability is expected between Novell's Multiprotocol Router and Cisco's line of routers. Additionally, portions of Cisco's CiscoWorks management suite are being ported to Novell's NetWare Management System (NMS). Cisco will support Novell remote-access technology for its dial-in server.

Router vendors are working with Novell to support the new protocols so that they can mix and match routers

Novell has also developed alliances with companies such as SynOptics to use the new switching technologies, such as ATM in the LAN environment in preparation for the next generation which will have a high volume of data applications, such as desktop video conferencing, multimedia and high-speed imaging, that rely on emerging network services. ATM is expected to provide sufficient digital bandwidth to simultaneously transmit voice, video, and data at speeds of more than 15 times that of conventional networks.

2.6.3 Connecting the Enterprise Network

NetWare also continues to extend its interconnection reach. As of this writing mainframe and midrange connectivity is supported for seamless access to IBM mainframes, IBM AS/400, Digital systems, UNISYS, and all UNIX systems using SNA, TCP/IP, and DEC LAT connectivity. Additionally, NetWare provides extensive dial-in and dial-out services and send-an- receive FAX serving capabilities. NetWare also enables remote independent workstations to dial-in and participate in the NetWare network.

Connects to most mainframes and midrange systems

Dial-in, dial-out, and FAX services

2.7 Network Application Enabling

NetWare services go beyond integration of multiple platforms and providing file and print sharing. Other services include data bases running on the server, messaging services for mail and data-exchange applications, imaging and document handling, and

NetWare and Telephony

NetWare 4.0 provides the ability to combine telephone and computer technology, thus giving a NetWare-connected workstation the ability to access and control telephone functionality. This capability, referred to as Computer-Telephone Integration (CTI) , enables workstations to control communications without being directly connected to the telephony equipment (no phone hookup is required at the workstation). NetWare provides the interface between the workstation and the PBX features and functionality.

This telephony server capability provides for the development of an integrated workstation and telephony applications, such as desktop call center, voice messaging, facsimile routing, automated voice response, and multimedia applications using Windows, OS/2, and Macintosh workstations. For example, in a call-center application the telephony server and application can determine where to switch a call and concurrently route the appropriate call-related information to that user's workstation.

The computer telephone integration is accomplished with:

- A telephony-server component (an NLM) that provides the application with control of the phone on the user's desktop and the monitoring of other telephones on the PBX switchTelephony Server library

- A PBX driver on the server and associated link hardware

- An optional server based application

- A PBX provides the functionality required to perform switching functions

- A client library which supports the telephony server API

The telephony client-server programming interface provides telephony control capabilities for a generic, vendor independent PBX environment. The API is based on the services and functionality defined by international standards for CTI implementations and the European Computer Manufacturer's Association (ECMA) definition of Computer-Support Telecommunications Applications (CSTA) CTI standard for the PBX environment.

multimedia services that will support playing full-motion videos, live broadcasts and video conferencing, and telephony services. In conjunction with third-party application developers Novell is also publishing a standard set of Netware application programming interfaces for such leading-edge applications as imaging, vide, and telephony (see telephony insert).

Novell has also recognized that the enterprise network boundaries have moved from the backbone network to the desktop, and that the desktop itself is changing with the changes in the workplace. Many offices are essentially out of the attaché case or the vest pocket. Handheld computers that merge voice, video, and digital data with computing are emerging and telecommuting has already taken hold in many companies.

There is now an emphasis within Novell and some of their key customer to identify the unique networking requirements that this new enterprise network will demand.

To grow the industry Novell is providing application enablers for a broad and diverse set of applications.

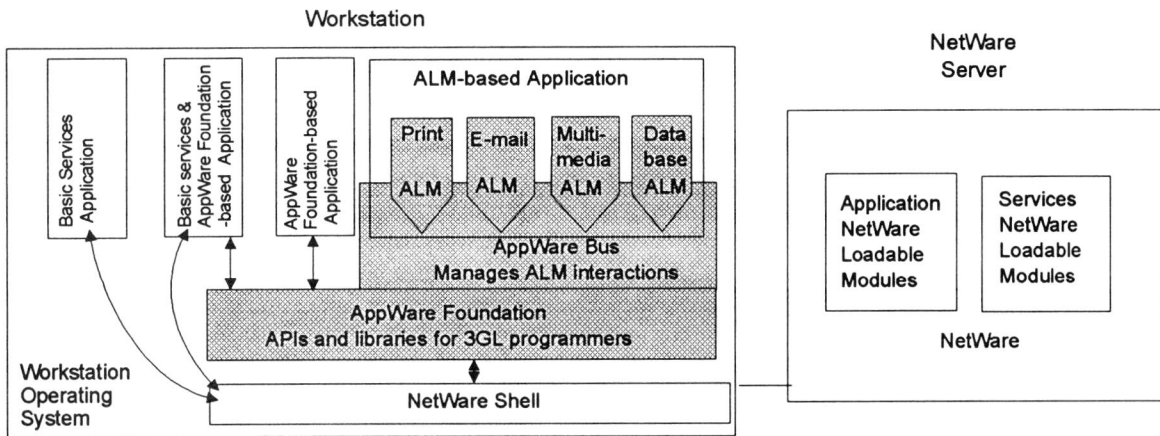

Figure 2-9 AppWare Structure

The NetWare environment currently supports a base of more than 300 application programming interfaces, which include such advanced network services as preprogrammed reusable modules that allow the developers to focus on their business application rather than on the inner workings of the NetWare environment.

Recognizing that an inhibitor to market growth is the speed with which applications can be built and the skills required, Novell has introduced an application development enabler - AppWare.

AppWare is a label for an approach and a set of workstation-based tools that focus on the time being expended by developers to support multiple workstation platforms and the time the developer spends in writing code to interface with the various NetWare-based applications and services. AppWare tools ease client-server application development. (See Fig. 2-9)

Fundamentally, AppWare is a tool kit of *middleware* that improves the developer's productivity by providing prebuilt AppWare Loadable Modules (ALMs) and AppWare services that run in the workstation to the developer. These ALMs and services provide the basic interconnection to the server-based applications and services that run as NLMs, and allow the programmer to focus on the application logic. AppWare includes four application development tools:

- AppWare Foundation Software Developer's Kit
- AppWare ALM Software Developer's Kit
- AppWare Bus ToolMaker
- Visual AppBuilder

AppWare Foundation includes basic services

The AppWare Foundation software developer's kit is composed of programming libraries and common cross-platform application programming interfaces (APIs) that carry out calls to specific operating systems, user interfaces, and network services.

These services include:
- Memory management

- Inter-application messaging
- File system
- Graphics
- Print
- International language support
- Windows
- Interactive help
- Multiple fonts
- Clipboard management
- Name pipes
- OLE
- Font scaling, transformations, and rotated text
- Palettes
- Off-screen imaging

Programs using these services will be source code compatible across AIX, HP-UX, Macintosh, OS/2, SunOS, Sun Solaris, UnixWare, Windows, and Windows NT platforms. (Check for the availability of support for OS/2 and Windows NT.) Moving from one platform to another requires a recompilation of the application. (Note that a fundamental understanding is that no environment unique services are used.)

AppWare Loadable Modules are self-contained, interchangeable software components that can be used to build applications. These ALMs reside on the workstation and can access the services provided by the local operating system and as well as use the AppWare Bus to access NetWare server-based NLMs.

AppWare Loadable Modules vendor provided or user developed object-oriented re-usable software modules that can range from simple utilities such painting a screen to more sophisticated network services such as accessing a database. These modules can provide end user visible function or can be combined with

AppWare programs are source compatible across multiple platforms

other ALMs and AppWare services to create comprehensive applications.

ALMs are created using 3GL (third generation language) programming tools (like C, C++, Cobol, and Pascal), interfaces with the AppWare Bus (a software engine that manages and coordinates the interaction of ALMs), and the AppWare Foundation libraries. The resulting ALMs can be accessed by 4GL and 5GL tools that use the AppWare Bus. Initial vendor-supplied ALMs include an ALM for connecting applications to the NetWare 4.x Directory services, an ALM linking Windows and Macintosh users to Novell's messaging engine, an ALM connecting DEC's Rdb back-end data base, and an ALM connecting to Sybase.

The Visual AppBuilder is a high-level programming tool that enables developers to construct applications by linking icons that represent prebuilt ALMs. Visual AppBuilder then uses the AppWare Bus software engine to actually link the necessary code and compile it into an executable file. Visual AppBuilder currently supports the Macintosh and MS Windows environments.

Collectively these application-enabling development tools provide a solid foundation for the successful implementation of client-server applications.

2.8 Novell and UNIX

In 1993 Novell acquired UNIX System Laboratories (USL) and Univel, which was a joint venture between Novell and USL. UNIX System Laboratories develops and markets the UNIX System V operating system. Univel develops and markets Unix-Ware, an advanced, 32-bit UNIX operating system that runs on Intel-based microprocessors.

Novell is using its experience in growing g the departmental marketplace to expand the use of UNIX while leveraging the NetWare facilities. Currently Novell provides a user-friendly UNIX desktop and server environment which allow the application to be integrated with the NetWare server and supports Unix systems with TCP/IP and runs on several UNIX platforms. This acquisition is expected to provide an even closer relationship with between NetWare and UNIX for the enterprise network. One such example is the introduction and availability of NetWare/IP which allows workstations with TCP/IP to access NetWare servers using standard TCP/IP and the NetWare/IP executable without the need for the IPX protocol stack.

2.9 Summary

NetWare has evolved from a simple file and print service into a comprehensive network platform and service. It has enabled a wide range of workstations to access NetWare services, as well as services provided by other vendors servers, minicomputers and mainframes. Despite the continued increase in function and expansion of tools and capabilities, the NetWare solutions continue to be focused on easy of implementation, ease of expansion and remain unobtrusive. I characterize NetWare as both an *underware* and *middleware* software solution. (The term *underware* implies that the software is invisible to the user and application. The term *Middleware* implies that while the underlying software services may be invisible to the user, the application program must use the *middleware interfaces to receive the requested services.)*

NetWare is still
- **Underware**
- **Middleware**
- **Unobtrusive**

As underware NetWare can be totally transparent to the workstation applications while providing server and network services. NetWare provides value add middleware to application developers who use NetWare provided APIs for NetWare Loadable Modules(NLMs) and for tools such as AppWare. NetWare also manages the underlying network interconnections, provides network services, and provides workstation support services. NetWare provides network management services and supports value added services that operate in conjunction with NetWare servers.

As of this writing, NetWare serves more than 66 percent of the worldwide LAN operating system market, supporting networks with DOS, MS Windows, OS/2, Macintosh, UNIX, DEC, IBM mainframe, midrange, and minicomputing environments.

Section 2

The Enterprise Network Environment

This section provides an introduction, background, and an overview of the business issues, challenges, and environment that have caused companies to alter their information system's infrastructure and tool kit.

It describes the current and future information systems (IS) challenges as IS responds to continually changing business demands and information systems technology. It introduces and describes how network computing using the appropriate network operating systems can provide responsive, viable, and manageable solutions to meet the new business and organizational demands.

This section covers issues faced by organizations, the reason that LANs, network operating systems, and Novell's NetWare are being used to address these issues. It goes on to test the NetWare-based solutions to ensure that they provide tactical solutions with the necessary flexibility to respond to the challenges of the 1990s in an IS context.

Chapter 3

Positioning for Success

3.1 Survival in the 1990s

In today's economy competitive companies focus on their customers' needs, the market forces, and the competition, paying close attention to their bottom line. To survive they must be agile, rapidly responding to constantly changing customer needs and options.

This emphasis on responsiveness to change and focus on the bottom line demands that even the most profitable companies constantly challenge their established business practices, organizational structures, and business tools.

Competitive companies focus:
- Customer
- Market
- Competition
- Bottom line

The entire company and its infrastructures are now under the microscope. The focus is on *flattening the organization*, *downsizing*, and *rightsizing*. The goal is to improve responsiveness by eliminating middle management and staff organizations and cutting operating costs by reducing the size of line organizations.

The information systems (IS) organization typically receives ongoing scrutiny because of its size, budget, and inability to respond to unique requirements. Most IS organizations are treated as cost centers and are a consolidation point for information technology staffs, computer equipment, data communications lines, and software. While the value of specific applications and projects are clearly tagged with such buzzwords as *mission critical* and *strategic weapons*, it is usually very difficult to establish an annual return on investment for the overall expenditure.

Targets:
- Big budget
- Big staffs
- Unclear ROI
- Responsiveness

Terms such as *downsizing*, *rightsizing*, *reengineering*, and *outsourcing* are being used to describe IS actions to better meet the needs of the business. However, some companies have made inroads on improving their agility while others continue to struggle.

Relationship between:
● **Control structure**
● **Operating systems**
● **Agility**

Those that are successfully implementing the newer technologies have recognized that there is a close relationship between their approach to control and the capabilities of the underlying network operating system technologies. That is, the operating system(s) must be able to meet the organization's control requirements. A company that is built around a strong central control model needs an network operating system that allows central control. On the other hand, a company that operates with multiple autonomous organizations needs a network operating system that allows autonomy.

An enterprise network usually requires a networking operating system that can support either or both control models in order to be responsive.

> **How does your organization measure up?**
> ● **Customer satisfaction**
> ● **Contribution to revenue**
> ● **Contribution to expense**
> ● **Ability to respond to business demands**

3.2 Competitive Success

Growing the market may be only way to keep competitive

The competitive companies of the 1990s focus on expanding the size of their market to grow their business and market share. Aggressive companies are constantly redefining the bounds of their market creating a formidable challenge to those trying to keep up. This consumer focused momentum appears to apply to all businesses providing hard product and services, educational institutions, as well as, government agencies. The other common denominators appear to include cost reduction and more productivity through empowerment.

Let's look the employees of any given company as consumers. Many of these consumers have desktop computers such as PCs, Macs, and RISC workstations, others use terminals to access minicomputer, midrange systems, and mainframe based applications. Some desktop users also use their system to access servers and other hosts. For the most part these consumers have the common goals of getting their job done as quickly and efficiently as possible.

From an IS context these consumers have a need to access data, update data, calculate, communicate, and generate documentation (text, graphics, voice, and image). These customers or potential IS customers have a need for information, connectivity, interconnectivity, application and technical support, and administrative assistance. They would prefer not to be technicians. In some cases, however, their demand is so strong they are building their own mini-IS organizations to meet their business needs.

IS can provide for these services, however, some major inhibitors have to be overcome to entice the consumer to buy the IS services. Additionally certain traditional IS provided services may have to be taken over by the consumer fro responsiveness and cost containment. The inhibitors to the effective use of the IS enterprise network tend to be organizational, cultural, and technical. (See insert on next page.)

We will explore these for an enterprise network environment and how NetWare might be used to meet these consumers' needs in the subsequent chapters of this book.

Competitive means:
- **Better quality**
- **Better service**
- **Minimum cost**
- **Empowerment**

3.3 More and Better for Less

Successful companies have discovered that in the complex business environment of the 1990s it takes more than a "back to the basics" slogan, reentrenchment, and a focus on cost reduction to maintain and grow their market share. These approaches do not provide the desired responsiveness, cost effectiveness, or competitive edge.

These companies found that the business environment of the late 1980s and early 1990s demanded more decisions more rapidly than ever before. Responsiveness was being stifled by traditional hierarchical controls. New approaches to address the

It takes more than "back to the basics"

Traditional controls stifled responsiveness

business needs of the 1990s had to be found. Decision processes had to be changed to respond to the need. (This change is sometimes referred to as *shifting paradigms*. Paradigms must

---

par•a•digm
An example that serves as pattern or model.
American Heritage Dictionary

---

shift when the fundamental premise for a business or technical model (paradigm) is no longer valid.)

The most frustrating aspect of paradigm shifts to enterprise network professionals is that shifts are usually introduced by people outside of their business. In the enterprise network business many networks are being driven by people applying FAX machines, cellular phones, and TV monitors to build their own networks. But paradigm shifts are really predictable if one pays attention to the momentum of the various industries and focuses on solutions that empower the masses to do something they want to do or want to buy.

> Some things must be done differently to grow the business, respond faster, and provide better product with fewer people for less cost.
>
> It takes more than "moving the chairs around" or "removing some chairs" to achieve the goals of rightsizing.

The most prevalent change has been to delegate more responsibility and accountability to line departments. The companies that have done this have discovered that this often provides better quality products and services in addition to greater responsiveness while providing cost savings. This *empowerment*, however, also challenges the existing infrastructure, management technologies, procedures, and tools which were often built for more focused control. This change therefore usually requires a reassessment of the control objectives, risks and technologies applied.

The companies that have seen the most benefits from delegating responsibility and accountability downward (empowerment) have an effective risk management process or may be in for a rude surprise. Over the years large companies have developed reliable "backroom" operational procedures and guidelines to protect the company. Many of the benefits of these procedures are taken for granted and delegating mission critical applications to organizations that don't address those exposures may prove very disruptive when problems arise.

Empowerment introduces greater risk

From an information systems standpoint this often means *empowering* the line organizations to resolve their own unique tactical information processing needs, often with inexpensive and less traditional technology. It also means that the IS organization must provide effective communication channels to ensure operational and strategic information availability and timeliness.

New *paradigm*: Departments may have do their own tactical information processing

Empowerment means:
- The line organizations need more information
- The information must be more timely
- More decision tools must be made available
- Ongoing risk assessments are required.

This specter of potential disaster makes it is very difficult for some infrastructures to give up or reduce their control. This concern is especially true for organizations that have developed extensive controls in order to deliver *guaranteed service levels* and *protect the corporate information asset*.

For some of these organizations it takes executive management pressure to break loose some of the responsibility and accountability (control) in other companies the internal departments may simple bypass the process and take their chances.

Control may be:
- Given away
- Taken away
- Usurped

The new desktop technologies and network operating systems, such as NetWare, make it easy for departments to take on some of the information systems responsibilities. This can be done with or without the IS organizations support.

If the IS organization doesn't understand these technologies, the more aggressive departments will solve their business problems without any IS influence or involvement.

Some Inhibitors to the growing IS Marketplace

Organizational
- Ownership and control of data
- Budget
- Measurements
- Responsibility
- Accountability

Cultural
- Knowledge of traditional environment and tools
- Knowledge of workgroup, LAN environment, and tools
- Terminology

Technical
- Connectivity complexity and controls
- Consistent data access interfaces
- Security
- Provision of timely and cost effective remote support
- Support for the wide variety of applications
- Provision of consistent service levels
- Provision for charging for service

3.4 Downsizing IS

Taken to extremes this delegation of an information systems responsibility to the ultimate users using less expensive technology is often referred to as downsizing [IS] - not to be confused with downsizing an organization to fewer people or flattening organizations, although these are frequently coincident.

In these downsized [IS] situations the traditional IS infrastructure and solutions are often discarded in favor of less expensive and more end user oriented solutions. There are many articles in the personal computer and LAN trade press that applaud these achievements and extol the significance of client-server computing and replacing mainframe and midrange systems with local area networks and saving millions of dollars. Figure 3-1 highlights the technology and price point dilemma that the IS organization must constantly assess.

Downsizing
- **Delegating IS Responsibilities**
- **Using less expensive equipment**

Figure 3-1 Downsizing Hardware Savings

Like most buzzwords in information technology, *downsizing* is used in several variations ranging from the elimination of a mainframe and replacing it by a midrange system or a server-based solution to moving a specific application off the mainframe onto a midrange with a LAN or a LAN-based solution. Unfortunately the distinctions often get blurred in the reporting. Perhaps even more disconcerting is the total absence of the organizational and control environments involved. Let's look at one such downsizing successes.

Read the articles carefully to determine how the term *downsize* is used

3.4.1 Downsizing to a Midrange System

The first downsizing example is a small manufacturing company that replaced its old mainframe, an IBM 4300 system using IBM's VSE operating system and IBM's CICS on-line transaction processing subsystem, with an IBM AS/400 midrange system and some new workstations (see Fig. 3-2).

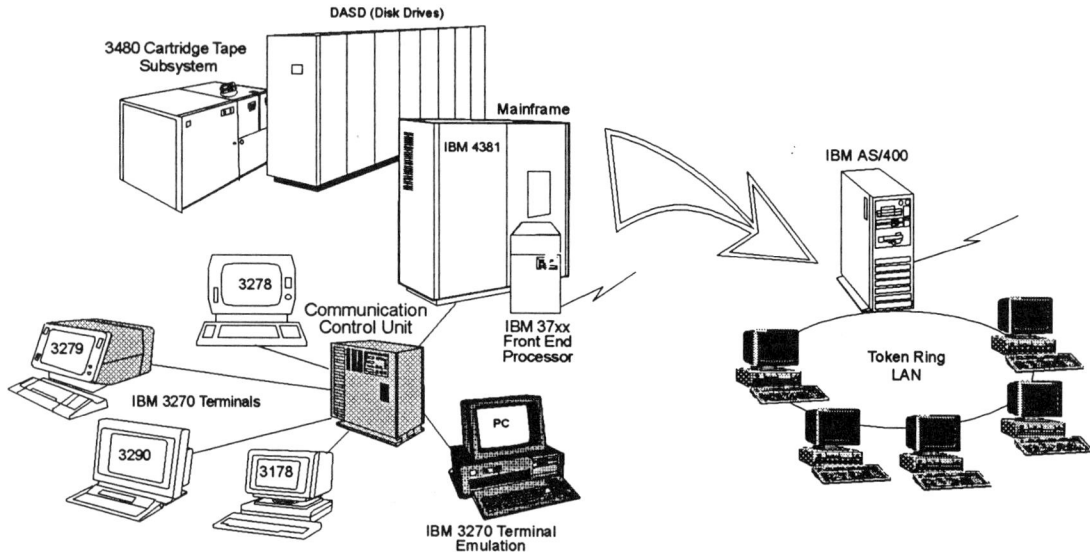

Figure 3-2 Downsizing to a Midrange System

A mainframe to midrange downsize example

On the surface it sounds like a mainframe is being downsized to midrange system. In fact, it is more of an old midrange technology being replaced with a newer midrange and desktop technology. The real value, however, comes from the change of operating systems and applications not the system hardware. (The IBM 4300 could have been replaced by a rack-mounted IBM ES/9000 to gain many of the newer processor and peripheral device savings if the sole criteria were the hardware configuration.) In this case, however, the new operating system reduced the systems management chores and significantly improved the company's ability to respond to new application requirements.

Despite the hardware differences the real benefit comes from the operating system and application software change.

The new system was justified on the savings in power, space, support skills, software license fees, and hardware maintenance fees. No fundamental control and support infrastructure changes were required. To extend the capabilities of the new workstations the company used IBM's PC Support (PCS) software, which let the workstations access midrange disk capacity (file folders) and exchange files.

A hardware software downsize with minimal infrastructure or organizational change

3.4.2 Downsizing to NetWare

Some companies that have replaced mainframes (usually mainframes from the lowend) and maidrange systems with workstations and servers (LANs). One such company, a small retail chain, replaced their IBM 4300 mainframe with multiple workstations and a NetWare server. The from and to configurations are depicted in Figure 3-3.

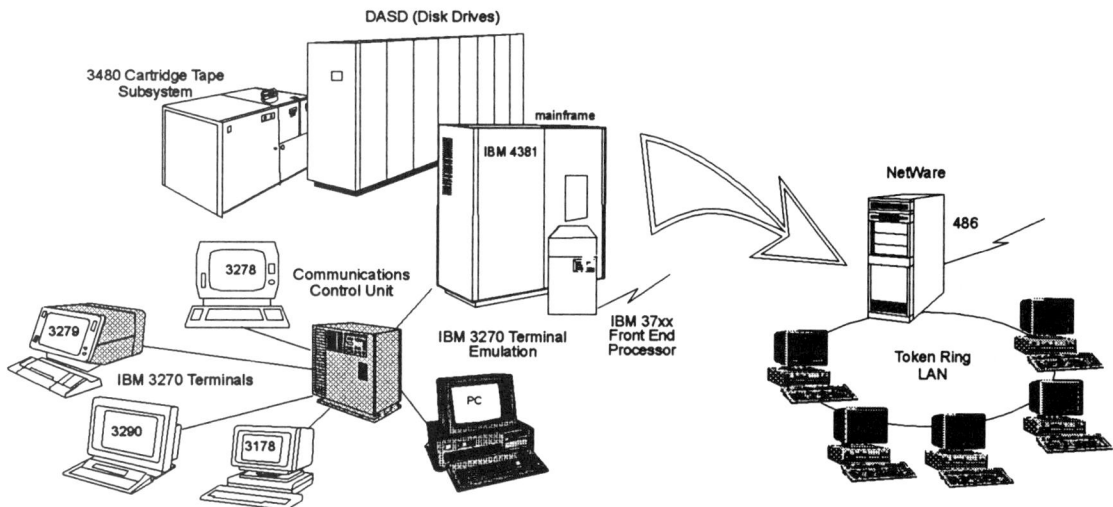

Figure 3-3 Downsizing a Mainframe to a LAN

From a hardware configuration standpoint, there doesn't appear to be any major difference from this example and the downsized mainframe to AS/400 example in Figure 3-2; however, there are some significant differences. The primary technical difference is the operating system. The primary management

The application moves from a host into each workstation

LAN can refer to the physical connection technology or the entire hardware and software configuration.

Multiple stand-alone minicomputer systems replaced with PC and server network

difference is the management of a centrally controlled system (the IBM AS/400) and a user controlled system (Workstations attached to a NetWare server). In other words, in this example (see Fig. 3-3) the application moves out of the host and into the workstation, and uses the server to provide common services. In the AS/400 configuration the applications resided in the host.

Another important difference between Figure 3-2 and Figure 3-3 is the way the users use the term *LAN*. In the 4300 to AS/400 downsize scenario the LAN was a token ring, while in the 4300 to NetWare the term *LAN* referred to the total configuration including the workstation, server, and the physical connection (the token ring).

From an organizational and control standpoint, the NetWare solution provides a better fit for organizations that are comfortable with user autonomy since only the shared resources such as common files and server-based applications are managed by the support organization. The workstations in this scenario are totally under the control of the user.

In the Figure 3-2 AS/400 scenario, the entire application and application resources are controlled by the AS/400. The desktop computers are used as terminals when accessing to the AS/400.

This downsizing solution met the company's immediate business needs and enabled the user departments to augment the IS provided applications with department specific applications that exploited the NetWare server capacity and data administration.

3.4.3 A Case Study

Let's look at how a state government IS organization replaced their aging standalone minicomputer-based judicial record keeping system with a new case management system that tracks court fines, fees, stores depositions, and keeps potential juror lists based on NetWare and an enterprise network solution. (This appeared as a success story in the March 22, 1993 edition of INFOWORLD, reported by Alice LaPlante on page 66 using the eye-catching headline of "Court Exiles Minicomputers, Scales Down with PCs.")

The old record keeping system used 44 stand-alone (not interconnected) Wang minicomputers that didn't have the capacity to keep up with the growing workload. Additionally it was getting increasingly harder for the application programmers to respond to new functional requirements in a timely manner using the COBOL-based applications. These shortcomings had resulted in long waiting lines for getting record information and little satisfaction in getting even simple questions answered.

The IS organization was faced with the choice of upgrading the existing systems or looking to a state-wide network solution that would respond to the current and future needs. The current systems cost more than $400,000 a year in hardware and software maintenance. Using the same technology would cost close to a half million dollars for the Wang systems, additional maintenance and the addition of programming staff.

Spend more money on stop-gap solution or select new solution

The IS team after much analysis selected a solution that was immediately responsive to the current needs, that used the existing programming staff, and that positioned for future growth. The new case management system which would cost $3.8M with $250,000 maintenance per year was cost justified with cost avoidance and improved service level.

Solutions aren't inexpensive

The new case management system was comprised of 14 HP9000 Series 800 systems which linked 800 PCs that were scattered throughout the state. The PCs hosted the data base and Windows client applications and used NetWare as the network operating system and TCP/IP as the network protocol. The existing programming team quickly became knowledgeable in using Windows-based object oriented programming, structured query language (SQL) and graphical user interfaces. This allowed them to implement the new system in 8 months and begin roll-out. The biggest challenge was retraining the users who were not used to working with Windows.

User training or retraining is an important consideration

This success story has several important aspects of a successful downsizing effort. The most rudimentary piece in the success of this solution was the general agreement of the IS organization and the users that the old system was broken and the technology did not match the needs of the business. Without this agreement the success is at risk from the start. Other important elements present in this case study that improved the odds for success include:

Downsizing success odds high when both IS and user agree on what is broken

- A definitive business problem
- Recognition that the existing solution is not extensible
- A existing standalone system which eases the roll-out
- Uses existing application staff
- The solution immediately provided better service levels and more functionality
- A solution that can easily to respond to capacity and functional changes
- Using tested desktop application enabling technology
- Selecting a network operating system that provides the necessary flexibility
- A thorough business analysis and cost justification
- Recognition that a robust solution requires up front investment ($3.8M) for longer term payback

NetWare was selected as the network operating system of choice because it provided the services needed and supported the interconnection protocols required, minimal skills were required to install and operate, support was readily available, and Net-Ware provided a solid platform for the administrating and managing the various networks.

3.4.4 What can You Expect from Downsizing

This judicial case management system case study reflects what can be done and some of the key management considerations of the downsizing effort. Unfortunately, the trade journals are full of articles that espouse success and neglect to describe the business problem and the key elements that assisted the company meet its objectives.

Solutions abound
- Open
- Downsize
- Rightsize
- Client-server
- Object-oriented
- Reengineer
- GUI

These articles typically highlight substantial savings and usually are riddled with multiple industry buzzwords. These include: *open systems*, *downsizing* and *rightsizing*, *client-server* technologies, *object-oriented* programs, *reengineering* existing systems, *graphical user interfaces (GUI)*,and *outsourcing*. Other articles describe exposures and problems based on some bad experience or based on scholarly analysis. The positive articles often lack credibility due to lack of specifics and the negative articles are often dismissed as the "old guard" thinking. In either instance, however, it is very difficult to come away from the article with a clear image of the problem, the solution and how the technologies were applied because of the state of our industry's terminology. As a direct consequence of this terminology fuzziness it is important not to jump to a conclusion based on the substance of these articles, whether they are positive or negative. The primary message that most of these articles highlight is that change is required and there are approaches that seem to work and there are approaches that are before their time.

Primary message
- **Change is required**
- **Multiple approaches**

Those companies that do the preliminary work have a greater chance of their solution withstanding the test of time, although surprises may still be ahead even for the most detailed efforts. A common observation from those who have begun implementing their downsizing plans with client-server technology is that client-server technology is expected to provide long term savings and productivity gains but is not an effective cost cutting measure.

So why are there so many articles that report quick successes? Because there are numerous projects with very aggressive schedules that that have very significant payback. These projects usually have very short installation periods and typically have a well contained scope, such as a specific department. For example the judicial case management case study that we just reviewed was only one portion of the state information system. Most downsizing projects are not enterprise-network-scale solutions.

In many cases a departmental team or specific application group is responsible a specific downsizing project. Using this *small bites* approach minimizes having to assess the over impact across a large enterprise network consumer base. This small bite boundary reduces the scale of the effort and the number of organizations involved in the decision making and the funding of the solution.

Downsizing can reduce the scope and the complexity and improve the timeliness of the solution.

In other words, downsizing can provide a way of getting your arms around a specific business requirement and the newer technologies provide some levers to meet the technical requirements in a timely and cost effective manner.

> ### How to Read Downsizing Articles
>
> Look for:
> - The original business problem being solved
> - The identification of the requirements
> - The approach used to reduce the options
> - How the robustness of the solution was tested
> - How the scalability was validated
> - The length of time the solution has been installed
> - User reactions
> - The associated support costs
> - The flexibility to change

More credibility when specifics described

A prime consideration is that the downsizing solutions do not preclude future enterprise growth. This is one reason that selection of the network operating system is so important at the onset. the appropriate selection will avoid major pain later on.

Implementation models don't clone or scale well

A second and equally important downsizing consideration is scalablity. That is, if the solution works for 15 users, will it work for 100 users, or for 1000 users? Unfortunately there is no easy way to clone the situation and map it from enterprise to another enterprise. There are few tools that readily determine where the design point of the solution is and how easily it scales. The larger scale downsizing projects typically entail several years of development and roll out because extensive design analysis and prototyping must be done to avoid major show stoppers later. We will hear about those projects that skipped these steps over the next several years.

Solution easier if no integration is required but selecting the appropriate networking operating system is fundamental

Downsizing is not a panacea but applied to the appropriate business problem the approach can provide substantial benefits.

3.5 Reengineering

3.5.1 What Does Reengineering Mean?

Reengineering is a term that refers to the process of re-examining existing applications and business problems outside of the context of the current implementation or tools. These new approaches require something more than "work smarter" or "work harder" in order to accomplish the desired objectives. The team or professional doing the analysis needs a grasp of the business problem and the ability to quickly and economically apply technology to address the business problem.

Successful approaches more than:
- Work smarter
- Work harder

The current reengineering tool kit includes desktop hardware and software, network operating systems, graphical user interfaces, standard network protocols, client-server applications, and object-oriented programming.

Most large enterprises have a reengineering initiative under way as part of their rightsizing focus. These reengineering efforts include replacement of older application systems or integrating of new technologies with existing application investments. To better understand how companies are successfully downsizing or rightsizing one has to understand the two dominant IS-centric approaches being used: *retooling* and *reengineering*.

Retooling is analogous to automating

Retooling is analogous to automating. Retooling upgrades the technology applied to an existing process to make it more cost effective, less error prone, and less labor intensive. Retooling can provide significant savings in a process, however, retooling rarely results in any major breakthroughs because the scope is usually confined to the existing process boundaries.

On the other hand, *reengineering* focuses on the business problem rather than the process. The reengineering effort begins with challenges to the original assumptions and *raison d'être* (reasons the application or process exists). Successful reengineering solutions require the analysis of current and future business. A quality reengineering plan must pass the "does not preclude" law of system architecture, as well as pass the accommodation of change test. Such solutions recognize that the user and some of the scaffolding hardware and software may change even before the system is fully implemented.

3.5.2 A Reengineering Case Study

**A reengineering
success story**

Let's look at a reengineering success story in a health plan new business unit of a large insurance company. The existing business system consisted of a paper process that often varied among the regional offices. It had grown extremely paper intensive, often requiring several binders to keep the information for a single case. Marketing and case workers could not keep up with workload.

A team was put together to design and implement a solution. The team examined the existing manual process and functionally decomposed it into discrete understandable pieces. The first design was to essentially automate each of the steps one-for-one, but upon review this was rejected by the team. Instead the team re-examined the elements of the process and evolved a different approach which eliminated several steps in addition to improving the overall productivity of the case workers.

**Reengineering focuses
on the business process**

After having designed the new system in functional context, the team determined that only flexible and affordable technologies could be considered for the building blocks. This is where the team initially ran into trouble.

For the most part, the team members were fairly knowledgeable in the desktop and LAN products available. However, as they moved from the general requirement such as a data base, project management tool, and GUI interface to identify the specific product they were surprised at the amount of product research required and the number of hard trade-offs they were forced to make. This part of the process took longer than any of the team had anticipated, but they worked through these challenges and emerged with a comprehensive new system.

Project used:
- **PCs**
- **GUI**
- **NetWare**
- **Client-server**

The new system included 100 PCs over multiple interconnected NetWare LANs. Each PC included various off-the-shelf software products that provided a Windows-based GUI user interface the client portion of the data base software and the project management software.

The new system helped marketing and the case workers to meet all their deadlines while handle 25 percent more cases. The new system also provides the ability share information among the various regional offices. The underlying technologies (NetWare and PC-based) provide the required flexibility to quickly add function, easily modify and grow with the business without any exceptional new expenses.

Reengineering and outsourcing sometimes intersect during the initial analysis. If the reengineering effort diverts the company's attention or resources to important but diffused areas, it may be more appropriate to redefine the requirements and interfaces of existing systems, and outsource the development, maintenance, and/or operation.

Outsourcing may be a form of reengineering

This outsourcing decision should be made as a business option based on the time to market, the impact on other equally high-priority items, the cost, and the degree of control the company has over changes to the outsourced solution versus the control they have on the in-house solution.

The primary considera-tion in outsourcing is the degree of flexibility it provides

Sometimes only portions of the reengineering solution are outsourced. The most common outsource elements are customer support and LAN support.

Top IS management would identify reengineering and client-server technology as the two most import keys to their ability to meet their measurements in the 1990s.

> **How quickly can your company respond to a business change that demands reinstrumentation or retooling?**
>
> **The answer is usually a function of the company's base tools (e.g., network operating system), the associated infrastructure, the skills available, and the availability of funds to make the change.**

3.6 Rightsizing

3.6.1 What Does Rightsizing Mean?

The term *rightsizing* may better describe the current focus on new technologies and approaches to applying information technology to business problems. Rightsizing is more than a euphemism for downsizing, those applying rightsizing approaches will

Rightsizing is not another word for downsizing

Rightsizing
- Reengineering
- LANs
- Networks
- Client-server

not necessarily be replacing the existing systems . Rightsizing can refer to the redistribution of responsibilities, accountability, and workload to those in the best position to execute for the benefit of their specific organization and the company. This addresses the biggest challenges the IS executive has today, shrinking IS budget and a scarcity of key skills.

Rightsizing options typically result from formal or informal reengineering exercises. Rightsizing solutions usually include using new technologies to augment the existing application, replace a portion of an existing application using newer technology, distributing specific IS functions to individual business units, selective outsourcing of specific portions of the application, or some combination of these. Rightsizing does not necessarily mean replacing the existing system with a new system that uses less expensive or more flexible technology, although in some cases that might be the result.

3.6.2 A Rightsizing Case Study

Business Problem:
- Containing/reducing cost
- Excessive stockpiling carrying costs and obsolescence
- Billing accuracy

Let's explore a medical care, multiple facility, 1000-bed hospital case study. This hospital, like most, has had difficulty in containing and reducing costs associated with medicine and medical supplies. This particular hospital has identified several problem areas that including billing errors and obsolete inventory. The old medicine and medical supplies dispensing system was a combination of a manual paper system and a mainframe-based backroom billing and inventory system. The IS organization was under severe cost-containment pressures.

After examing the business requirements, technical capability, and the logistics problems associated with gaining better control of the dispensing of medicine and supplies, the IS team concluded that a new medical facility materials management system was required. The solution attacked the primary problem at the root. The data needed to be captured at the source, needed to be entered with minimum opportunity for error, and needed to be sent to the mainframe application inventory and billing applications.

Rightsizing project:
- focus on the problem
- leverage the old
- leverage new

The technical solution was to populate the hospital with laptops and desktop PCs with bar-code readers. This allowed for easy and accurate data entry when dispensing the medicine and medical supplies. Both the desktop and laptop PCs were connected to a NetWare LAN. To assist the hospital staff in using the new data entry system a Windows-based GUI front-end was developed to prompt the user and to launch the data transfer to the mainframe form the PC. An electronic data interchange (EDI) connection was installed for electronically ordering supplies.

This solution would cost $250,000 for software and network hardware with an annual $50K for support. This proposed expenditure appeared to pay for itself in savings over the first year. It was estimated that the improved inventory control would provide a 25 percent reduction in stock, saving more than $100,000 annually. The elimination of the obsolete inventory was estimated to save $150,000 in the first year.

Additionally savings were realized immediately in staff productivity by the elimination of the data entry from the old paper forms, as well as in the elimination of the paper documentation and training to fill out the forms. The new system also reduced the labor associated in managing the supply inventory and the EDI allowed for lowering the economic order quantity since less safety stock was now required.

The project was implemented over four months using PCs and NetWare. NetWare and the Windows software on the PCs allowed the team to use available skills and provided the desired flexibility for future growth and functional enhancements. The biggest complaint upon completion of the project was that the analysis of options and cost justification took longer than it took to implement the system.

Rightsizing
- **identified specific problem**
- **augmented with new approaches and technology**
- **cost justified with immediate savings**
- **selected technologies that minimize risk**
- **encompasses downsizing**

3.6.3 Yours, Mine, and Our Model

Boundaries for support must be set up

Rightsizing often entails the introduction of new technologies that require the using department or user to take on specific responsibilities. This requires that well-defined boundaries be set up between those aspects of information access, processing, and management that lend themselves to being delegated away from the traditional controls and processes and those that do not. The determination of these boundaries are the gray area that most companies are struggling with.

Yours, mine, ours model leverages the strengths of each organization.

Figure 3-4 conceptually portrays the relationship frequently encountered during rightsizing. The diagram is intended to emphasize that the relative size differences of systems managed by the normal IS organization versus the number of desktop com-

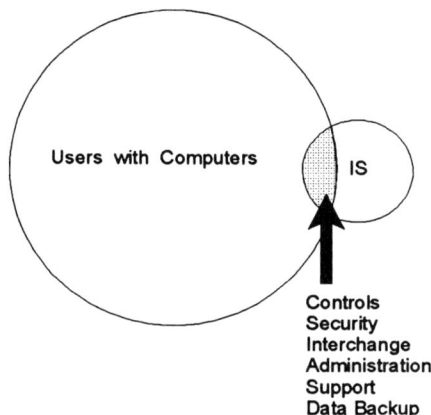

Figure 3-4 Yours, Mine, and Ours Model

puters managed by the users. I refer to this relationships portrayed in the diagram as the *yours*, *mine*, and *ours* model. This model is intended to identify the boundaries between user and IS responsibilities. (Obviously the *yours* and the *mine* references will change between the user and IS based on which is looking at the model, but the relationships appear to remain constant. For example, the *your* portion of the model might represent the user owned and managed systems and resources if viewed by and IS organization member.

In an enterprise network of the 1990s it is doubtful that IS can afford to exert the kind of control at the user's PC that were exerted on mainframe and mini applications. Most IS organizations now expect that each user or user department has some degree of responsibility for the local user PCs.

The IS portion of the model represents the domain IS of enterprise network-managed resources. Resources within this boundary are entirely under the IS control. The IS organization grants access to authorized users and protects their service level. This portion of the model provides the traditional infrastructure, controls, and applications.

The *ours* portion of the model refers to those services and applications that can overlap between the department and the enterprise network IS organization. This area is usually associated with agreements between the various organizations as to who has the control for which value added service. The *our* portion of the model is the the most difficult because this is where the technology and the organizational and control requirements are really put to the test.

For example, if the network operating system doesn't readily allow the IS organization to provide the management support or control required by the user (consumer), the *our* portion of this model can represent substantial overhead and expense. The other alternative is that the IS organization take risk and hope that the areas not covered will not impact the service. One of the reasons NetWare is so popular in rightsizing projects is that it provides the most flexibility in this area.

 For simplicity I characterize the *ours* area as touching on access controls, security authentication and management, interchange connectivity, user administration, help desk and user support, and data backup and recovery. These tend to be the most common services that an enterprise network user needs.

So why is delegating associated with rightsizing? Because most IS organizations are not in a position to take on the additional workload required to support the desktop systems and the users are not in a position to provide the administrative and data management services required for a production system. The network operating system you select will determine your delegation flexibility and the tools available.

> Rightsizing approaches address the business needs with technical solutions that meet the customers objectives in a timely manner by using a mix of existing and less expensive technologies. The solution may involve delegating certain responsibilities to the customer or from the user to the IS organization.

3.6.4 The Formula for Rightsizing Success

Companies that have easily and successfully "rightsized" have typically had many of the prerequisite change agents such as a

$$success = profitable,\ competitive,\ measurable\ improvements$$

funded project and an appreciation of the application.

Successful rightsizing:
- **Grassroots**
- **Demonstrated value**
- **Experimentation**

The pre- or co-requisites to success are:
- Common agreement that change is required
- Benefits reflected immediately on implementation
- User willingness to use new interfaces and accept new responsibilities
- Tools to support the new applications
- Robust technologies
- Availability of the required skills
- A solution that is flexible and scales

Some of the elements of these key ingredients have typically been well under way long before the company mandate in many of the companies that have successfully rightsized. In those companies the market-driven individuals, departments, or divisions had already focused on ways to demonstrate value. This focus drove them to experiment with newer technologies and other uses of existing technological investments. The network operating system is usually a significant piece of the technical solution since it can expand or limit the options.

3.7 How Agile Is Your Company?

A company can determine its agility by reviewing its ability to effectively respond to change. The parameters are:

- Time to make the change
- Cost of the change and the funds available
- Ability to meet current requirements (time and funding)
- Flexibility for new demands (time and funding)

Effective response requires:
- **Time**
- **Dollars**
- **Resource for old and new**
- **Flexibility**

The time to make a change is usually a function of the company's ability to leverage existing investments, introduce a new technology, or marry previous technology and infrastructure investments with new technology. The network operating system can directly influence your company's agility.

Survival in the 1990s requires:
- **A focus on the business dynamics**
- **A willingness to empower to achieve common goals**
- **The ability to separate technical content from hype**
- **A willingness to give up some control**
- **The ability to recognize opportunities**
- **The ability to select robust technologies**

The current focus is on client-server and reengineering technology. The network operating system is a critical element.

3.8 Summary

To this point in the book we have discussed some of corporate computing issues associated with downsizing, rightsizing, reengineering, and outsourcing the existing application systems and support infrastructure. In brief :

- Downsizing involves the changing of hardware, software and sometimes the control model.

- Reengineering involves the applying new approaches and new technologies to replace old processes.

- Rightsizing involves the augmenting of the existing information systems solutions with new less expensive technologies. Rightsizing encompasses downsizing and reengineering

Now we come to the rub: there is even a more powerful *upsizing* movement.

Chapter 4

Upsizing

The early 1990s will probably be remembered most for major political upheavals, increased global competition, increased and conflicting economic and business pressures and radical corporate cultural, structural, and organizational changes. There is little likelihood that the pace will slow in the near future. One such change encompasses the dichotomies associated with *rightsizing* and *upsizing* using the *enterprise network*.

This *upsizing* is the basically the label used to describe the movement of departmental systems into the enterprise network. The departments to have their grassroots developed applications, workstations, and local-area networks (LANs) participate in the enterprise network in order to access enterprisewide data, share enterprisewide resource, and benefit from the security and support provided by the enterprise network infrastructure.

Rapidly changing technologies

**Lots of change
Lots of choices**

Forces:
● **Rightsizing**
● **Upsizing**

4.1 Converging Pressures

From an enterprise network providers are seeing an unusual convergence of two very significant trends (see Fig. 4-1):

- Business pressures to *rightsize* infrastructure applications (use new network technologies)

- Departmental pressure to *upsize* (use corporate managed network and resources)

The *rightsizing* pressures are driving the IS infrastructure to look to new approaches of providing more services using the very technologies that the depart-

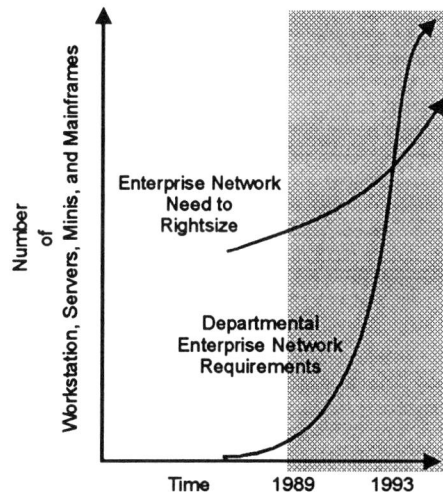

Figure 4-1 Upsizing Pressures

mental users are asking the IS organization to help manage.

Many user departments have already implemented their own NetWare networks and with server based applications and they are now pushing to *upsize* these local information systems into the IS infrastructure. These departmental organizations want to use the corporate networks, to access IS managed data, and to use IS administrative and support skills whenever possible as identified in the yours, mine, and ours model.

When the rightsizing and upsizing trends are closely scrutinized it becomes clear that the effective use and management of new workstation technologies (e.g., desktop, laptop, notebook, and hand-held computers) are at the core of the trend and the dichotomy. The IS opportunity, or challenge, centers on its ability to effectively support and empower the user while providing corporate-wide service levels and asset protection.

The primary point of convergence of both the user departments and corporate computing organizations is the *enterprise network*. This enterprise network is very dependent on a comprehensive network operating system and system management tools.

Convergence of corporate and departmental computing

The point of intersection is the support of the end-user workstation

Convergence of corporate and departmental computing

4.2 The S-curve Is a Key

The focus is now on the ability to share resources among multiple workers and the ability to support the workers and their work environment from a remote location. The three most compelling and recurring reasons for integration are:

Focus:
● **Share resources**
● **Remote support**

- Sharing physical resources
- Sharing data
- Sharing skills and knowledge

Many IS organizations are struggling with the ever increasing rate of change and increasing demands on the enterprise network, however, the changes and the associated requirements are predictable. Knowing the upcoming changes and motivations will help you position your support infrastructure to be ready for the next stage.

The changes and the motivation are predictable

Reasons to Interface or Integrate

Sharing physical resources:

- Minimize redundant costs
- Maximize the efficiency of existing investments
- Resources include processor cycles and main storage, printers, disk storage, and communication lines
- Save desk space and office space

Shared data:

- Access and update common data in a timely manner
- Avoid cost, time,and errors of re-entering data into other applications
- Access shared file and shared data base systems
- Enable sophisticated security and performance controls

Sharing skills and knowledge:

- Maximize the quality of service
- Eliminate replicating skill or knowledge at each location

I use an S-curve chart (see Fig. 4-2) to help me understand, forecast, and communicate the upsizing phenomena. This S-curve was derived from Richard L. Nolan's stages of EDP growth model. (The label S-curve comes from the shape of the

S-curve derived from Nolan's stages of EDP growth

curve as the applications evolve.) This model was the result of studying the information systems growth of several Fortune 100 companies in terms of their users-driven applications, their needs, and their budgets vis-à-vis the requested enterprise IS involvement.

The S-curve depicts information systems involvement as the user evolves from separate organizational systems to systems that require enterprisewide systems integration. The S-curve highlights that user solutions evolve through three stages, which I characterize as (1) departmental standalone solutions, (2) interdepartmental resource, (3) enterprise network integration. This was first described at an IBM users' group meeting, Guide 48, in 1979, as part of a discussion on programming "Languages in a Distributed Environment."

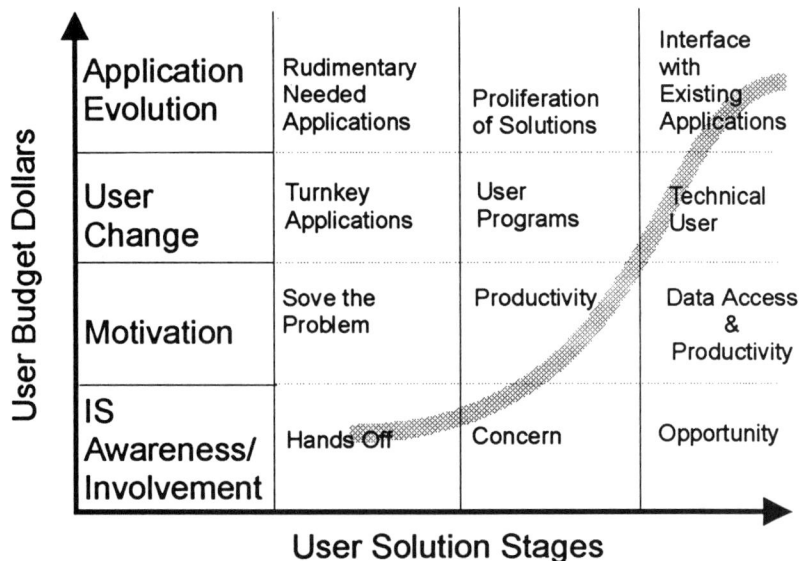

Three stages:
- **Stand alone**
- **Resource sharing**
- **Integrated**

User Budget Dollars			
Application Evolution	Rudimentary Needed Applications	Proliferation of Solutions	Interface with Existing Applications
User Change	Turnkey Applications	User Programs	Technical User
Motivation	Sove the Problem	Productivity	Data Access & Productivity
IS Awareness/ Involvement	Hands Off	Concern	Opportunity

User Solution Stages

Figure 4-2   Stages of User Application Development

The user driven application(s) move(s) through the stages accompanied by additional user expenditure, demands for additional user skills, until the user crosses a threshold where either too much time or too much money is required to continue. At this stage, usually the integration stage, the enterprise network organization is sought out for help. (The help request may come in the form of an outsourcing contract.)

> The S-curve evolution begins with dedicated resources (equipment and applications to a person, department, or organization) and evolves through multiple stages of integration until there is a need to find a coordinator to manage the sharing of key resources and data.

If you notice the IS Awareness/Involvement row on the S-curve diagram in Figure 4.2, you will note that the value of IS involvement increases in the most in the third stage. A natural corequisite for the enterprise network integration stage may be to write new applications, reengineer, or buy new applications. This may be easier when the user department has evolved to this stage since there is a better appreciation of the value and the cost, an appreciation that wasn't there during the first two stages.

User finds threshold:
- Cost
- Skill
- Time

> User information systems spending habits are predictable and follow an S-curve. The evolution is closely tied to affordability, skill, and time expended.

4.3 An Example S-curve Scenario

Let's explore a representative enterprise network scenario. In this scenario a specific department whose users all have personal computers that are connected to a mainframe to access the on-line business transactions also use their workstation as a personal computer to run spreadsheets and do personal letter preparation. The users use the desktop computer in two modes: a terminal access to the host applications and a personal desktop tool.

In the first stage the users are all very satisfied with the newly found tools that enhance their individual productivity. Their primary considerations are how to get their output printed at a

Dual use PCs:
- Terminal access
- Personal desktop

First Stage:
- Dedicated printers
- Swapping diskettes
- Workgroup computing

local printer and how to exchange files. After various attempts at meeting these requirements our representative department users recognize that they cannot afford the idealized solution of a dedicated local printer per desk and a personal computer with infinite disk space. Additionally, the passing of diskettes back and forth is far less than productive.

Second Stage:
- Resource sharing
- Local support
- Interconnectivity

To address these needs the department looks to some more sophisticated solutions that allow sharing of resources. One such solution might be the introduction of a peer-to-peer or workgroup network that allows the workstations to share resources. This brings with it some sensitivity to the existing software and connectivity. As user productivity wanes due to logistical conflicts stemming from in sharing individual workstation resources, the value of a dedicated server emerges.

This recognition usually marks the beginning of the transition into the second stage. The second stage is marked by the emergence of a local information technology support team (formal or informal) that keeps the user workstations and connectivity intact. This second stage is fraught with technical and local business trade-offs regarding backup and security (if any) software to be used, and so on.

Additionally, even if the mainframe application access is the same, other network connectivity considerations begin to arise regarding the server and workstation. This is also the stage in which some departments begin interconnecting local networks with other departments.

Third Stage threshold:
- More skills
- Increased expenditures
- Increased time
- Owner identification
- Outside help

As the internetwork dependencies increase, the individual users and/or management realize that they may be spending too much time on information technology issues as opposed to getting their work done. This marks the entry into third stage: the integration stage. At this stage, several options arise: a loose federation of departmental users can evolve to try to share common resources with no clear owner of the network, the enterprise network organization can be sought out for help, or an outside source can be engaged to provide the network service and support. It is in this third stage that there is a clear opportunity for IS to pick up cash paying customers.

Third stage of the S-curve is an IS and departmental opportunity.

4.4 Multiple Iterations of the S-curve

From an enterprise network organization standpoint several significant observations can be made regarding user solutions and the S-curve evolution, however, I will have to digress to explain them.

4.4.1 First Iteration- General Purpose Mainframes

When I first introduced this user budget driven S-curve, the characterization was based on the evolution from multiple specialized systems in the 1960s and early 1970s to general purpose mainframes with operating systems that had been designed to maximize resource sharing. This was the consolidation to the mainframe S-curve, and the solution for sharing was to be part of the subsystem environment.

First tracked S-curve:
- Consolidation to mainframe
- Applications part of same subsystem

4.4.2 Second Iteration - Minis

By the late 1970s and early 1980s the press was filled with numerous articles foretelling the imminent end of the mainframe - (the mainframe was to be obviated by minicomputers). Hundreds of thousands of minis and midrange processors were installed during the 1980s, and the users of these systems evolved through a second iteration of the S-curve, but the mainframe remained.

Second S-curve:
- Minis and midrange
- But mainframes remained
- Sharing meant interoperability

When the mini-based applications evolved into the third stage (the enterprise integration stage) the industry looked for *interoperability* solutions. Interoperability solutions were intended to mask the differences between the various systems, to protect the existing investments and form an integrated enterprise network. This intention made sense for a subset of the application base, but many applications were hampered by hardware and operating

Interoperability solutions not complete and cost too much

Currently:
- **Over 100K mainframes**
- **Over 1M minis/midrange**

system constraints and differences. At that time the solutions were too expensive for many companies and volumes were too low to allow the vendors to bring the price down.

As of this writing there are more than a hundred thousand mainframes and close to one million minis and midrange systems, including IBM S/38s and AS/400s or DEC VAX systems, to name just a few.

> **Human history becomes more and more a race between education and catastrophe.**
>
> *H. G. Wells*

4.4.3 Third Iteration - *Network Computing*

LAN could be likened to distributed mini/midrange

Many companies are currently experiencing the third S-curve iteration, which I refer to as *network computing*. Most IS professionals saw this coming, but were not sure how to influence it. In fact, the evolution took a little detour because the personal computers played a dual role, first as terminals (with hardware and software terminal emulation) and second as a private tool set. As soon as the need for sharing resources emerged, LAN operating systems were introduced and the curve was true to form.

The difference is that the vendors designed the minis and you get to design the LAN

These LAN solutions could be likened to *distributed minis* or *midrange systems*. There are just two significant differences: it is a *build-it-yourself* system and it is often designed by individuals with no consideration of sharing. (Most minis and midrange systems, such as the IBM AS/400, are complete industrial strength turnkey-type systems.)

Very difficult to sort through the options and trade-offs

This build-it-yourself approach provides enormous flexibility, with the components usually within the scope of a department's discretionary budget. The challenge for the department or division manager is to make sure that the solutions meet the requirements in an environment where the technologies themselves are often enshrouded with jargon and fuzzily defined terms.

For example, the billing department would like to have ready access to the order data base in the sales department for the price of a common data base is too expensive for either department individually, considering the product price, hardware, and support. The solution is an interdepartmental network and the management issues that come with it. Welcome to stage two!

Company moves to third stage of S-curve for printer support

Let's look at a stage 2 exit threshold example. This company has already established itself in stage 1 with LANs and printer sharing. The problem was that many of the user departments were losing printer output and significant time waiting for this output. I can remember people in tears as they told me about their output problem. They showed me several pages of strange characters and number combinations across several pages. When I suggested that they reprint it, I was told that the particular accounting program being used only printed this report once—and here it was! The workers were ready for the obvious solution, a dedicated printer for those that needed one. This solution would cost in excess of $300,000 in capital expenditure, maintenance, and supplies for the company.

The chief financial officer suggested that other avenues be explored, even though the lost financial reports were within his department. The company's IS staff was approached to suggest an alternative. An information systems specialist was assigned to provide a robust print support structure for the existing printers and make the appropriate upgrades as well as to work with the software vendors to better understand or resolve their product frailties. This alternative resulted in a satisfied user community and a savings of $200,000 of the projected $300,000 cost.

The third S-curve iteration makes extensive use of personal computer and local area network technology. The LAN operating systems make common LAN resources, such as files and printers, available to DOS, Windows, OS/2 UNIX, and Mac workstations for network computing. Network computing entails the evolution of interconnecting local and remote LAN computing with different personal computer, mini, and mainframe systems. The current industry buzzword for this enterprise network technology is *internetworking*.

Third S-curve uses:
- LANs
- Personal computer
- Network computing

Our enterprises now have over 150 million personal computers worldwide, more than 8 million LANs, as well as most of the

Currently over:
- 150M PCs
- 8M LANs
- 1M minis/midrange
- 100K mainframes

30 percent of the PCs connected to LANs but growing

Many companies are using NetWare for Stages 1 and 2 of the network computing S-curve

NetWare product evolution is tracking Fortune 1000 network computing S-curve

With NetWare 4 Novell is supporting Stage 3

minis and mainframe systems of the previous iterations, since most of them still run mission critical workloads.

Probably less than 30 percent of these LANs are currently internetworked among minis and mainframes. But the demand is accelerating with the need to provide interconnectivity not only with the traditional LAN and wide-area network (WAN) connectivity but also with sophisticated dial-in technologies and wireless approaches.

If you were to take a cross section of enterprises today, you would find that each enterprise has organizations at various stages within the S-curve and within various iterations of the S-curves (e.g., some organizations' applications are completely on the mainframe, other organizations' applications may be completely on minis, etc.). It is this variety together with potential difficulty in integrating the old with the new technologies that causes many organizations to ponder tactical or strategic decisions — in the meantime the decision is end-user driven. For many enterprises this decision has resulted in a new S-curve with NetWare.

It is interesting to note that NetWare's product evolution very closely tracks current network computing S-curve: a departmental solution, interdepartmental solutions with network management, and now the focus is on all aspects of enterprise networking as practiced by the Fortune 1000 companies.

Now the challenge for both the enterprise and Novell NetWare-based products is to smoothly evolve into the third stage of the curve. The rest of this book discusses the managerial issues and technical considerations of how NetWare can meet your enterprise requirements.

4.4.4 Iterative S-curve Attributes

The S-curve evolution and iterations can be used by enterprise network management to identify where they are and anticipate what they must do next.

The following is a list of what has been learned to date in an enterprise network context:

- The upward evolutionary movement is directly associated with the need to share either resources or data.

- Each successive technology S-curve tends to bring more users who collectively have more dollars to solve the problem.

- The new technology does not typically build on the past, in fact, it often appears to provide overlapping solutions.

- The new technology does not usually replace the old, however, it often adds more potential for integration complexity later.

- Once in the integration stage of a particular S-curve, the users tend to stay there until their information processing needs exceed the ability of the IS organization's ability or desire to support the need.

- Users in the integration stage that are unsatisfied look for other avenues. If a user or departmental system is affordable, another iteration of the curve begins. The likelihood of this movement is increased coincident with the introduction of new solutions with lower price and skill points.

- The number of user organization personnel that could be characterized as IS professionals outside of the enterprise network traditional IS organization increases with each S-curve iteration.

4.5 Good News - Bad News

From an IS viewpoint the entry into the third stage of the S-curve is usually a good news-bad news theme.

The good news is that folks with money are at the gates.

The bad news is that the easy work has already been taken care of the at one price point and that they now want to do the tough part to be done at the same price point! A typical corequisite for the integration stage is to write new applications, reengineer, or buy new applications since the departmental solutions don't necessarily scale well.

Additionally, many enterprises are already supporting at least two iterations of the S-curve and that the third repetition has more systems by two orders of magnitude.

Good news - bad news
- Want IS help
- The easy part already done

Figure 4-3 depicts the three stages and highlights the relative volume and budget implications of each of the last three iterations (mainframe, mini, and now network computing). Each S-curve begins with department-initiated and controlled applications and equipment and then moves through the three stages. The evolution in each stage is marked with additional user expenditure and the need for additional skills until a threshold is crossed.

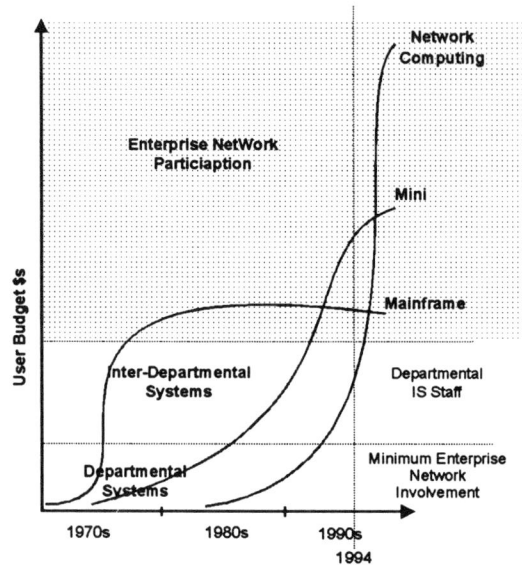

Figure 4-3   S-curve Iterations

Users stay until:
- Service not adequate
- New options available

The users stay in the third stage until their needs are not satisfied and an alternative solution is available. The most common need not satisfied is responsiveness. Each successive S-curve stage is marked with the user's willingness to do more themselves and make tough trade-offs to achieve the responsiveness they desire.

Good news
- Technology better
- Internetworking affordable
- Techniques to direct budget and energy momentum

The good news is that technology has improved, the cost of new internetworking solutions has come down dramatically, and if a way to channel the user budget dollars can be found and if the users are willing to do some IS work, a very responsive information model can be achieved.

Good news :
- The third stage is an IS opportunity
- There is a lot of money available
- Technology better
- Less-expensive-internetworking options
- Lots of user budget dollars
- Lots of user momentum

Bad news:
- The easy work has already been done
- Many more components to manage
- Large diversity in existing user solutions
- Minimal IS budget for the new solution

4.6 Watch the Budget

There are some very compelling observations that can help an enterprise organization determine what the most appropriate support model is, given where organizations are in their evolution. Using this S-curve you can predict the next stage or influence the next action. Most companies are now in the first two stages of the third S-curve iteration. Some organizations in these companies are pushing at the third stage.

Use S-curve to predict the organization's next step

If you use the S-curve analysis you can see that departments have more money and more resources than the IS organization. You should also be aware that the true costs of supporting the first two stages of the S-curve are often hidden. As soon as the third stage is entered and handed to a service provider the expense becomes very visible. Unless the enterprise network organization recognizes this up front, there might not be enough money to do the job effectively. Another consideration, that the enterprise network provider must be sensitive to, is that even if the budget

Watch the budget:
- Stages 1 and 2 have hidden costs
- A single enterprise network budget makes a big target

were large enough to do the job, the large budget makes a much bigger target than the stage one and two implementations.

Creative techniques to protect the budget must be built into the third stage solution. Even so, some companies have found successful ways to share the risk and the budget. These considerations have immediate and long range management, organizational control, and technical culture considerations.

Creative techniques to protect budget required

> **The S-curve can help you anticipate and provide enterprise network services.**
>
> **Care must be taken to watch the budget and funding to assure that these are representative and protected.**
>
> **Creative techniques to protect the budget are required.**

4.7 Managing Change

4.7.1 Anticipating Change

Differentiator: Anticipating Recognizing Managing change

The primary information technology challenge for most companies in the 1990s is to successfully anticipate, recognize, and manage continuous change.

To successfully manage the introduction of technological change the enterprise network organization must:

- Know where it is
- Have a vision of where it would like to be
- Be in a position to alter either or both of the above *quickly*
- Understand the motivation for change

Models need revision

Determining where the enterprise network is in the evolution curve is probably one of the biggest challenges faced by business and technical professionals today. The difficulty stems from the number of different organizations involved and their potentially diverse objectives. Different controls and motivations for each may be required for a successful integration.

For example, some organizations might be happy with a subsecond response time for their on-line transactions while others might expect a close to instantaneous response time, depending on where each is on the evolution curve and their view of the business priorities. Who would put up with subsecond time if instantaneous response time were technically possible? Organizations that can't afford the high-bandwidth connection required or don't want the responsibility for protecting corporate data locally might easily opt for the slower response, considering the options.

4.7.2 Doing More with Less

Some companies that have recognized the need to support rapid change have begun to use what I refer to as judo.

> **judo** - A sport, usually used for self-defense, that uses the principles of balance and leverage to turn an opponent's energy to one's own advantage.

Judo - leverage the departmental and user momentum

These companies leverage the departmental and user momentum to respond to the business pressures. The IS organizations in these companies provide the user departments with NetWare and some basic interfaces and help them with the implementation of security, asset protection, and data integrity control. Using this approach these IS organizations enlist the departments to implement the less complex client-server-based applications while containing the the IS costs. They use NetWare because it introduces the least amount of risk into their support structure.

When you focus on the sheer number of the your company's computer-literate business professionals and the enterprise network infrastructure population, it becomes obvious that unless the enterprise develops ways of leveraging the momentum of the users in the way it controls administratively, it cannot keep up with the ever increasing requirements and ad hoc solutions at the department level. Ergo, my suggestion to use judo.

NetWare:
● Low risk option

Based on previous behavior we expect that department LANs will want to help form the enterprise network, especially as the complexity of managing their own local network increases.

4.8 Sharing Control

Several shared models have evolved over time (see Fig. 4-4).

4.8.1 Central Control

In the early 1970s a strong central control model emerged to support the distributed computing systems in retail stores, banks, and grocery stores. This central control model was characterized by distributed computer systems whose programming and management was entirely from some remote IS location. The point-of-sale systems were distributed throughout the country. The stores or agencies typically purchased the equipment and the support from the IS organization. The applications were designed to provide access to both local and host-based data via authorized transactions. Based on the location of the data or transaction the teller, agent, or store clerk received local or remote response time. The objective was to minimize the dependency on the remote data access during normal operating hours. These distributed systems were augmented with vendor supplied sophisticated remote control mechanisms, including software distribution, remote diagnosis, remote change management, and data upload and download capabilities. For the most part the users were responsible for keeping the power on and letting the maintenance engineer into the locked room when it was necessary.

4.8.2 Distributed Control

By the late 1970s and early 1980s another variation of distributed systems emerged. This was the second stage of the S-curve, in which user organizations took control of their needs by purchasing, installing, and operating their own systems. These systems can be viewed as using distributed control with distributed computing. For example, the many engineering organizations installed and ran DEC VAX systems to support their design and development efforts, while the commercial organizations in the

Users
with
Computers

IS

Delgated
and
Shared
Controls

Which Model Works?

Central Control with Distribute Computing?
Distributed Control with Distributed Computing
Some Combination of the Above?
Yours, Mine, and Ours Model?

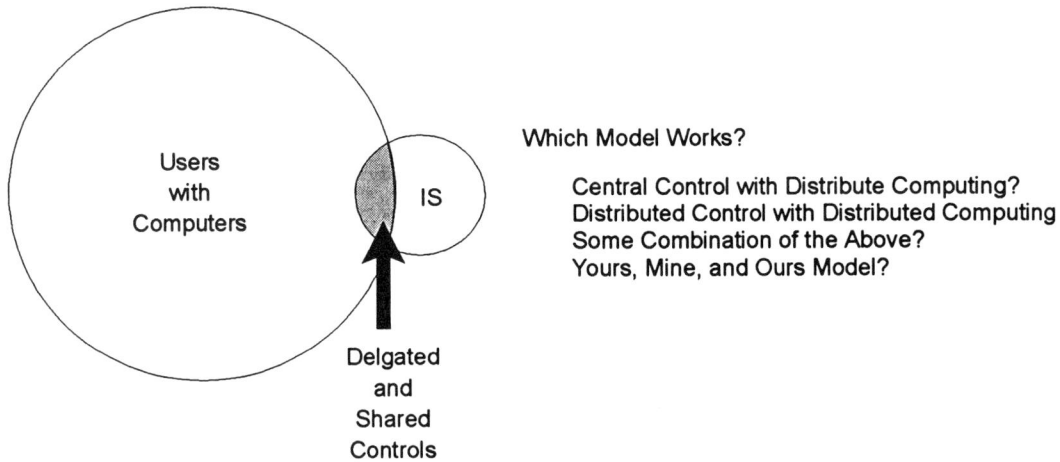

Figure 4-4   Control Models

same companies installed midrange systems, such as the IBM
AS/400 with turnkey applications. Although these systems were
considerably less complex to operate than a mainframe, in general
a trained operator and programming staff were required. Sometimes the programming staff was an outside firm that was on
retainer. These systems were typically controlled locally and only
the vendor used some remote diagnosis capabilities to help isolate
hardware problems.

4.8.3 Mixed Control

As the independent distributed systems began connecting into the
enterprise network, the distributed and central control aspects of
the systems began to merge. The enterprise network organization
had to become involved with the software definitions for connecting the distributed systems into the enterprise network. This
involved controlling the network-specific addressing, network
usage, and network problem determination for each specific
system. The overall control objective was protect the other users

on the network while assuring quality response time (consistent) and meeting the network availability objectives for that system.

4.8.4 Yours, Mine, Ours Control

Figure 4-5 Control Challenge

With the significant growth of desktop and mobile computing the traditional models for controlling or supporting distributed systems fail under the sheer weight of all the possible combinations and permutations associated with the hardware being used, the software being used, the controls, and the change of controls. (Figure 4-5 characterizes the challenge, to run with multiple different loosely connected boxes and one's back. The only solution is that each box also has some capabilities to help stay on.) This type of environment seems to demand a *yours*, *mine*, and *ours* model approach.

This model recognizes that in the enterprise network of the 1990s, there will be products, equipment, and management responsibilities that belong to the user. Likewise there are responsibilities that belong solely to the IS organization managing the enterprise network.

There will also be responsibilities that overlap or are shared. These latter responsibilities are usually responsibilities that cannot be completely executed by either the user or the enterprise network organization. The user delegates them to the enterprise network organization and the enterprise network organization may delegate some of them to the user organizations.

Yours, mine, and our model uses judo

NetWare is currently the most flexible network operating system that can support this model for the network, servers, routers, as well as to some degree the workstation.

4.9 Preparing for Change

Technology:
- Even more critical
- Part of employees' tool kit

4.9.1 The Role of Technology

The easy parts of the planning-for-the-future process is recognizing that information technology is playing an ever increasing role in a company's ability to compete and to achieve the required return on investments, as well as recognizing that equipment and software that were once solely in the domain of the IS organization are now as much a part of the user's standard personal and office tool kit as a pad of paper is.

4.9.2 Watch the First Step

The difficult part of the planning process is determining the first step! There just seem to be too many choices and none seem to give us the confidence that it will serve us for the next 3 years, much less the next 25 years, as many of the current installed technologies have.

> **The last application lasted 25 years. What is the encore application life span?**

The dilemma at the enterprise decision level is typically the large multipliers associated with a decision. For example, even at volume discounts 2000 workstations costing $5000 per seat has between six and seven zeros to the left of the decimal point. This doesn't even consider any subsequent software and hardware upgrade costs. If the hardware platform doesn't support an as yet unspecified critical application, there could be significant user dissatisfaction. The result is often "analysis paralysis" or a quick "you bet your job" decision. On the other hand, every day that the selection is deferred some department in your organization is making a decision for the enterprise network by solving their business problems.

> **Enterprise decisions cost more than department unique decisions**

> **Indecision is a decision**

At an enterprise level the primary focus is to pick the right technologies that meet the user's needs today, one that doesn't introduce a significant support cost, one that doesn't cause us to impact the bottom line with unexpected write-offs, and one that we are sure will not create a major problem for tomorrow.

4.9.3 How does Yours, Mine, and Ours Fit?

> **Giving control to the user gives control to the enterprise network**

The yours, mine, and ours approach reduces the complexity of the decision process by allowing the user departments to select their own technology with their own budgets, and letting IS focus on providing volume purchase discount prices. However, it usually takes a CIO, an enterprise network administrator, and LAN administrators to make this work.

The CIOs in these companies focus on the overall direction that the solutions are taking the company in both a tactical and strategic time frame. Their focus is typically on the business directions and techniques to orchestrate and *apply technology* to make and keep the company profitable and competitive. Given a vision from the CIO the network administrator can lay the groundwork for that eventuality.

The enterprise network administrator (may be a single person or department) is responsible for administrating the boundaries between the *yours* and *mine* and coordinates the *ours*. The enterprise network administrator typically has the best understanding

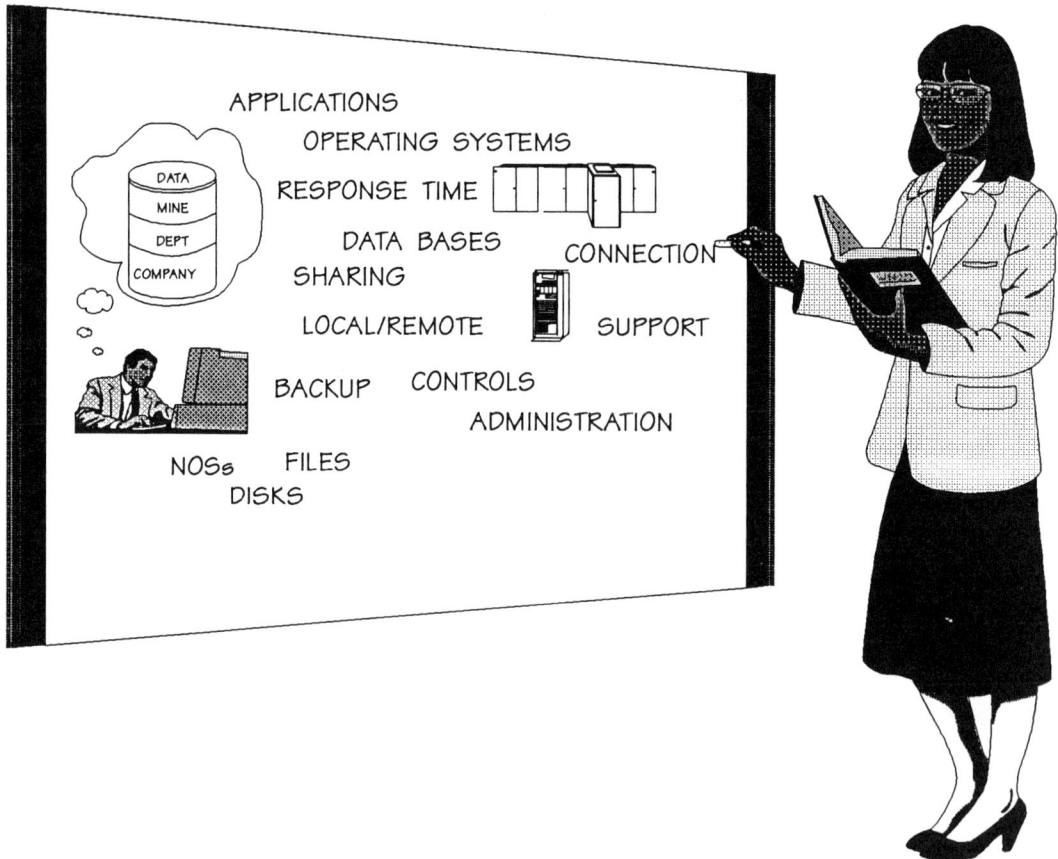

Figure 4-6 Enterprise Network Administrator

of the various environments and must find ways to accommodate these in an economical manner. (See fig. 4-6.)

Enterprise network requires a NOS

The CIO and the enterprise network administrator(s) recognize that the selection and implementation of the appropriate *network operating system (NOS)* has a major impact on the ease with which the enterprise network can be supported. The selection of the right NOS can dramatically impact the enterprise network's responsiveness to today's and tomorrow's needs. This responsiveness demands that the enterprise network organization be influential in in selecting the NOS within the enterprise.

This can be most effectively achieved if the NOS selected is well suited for both local and remote control and can easily fit into the department without enterprise network staff involvement. With the right NOS each local LAN administrator is essentially an extension of the enterprise network infrastructure.

The right NOS can let you use judo

Figure 4-7   Department LAN Administrator

The local LAN administrator's focus is on keeping the departmental LAN operating, backingup the data, and connecting to the mainframe or midrange system. Typically, the responsibility is limited to a single LAN and for the most part a single workstation environment, for example., Macs, DOS/Windows, OS/2, or UNIX. (See Fig. 4-7.)

If the LAN administrator is on the team the enterprise network organization is able to focus on how the users can interconnect with the enterprise applications.

The alternative is not very attractive. If the yours, mine, and ours model is not implemented the enterprise network organization may not have the influence in the selection of the building blocks. The result is subsequent integration challenges.

For example in companies where the model isn't being applied, it is not uncommon to have many different types of routers that cannot communicate with each other. How does this happen? The answer is, one interconnection (two units) at a time! Unless the LAN administrator that is interconnecting a few departmental LANs selects a router that is compatible with the rest of the enterprise, they might not interconnect. Similarly, the various interconnect technologies might not support the same protocols, or have common systems management interfaces, or even have the same level of remote diagnostic functions.

From an enterprise network standpoint the number of choices is considerable; however, the issues that must be considered from the start, are the budget to develop and support the internet, the tools available to manage large numbers of interconnections with very different workload characteristics, and skills required to support the LANs and network interconnections.

4.9.4 How to Staff the Enterprise Network

Who should you train?

Training is another important consideration that has many enterprise network organizations scratching their heads. Should new professionals be hired to support the LANs? Should the existing staff be retrained to support the LANs? Should the current LAN administrators from the departments be asked to augment the network management and support staffs?

There are no simple answers to these questions. Some companies have taken the hire-the-new-skill approach. This has been
extremely effective as long as the responsibilities match the
individual's skills. When the questions start dealing with mainframe connections or its use, the skills of the LAN operators tend
to be fewer. Other companies have made major investments in
retraining some of their existing network management staffs to
support LANs. Here again the results are mixed. Many experienced network support professionals become very frustrated with
the hacking approach to resolving problems. The lack of precise
documentation and a general lack of rigor encountered when
trying to resolve workstation-and LAN-related hardware and
software problems cause many professionals to look for new
opportunities.

There isn't a single answer

Which approach to training is best for your organization?
Again the answer is the your, mine, and our model. Departmental
LAN administrators are well suited for departmental roles, and
when given some enterprise network infrastructure support, can
be extremely helpful in supporting the network and making sure
that the right hardware and software are used. Similarly the need
for highly skilled enterprise network professionals, familiar with
IBM's SNA software can make a big difference in providing
quality service. There is also a need for the split-personality
professional. This individual is able to work on both the LAN and
the traditional enterprise network side. These professionals are
usually grown from within the IS organization, since the required
mainframe and SNA skills and experience cannot be acquired
without several years of exposure and hands on involvement.

Use LAN skill, IS skill, and enterprise network skill, probably three different people

The only consistent answer appears to be to select a NOS that
is widely used, supports the most environments, and has a large
and diverse customer base. This gives the company the most
personnel flexibility and keeps the personnel in the mainstream.

NOS criteria:
- **Widely used**
- **Supports all environments**
- **Large customer base**

4.10 Summary

In this chapter we have reviewed techniques of identifying where
in the enterprise evolution cycle your company and its various
organizations are using the S-curve. We have reviewed an approach to give up some control using the yours, mine, and ours

model in order to gain control of the enterprise direction and leverage the momentum of the users. We have also identified that the network operating system is key element of this approach.

> The criteria for an enterprise network operating system are that it be widely used, supports all the potential user environments, and has a sufficiently large customer base to assure that continued enhancements are forthcoming. If this condition is met, the enterprise applications can easily be implemented on the network operating system server, leaving only workstation-operating-system specific interfaces to be developed.

In the rest of this book I identify NetWare and NetWare-based and NetWare compatible products and that can be applied to leverage your current enterprise network investments, position your company for growth, and integrate them into the worker's environment.

> **Picking the right networking operating system can provide the enterprise with the glue between the desktop and the existing enterprise resources.**

First, let's look at the services that Novell's NetWare provides.

Section 3

The NetWare Building Blocks

This section describes some of the elements of the NetWare product line that you will probably encounter as you assess approaches to extending your enterprise network.

The NetWare products and the complementary products have been selected for their applicability to integration into the enterprise network. These products are described only to the depth that is necessary to build an understanding of what the product is and how its implementation or functions support the integration effort. A direct consequence of this approach is that some topics are covered in a very broadbrush manner while other topics are presented in to much more detail. The depth of coverage is the direct result of the number of questions I have encountered on the topics. NetWare for system application architecture (SAA) is covered only as the product in this section. It should be understood that NetWare for SAA is the cornerstone of the NetWare and system network architecture (SNA) network and host integration. Details of NetWare for SAA are spread throughout the entire book.

After reviewing this section you should have a conceptual appreciation of how the NetWare architecture and product line provide many of the basic building blocks that are required in extending the boundaries of the enterprise network.

The primary focus is on how NetWare is structured, and how this structure is packaged to provide discrete or combined building blocks that when merged together can be applied to meet the user and management objectives of the enterprise network.

Chapter 5

The NetWare Structure

5.1 The Conceptual Architecture

NetWare has a very straightforward conceptual architecture that lends itself to to many different environments. As depicted in Figure 5-1, the NetWare superstructure can be characterized as an executive system, a file system for the executive system, and a software bus. All the services and drivers plug into the software bus just as adapter cards plug into the slot in microcomputers. Novell provides their services as NetWare loadable modules (NLMs), and other NLMs can be added to support user or vendor applications.

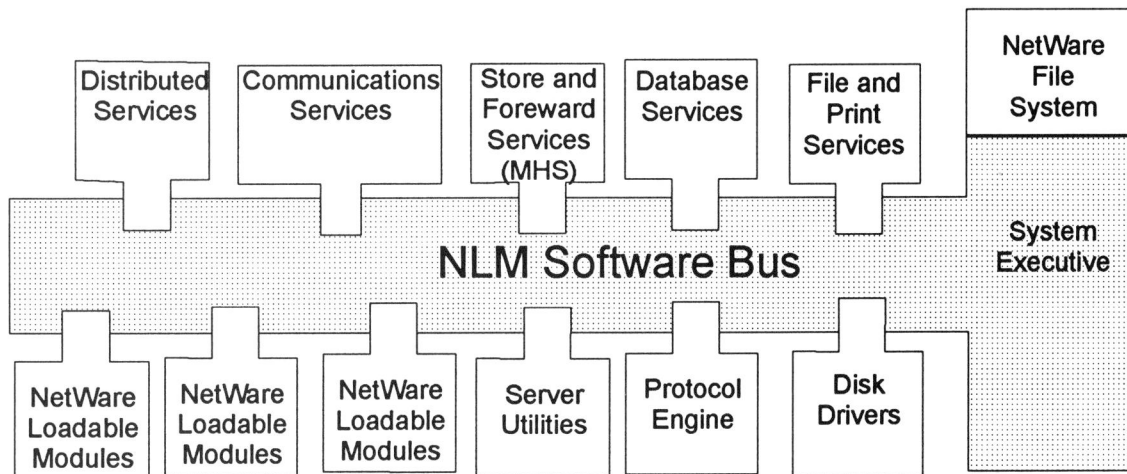

Figure 5-1   NetWare Architecture

For those of you familiar with IBM's CICS, you might liken NetWare to it in that the NLMs all run inside the operating system space. This provides a high-performance low-overhead implementation, but requires close attention to avoid ill-behaved NLMs from compromising memory. NetWare provides an OS Protected Domain that protects the other NLMs. (Not all NLMs can run in the protected domain.)

The NetWare architecture allows the NetWare operating system to be configured with and without general server services. The basic platform is referred to as a *runtime NetWare*. This configuration is used when NetWare is packaged for providing a specific service such as a multiprotocol router or hub manager.

5.2   NetWare as a File Server

We will at look the many NetWare services throughout this book but the most generic is the file server. The file server structure (see Fig.5-2) provides a basis for storing and sharing files across multiple workstation platforms. 1For example, the NetWare files

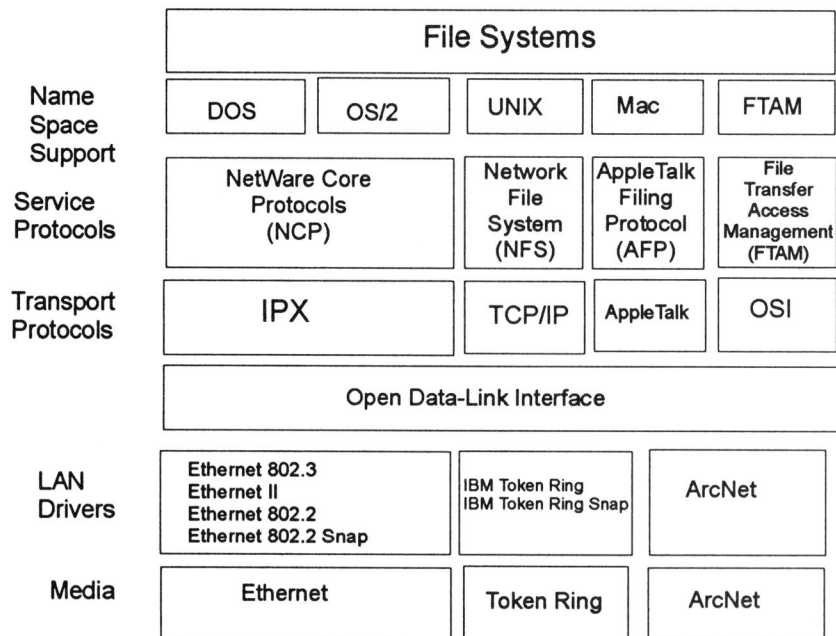

Figure 5-2   NetWare Files Server

services supports DOS, Mac, OS/2, UNIX, and Windows' workstation access to common files.

Figure 5-3 depicts the transfer and file protocols required to
to support the file server functions. As in any client-server

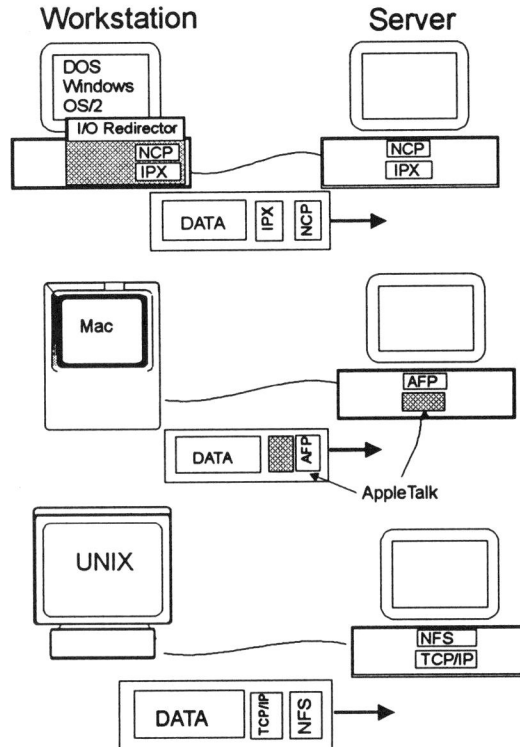

Figure 5-3   Workstation to File Server Protocols

implementation, client software is resident in each of the workstations. The appropriate matching server logic resides in the
NetWare server. various protocol stacks and services involved.

NetWare provides a client software shell for DOS, Windows
and OS/2 environments. This shell provides an input/output (I/O)
redirector that lets the workstation access disk drives and files on

the server, as if they were physically attached to the workstation. When the users bring up their systems they log in into the appropriate server(s). The shell then presents the user with a one more virtual disk drives (.eg., drives D, E, and F) which contain the directories and files that the users are authorized to access. These drives look and behave just as any other local workstation drive to the workstation user.

The shell captures the data request or data and packages it in the NetWare core protocol (NCP) and then uses the NetWare internetwork packet exchange protocol (IPX) to send and receive the data to and from the server.

Macintoshes, UNIX, and OSI compliant systems provide their own client software which interfaces with the appropriate NetWare server provided interface. For example, Apple's Macintosh workstations can use the AppleTalk File Protocol (AFP) software and interface to interface with the NetWare server (see Fig. 5-2 and 5-3). Similarly, UNIX systems can use TCP/IP and the Network File System (NFS) software to access the NetWare file server. Systems with OSI's file transfer, access, and management (FTAM) can also access the NetWare server. The Names Space Support provides the accommodates the various naming conventions and access idiosyncrasies of the workstation operating systems and access methods.

The NetWare file server provides controlled shared access to files, however, the NetWare file server software does not provide any assistance in sharing the data content. This responsibility belongs to the applications.

For example, if a Windows user stores a document generated using Microsoft Word on the file server and it is then accessed by a user using Word at a Mac workstation, Word detects the different internal format and makes any required adjustments in the document. Companies like Microsoft and WordPerfect have focused on these conversions and provide extensive filters that convert one format to another, but care must be taken to assure that the conversion is 100 percent complete.

Having looked at a simple service end-to-end connection in Figure 5-3, we can now focus on the real essence of the underlying robustness of the architecture.

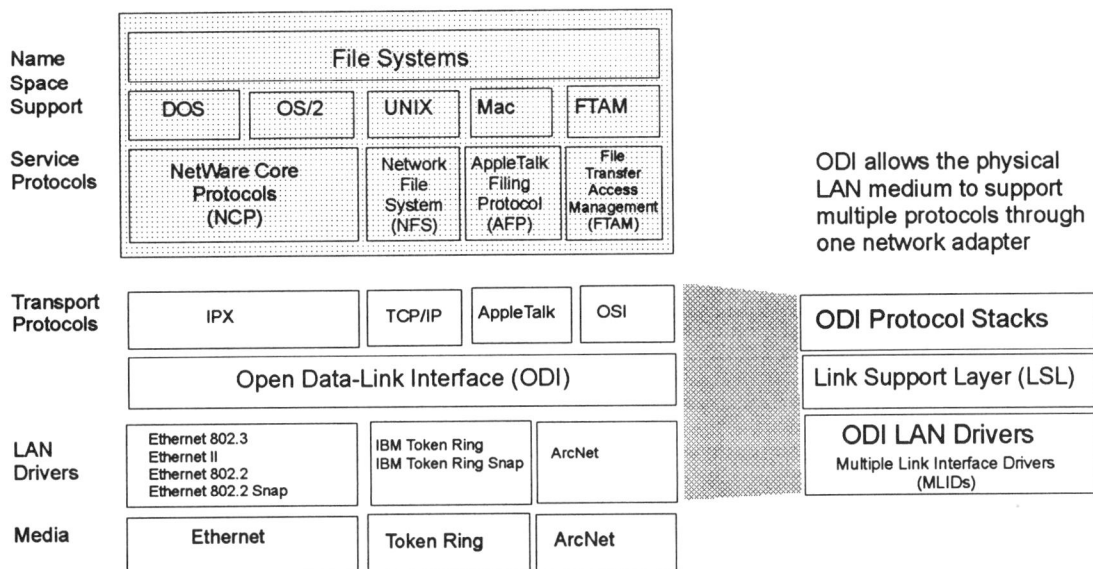

Name Space Support	File Systems				
	DOS	OS/2	UNIX	Mac	FTAM
Service Protocols	NetWare Core Protocols (NCP)		Network File System (NFS)	AppleTalk Filing Protocol (AFP)	File Transfer Access Management (FTAM)

ODI allows the physical LAN medium to support multiple protocols through one network adapter

Transport Protocols	IPX		TCP/IP	AppleTalk	OSI	ODI Protocol Stacks
	Open Data-Link Interface (ODI)					Link Support Layer (LSL)
LAN Drivers	Ethernet 802.3 Ethernet II Ethernet 802.2 Ethernet 802.2 Snap		IBM Token Ring IBM Token Ring Snap	ArcNet		ODI LAN Drivers Multiple Link Interface Drivers (MLIDs)
Media	Ethernet		Token Ring	ArcNet		

Figure 5-4   NetWare Open Data Link Interface

5.3   The NetWare Networking Architecture

As a networking operating system the NetWare server must support a multitude of protocols. To enable shared usage of the communications adapters and standardize communication adapter driver software access NetWare use an open data-link interface (ODI). Figure 5-4 depicts NetWare's ODI architecture and maps it to protocol stacks, a link support layer (LSL), and a multiple link interface driver (MLID). I have shaded in the file service protocols to differentiate them from the networking protocols.

The open data-link interface allows multiple communication protocol stacks to pass through a local-area network (LAN) adapter card at the same time. Prior to the implementation of ODI MLIDs, each protocol stack was supported by a unique LAN adapter driver. This necessitated a separate LAN adapter for each protocol stack supported. For the example, three LAN adapter

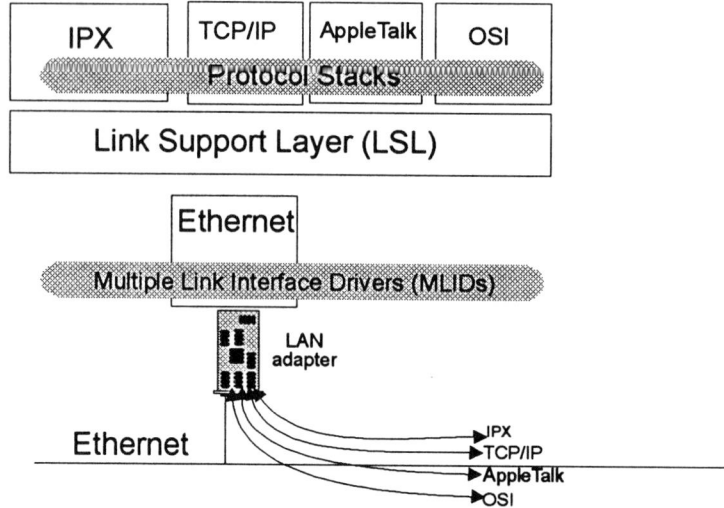

Figure 5-5   Multiple Link Interface Drivers

cards would be required to connect IPX, TCP/IP, or AppleTalk to an Ethernet cable. In contrast an ODI MLID allows all three protocols to concurrently pass through the common network adapter as depicted in Figure 5-5. Each hardware adapter typically requires a unique ODI MLID that supports multiple protocol stacks independently of the media frame type and stack protocol.

The LSL software as depicted in figures 5-4, 5-5, and 5-6 provides an interface between the drivers and the protocol stacks.

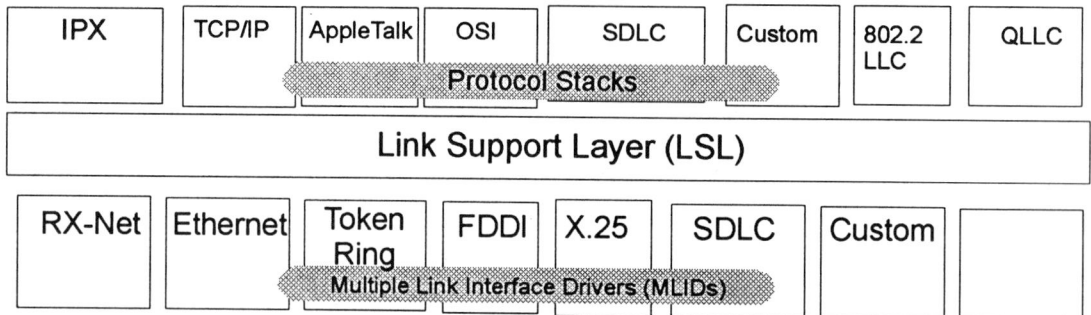

Figure 5-6   Link Support Layer

This essentially acts as a switchboard, directing the packets between the appropriate drivers and protocol stacks. Figure 5-6 depicts the same ODI architecture, only this time I have added some wide-area network (WAN) connectivity.

Until now in the discussion we have looked at NetWare as a server. That is, the workstations request services from the server. Access to the server is accomplished by each workstation having a NetWare-provided workstation shell as a client or using workstation native client software that the NetWare server supports.

5.4 NetWare as a LAN Router

Now let's look at NetWare as a transparent router or hub. The NetWare architecture lends itself naturally to providing router services. For example, Figure 5-7 depicts a simple Token Ring to Ethernet router using NetWare and an NLM that essentially provides the address mapping. In this example all that was required to implement this router was to place a Token Ring and

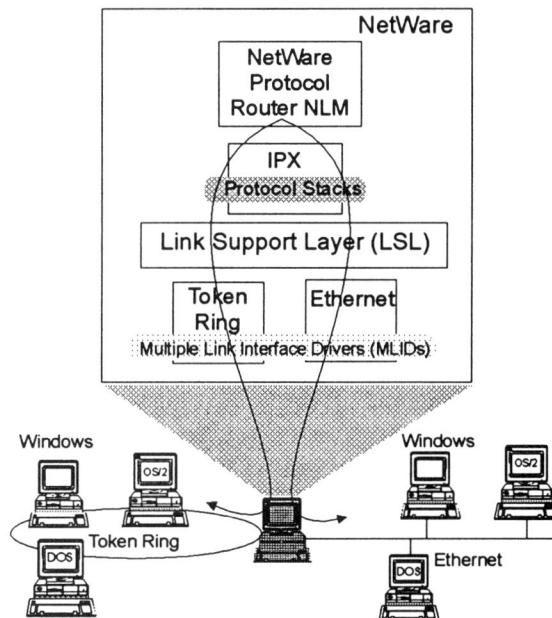

Figure 5-7   Local Router Example

an Ethernet adapter into the "router server" and add the NetWare multiprotocol router NLM.

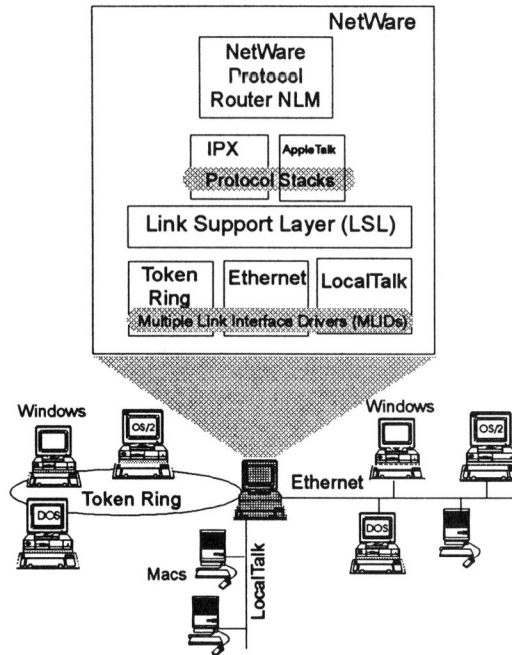

Figure 5-8 Local Multiprotocol Router

Figure 5-8 depicts a mixed-protocol stack example. In this diagram the workstations sing IPX on the Token Ring LAN can communicate with the workstations on the Ethernet using IPX. Similarly, the Macintosh workstations can communicate through the router using AppleTalk.

5.5 NetWare as a LAN-to-LAN Router

The NetWare local router architecture can also be extended to interconnect remote locations, as depicted in Figure 5-9.

Figure 5-9 depicts the same multiprotocol routing structure as seen in Figure 5-8, except that the Ethernet LAN is remote from the Token Ring and LocalTalk LANs. Novell's NetWare Multiple Protocol Router Plus or Newport Systems Solutions Inc.'s LAN^{2}LAN Router NLMs extend the LAN across the WAN. These NLMs, in conjunction with the respective communication adapters in the sever, provide a NetWare based WAN router.

The resulting implementation differs from the local environment in that remote multiprotocol routers must mix the protocols

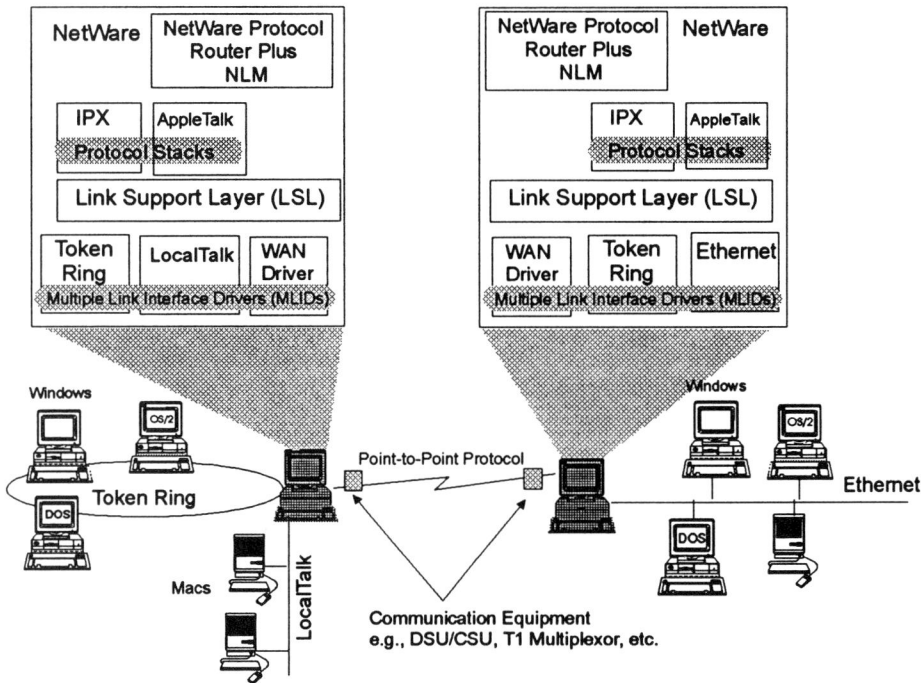

Figure 5-9   Remote NetWare Routers

(see characterization in Figure 5-10) that they are routing and either carry the client protocols to the target router with a proprietary protocol or encapsulated in a public protocol (e.g., IP).

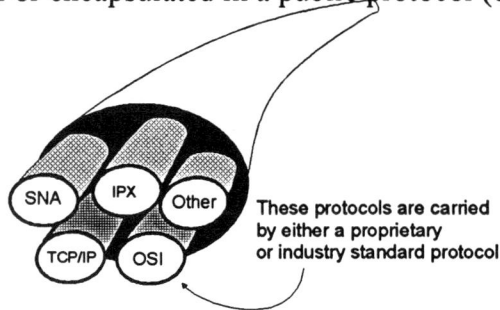

Figure 5-10   Multiple Protocols on Same Wire

These mixed protocol routers can be used to transfer a single protocol such as IPX between remote locations or mix the protocols. Typical protocol support include any protocol supported by the NetWare LAN environment.

The NetWare architecture provides more flexibility than a traditional router. The NetWare architecture allows a router to be built using standard off-the-shelf PC hardware and standard LAN and communication adapters, and to be operated using familiar NetWare interfaces and controls. Additionally, when using NetWare a separate router is not required at each location. Routers encapsulate the protocols they carry in their unique protocol to achieve control and performance. In routers the router logic therefore must be on both ends of the pipe.

Because the NetWare environment supports both file server and routing capabilities, the router logic can be on a server on the receiving end or on both ends, or run as dedicated routers using

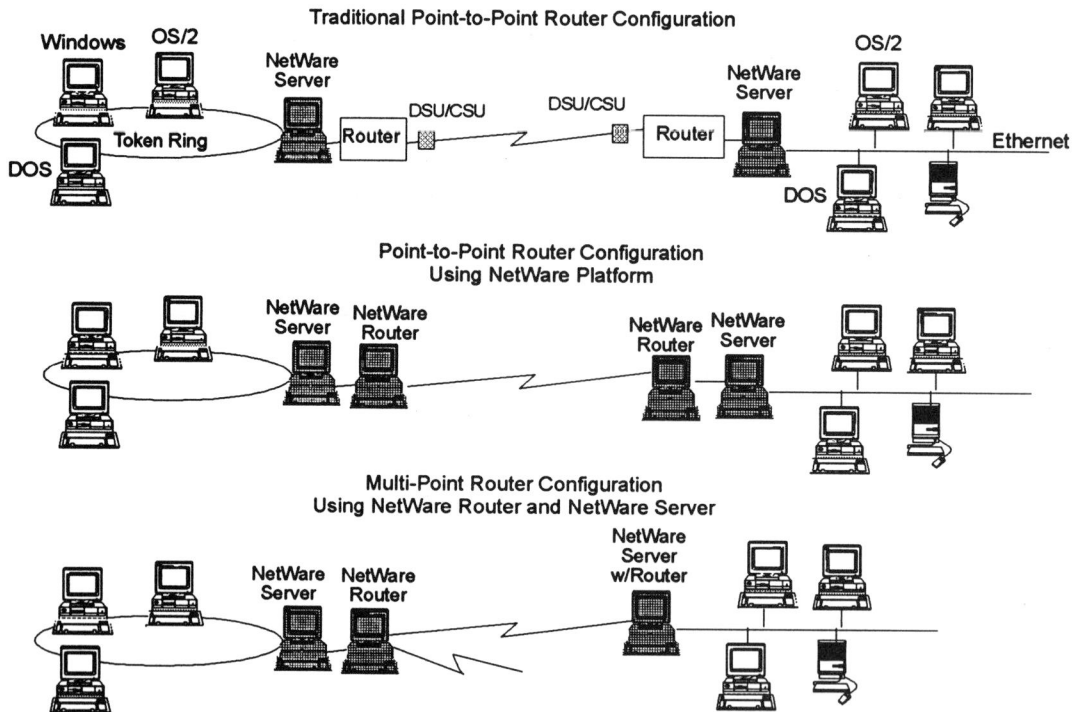

Figure 5-11   Remote Router Configuration Examples

a runtime copy of NetWare. Figure 5-12 depicts the options available for connecting NetWare LANs.

The first configuration uses a standard point-to-point router configuration; the second configuration shows the router replaced by a NetWare router. Notice that the digital service unit/channel service unit (DSU/CSU) can be placed inside the NetWare router using a card-type DSU/CSU.

Another configuration option that is expected soon is a connection between a NetWare Multiprotocol Router and high capacity routers such as provided by Cisco and Wellfleet. The combination of the two technologies solves a major price point challenge for the small NetWare LAN organizations that can't afford the outboard router but need to share the enterprise network backbone which is comprised of these high capacity routers.

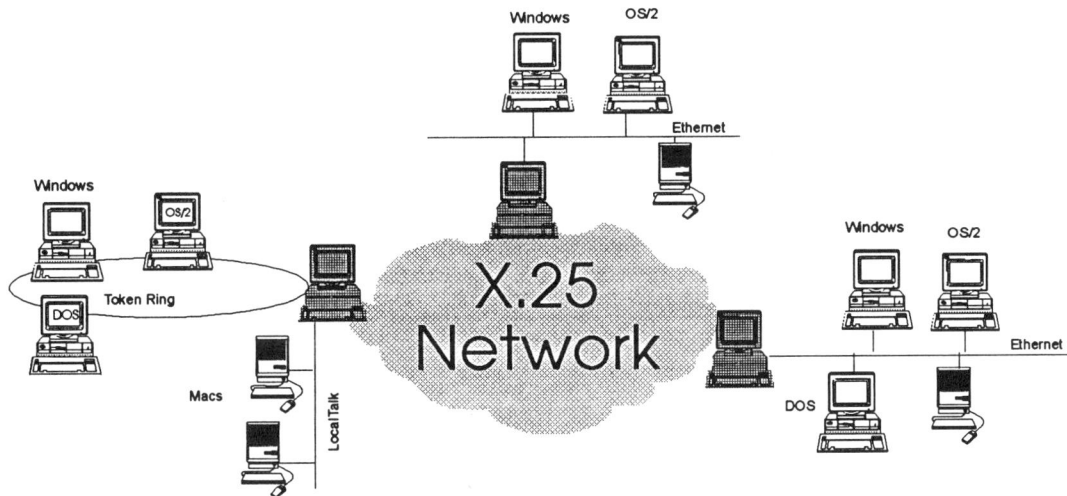

Figure 5-12   Routing over an X.25 Network

5.6 NetWare over Public Switched Networks

To this point I have described NetWare in the point-to-point routing context. That is, that the routing is from one router directly to the target router. This can become very expensive when one considers the number of leased lines that could be required required.

An alternative is to use a switched network, which essentially acts as the routers. Typical public switched networks support by X.25 networks or Frame Relay service. Figure 5-12 depicts a switched network configuration. In this configuration the server and multiprotocol router are combined. Unlike the point-to-point configuration only one wide-area network (WAN) connection is required per server since the switched network provides the virtual circuit to each destination location.

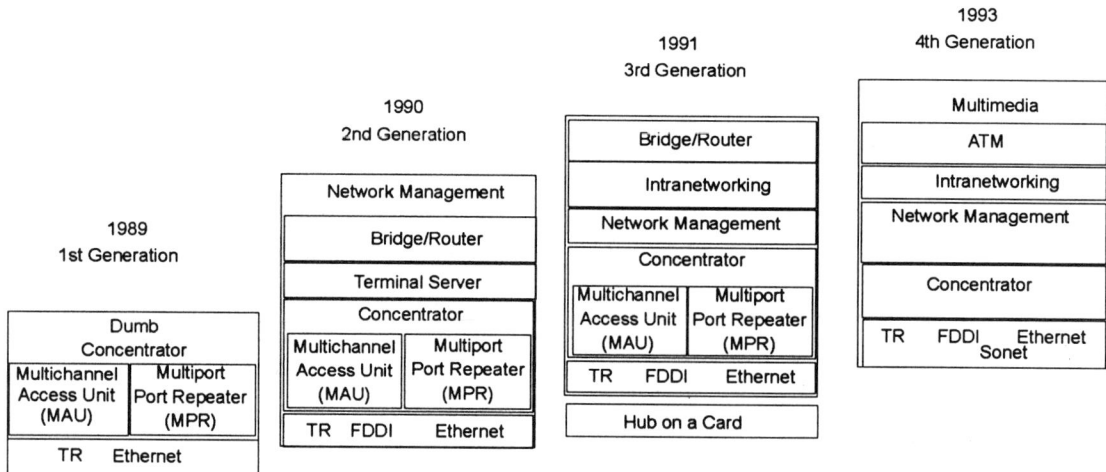

(Source: The Yankee Group,
Smart Hubs' Market, Value, and Players,
Communications & Computer News,
2/92, pp. 1, 14.)

Figure 5-13   Smart Hub Evolution

5.7 NetWare as a Hub Manager

NetWare can also be used to build a hub. Hubs are used to provide a common physical connection point for the LAN-connected workstations. Wiring hubs (sometimes referred to as *wiring con-centrators* or *dumb hubs*) are comprised of built-in repeaters. These hubs perform signal reception and retransmission. Some hubs (smart hubs) support multiple network types and provide some network management, such as statistics, isolate problem connections, and provide remote control. Even more recently a new term, enterprise hub, has emerged that includes LAN, WAN, and network services on the same hub. (See Figure 5-13 for a snapshot of how the hubs have evolved.)

Traditionally, these hubs and wiring concentrator services have been provided with proprietary stand-alone hardware equip-

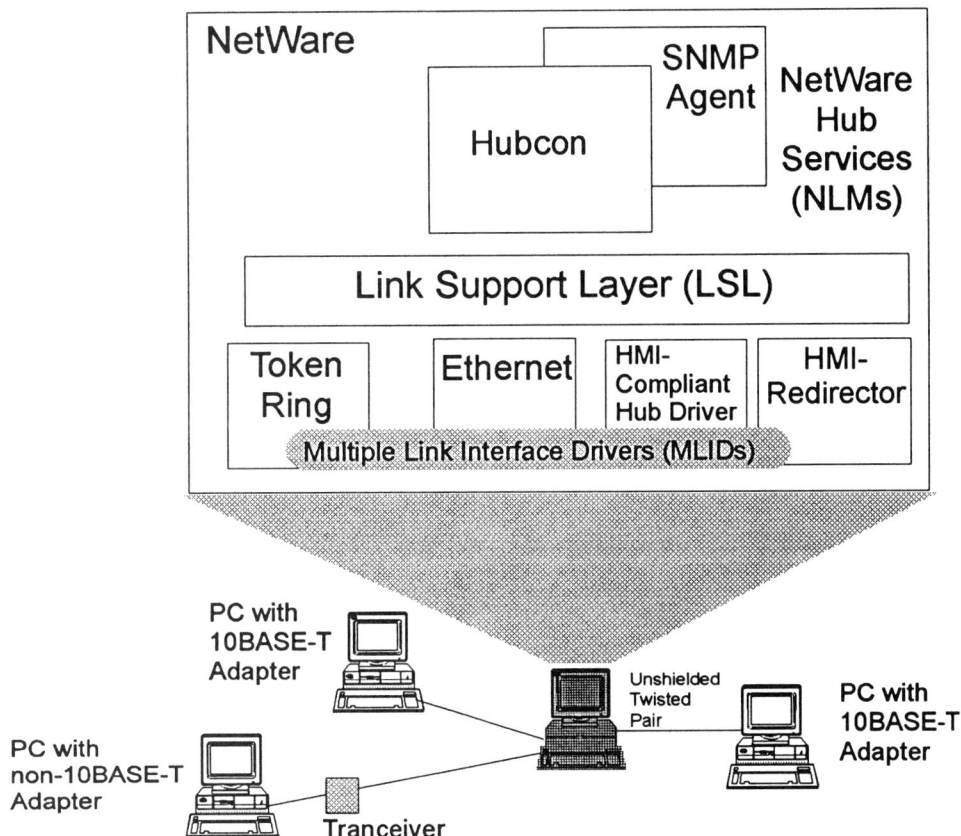

Figure 5-14   NetWare Hub

NetWare Hub Services Statistics

System Statistics

- Number of hubs within the server
- Number of hub adapters per hub
- Number of ports per hub adapter
- Hub adapter manufacturer
- Hub adapter version number

Hub Statistics

- Hub health
- Hub usage
- Hub throughput
- Hub collisions
- Hub very long events

Per-Port Statistics

- Port name
- Log-in ID
- MAC address of attached device
- Number of address changes
- Link state
- Readable frames
- Readable bytes
- Collisions
- Late collisions
- Errors
- Auto partition count
- Very long events

ment. Over the last few years, however, hub cards that fit into the PC have become available.

To take advantage of this technology flexibility Novell has introduced the Hub Management Interface (HMI) standard, which is an extension of the ODI standard. The HMI standard enables hub hardware to communicate with NetWare. (HMI hub implementations range from inexpensive hub boards to sophisticated high-end hubs.) Novell also offers a set of NetWare loadable modules, NetWare Hub Services, that enable the NetWare server to monitor the network traffic of the HMI-compliant hub hardware and provide local and remote access to the information (See Fig.5-14.)

Using these NetWare Hub Services an administrator can remotely access detailed information about the traffic generated by each port, the name and physical address of the station, the amount of traffic being generated, and the type and quality of errors being generated by the port in question. (See insert for list of NetWare Hub Services Statistics on previous page.)

These NLMs are managed the same as any other NetWare components. The hub specific services can be accessed though an simple network management protocol (SNMP) management console, from a remote PC, or from the NetWare management system (NMS). The administrator can view the hub back panel as well as see a port mapping. The NetWare Hub Services NLMs enable the automation of the management of HMI-compatible hubs and provides detailed network information ranging from the hub to the individual port. NMS also enables the management of multiple hub adapters in a single server and multiple hub adapters in multiple servers, all from a single management platform.

The NetWare architecture allows Novell's customers to leverage NetWare's LAN connectivity support and routing capabilities with the services to provide a very powerful enterprise hub in a single NetWare server. Multiple vendors provide HMI-compliant hub cards. The opposite is also evolving, some vendors already use NetWare on their hubs. In fact, Networth has packaged their product such that the users can add application NLMs to the NetWare server on the hub.

5.8 Summary

In summary the NetWare operating system is architected to for maximum server and network operating system flexibility. The operating system can provide basic file services to a wide variety of workstations and can be used to build relatively inexpensive routers and and hubs that can be run within an existing file server or as a separate service on a runtime version of NetWare. A key benefit of this architecture to the system administrator is that systems management retains the same NetWare touch and feel for the various network capabilities. This architecture also provides a very low entry price to have some very sophisticated services. These services can be scaled by increasing the hardware capacity and separating the workload among multiple specialized servers.

Now let's explore how this base architecture is applied to more sophisticated network applications.

Chapter 6

NetWare and Dial Services

6.1 Introduction

While leased-line and switched-network access are extremely important there is an everincreasing demand to extend the network to remote locations via dial-up connections. The reasons for remote dial-up vary from the need for mobility of the workstation and the user to the economics of only paying for the WAN connection while it is being used.

From a conceptual point of view a workstation dials the remote LAN port, logs in and begins work. Unfortunately, while the concept is sound the low-speed WAN connection may have some major drawbacks depending on the application.

to better understand the trade-offs and options consider a user with a laptop who has dialed into the NetWare LAN over a low-speed dial-up line. Let's further assume that this user's program needs to access a file that is stored on the remote NetWare volume.

The user has two options options to access this data, and the resulting differences are significant.

In the first scenario, our user dials into the LAN, logs in as a NetWare user and begins to interact with LAN resources as if locally connected. Every input/output (I/O) between the disk and the application could travel across the dial-up line. From a user standpoint the time it takes to access the data seems like an eternity.

This example uses what is referred to as a *remote node configuration*. In this configuration the computing is done at the mobile workstation and all the data including network protocols are transferred from the server on the other end of the wire. Figure 6-1) depicts a remote node configuration. This remote nodeconfiguration includes software in the laptop which connects through a dedicated PC dial-in server to the NetWare LAN.

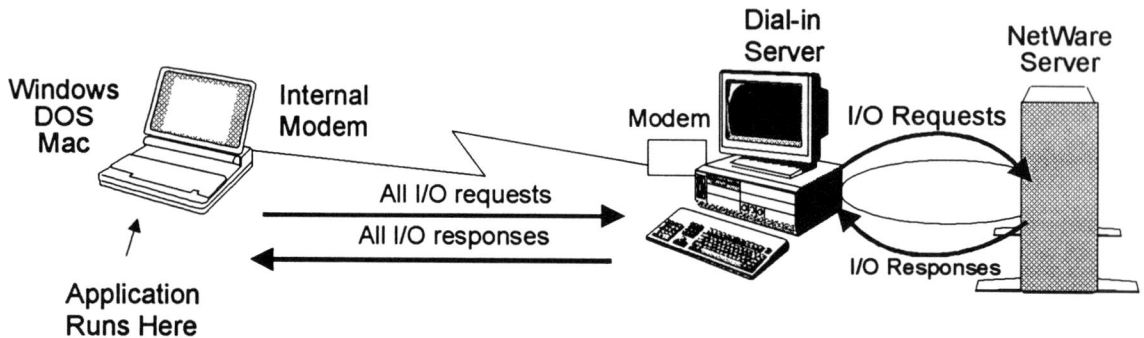

Figure 6-1 Remote Node Configuration

The remote node configuration is ideally suited for participating in a remote LAN incidental data access, E-mail and file transfers. It is relatively easy for the user since all the programs and services work the same as if they were locally attached to the NetWare LAN, although the response time is usually slower.

In our second scenario the laptop user dials a remote PC or access server, logins in on the local NetWare LAN and initiates the same file access application. This time response time is much faster than when using the *remote node configuration*. (See Fig. 6-2.)

This configuration turns the laptop into a local screen and keyboard to the remote PC or access server. This approach signicantly reduces the network traffic sincethere are typically less keystrokes and screen output than I/Os between the workstation and the server.

Remote Control

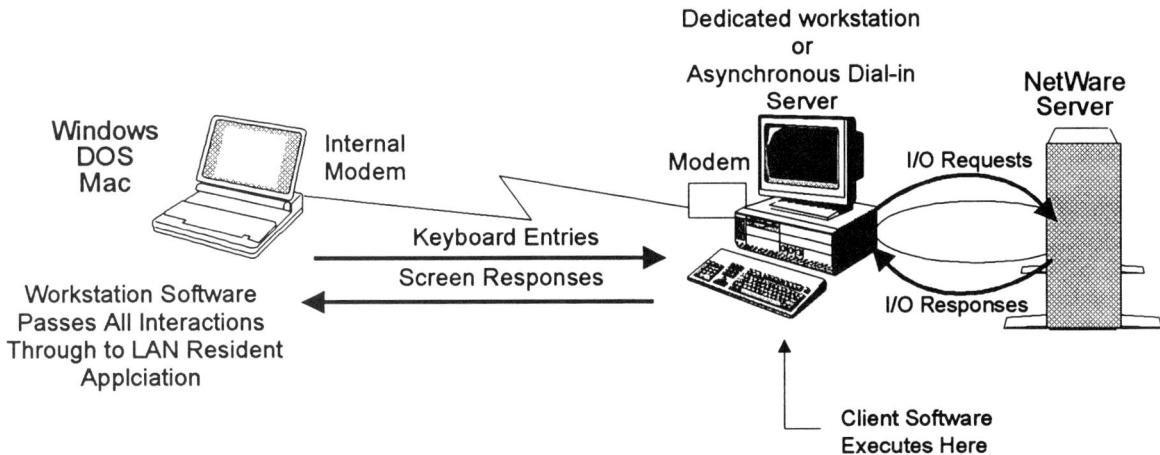

Figure 6-2   Remote Control Configuration

6.2 Some Remote Control Configurations

There are several approaches to supporting remote control access over dial-up connections. One way is to have a one-for-one relationship, that is to have workstations on the NetWare network with remote-control software and dial-in ports and modems dedicated to serving dial-in users. There are several products that provide one-to-one remote control access, including Timbuktu (Farallon Computing), Proxy (Funk Software), Carbon Copy (Microcom Systems, Inc.), pcANYWHERE (Symantec Corporation), and Co/Session (Triton Technologies). Figure 6-3 shows an example using pcANYWHERE as the remote control software. In general these remote-control software products require withboth the remote workstation and the LAN-connected workstation have that vendor's software. This solution can become very expensive because of the number of LAN-resident workstations that might be required.

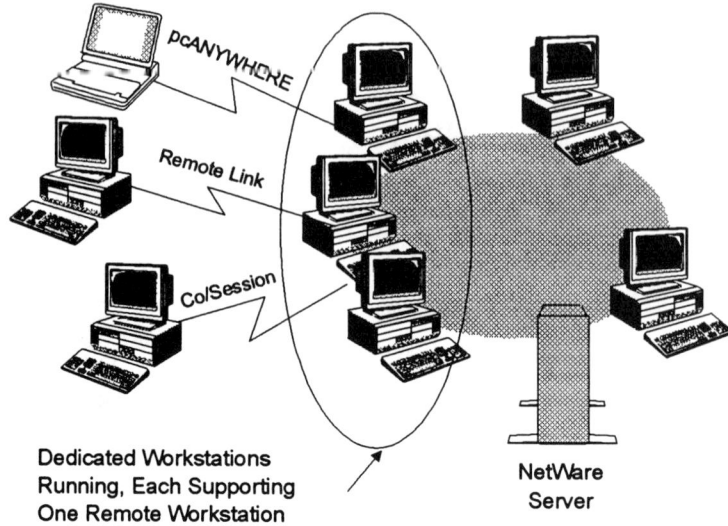

Figure 6-3 PC-to-PC Remote Control Configuration

Another approach is to use multiple processor system solutions as depicted in Figure 6-4. These solutions use multiple processors in a common enclosure. This allows a real system image per port while reducing the overall costs. Multiple-processor system solutions include: LAN Central Station (Cubix), Flex-

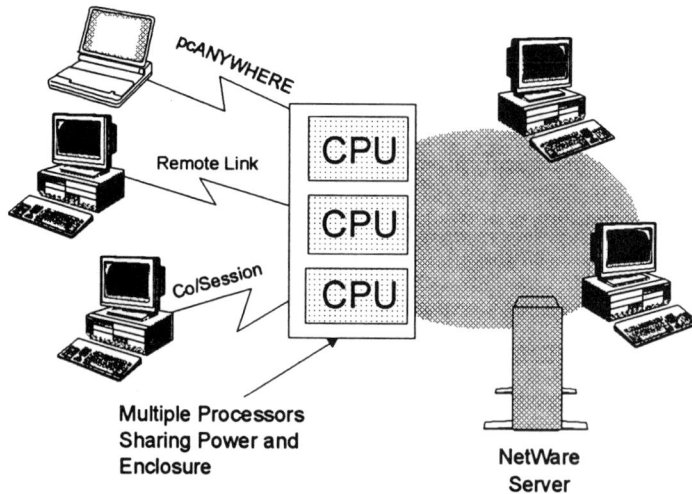

Figure 6-4 PC-to-PC Multiprocessor Server

Com (Evergreen), Communiqué (IWI), and Chatterbox NRS (J&L Information Systems).

A way of futher reducing the hardware redundancy is to provide a software based server that supports multiple simultaneous users in a single CPU system. This approach has been implemented with products such as Citrix's A+ for NetWare and Novell's NetWare Access Services. Novell's NetWare Access Services supports 16 remote workstations on the same physical system (see Fig. 6-5). This solution costs the least. The only draw-back with a software solution is that not all software can run in the virtual environments supported. For example, Windows might only run in standard or real mode, while your application might require enhanced mode to operate. In other words, the software solution requires an evaluation of the applications that will be run in the server to ensure that the requirements are met.

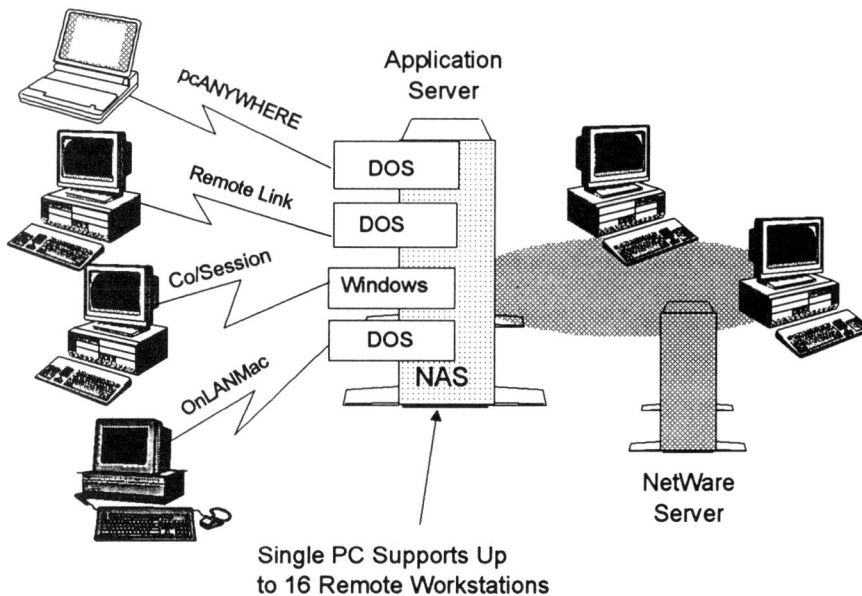

Figure 6-5   PC-to-NAS Server

6.3 NetWare Access Services

NetWare Access Services (NAS), which was acquired from Novell by Citrix Systems, Inc. is software that slices a dedicated PC into as many as 16 virtual machines to support 16 simultaneous remote-control users. The NetWare access software together with the dedicated PC are often referred to as *application servers* and *access servers*. Each virtual machine and its operating system environment allows one workstation or one terminal to connect to the NetWare network. In addition to facilitating remote control capabilities to DOS, Windows, and Macintosh, NetWare Access Services supports over 30 different types of ASCII terminals, including VT-100, IBM 3101, Wyse 50, and ANSI displays. This enables ASCII terminal users to have PC workstation capabilities. (Servers that are used to support terminals are often referred to as *terminal servers*.) Figure 6-6 depicts two NetWare Access Services servers, one being used as an application server by providing DOS and windows environments for PCs and Mac workstation remote control access, and the other being used as a

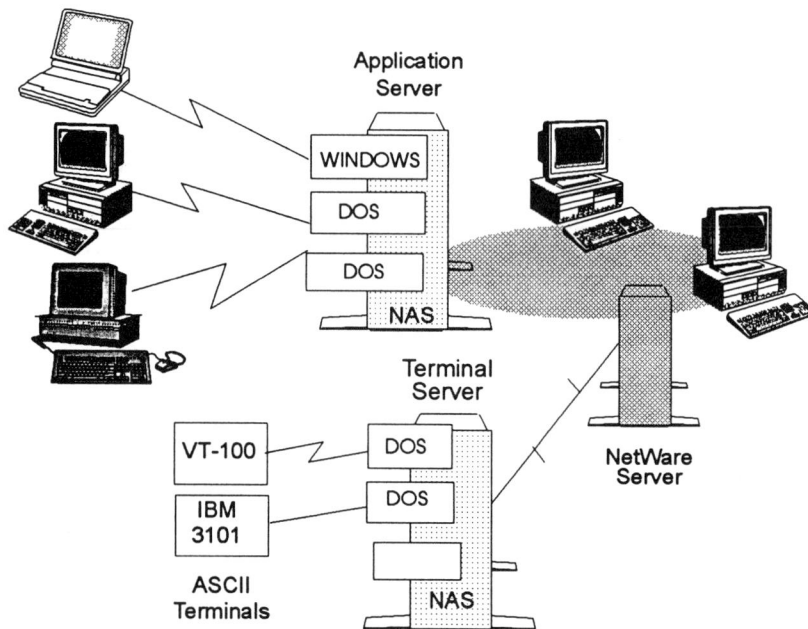

Figure 6-6 Application and Terminal Server

terminal server. (The terminal and workstation support could also be combined in a single server.)

Each workstation can access the NetWare Access Services server through a remote control interface on the workstation. This remote-control service can be invoked with a specialized interface or the workstation can emulate a terminal. Once the connection is established the workstation or terminal can use any of the services that a LAN-connected authorized NetWare user can access. Only screen updates, keystrokes, and mouse signals travel over the communication connection.

The NetWare Access Services product includes PC and Mac workstation software via OnLAN/PC and OnLAN/Mac. These programs allow a user to connect to the network through menus. OnLAN/PC includes several user utilities, scripting, automated procedures, screen record and playback, and troubleshooting diagnostics. OnLAN/Mac uses the conventional Macintosh user interface to access standard DOS applications on the application server. NetWare Access Services also allows users to transfer DOS and Macintosh files to and from the NetWare network. Printing is supported from all workstation types, including ASCII terminals and Macintosh computers. A user can specify if an application is to print on a NetWare-based printer or a remote printer connected directly to the workstation.

Some representative communications software examples that might be run in the NetWare Access Services server to access the NetWare network or business application are listed below:

- Crosstalk Mark IV Digital Communications Associates
- Crosstalk for Windows Digital Communications Associates
- eMail Da Vinci Systems
- NACS/NASI Novell
- NetWare 3270 LAN Workstation for DOS
- Novell LAN Workplace for DOS
- Novell NETBIOS Emulator
- Norton pcANYWHERE /LAN - Symantec

- Procomm Plus NCSI/NASI (network) DataStorm Technologies
- Procomm Plus DataStorm Technologies

The second important use of the NetWare Access Services is to enable PC access from ACII terminals. A representative list of the ACSII terminals includes:

Ampex 230
ADDS Regent
ADDS Viewpoint
ANSI Standard Beehive 4/78/DMS
Dasher D410/D460
DEC VT-52
Digital Microsystems
Esprit III Falco
FAME III
Hazeltine 1500
Hewlett-Packard
IBM 3101
Kaypro
Kimtron KT-7 PC
Link PCTERM
LSI ADM 3A
OnLAN v1.0x
OnLAN v1.2x and above
OnLAN v1.3x with parity
Prime PST100 Qume (102/108)
Soroc
Tektronix
Teleray
TeleVideo
Visual V330 (DG)
VT-100/200 1
VT-100/200 IBM font
Wyse 50/100/300
Zenith Z-19
Zenith Z-29

Workstations and ASCII terminals can be connected directly to NetWare Access Services through a properly wired RS-232 null modem cable.

Remote users can connect to NetWare Access Services over asynchronous dial-up or leased lines, public or private X.25 packet-switching services, ISDN services, and multiplexer connections. Communication adapter support is provided from vendors such as Microdyne, Newport Systems Solutions, and Digiboard. Data rates for the asynchronous connections can reach 38.4 kbit/s, however, these rates are dependent upon the communication adapter type (see Fig. 6-7).

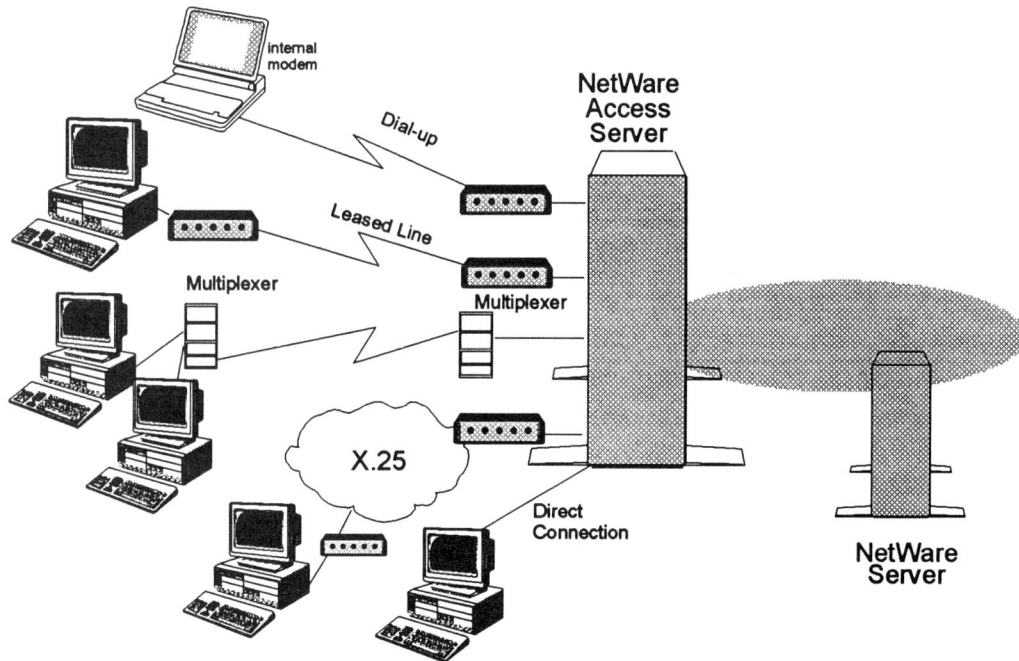

Figure 6-7   NetWare Access Services Connectivity

Because remote control minimizes network traffic some users use NetWare Access Services for accessing applications and data across NetWare networks that extend across multiple internet nodes or a WAN. In this case, the NetWare Access Services connected workstations are on the NetWare LAN using Internetwork Packet Exchange (IPX) or AppleTalk protocols. Figure 6-8 depicts this scenario for a workstation user on a NetWare LAN that is WAN connected to a remote NetWare LAN. The user invokes the remote control software in the workstation and uses the NetWare Access Services server on the remote LAN to execute the application. This example is the ideal for files-server-intensive applications since only a small percentage of the I/Os cross the WAN.

It is also ideal for locally attached Macintosh computers that need to run DOS applications. Macintosh users can integrate DOS access onto their Macintosh workstations, and local PC users can use NetWare Access Services as an application server.

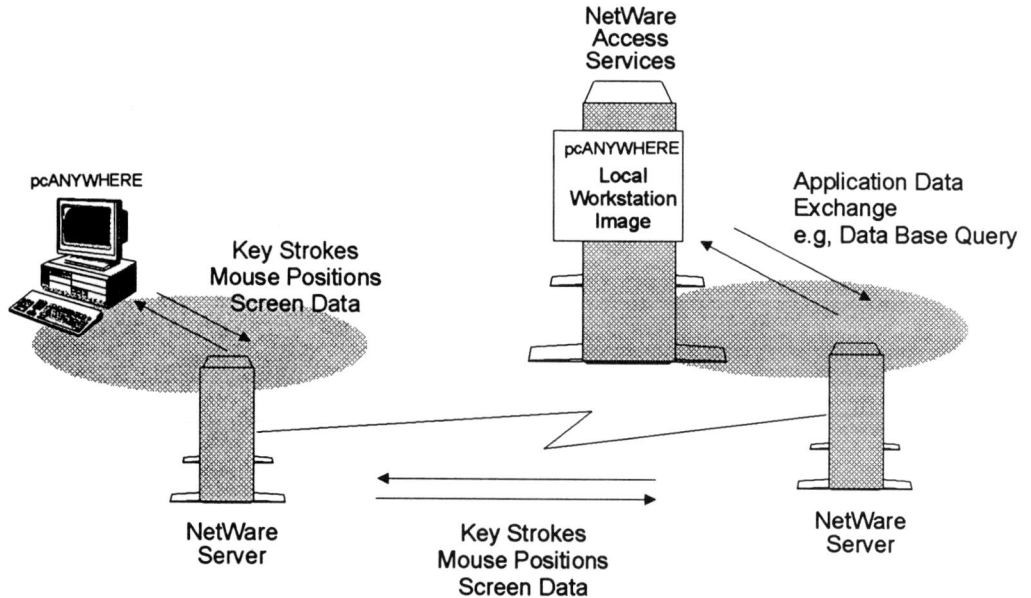

Figure 6-8 Remote Control Reduces Network Traffic

NetWare Access Services uses standard NetWare access controls to prevent unauthorized access. Such controls include user name and password checking. Additionally, NetWare Access Services provides a dial-back feature to ensure that the person calling is at a minimum where that user is authorized to access the network. The NetWare network supervisor can also limit a user's or groups of users access based on the NetWare profile in the NetWare directory.

NetWare Access Services can also be used to enable access to mainframes and AS/400 by passing key strokes and screens through to the NetWare Access Services server resident terminal emulation software in order to interface with system-network-architecture (SNA) communication gateways. Similarly UNIX hosts can be accessed through Novell's LAN WorkPlace for DOS.

6.4 NetWare Connect

NetWare Connect is an integrated set of NetWare loadable modules (NLMs) designed to support efficient NetWare network connectivity to remote and mobile users using either remote-control and remote-node connectivity. It is essentially a NetWare server-based front-end processor for a NetWare network. NetWare Connect incorporates Novell's NetWare Asynchronous Communication Services (NACS) product, which provides modem sharing and management.

NetWare Connect provides:

- Modem pooling
- Dial-in control services
- Dial-out services
- A NetWare enabled workstation to NetWare connection
- A workstation to workstation connection
- A workstation to application server connection

Figure 6-9 conceptualizes Netware Connect services as modem pooling that includes selecting the appropriate dial-out port and routing the dial-in traffic to the appropriate Netware LAN-connected workstation or server. This routing is accomplished by specifying specific ports to specific applications. For example, ASCII terminals might always be directed to the Netware Access Services server as a terminal server. The target service might also be selected as part of the log-in process. NetWare Connect

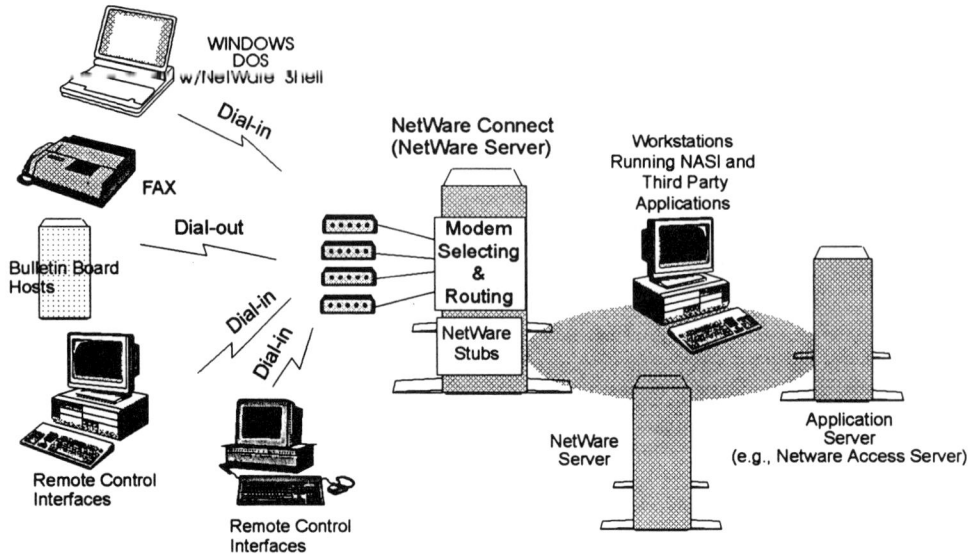

Figure 6-9   Modem Pooling with Netware Connect

provides modem independence to applications that use the Net-Ware Asynchronous Services Interface (NASI), which supports using the same generic modem initialization regardless of the port and modem type they connect to once the administrator maps the modems.

As part of its control role NetWare Connect lets the administrator establish and enforce call time limits, restrict users to certain ports, restrict users to specific services, and to provide dial-back to specific numbers. NetWare Connect can also maintain an audit trail that records information about each dial connection.

NetWare Connect also provides the appropriate, what I refer to as, "NetWare stubs" to support the remote node connection and IPXWAN traffic.

NetWare Connect allows remote users of DOS, Microsoft Windows, and Apple Macintosh computers to both dial into and dial-out of NetWare LAN. NetWare Connect supports AppleTalk, IPX, and Transmission Control Protocol/Internetwork Protocol (TCP/IP) protocols over the wire.

Figure 6-10 depicts the NLMs that provide the connectivity services.

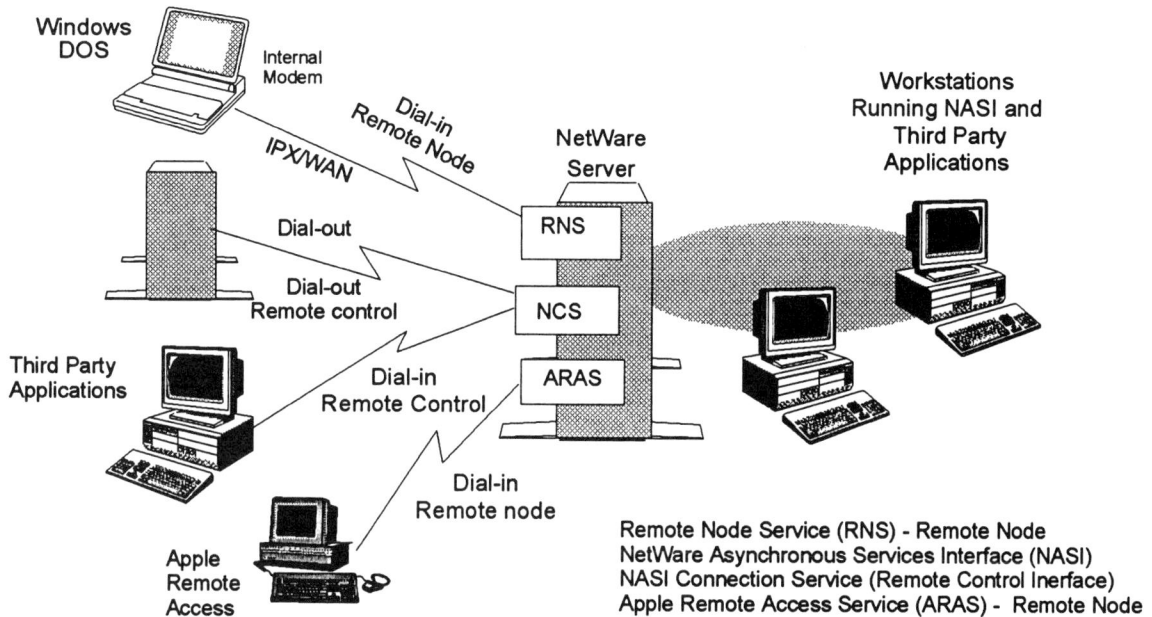

Figure 6-10   NetWare Connect Connectivity

These three NLMs are associated with the appropriate client software in either the remote or local workstations or both. They can be used to control of a remote workstation from a local NetWare connected workstation. The three NLMs and their associated client software include:

- *AppleTalk Remote Access Service* (ARAS), which allows Macintosh clients with AppleTalk Remote Access to dial in and become *remote nodes* on the NetWare LAN. OnLAN/MAC remote control also uses AppleTalk Remote Access.

- *Remote Node Service* (RNS), which allows DOS clients with RNS NetWare Remote Node (NRN) support and the Dial utility to dial in and become *remote nodes* on the NetWare LAN.

- *NetWare Asynchronous Services Interface (NASI) Connection Service* (NCS), which establishes a logical connection between a NetWare Connect port and a DOS or Microsoft (MS) Windows workstation. Using this capability, dial-in users can use a third-party application to remotely control a dedicated workstation (or application on an application server) on the LAN. Similarly a NetWare LAN workstation user can dial-out of the network with third-party applications using a modem from the pool available to the NetWare Connect server via NCS. NSC NASI software and a third party application are required.

Each of the NetWare Connect services on the server requires a corresponding client component that is installed on the workstation. Remote control is achieved using the NetWare Asynchronous Services Interface (NASI) connections, which allows remote users to connect to NetWare Access Services, workstations, or other application servers that support the interface. The third-party application must support NASI or Interrupt 14. NASI-compatible or Interrupt 14 terminal-emulation software (see the following list) can also be used to directly access minicomputer hosts such as DEC, Prime, Data General, and Hewlett-Packard. The NetWare Connect product includes the NASI workstation modules for communication between the workstation and the server. When the NASI.EXE is loaded it prompts the user for a NetWare user name, password, and session name unless these options have been disabled.

NASI-compatible DOS-based terminal emulation programs:
Anzio — Rasmussen Software
Blast Professional 10.5 — U.S. Robotics, Inc.
CROSSTALK Mark IV v2.1.1 — DCA
Minisoft HP 2392 — Minisoft
pcANYWHERE IV LAN v4.5 — Symantec

PC-Term — Crystal Point Software
Procomm Plus v2.0 LAN — Datastorm Technologies
Qmodem Pro 1.0 — Mustang Software
Reflection — Walker, Richter & Quinn
Relay Gold LAN — Microcom Systems, Inc.
Smartcom Exec 2.1 — Hayes Microcomputer
Smart Term v3.0 — Persoft , Inc.
Softerm PC — Softronics
Telepathy — Extrasensory Software
VSCOM for Novell LAN 7.9 — M/H Group
Zstem LAN — KEA Systems

NetWare Connect works with third-party remote-control applications,-including pcANYWHERE, Co/Session and Carbon Copy, Reach-out LAN, and application servers, such as Citrx Systems's NetWare Access Services and WinView. When more than one remote control host PC is set up, NetWare Connect presents a list to select from.

From a dial-out standpoint NetWare Connect allows users on the NetWare network to and connect to bulletin boards, X.25 and ISDN services, remote workstations, FAX machines or FAX-enabled PCs, and asynchronous host systems. Multiple users can share the same physical connection for some of the bulletin board services such as CompuServe and NetWire.

NetWare Connect NLMs can run on any NetWare 3.x server. A user can optionally use the NetWare Runtime 3.x software included with NetWare Connect to set up a dedicated server. The placement of the NetWare Connect services on a dedicated server or shared server is a function of the workload. It is recommended that no more than 64 ports be used per server.

NetWare Connect can be centrally administered via various management tools, such as Simple Network Management Protocol (SNMP), Novell's NetWare Management System (NMS) product, or a NetView console.

NetWare Connect includes several dial-back options that provide security and reverse phone charges.

NetWare Connect supports the COM ports on the server or third-party communications adapters. Communications adapters installed in the server support connections via direct cable, modem, multiplexer, and X.25 public data networks. The adapters must comply with the Novell Asynchronous Input/Output (AIO) specification for asynchronous, X.25, ISDN, and other types of connections. NetWare Connect supports dial-up modems with features such as error correction, data compression, V.32, and speeds up to 115.2 Kbps.

Chapter 7

NetWare SNA Access

7.1 SNA Connectivity Evolution

As discussed earlier many enterprise networks include one or more IBM mainframes and AS/400 midrange computers. These hosts typically had display terminals attached with which the user accessed the business applications. (A typical IBM mainframe configuration in the 1980s might have been configured with an IBM systems network architecture (SNA) backbone network, a communication controller such as the IBM 3174, and multiple IBM 3270 displays as depicted in Figure 7-1.)

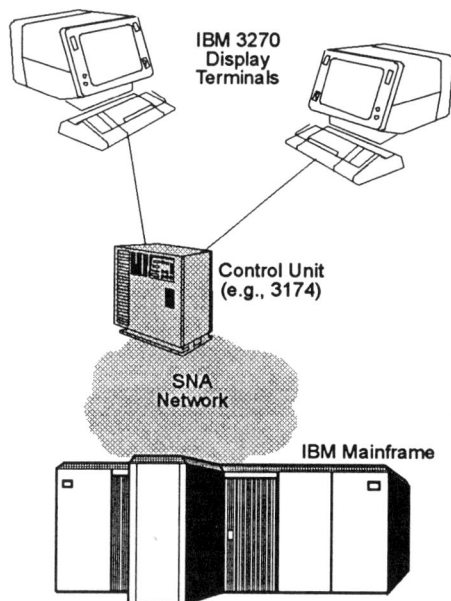

Figure 7-1   Typical IBM Mainframe Access in the 1980s

As personal computers began to appear on the user's desktop, the 3270 terminals were replaced and the function merged into the PCs. The PCs would be loaded with some 3270 emulation software and a communications adapter card that connected to an IBM 3174 cluster controller through coax cables. (See Fig. 7-2.) The user could hot-key between the 3270 display on the screen

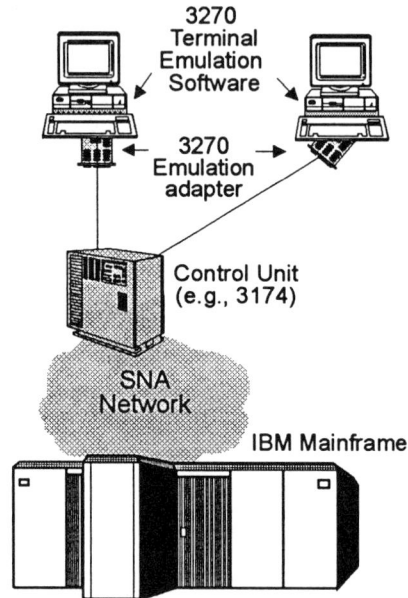

Figure 7-2   3270 Terminal Function Merged into PC

and the other personal computer applications.

This emulation software consumed quite a bit of workstation memory. Additionally, if the workstation user also needed local-area-network (LAN) connectivity, a LAN adapter card (often referred to as *network interface card*) was required in addition to the communications card (see Fig. 7-3). This meant that a second cable was required, it increased the cost of each workstation, it reduced the number of slots available for peripherals, and it took more memory away from the business applications.

The first step to reduce these impacts was to connect the workstation to the LAN cabling system and upgrade the 3174 to support Token Ring connectivity (see Fig. 7-4). This eliminated one of the two cables in the walls, but still required two LAN

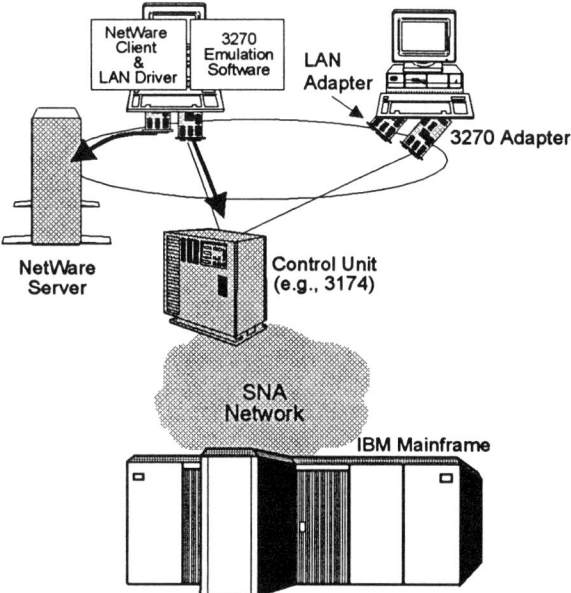

Figure 7-3   PCs Connected to 3174 and NetWare Server

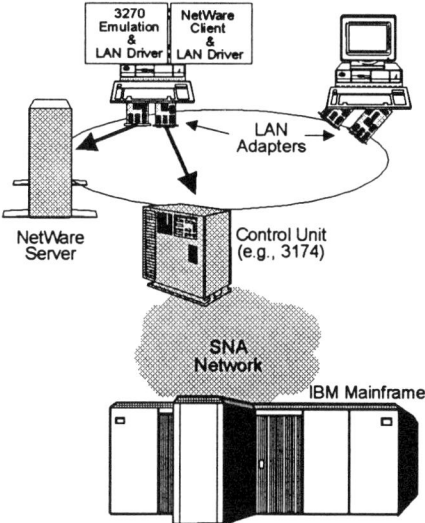

Figure 7-4   Common Media Connection

connections to the wall because two different drivers were required. The LAN communication drivers used for network oper-

ating systems server was not compatible with the system network architecture (SNA) communication drivers. As a result one LAN adapter card was required for the local network operating system and a second LAN adapter was required for the communications controller access.

The next evolutionary step was to use a networking operating system communication driver that supported connectivity to both the networking operating system services and the communications controller.

The easiest solution here was to replace the PC 3270 emulation software and communications controller. The communications controller was replaced with a *communications server* (an SNA *gateway*) that received the screens from the workstation and presented them to the SNA network the same way a 3174 would.

In the NetWare context Novell sold NetWare 3270 LAN Workstation for DOS, which worked hand-in-hand with the NetWare SNA Gateway software. (See Fig. 7-5.) The NetWare gateway software ran on a dedicated workstation. This solution enabled a PC to communicate with the file server and the communications gateway directly using a single adapter card and a single cable to the wall. It also reduced the memory requirements

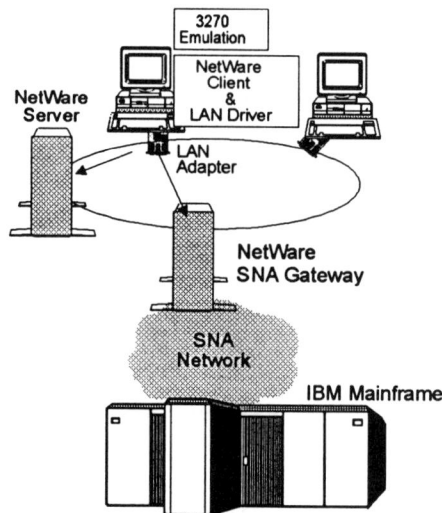

Figure 7-5 Communications and File Server Access

for the communications since only one communication driver was required.

As in any user driven technology solution the customers were still not happy because the workstation portion of the SNA communications stack still took up too much of the workstation's 640K memory and not everyone wanted to dedicate an additional PC for SNA communications.

To address the first part of the requirements many 3270 emulation vendors shrunk the amount of SNA stack processing in the workstation and added more of the stack in the SNA gateway (communications server). Novell went one step further. It developed an SNA gateway service that ran in the same server as the other networking operating services (see Fig. 7-6). This service, NetWare for SAA (system application architecture), has provided a comprehensive basis for NetWare network SNA host, midrange, and LAN-to-LAN over SNA network connectivity.

Netware for SAA also addressed several other subtle but very import issues. The first issue was that most 3270 emulator ven-

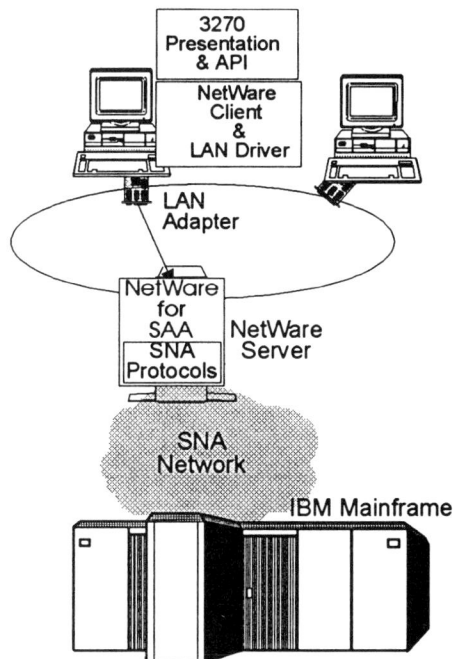

Figure 7-6   NetWare for SAA Runs with File Server

dors had implemented proprietary connections between the workstation resident 3270 presentation and application interfaces and their gateway. This meant that many of Novell's potential customers didn't want to use NetWare for SAA because they enjoyed and were unwilling to give up some the unique presentation attributes and features provided by their vendor. The solution was to adapt Netware for SAA as a NetWare network service to the various vendors' workstation resident 3270-emulation client software (see Fig. 7-7). This had two benefits: the 3270-emulation software vendor no longer had to focus on the hardware aspects of the SNA connection, and the vendor didn't have to get involved in the network management. These responsibilities fell on Novell's NetWare for SAA, which was really mare a comprehensive SNA communications subsystem than a gateway since it provided extensive management services beyond the traditional gateway service.

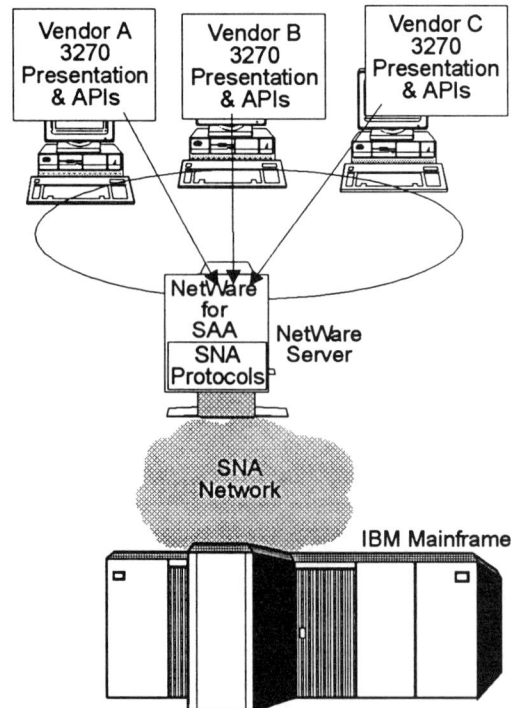

Figure 7-7 NetWare for SAA as a Multivendor Gateway

7.2 NetWare for SAA

NetWare for SAA is a set of NLMs, that provides SNA connectivity to IBM mainframes and AS/400s (see Fig.7-8).

A NetWare for SAA server for a host connection:

- Supports 508 host sessions with two host connection (2 PUs)

- 506 DOS, Windows, OS/2, and UNIX users (two sessions are reserved for internal use) or 200 Macintosh users

- Supports up to 253 AS/400 connections using IBM's Advanced Peer-to-Peer Networking (APPN) protocols from a single server (only one PU is supported for the AS/400 attachment)

- DOS and OS/2 workstation users with IBM's PC Support/400 (IBM's PC to AS/400 integration software) can simultaneously access up to 128 AS/400s over Token Ring or Ethernet using emulated terminal to AS/400 protocols

- One PC Support user can simultaneously access 32 AS/400s using (APPN)

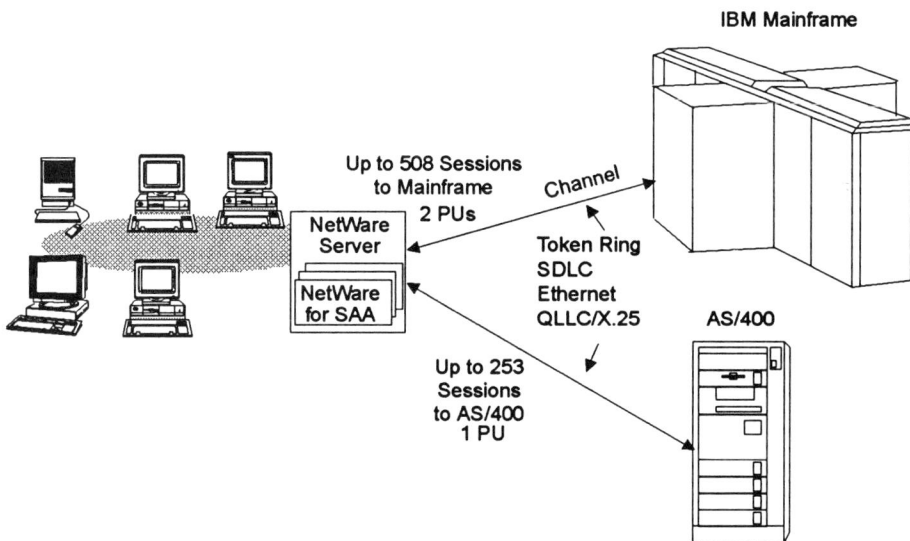

Figure 7-8   NetWare for SAA

NetWare for SAA supports a variety of DOS, Macintosh, MS Windows, OS/2, and UNIX workstation-based IBM 3270 and IBM 5250 emulators (see Fig.7-10). These include emulators from such vendors as:

- Avatar Corporation
- Attachmate Corporation
- Digital Communications Associates, Inc. (DCA)
- Dr. Materna
- Eicon Technology Corporation
- IBM (PC/Support/400)
- Network Software Associates, Inc. (NetSoft)
- Systems Strategies, Inc.
- Wall Data, Inc.

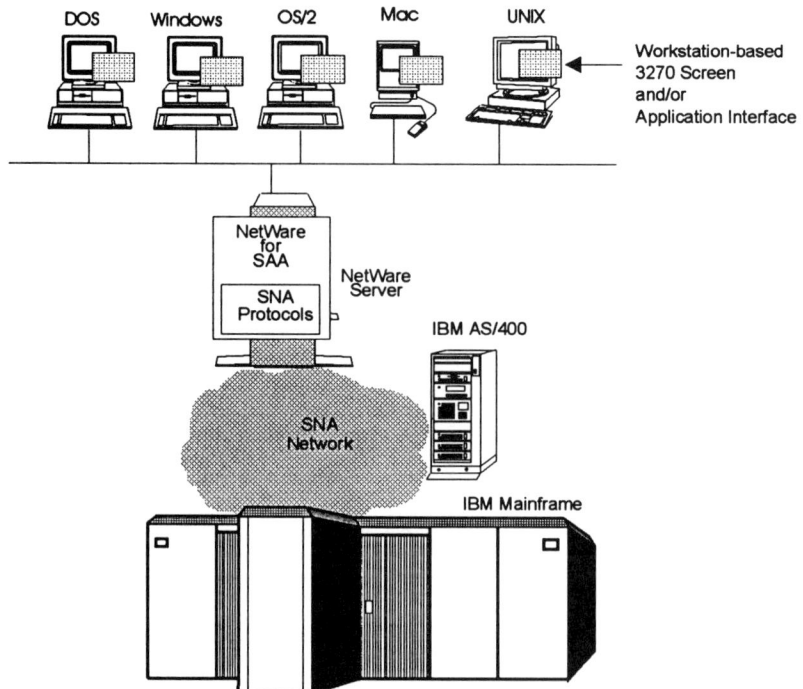

Figure 7-9 NetWare for SAA Workstation Support

Novell has transferred the marketing and support of the Net-Ware 3270 LAN Workstation for DOS, NetWare 3270 LAN Workstation for Windows, NetWare 3270 LAN Workstation for Macintosh, and NetWare 3270 Vector Graphics Option to Attachmate Corporation.

These emulator products allow workstation users with connectivity to NetWare to access the CICS, TSO, CMS, and OfficeVision and AS/400 applications through a variety of presentations.

Several vendors provide what is sometimes referred to as *FrontWare*, which is comprised of software that allows a programmer to add a different presentation to the data arriving at the workstation. The *FrontWare* receives the screen image, but rather than passing it on to the user, the data are either remapped to a graphical screen presentation or combined with some local data before being presented. *FrontWare* tools on the market include Attachmate NOW!, Easel, Mozart, and RUMBA's Visual Basic Toolkit.

NetWare for SAA now provides a NetWare-based software platform that supports:

- A multitude of third party workstation SNA interface software and terminal-emulation programs

- Numerous server-to-host and workstation-to-host-based applications that support the business applications

- Electronic mail gateways, such as NetWare Message Handling Service (MHS) to IBM's Distributed Office Support System (DISOSS) and OfficeVision

- Tools to manage the network

- Support for mainframe and AS/400 applications to print on NetWare printers

- An SNA-based router allowing internetwork packet exchange/sequenced packet exchange (IPX/SPX) traffic to use SNA corporate backbone

The NetWare for SAA NetWare loadable modules (NLMs) support data flows from the workstation or from within the server an pass data on in the appropriate SNA protocols. Figure 7-9 depicts the data flow arriving from emulation software on a

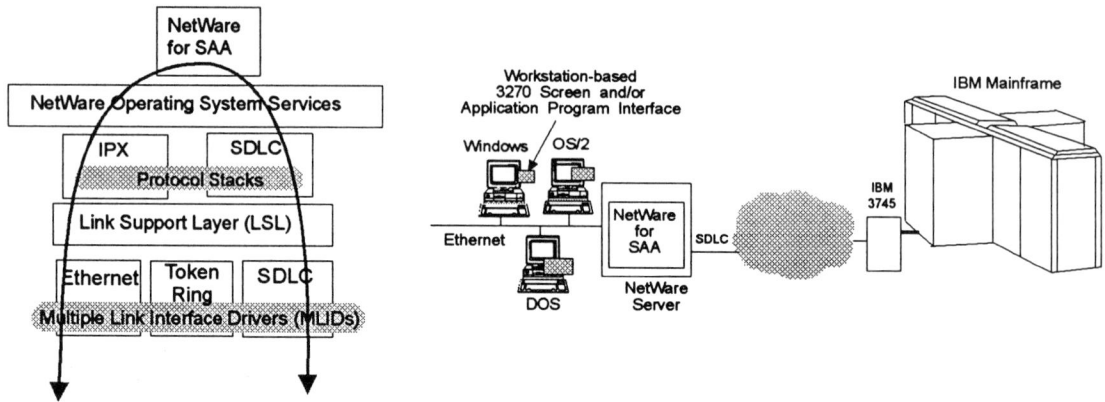

Figure 7-10   NetWare for SAA Data Flows

workstation connected to the Netware server via Ethernet. In this example, a 3270 emulation program in the workstation uses IPX to send the data to the NetWare resident NetWare for SAA NLMs. The NetWare for SAA NLM provides a gateway service and converts the data into synchronous data-link control (SDLC) protocols that move down through the protocol layers and into the SNA network up to the mainframe.

7.3 NetWare Server-based SNA APIs

By separating the workstation emulation support from the SNA connectivity services, NetWare for SAA does not really remove itself from the need to support the external SNA application programming interfaces (APIs) such as programmable device emulation interfaces or advanced program-to-program communications (APPC) and Common Programming Interface-Communications (CPI-C) interfaces, since with this architecture vendors and corporate developers would develop NetWare server-based applications that needed the SNA services.

NetWare for SAA supports IBM's LU6.2/APPC CPI-C and Emulator High-Level Language Application Programming Interface (EHLLAPI). The APPC CPI-C support is really the NetWare for SAA name sake, since it is IBM' SAA common programming interface for communications (CPI-C).

NetWare for SAA also provides support for IBM's customizable LU, referred to a LUA. This LUA API supported the IBM LU0 SNA protocols. This API allows software vendors and corporate developers with existing LU0 applications to leverage the capabilities of NetWare to consolidate their network connectivity and management using both NetWare and NetView. (Many branch banking software applications use the LU0. LU0 enabled custom and streamlined protocols use the SNA envelope without incurring the overhead of some of the generic SNA communications management support.)

7.4 NetWare for SAA Network Management

Because NetWare for SAA had assumed the role of the SNA communications subsystem on the NetWare network, extensive network management facilities and interfaces also had to be provided. NetWare for SAA includes an Open NetView API that allows software vendors to provide their hardware or software products with the ability to both generate alerts to NetView and respond to received requests from from NetView.

NetWare for SAA provides two different but complementary network management mechanisms and facilities. These two approaches are often referred to as *host-based* and *network-based* or *mainframe-centric* and *LAN-centric* network management approaches. My experience has been that both approaches are used when doing end-to-end problem determination and tuning of an enterprise network. Those network management tasks that are easy to automate or already part of the NetView-based infrastructure tend to be host-based and those tasks that require more analysis are typical done via the NetWare LAN-based administrative and analysis interfaces.

Using NetWare for SAA, the NetWare servers and NetWare for SAA servers attached to the enterprise network can be directly supported by NetView automated procedures and the NetView support infrastructure. Using the NetWare for SAA facilities, the servers are monitored and appropriate actions taken.

NetWare for SAA is implemented as a NetView Entry Point and generates alerts for errors detected by NetWare file services as well as for data-link and protocol-level errors detected on the host link. A RUNCMD interface (RUNCMD is a NetView command API that forwards commands to a remote operating system) on the mainframe enables the host operators to monitor and control the servers. Sterling's NetMaster and Solve:LAN for NetWare, can also be used to support remote monitoring and control of NetWare servers.

Novell also provides a NetWare for SAA Tools software development kit for developing distributed NetWare-to-host applications for the NetWare for SAA environment. The tool kit includes NetWare for SAA LU6.2, NetWare 3270, Open NetView API, and LUA tools.

NetWare for SAA provides and is augmented by a comprehensive set of network management and administrative tools that are accessed from workstations on the NetWare network. For example, Novell provides a a Windows-based NetWare Management System (NMS) that includes Novell's NetWare for SAA Services Manager. NetWare for SAA Services Manager provides network management capabilities for monitoring, controlling, diagnosing, tuning, auditing, and maintaining multiple NetWare for SAA servers anywhere on a NetWare network. Examples of the types of capabilities include

- Real-time status information on active host sessions
- Diagnostic LU traces
- Historical information on user profiles
- Data for security and billing purposes
- A centralized control and configuration distribution feature
- A centralized configuration backup

NetWare's Remote Management Facility (RMF) allows supervisors to dynamically control and configure NetWare for SAA servers from a remote workstation.

Through different windows, NMS allows you concurrent access to IBM NetView, SunNet Manager, HP OpenView, SynOptics Cabling Management Services, and Novell Service Management Software.

7.5 NetWare for SAA Connectivity

NetWare for SAA supports host SNA session connectivity via:

- 10-Mbit Ethernet - NetWare for SAA can connect through an Ethernet host link to a 3172 controller, a 37xx communications processor, a 9370 host processor, or an AS/400 minicomputer

- 16-Mbit Token Ring - NetWare for SAA can connect through a Token Ring host link to a 3172 controller, a 3174 controller, a 37xx communications processor, a 9370 host processor or an AS/400 minicomputer

- SDLC

- QLLC/X.25 - NetWare for SAA can connect through a qualified logical-link control (QLLC) host link to an X.25 network. The required Call Support Layer (CSL) software is included with NetWare for SAA. Hardware and driver support are provided by Novell and Newport Systems Solutions, Inc.

- IBM S/370 channel - Netware for SAA can be used to directly attach NetWare connected workstations and server applications to the mainframe without the overhead of an additional cluster controller or front-end processor. Systems currently available include Bus Tech's IBM 3172-BT1 and Memorex Telex's 9430 Enterprise Gateway (see Fig.7-9).

The mainframe channel attachment scenario deserves more attention. Figure 7-9 describes three local connection options:

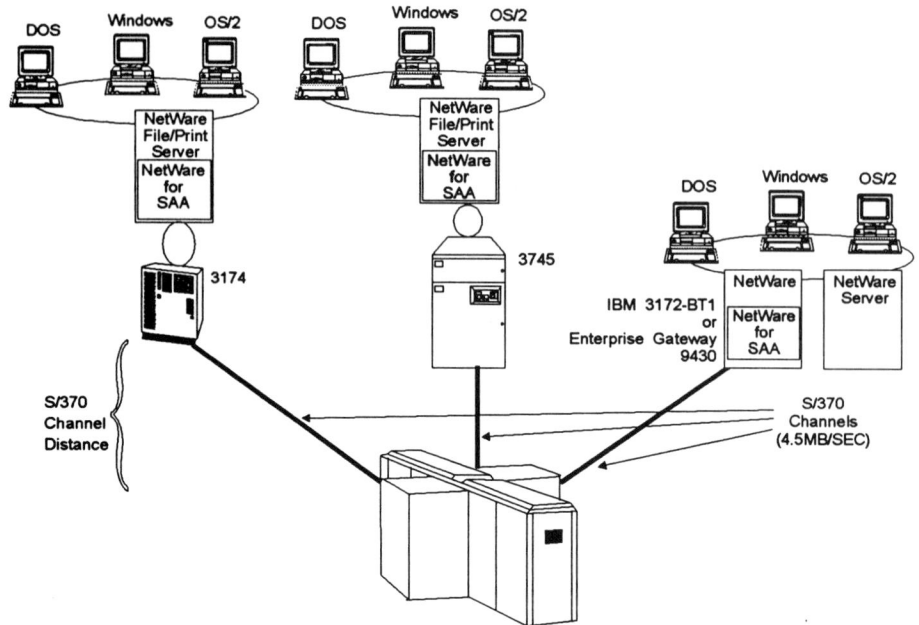

Figure 7-11   IBM Channel Attachment Options

A Netware for SAA in a file and print server connected via a Token Ring connection to an IBM 3174 that is channel attached to the mainframe

A Netware for SAA in a file-and print-server connected via a Token Ring connection to an IBM 3745 communications front-end that is channel attached to the mainframe

A Bus Tech Inc. IBM 3172-BT1 or Memorex Telex Enterprise Gateway 9430 channel attached to the mainframe

I have presented these this way to clarify the various relationships. The first two configurations that connect to IBM's communications controllers via Token Ring show NetWare for SAA in a generalized server. The third configuration with the channel attachment from NetWare for SAA server is intended to highlight that the 3172-BT1 and the MT 9430 servers are exclusively communication servers. Both of these channel attached servers have been customized as communication controllers rather than generalized servers which ensures even higher availability.

A more subtle consideration that one might miss is that IBM currently supports two channel architectures, the IBM S/370 parallel channel and the IBM Enterprise Systems Communication Architecture (ESCON) serial channel.

The IBM Parallel channels support data rates up to 4.5 MByte per second and can connect with controllers with 400 feet without channel extenders. The IBM ESCON channels have a much higher data rate (10M Byte per second) and extend 3 kilometers and up to 9 kilometers (5.6 miles) with two ESCON directors. Additionally the ESCON fiber channels are significantly less bulky and more secure. IBM's S/370 and S/390 mainframes support the parallel channel and the S/390s (the ES/9000 system line also supports ESCON channels).

Having described the S/370 and ESCON channel connections, note that all NetWare for SAA channel connections are currently made through a communications controller and that BTI and Memorex/Telex provide a hybrid controller that runs a runtime version of NetWare and NetWare for SAA in the same unit. We'll discuss these and other channel connections options in the Server chapter when discussing how to use the mainframe as a server.

For now, you should note that the channel data rate is not usually a constraint on the configuration, the constraints are typically a function of the server(s) feeding the channel connected controller and the aggregate throughput of the feeding networks.

When compared to the alternatives, most companies that use communication servers have been very happy with the data transfer performance.

7.6 The NetWare Backbone

There is a second major option that the channel-attached Net-Ware-based communications server offers: the concept of a virtual SNA network. The virtual SNA network as conceptualized in Figure 7-10 is comprised of interconnected NetWare mutliprotocol routers and NetWare servers, with a single communications server with NetWare for SAA at the mainframe site. This configuration now has an NetWare backbone network and an SNA interchange at the mainframe using the channel connection. (The

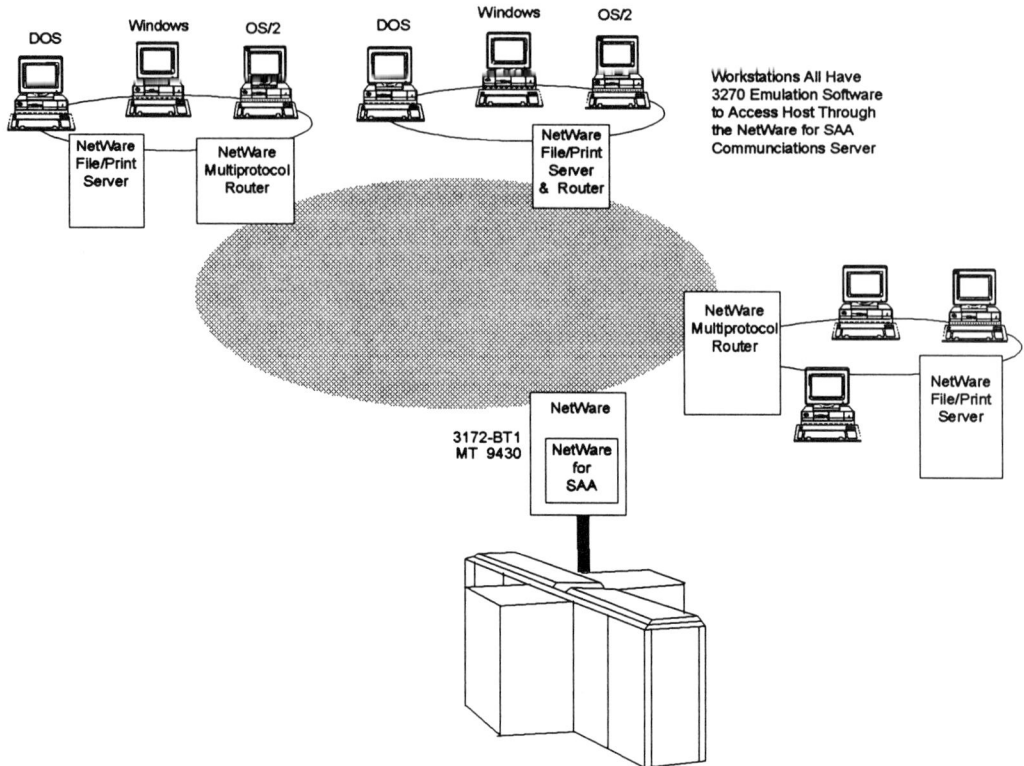

Figure 7-12   A NetWare SNA Backbone

configuration depicted supports up to 506 sessions.) Additional communications servers would be used to increase the network.

The backbone could also be built using bridges, hardware routers, and various multiprotocol routing packages.

The physical connection technologies, data rates, and sources are described in Table 7-1.

NetWare for SAA provides the following SNA support:

• Physical unit (PU) types

• PU Type 2.0

• PU Type 2.1 LEN

• Logical unit (LU) types supported

• LU Type 2 terminal display sessions emulating 3270 terminals

- LU Types 1 or 3 printer sessions
- LU Type 6.2 sessions
- LU Type 0 sessions

Table 7-1 NetWare for SAA Hardware Connections

Connection Type	Data Rating	Adapter Source
Ethernet	10 Mbits	ODI v4.0 compliant adapter
Token Ring	16 Mbits	ODI v4.0 compliant adapter
SDLC	64 Kbits	Eicon Technology IBM Microdyne
QLLC/X.25	64 Kbits	Newport Systems Novell
IBM S/370 Channel	4.5 Mbytes	Bus Tech Inc. 3172 BT1 Memorex Telex 9430

7.6 NetWare for SAA as a PU Concentrator

NetWare for SAA can be used to concentrate other SNA communication controllers and systems with SNA communications software. This support is SNA capability is referred to as *downstream* support, *downstream physical unit*, or *downstream PU* support. The unit that provides this downstream PU support is often referred to as *PU concentrator* to describe the role the unit plays in the network.

Downstream PU device support allows a NetWare for SAA server to have other NetWare for SAAs, OS/2 SNA gateways, OS/2 Communications Manager/2 clients, PC/3270 clients, Attachmate EXTRA! clients, 3172 or 3174 cluster controllers or AS/400s all be connected into one Netware for SAA server (see Fig.7-11).

The downstream device appears as a PU2.0 to the NetWare for SAA server, and NetWare for SAA provides a host connection and LU allocation for the downstream PU. Using the downstream

IBM Mainframe

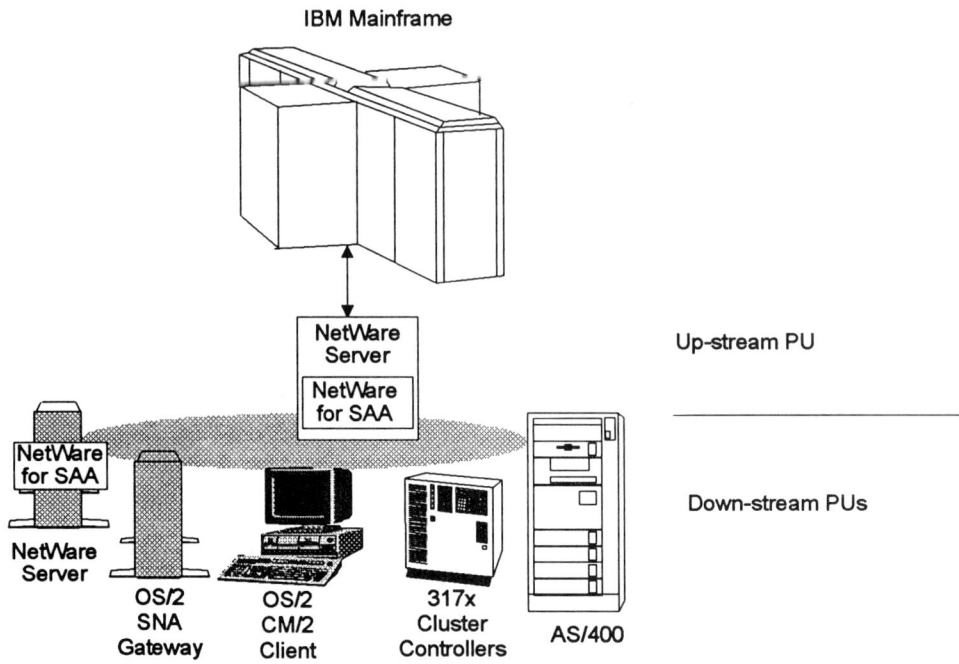

NetWare
Server

NetWare
for SAA

Up-stream PU

NetWare
for SAA

Down-stream PUs

NetWare
Server

OS/2
SNA
Gateway

OS/2
CM/2
Client

317x
Cluster
Controllers

AS/400

Figure 7-13   NetWare for SAA as Concentrator

capability increases the configuration flexibility and reduces the number of PUs defined in the host.

7.7 NetWare for SAA and the AS/400

NetWare for SAA provides the connectivity between worksta-tions and the AS/400. This connectivity support, together with workstation-based 5250 emulation software on each workstation enables workstation users to access AS/400-based applications. NetWare for SAA is completely compatible with IBM's PC Support applications and application programming interfaces (APIs), as well as third-party applications.

Using PC Support software, NetWare clients can access AS/400 applications from anywhere in a network. This allows the workstation users to access the AS/400's Shared Folders, use the virtual print capabilities, transfer files, issue remote com-mands, and issue remote SQL requests. IBM PC support is also discussed in the Section 4 in the DOS and Windows Chapter.

NetWare for SAA enables each workstation user to concurrently access as many as 32 AS/400s. A single NetWare for SAA server can provide simultaneous access to as many as 128 AS/400s over Token Ring or Ethernet (see Fig.7-14). It the connections using the NetWare for SAA server are APPN sessions, as many as 253 AS/400s can be simultaneously accessed.

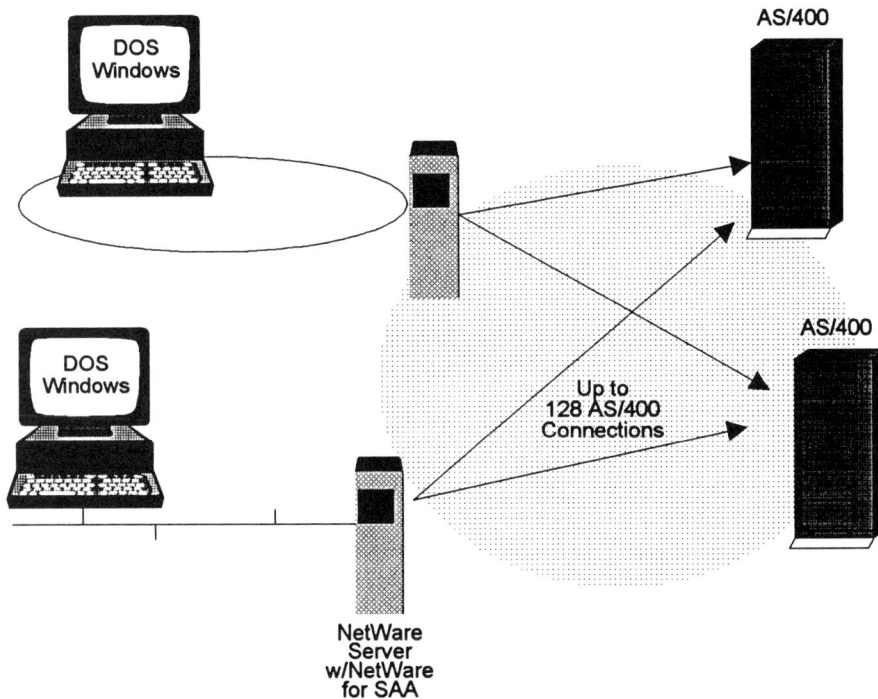

Figure 7-14   NetWare Accessing Multiple AS/400s

7.8 NetWare HostPrint

NetWare HostPrint is an NLM that coresides with and uses a NetWare for SAA server. It enables users to send mainframe and AS/400 print outputs directly to NetWare-based printers. Each server can support only one NetWare HostPrint NetWare loadable module (NLM), which can support up to 128 SNA sessions.

NetWare HostPrint is an IBM 3287 LU1 and LU3 printer emulation program that can have up to 128 printer appearances to the host. Each NetWare HostPrint session requires a dedicated logical unit (LU) configured for NetWare for SAA. A workstation based configuration utility provides the coordination to tie each 3287 session to the target NetWare printer queue. The host sends the IBM 3287 output to the appropriate network address just as if it were sending the output to a specific printer on the system network architecture (SNA) network. NetWare HostPrint accepts the data stream and routes directly to the configured NetWare print queues. Once on the server the output can be routed and managed the same as any other NetWare printed output produced by NetWare Print Services or other print products.

Figure 7-15 depicts four representative print output configurations options (A though D) connected to a common mainframe. Configuration A is an IBM 3174 with an attached IBM 3287

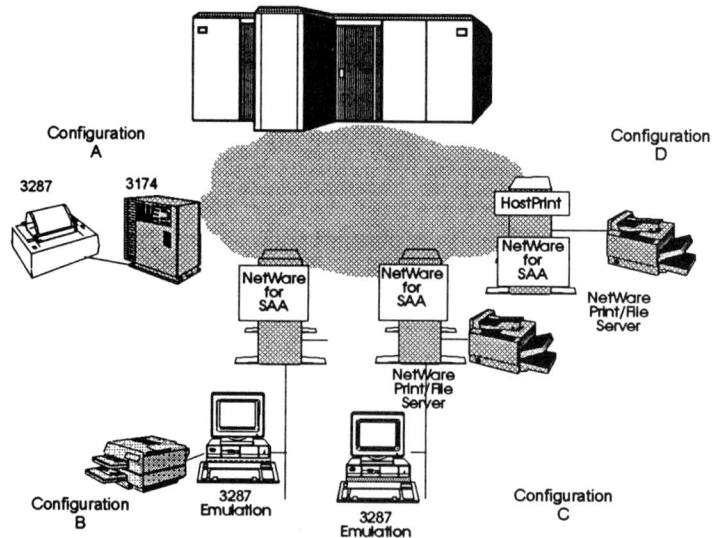

Figure 7-15 Mainframe-to-LAN Printing Options

printer. This configuration represents the hardware environment being emulated in the other three configurations. In configuration B the 3174 and 3287 printer have been replaced with a NetWare server, NetWare for SAA, and by a workstation that emulates the 3287 with a printer attached. NetWare for SAA in this configuration simply passes on LU1 or LU3 data streams. The server in this configuration could be a run-time version with only NetWare for SAA capabilities.

Configuration C depicts an environment which has moved the printer from the workstation to the NetWare server. In this case the NetWare server provides file and print services to the server attached printer and runs NetWare for SAA.

Configuration D eliminates the need for a workstation based emulator by running the NetWare HostPrint NLM and using the NetWare print service. NetWare HostPrint print jobs are forwarded to the NetWare print system and can then be managed as any other print job. Additionaly, a printer control utility panel that allows dynamic changes to the emulation characteristics is included.

As a general comment these configurations are very trivial in that only one printer is required in each configuration. If the mainframe output were to be sent to different printers in configuration B, multiple workstations with 3287 emulation programs would be required. The NetWare HostPrint implementation eliminates the need for one or more workstations to be dedicated to emulating an IBM 3287.

NetWare HostPrint can also be used to support AS/400 output. The AS/400 must be set up with a 3x74 controller and IBM 3287 definitions. This allows AS/400 users using any AS/400 terminal emulation or IBM 5250 terminals to use the NetWare HostPrint (see Fig. 7-16). The NetWare HostPrint printer emulation supports the SNA Character Stream (SCS) protocol. Most IBM line-mode printers use SCS to control printing. These printers include 3812, 3816, 4214, 4234, 4245, 5219, 5224, 5225, 5256, 5262, 6552, and 6262. The IBM 5256-03 is functionally equivalent to the 3287.

Intelligent Printer Data Stream (IPDS) protocols and Advanced Function Printing Data Stream (AFPDS) are not supported by NetWare HostPrint, but AS/400 users can use PC Support/400 to support these printing services. NetWare HostPrint also provides automatic queue reconnection when the output is being sent to remote printers over wide-area network (WAN) connections.

AS/400

Figure 7-16   NetWare HostPrint and the AS/400

7.9 NetWare SNA Links

NetWare SNA Links is a software router that encapsulates NetWare's Packet Exchange/Sequenced Packet Exchange (IPX/SPX) packets with an SNA envelope and sends the resulting envelopes across the network using LU6.2 protocols (see Fig. 7-17).

NetWare SNA Links is an NLM that works with NetWare for SAA to provide local-area-network-to-local-area-network (LAN-to-LAN) communications over existing SNA networks. NetWare SNA Links allows departmental NetWare users to use the main corporate SNA to provide their inter-LAN NetWare communications with minimum expense by connecting remote NetWare servers across the SNA network.

Windows   OS/2

UNIX

Netware
Services

NetWare
SNA Links

NetWare
for SAA

NetWare
Services

SNA
WAN

IPX/SPX

Netware
Services

NetWare
SNA Links

NetWare
for SAA

NetWare
Services

Mac

DOS

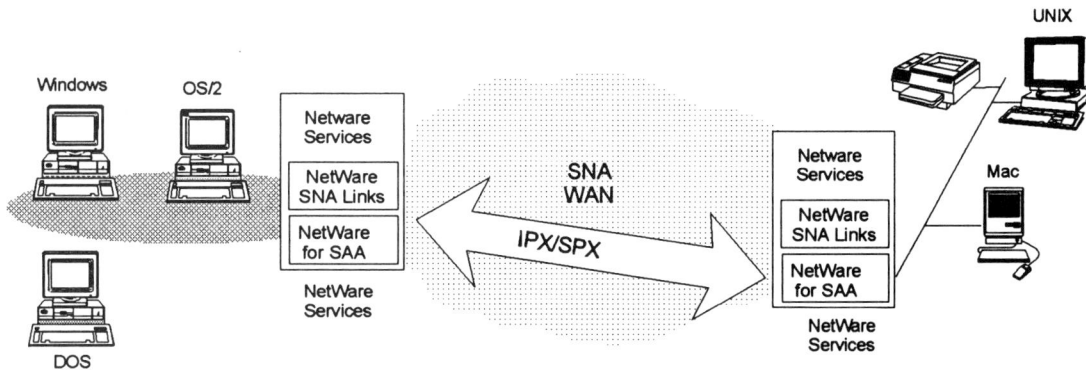

Figure 7-17   LAN-to-LAN with NetWare SNA Links

NetWare for SAA and NetWare SNA Links users can access
mainframe or AS/400 applications and remote NetWare LANs
connected via the SNA or AS/400 network using a single physical
connection to the wide area network.

Once the Netware for SAA has been installed SNA Links runs
on the existing hardware and with the existing communications
adapters. NetWare SNA Links and NetWare for SAA software
must be co-resident and appear in all NetWare nodes expected to
be interconnected. Typical applications include file transfers,
remote NetWare administration, remote user support, and remote
workstation administration.

NetWare SNA Links is configured by the LAN administrator
to interconnect the various NetWare servers with unique sessions,
usually a pair per connection. For example, Figure 7-18 depicts
three NetWare servers that are interconnected with three SNA
Links connections. Each connection is comprised of a unique LU
with two sessions. Figure 7-18 depicts a configuration using
three LUs and six sessions. The connections are between SNA

Links server B and server A, server B and server C, and server C and server A.

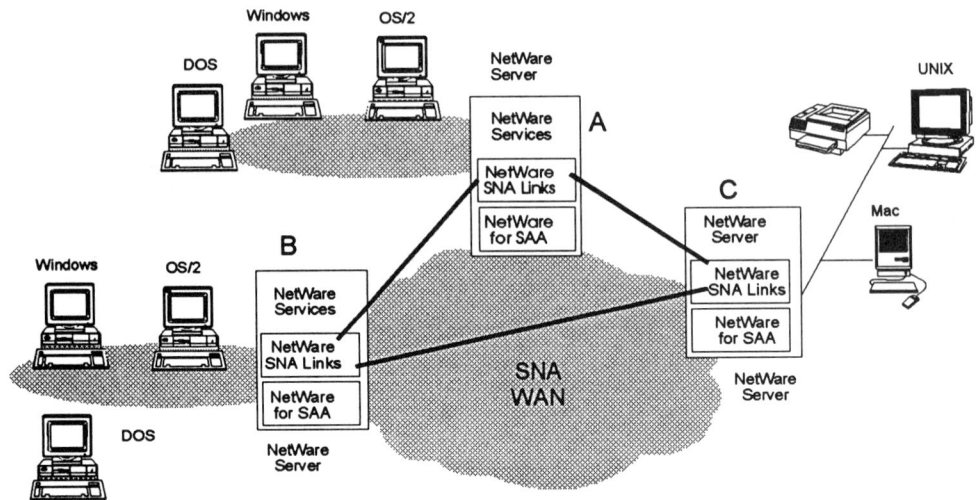

Figure 7-18   A NetWare SNA Links Configuration

NetWare SNA Links is a state-of-the-art SNA peer-to-peer service. It uses LU6.2 independent sessions, which requires physical unit (PU) T2.1 support. This support provides the desired dynamics, however, T2.1 support is relatively recent, and care must be taken to ensure that the SNA network and 3174 configuration's prerequisite support levels are installed prior to installing SNA Links. The SNA Links connections are made through NetWare for SAA as PU T2.1 connections. PU T2.1 support enables independent peer-to-peer SNA network connections, this means that the communications software can establish a connection between two end-points without any intervention by a third party service. However, in a shared SNA network or AS/400 network context, it still means that a front-end processor such as IBM's 3745 or the AS/400 network hardware and software are involved in the connection and the data flow.

Figure 7-19 depicts the logical connections and the physical connections. Note that the SNA *backbone cloud* involves a communications front-end processor such as an IBM 3745 as the

switching focal point for the traffic among the servers and a
mainframe for managing the front-end processor.

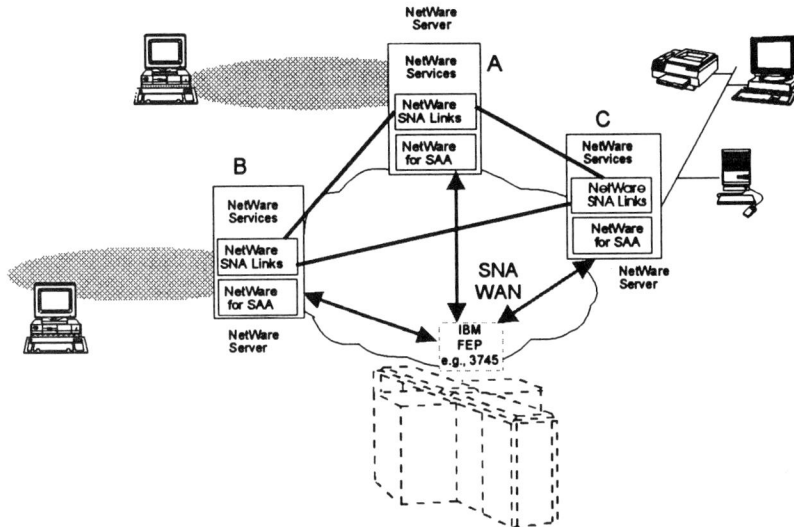

Figure 7-19   SNA Links Physical and Logical Paths

Figure 7-20 depicts a simple AS/400 network (simple because
only one AS/400 is included). In this example the data path flows
through the integrated communications adapter in the AS/400 and

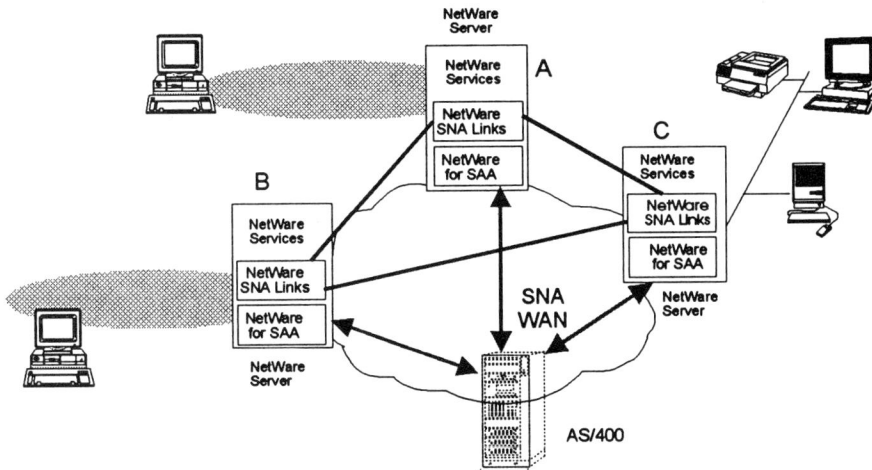

Figure 7-20   An AS/400 Network and SNA Links

uses some of the AS/400 operating system communications support.

SNA Links networks can also be cascaded. For example, assume that only servers B and A and servers A and C of the configuration as depicted in Figure 7-21 are connected via SNA Links.

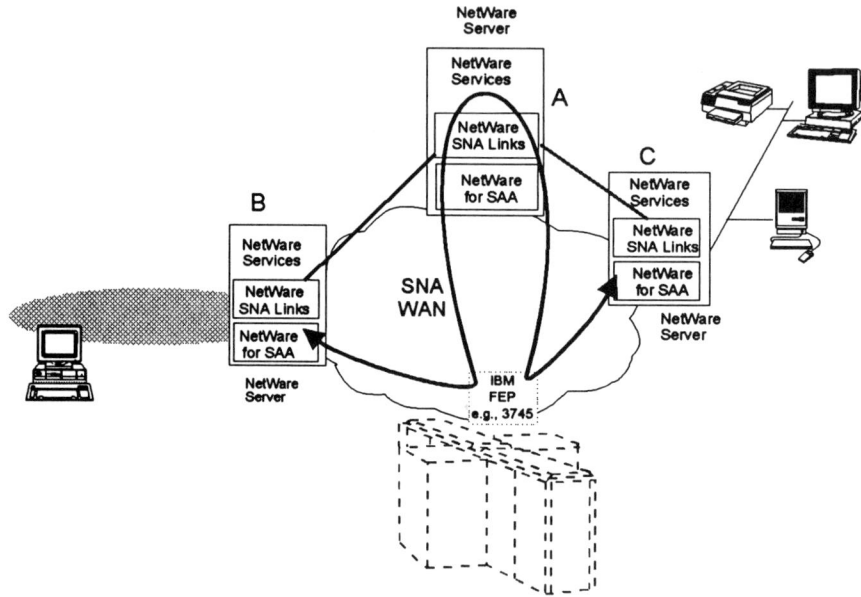

Figure 7-21   A SNA Links Cascading Example

In this case server A routes the traffic between the two legs. A request from a user connected to server B needing services from the C server would travel as an encapsulated IPX/SPX request from the server B's SNA Links to server A's SNA Links into NetWare and then be reencapsulated and sent from server A's SNA Links to server C's SNA links where it would be deencapsulated and serviced.

In this cascade configuration you should note the path from B to C passes through the front-end processor twice. Into the front-end processor, to the server A, through server A, back to the front-end processor and then out to server C.

Because SNA Links uses state-of-the-art SNA features it is important to make sure the co-requisite software and communication controller(s) are current. For a NetWare SNA Links server attached to a 37xx front-end processor through an synchronous data-link control (SDLC) or Token Ring connection the IBM Network Control Program (NCP) and Virtual Telecommunications Access Method (VTAM) software must be a the following levels:

- NCP 5.2 or later on the 3720 or 3745 front-end processor
- NCP 4.3 or later on the 3725 front-end processor
- VTAM 3.2 or later on IBM's MVS and VM operating systems
- VTAM 3.4 or later for IBM's DOS/VSE

If the NetWare SNA Links is connected downstream from a 3174 attached to a front-end processor the following software and hardware levels apply:

- NCP 5.2 or later on a 3720 or 3745
- NCP 4.3 or later on a 3725
- VTAM 3.2 or later for MVS or VM
- An IBM 3174 with Configuration B, revision 4.0 and RPQ 8Q0880
- VTAM 3.4 or later for DOS/VSE

If the NetWare SNA Links is connected downstream from a 3174 attached to the mainframe through a channel connection the following software and hardware levels apply:

- VTAM 3.4 or later for MVS
- VTAM 3.3 or later for VM
- 3174 with Configuration B, revision 4.0, and RPQ 8Q0880

If the NetWare SNA Links is connected to an IBM 9370 through an SDLC or Token Ring connection the following software levels apply:

- Any version of Telecommunications Control Subsystem
- VTAM 3.3 or above for MVS or VM

If the NetWare SNA links is connected to an AS/400 through an SDLC or Token Ring connection the AS/400 must be running OS/400, Release 1.1

The primary sensitivity here is for planning purposes since most NetWare for SAA connections installed today use PU T2.0, a dependent PU connectivity with the mainframe, and run with earlier SNA software and hardware levels.

7.10 Summary

In summary NetWare provides some solid base of NetWare-based building blocks to support integrating the NetWare network with the enterprise network's SNA-based applications and the enterprise's SNA backbone.

The NetWare-based building blocks allow the company to select the appropriate products and fit their management into the appropriate systems management infrastructure. Additionally, the previously non-SNA-related NetWare building blocks, such as Netware Connect and Netware Access Services work hand in hand with NetWare for SAA to enable enterprise-wide accessibility to the enterprise network and its information and computing resources.

Chapter 8

Other NetWare Building Blocks

8.1 NetWare and Digital Equipment's LAT

It is estimated that their are approximately 50,000 sites that use the Digital Equipment Corporation's Virtual Address Extension/Virtual Memory System (VAX/VMS) systems. From all indications many of these sites also have NetWare servers. Until late 1993 there was no direct way for NetWare users to access these VAXs without imposing additional overhead in each workstation. NetWare for LAT is a new NetWare-to-VMS host connectivity product enabling NetWare customers to transparently access VAX/VMS and NetWare services from any workstation attached to the NetWare network. No special software is required on the DEC host. NetWare for LAT provides the protocol processing, security, and management to access multiple VAX/VMS hosts by interfacing with DEC's Local Area Transport (LAT) protocol.

NetWare for LAT is a set of NLMs that provide up to 128 users simultaneous access to NetWare and VMS applications over any NetWare-supported topology including Token-Ring, Ethernet, and Arcnet using IPX/SPX, Transmission Control Protocol/Internet Protocol (TCP/IP), or AppleTalk protocols. As with most NetWare products of this type, NetWare for LAT can run on a shared or dedicated server. It is an integration platform used by many third-party vendors, which are developing applications to further integrate the NetWare and VMS environments with terminal emulation, file transfer, E-mail services, and printing services.

NetWare for LAT removes the need to support multiple protocol stacks to access both NetWare servers and VAX/VMS systems. Prior to NetWare for LAT, the NetWare-connected user workstations had to support LAT or DECnet protocols in addition to LAT on each client workstation if they wanted to access both NetWare and DEC VMS services. With NetWare for LAT, terminal emulators can use IPX/SPX or TCP/IP protocols to connect to NetWare for LAT, which in turn communicates with the VAX/VMS system using the LAT protocol over the Ethernet LAN, as depicted in Figure 8-1. NetWare for LAT supports various vendors' terminal emulators for DOS, MS Windows, Apple Macintosh, OS/2, UNIX, and MS Windows NT workstations.

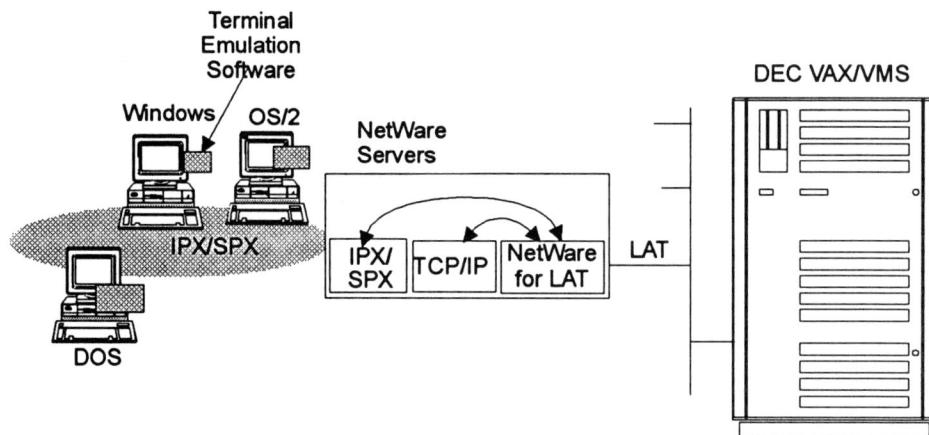

Figure 8-1   NetWare for LAT

Customers can now use their existing TCP/IP-and IPX/SPX-based NetWare networks to connect to all DEC hosts. Using the NetWare server and NetWare for LAT eliminates the need to use terminal servers or to bridge LAT or route DECnet across their WANs. NetWare for LAT provides developers an open platform to further integrate VMS and NetWare services. These vendors are providing terminal emulation that interfaces with NetWare for LAT or supplements interoperability services.

InterConnections, an Emulex company, provides Leverage Gateway Services, a set of NLMs that provides a LAT terminal interface, bidirectional printing, and file transfer for both VMS and UNIX environments. It also includes an simple network management protocol management information base (SNMP MIB) that allows the administrator to monitor and manage the Gateway Services and the traffic it is handling from any network display or management tool that supports SNMP (see Fig. 8-2).

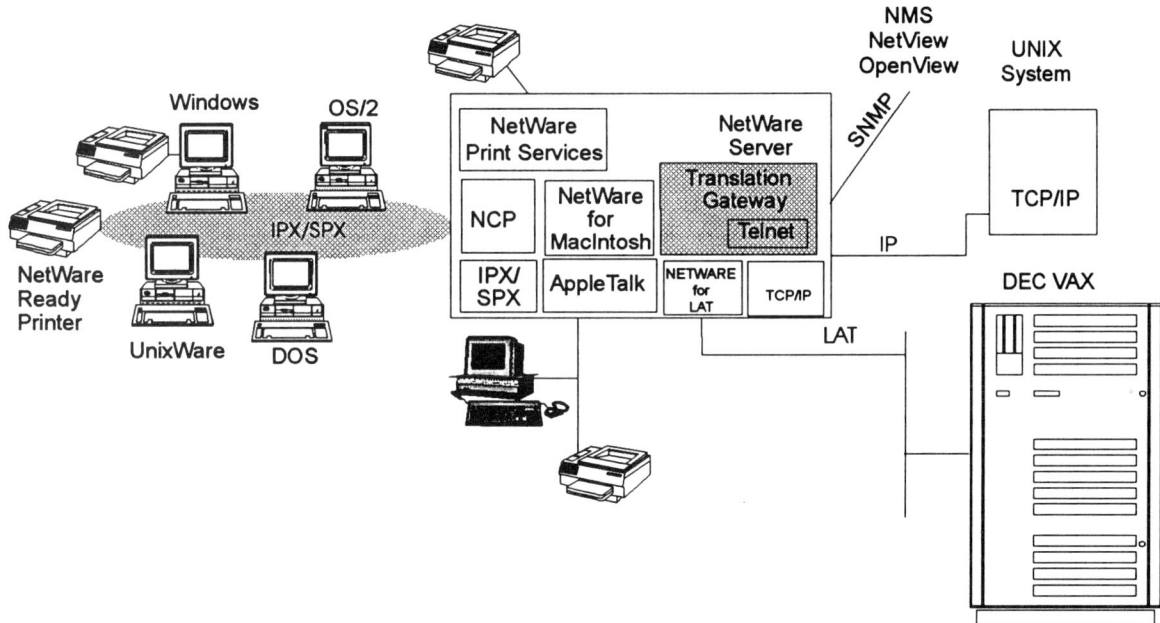

Figure 8-2   Interconnection Leverage Gateway Services

This product allows NetWare users and terminal users to access UNIX systems via Telnet. Likewise UNIX users can access VMS applications. The workstation application uses normal terminal emulation products that use the IPX/SPX protocol stack to communicate to the NetWare server-based NLMs. The InterConnection's NLMs in turn route the access through their Telnet module to access the UNIX system. The same scenario is applicable for terminals connected to NetWare for LAT and

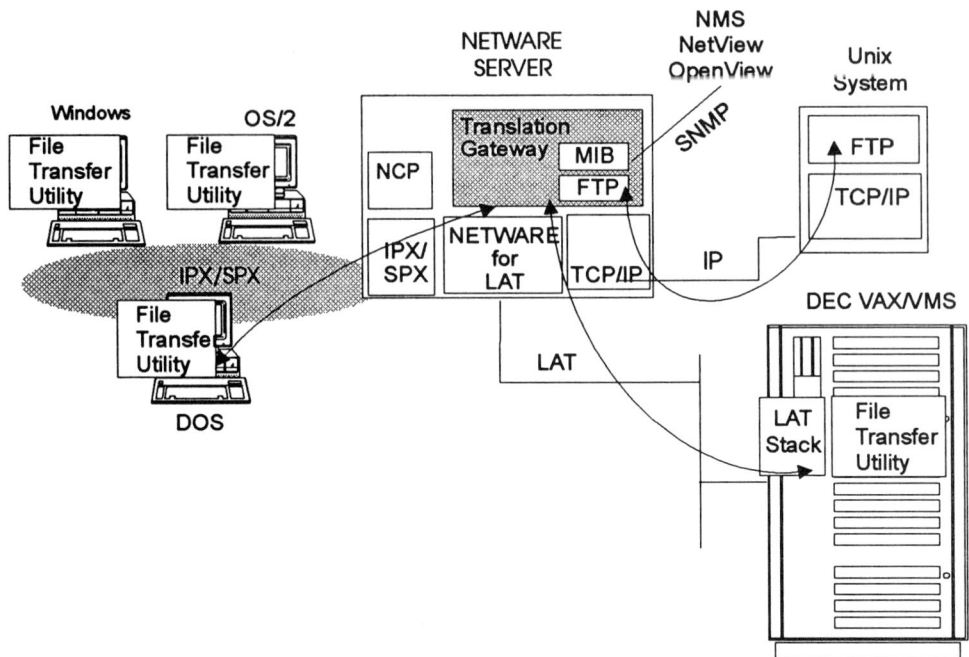

Figure 8-3   File Transfer Example

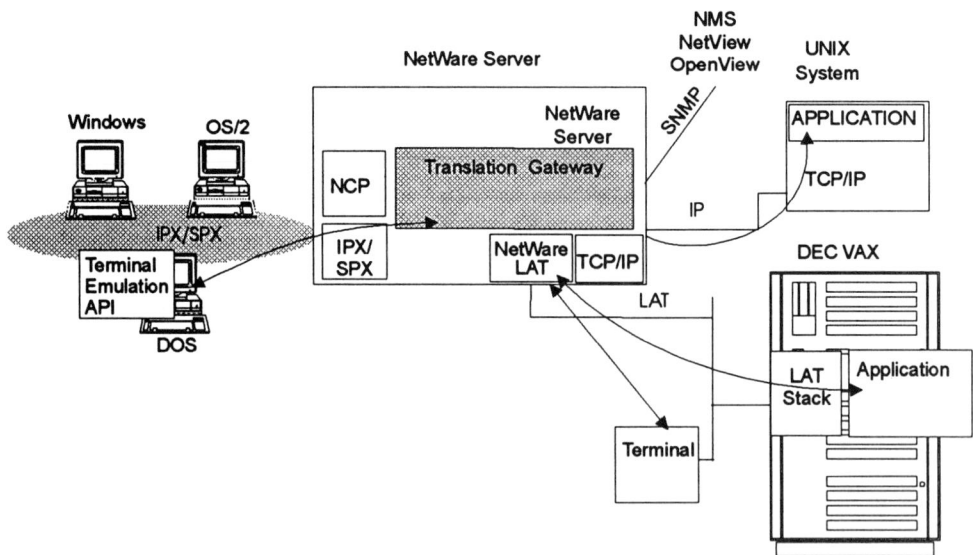

Figure 8-4   Terminal Gateway to UNIX

UNIX users wanting to access VMS applications. In each case no additional protocol stacks are required (see Fig. 8-3).

Using an InterConnection's utility on the PC and on the VMS systems allows users to transfer files among NetWare-connected workstations, VMS systems, and systems with TCP/IP with File Transfer Protocol (FTP). InterConnections' Leverage Gateway Services file transfer NLM provides the necessary conversion and routing to the target environments. This enables NetWare-connected workstations to use only IPX/SPX protocols, VMS systems to use the LAT protocol and UNIX or other systems to use TCP/IP in order to exchange files (see Fig. 8-4).

This InterConnections product also provides transparent printer sharing (output routing) among the different environments. That is VMS- TCP/IP-, and NetWare-attached workstations can route output to printers on any NetWare for LAT server interconnected system printer. For example, users can print VMS files on a NetWare printer, and a NetWare-network-connected

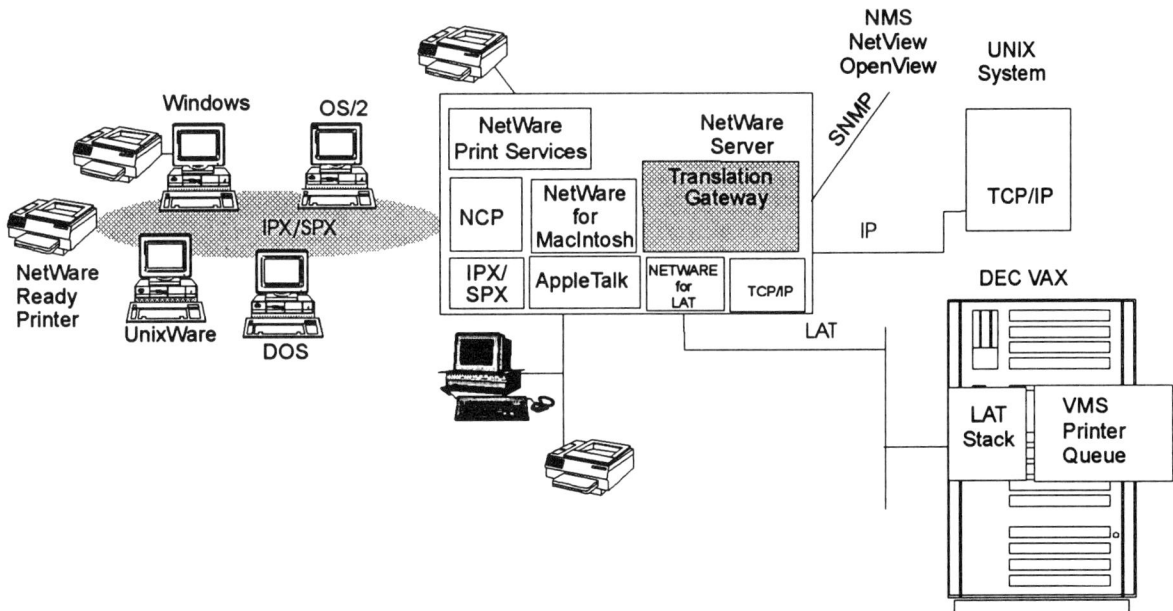

Figure 8-5   Output Routing Example

workstation user can send files to be printed by the VAX printer. The Leverage Gateway Services provide the same capabilities to a UNIX platform. This routed print capability should work for any output that is handled by the NetWare server. For example, the output from Mac workstations attached to the server and the output from UNIX workstations attached to the server can be

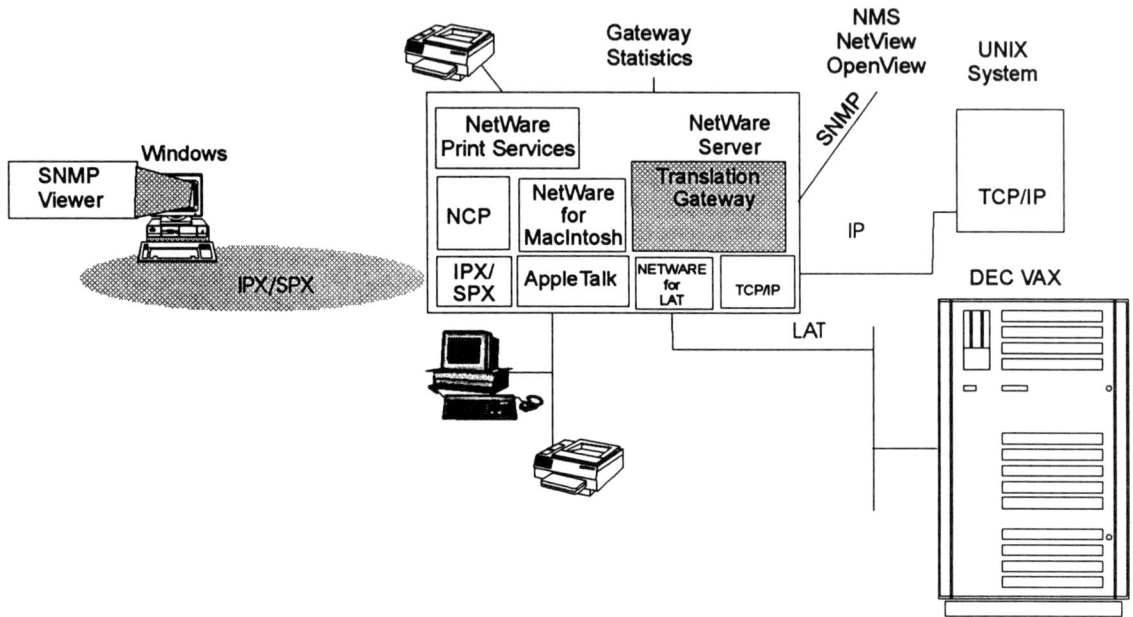

Figure 8-6   Windows-based Monitoring

routed to the VMS- or TCP/IP-connected systems (see Fig. 8-5).

InterConnections also includes a management facility as part of their product. The NLM's activities can be monitored via an InterConnection's SNMP-accessible module. Traffic through the gateway and logged-in users information can be accessed and displayed via any SNMP displayer as well as via the Windows-based service that InterConnections provides. Since NetWare supports SNMP flows over IPX, this tool can be used without adding a TCP/IP stack (see Fig. 8-6).

Another company, Firefox, Inc., provides NOV*AX for Net-Ware, which is an NLM that provides VT100 and VT200 terminal emulation that uses the NetWare for LAT capability. The workstation traffic to this NLM is carried in IPX/SPX protocols.

Meridian Technology Corporation provides SuperLAT Host-Print, which is an NLM that enables NetWare-attached users to print to Digital printers and Digital users to print to NetWare-attached printers.

Wingra Technologies, Inc., is offering Digital-to-Netware direct mail exchange capabilities using NetWare for LAT.

Other interconnectivity companies, such as Diversified Computer Systems, Inc., KEA Systems Ltd., Meridian Technology Corp., Persoft Inc., Polygon Inc., Simware Inc., Wall Data Inc., and Walker Richer & Quinn Inc., have also declared their intent to provide DEC interoperability enhancements that use NetWare for LAT.

8.2 NetWare MHS

8.2.1 Overview

Novell provides three NetWare MHS products that which all support workgroup messaging for applications that use Novell's native Netware MHS API, the Standard Message Format (SMF): two DOS-based messaging versions, NetWare MHS 1.5N and NetWare MHS 1.5M, and an NLM-based NetWare Global MHS. All three are fully compatible with each other.

Collectively this product line provides MHS-compatible messaging to NetWare and non-NetWare in the enterprise network, allowing the users the freedom to choose from over 150 DOS, MS Windows, Macintosh, OS/2, and UNIX operating system applications, gateways, and utilities that can use NetWare's Global Message Handling Service.

The NetWare MHS 1.5 products provide messaging services for environments that do not include NetWare 3.x/4.x, such as NetWare 2.x, NetWareLite, LAN Manager, and Artisoft's LAN-tastic. All of these services run as a dedicated Message Server.

Each NetWare Global MHS server consists of a set of NLMs that provide store-and-forward messaging services, including

E-mail, workflow automation, calendar and scheduling, and fax services for up to 1000 mailboxes. It is expected that an enterprise will contain multiple NetWare Global MHS servers that pass messages among themselves and the users. These servers often provide internetwork messaging across enterprise boundaries.

The NetWare Global MHS NLMs support NetWare's native IPX/SPX and three optional protocols NLMs that enable interoperability across the enterprise network. These protocols are:

Simple Mail Transfer Protocol (SMTP) for connecting UNIX and TCP/IP networks.

Systems Network Architecture Distribution Services (SNADS), for connecting to IBM mainframe and midrange messaging systems such as OfficeVision/400 and DISOSS.

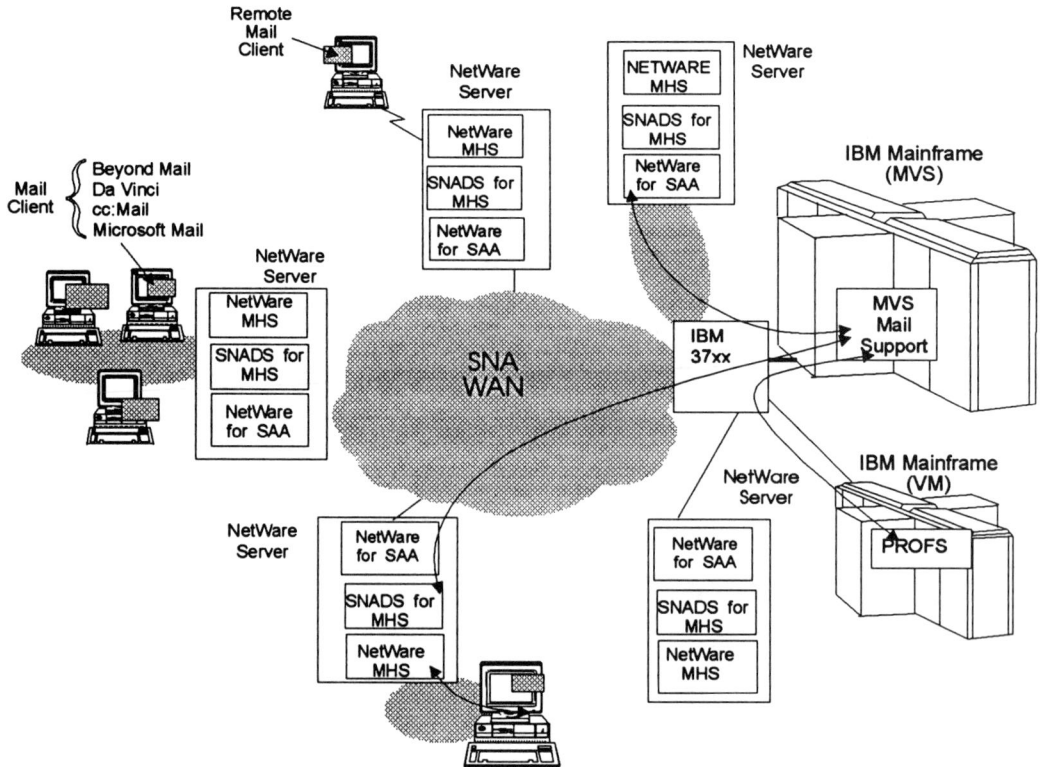

Figure 8-7   NetWare Global MHS with SNADS

X.400 for OSI mail networks using Retix X.400 for NetWare Global MHS, for connecting to public mail networks and OSI based messaging systems.

These optional protocol NLMs can be installed in one or more NetWare Global MHS servers, together with other services or as dedicated messaging servers.

NetWare Global MHS includes built-in directory support for NetWare networks, which aids the administration in addressing information. These services include automatic directory synchronization by using a directory data base that is kept current across the participating servers. Additionally, NetWare Global MHS includes some administrative tools needed to add users, configure network communications, monitor the server performance, manage disk space, and handle error reports.

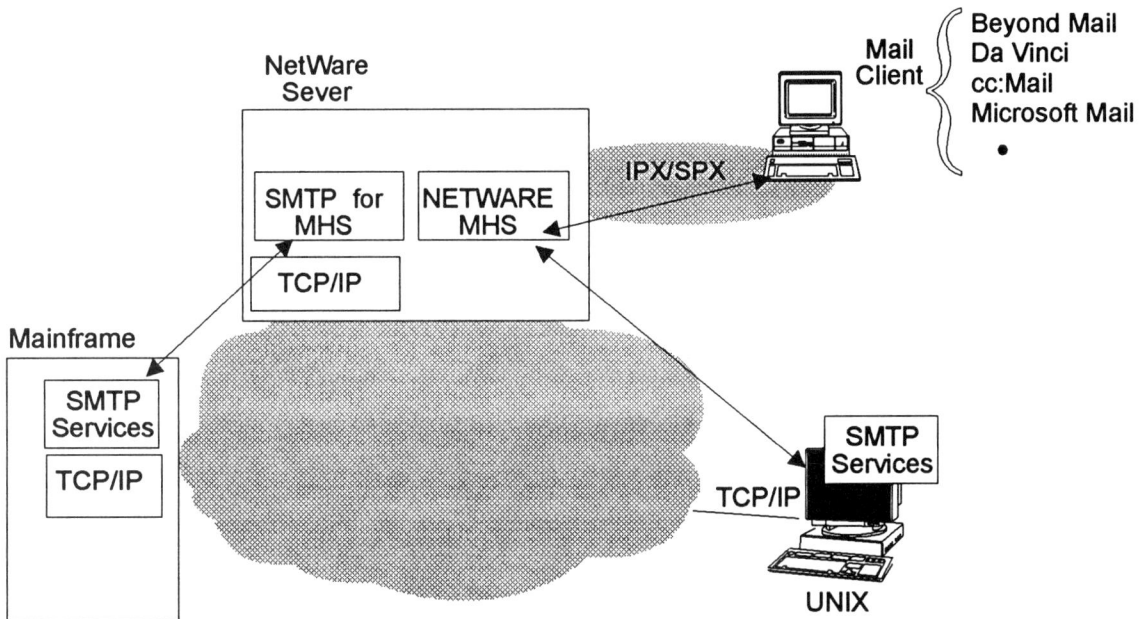

Figure 8-8   SMTP for Global MHS

8.2.2 SNADS for NetWare Global MHS

In order to exchange messages with IBM mainframe and midrange systems NetWare Global MHS provides an optional

SNADS for the NetWare Global MHS protocol module. This software enables NetWare servers to exchange messages with IBM SNADS-based office system products or products that interoperate with SNADS (see Fig. 8-7).

SNADS for NetWare Global MHS uses a single NetWare for SAA session to access the mainframe or midrange systems' IBM office system products. SNADS routing information is integrated into NetWare Global MHS. This product is both serialized and stratified to charge only for NetWare resident mail box messages. For example, a 20 user version enables 20 registered NetWare Global MHS users to exchange messages with an unlimited number of the mainframe based users.

8.2.3 SMTP for NetWare Global MHS

To exchange mail with UNIX users NetWare Global MHS provides an optional SMTP for NetWare Global MHS NLM, which enables the message exchange through TCP/IP networks, including the Internet. With SMTP for NetWare Global MHS, you can

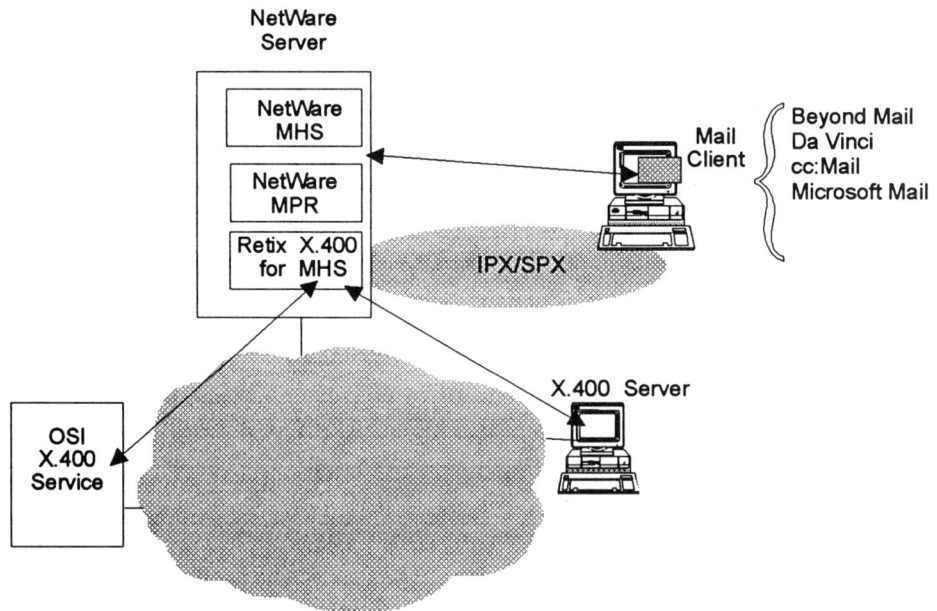

Figure 8-9   X.400 and Gobal MHS

send messages between NetWare Global MHS servers using the NetWare TCP/IP transport (see Fig. 8-8).

The NetWare Global MHS servers maintain directory continuity with the SMTP-connected UNIX system workgroups by exchanging directory information with them and distributing the information among the NetWare Global MHS servers

SNMP administration functions are integrated with NetWare Global MHS to provide a single point of management.

8.2.4 X.400 for NetWare Global MHS

Retix X.400 for NetWare Global MHS is a set of NLMs that enable NetWare users to exchange messages and files over existing open systems interconnections (OSI) and X.400 networks. This exchange can be with users of public E-mail services, host-based messaging systems that support international X.400 messaging standard messages, and remote Global MHSs.

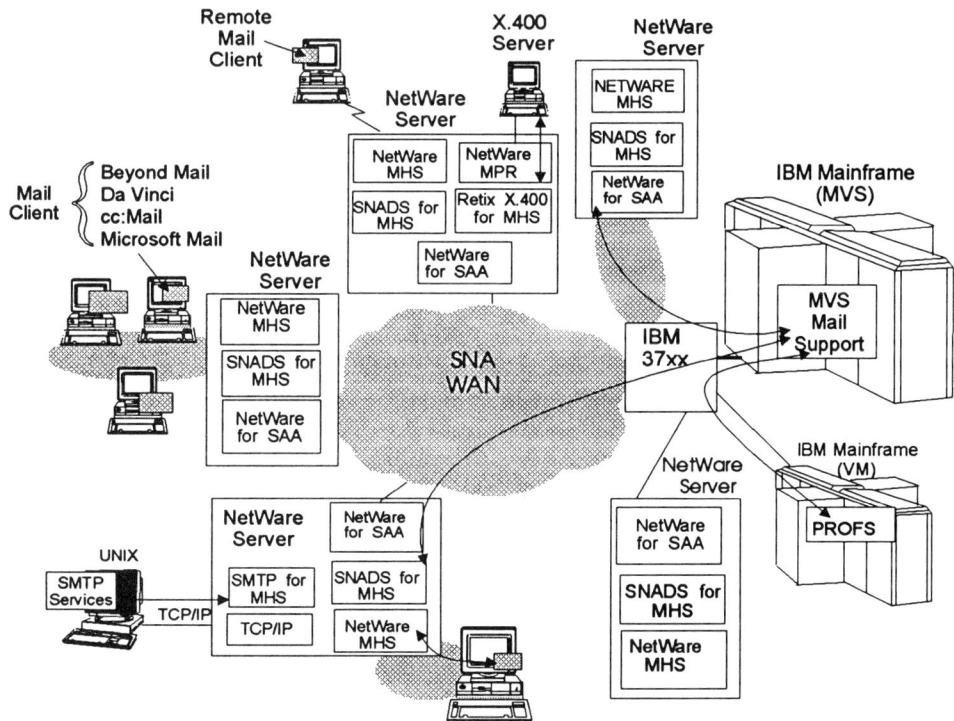

Figure 8-10 An Enterprise Network Configuration

X.400 for NetWare Global MHS has corequisites of NetWare Global MHS and NetWare Multiprotocol Router (or OSI Transport) (see Fig. 8-9).

8.2.5 An Enterprise Configuration

Figure 8-10 depicts a typical enterprise network that is exchanging E-mail using the NetWare Global MHS servers and a typical mix of workstations and servers and mainframes. This configuration could be made significantly more complex, but the concepts of attachment are consistent. The IBM PROFS or Office Vision/VM do not have a SNADS service, so the messages must first go to the MVS DISOSS-based mail support and then be routed to and from VM via a SNADS bridge using VM's RSCS and MVS's JES2 for interconnectivity.

8.3 NetWare Data-Based Tools

Because of its broad usage across the industry there are numerous data base vendors that run certain products on the server. These products can also interface with the vendor's other supported platforms. These data base products include:

- SQLServer for NetWare from Sybase
- SQLBase from Gupta Technologies
- Online for NetWare by Informix
- Ingres Server for NetWare by Ingres Limited
- Progress NLM Server by Progress Software

Novell supports distributed data applications with NetWare Btrieve, NetWare SQL, and OracleWare as facilities to enable application development.

NetWare Btrieve is the server-based version of Btrieve, Novell's industry-standard, key-indexed record manager. NetWare Btrieve is a core component of the NetWare operating system and is used by many Novell products, including NetWare for SAA, LANtern Services Manager, NetWare Management System, NetWare MultiProtocol Router Plus, and NetWare

Global MHS. It is also used by many application vendors for NetWare-based applications and services.

Worksation applications send a request to NetWare Btrieve through the Btrieve Requester on the client workstation using NetWare communication protocols. NetWare server-based applications use Btrieve on the server. NetWare Btrieve provides data base activity logging, rollback and forward apply from the last backup capabilities to provide data protection and integrity.

NetWare SQL (structured query language) is a relational data access system that enables NetWare users to simultaneously and transparently share data generated by Btrieve-based applications. It is tightly integrated with NetWare and can be managed as a component of the network using standard NetWare backup. Administrative procedures and security apply to NetWare SQL database files.

NetWare SQL can be used on a runtime version of NetWare if a dedicated database server is desired for the NetWare SQL applications. NetWare SQL provides database administrators with the capability of controlling access to data base elements. The NetWare SQL product includes a complete set of tools for data management, including the NetWare Btrieve record manager engine; NetWare SQL relational engine; client requesters for DOS, OS/2, and Windows workstations; Macintosh DAL interface; an interface to Gupta SQL Windows; DataLens Driver for accessing and updating Lotus 1-2-3 data; and Xtrieve PLUS 4.11, an interactive data-query system with a flexible report writer.

OracleWare is an enterprise system for accessing, managing, distributing, and storing business-critical information.

NetWare SQL provides direct access to Btrieve-based data from multiple desktop platforms and applications. Because NetWare SQL uses NetWare Btrieve as its underlying record manager, applications written for either product can share data. Novell also provides developer's toolkits for NetWare Btrieve and NetWare SQL.

OracleWare was developed by Novell, Inc., and Oracle Corporation to deliver an enterprise system for accessing, managing, distributing, and storing business-critical information. It combines the NetWare operating system, the ORACLE7 database, and Oracle Office into a single integrated and powerful package. The OracleWare System includes Oracle 7, Oracle Office, and Oracle Glue. It is what might be referred to as a focused packaging effort which, I differentiate from those systems that wrap around a group of disparate products that only share the wrapper and the vendor's logo. In the OracleWare System a concerted effort was made to apply tools and prepackaging to provide a NetWare-based office environment that provides the normal departmental networking services, such as file and print and, network management, and augments these with information storage and retrieval capabilities, transaction processing using OR-ACLE7 and messaging, calendaring, and scheduling services from Oracle Office.

Oracle Corporation provides tools for writing applications that are compatible with OracleWare and Novell provides Btrieve, NetWare SQL, XQL, and Xtrieve PLUS developer's kits for writing applications that take advantage of NetWare Btrieve and NetWare SQL.

Chapter 9

The NetWare Building Blocks Summary

In this section we have discussed how NetWare is structured. The most important aspect of this structure is the similarity to a hardware bus structure in a software context. The operating system is essentially a resource manager for its own environment and a router (bus) that routes messages among NetWare Loadable Modules (NLMs) and device drivers (MLIDs) Novell application and network management vendors and users can add their respective software into the NetWare Server as NLMs. Communication card vendors add their ODI-compatible drivers as MLIDs.

The NetWare operating system can be used with and without the file server and printer server functions. This is referred to as a real-time version of NetWare, and is used when the user wants to use NetWare as a dedicated server such as an application server, data base server, or communications server.

The NetWare file server provides a basis for storing user's files and sharing the files among multiple users each of whom may be in a different environment. The file server works in conjunction with a workstation resident NetWare shell, which for the DOS, Windows, and OS/2 environments. This shell can be viewed as including the file and print redirector services and the NetWare Core Protocol (NCP), Sequenced Packet Exchange (SPX) and Internetwork Packet Exchange (IPX) protocols and local-area network (LAN) drivers that are necessary to communicate with the NetWare server. No Netware shells are required in Mac and

UNIX workstations, since NetWare provides the server interfaces to existing Apple and UNIX operating systems that have the NetWare server resident for the Macintosh set of NLMs and the NetWare network file system (NFS). The services are accessed using AppleTalk and Transmission Control Protocol/Internet Protocol (TCP/IP) respectively.

Since the fundamental NetWare structure is a router, a NetWare server can easily be turned into a LAN and/or wide-area network (WAN) multiprotocol router with the various communications drivers and some control NLMs. Similarly, by adding subdrivers to support a hub card or connections to hubs, the NetWare server can become a hub manager. Combined with the routing this might be referred to as a communications management server.

NetWare communications routing and connectivity include connectivity from the various LAN technologies, such as ArcNet, Ethernet, and Token Ring, and WAN technologies, including dial leased, and switched networks that use various line speeds ranging from 1200 bps to T1; Frame Relay; and asynchronous transfer mode (ATM). AppleTalk, IPX/SPX, Digital's LAT protocols, IBM system network architecture (SNA) protocols, and TCP/IP are supported.

Novell provides complementary dial-in and dial-out capabilities under the name of NetWare Connect. These NLMs work with other vendor's remote-control application software and provide remote-node support to connect dial-in workstations as if they were locally attached. These dial-in and dial-out services can be combined with the other NetWare communications products, such as NetWare for SAA (system application architecture) (a full-function NetWare-based SNA subsystem), NetWare SNA Links (a NetWare for SAA-based LAN-to-LAN over SNA routing capability), TCP/IP WAN services, and all the local-area network protocols to provide enterprise network access from any workstation.

Novell also provides a messaging capability that provides store-and-forward services to any application that uses NetWare's standard message format (SMF). NetWare Global Message Handling Service (MHS) NLMs can be placed throughout the enterprise to provide mail boxes and to forward mail to destinations across and outside the enterprise. The MHS capability is augmented with the ability to exchange messages with mainframe and AS/400 networks using system network architecture distribution systems (SNADS) for NetWare Global MHS, with TCP/IP-based systems using a simple mail transfer protocol (SMTP) for NetWare Global MHS, and with open-system-interconnection-based (OSI) services using the Retix X.400 for NetWare Global MHS NLM. The MHS product line provides an extensive enterprise-network-wide messaging service that uses an X.500 directory approach. The key distinction is that X.500 doesn't support IPX/SPX and Novell's implementation does.

To provide network management, NetWare supplies multiple-network management tools that interface with existing infrastructure tools such as NetView and the various simple network management protocol (SNMP) implementations. Additionally, NetWare supplies its own NetWare Network Management System (NMS), which provides interfaces and services to the NetWare network manager. NMS also provides access to SNMP implementations.

To support the management of desktop software Novell has a comprehensive NetWare Navigator product line. This software provides the ability to distribute data and software to the workstation and to install it automatically. This product line supports both NetWare-and non-NetWare-connected DOS, Windows, and OS/2 workstations.

NetWare provides an excellent base for various data management products, including the major industry data base systems. These include SQLServer for NetWare from Sybase, SQLBase from Gupta Technologies, Online for NetWare by Informix, and Ingres Server for NetWare by Ingres Limited.

To augment the development of these data bases for the NetWare environment and to provide corporate developers with a solid basis Novell supplies several data-management-oriented products, including NetWare Btrieve, NetWare SQL, and OracleWare to facilitate application development.

Overall the NetWare product line provides an extensive cohesive platform that can be used to extend and integrate the desktop and its applications into the enterprise networks. Many vendors and enterprises are using these platform components and extending functions to meet their specific needs and marketplaces.

Section 4

The Elements
of the Enterprise Network

This section describes some of rudimentary elements of the enterprise network. The material is presented from a conceptual right very specific workstation and NetWare considerations. This section describes the non-IS networks and the workstation environments and then brings these into the enterprise network context with specific interoperability and enterprise network management implementations.

Chapter 10

An Enterprise Network Profile

10.1 Introduction

Although everyone believes that information technology plays an ever increasing role in a company's ability to compete and achieve the required return on investments, most of us aren't quite sure which technologies to choose.

Pieces of the puzzle:
- Workstations
- Client-server
- Network computing

We are told that *workstation, client-server,* and *network computing* technologies are at the apex of computing in the 1990s. Proponents of these technologies emphasize the benefits of using newer and less expensive hardware and software that have reduced user skill requirements. These advocates predict that a company that does not embrace these new technologies could quickly move from the competitive driver's seat to a passenger seat. The primary challenge is to integrate these technologies without incurring the costs typically associated with providing service in complex environments or being forced to make strategic decisions before being ready.

Having said this, it should be pointed out that it has become apparent that the use of these technologies can become the bridge or the moat that integrates or separates the company's information assets. Additionally, the ways to apply these technologies without significant unexpected expense, mismanaged expectations, and turmoil is often far from clear. The results depend on the integrator's grasp of the technologies and the company's approach to implementation. To add to the latter challenge, new concepts and products, including new approaches for such key applications as image, voice, and video, are being continuously promoted.

Purpose:
- Interconnectivity
- Access to applications
- Access to information

One way to increase the odds of success is to never lose sight of the goals of the company's enterprise network. The foremost of these goals is to effectively and efficiently provide users with interconnectivity and access to applications and information.

Novell's NetWare product line focuses on workstation integration, exploiting and enabling client-server technology, and network computing. NetWare can be used within the enterprise by individual departments that are totally independent of the enterprise network, or it can be fully integrated into the enterprise network as a workstation consolidation mechanism as well as a major portion of the delivery infrastructure.

NetWare:
- Consolidate workstations
- Interconnectivity
- Part of physical network

NetWare products are usually easily installed and operated by departments and workgroups to meet their immediate sharing and communications needs. Departmental NetWare networks can also be interconnected using relatively straightforward techniques. Integrating NetWare into an enterprise network can also be relatively easy or, on the other hand, very hard. The degree of ease is a function of the level of integration desired and the management approaches applied.

10.2 What does Integrate Mean?

Given the need to extend the enterprise network boundary, it is important to know that there are minimum risk paths that can be used to integrate the workstation and network technologies into the enterprise network. A few companies have found that the formula for their path is far easier and far more resilient where change is concerned than the others. We'll explore these now.

---

integrate

1. To make into a whole by bringing all parts together; unify.
2. a. To join with something else; unite.
   b. To make part of a larger unit.

American Heritage Dictionary

Integrating NetWare into the Enterprise Network

The first step in selecting your path is to make sure that the objectives are clear and understood. Terminology has gotten many companies off on the wrong foot and over committed. If the goal is to provide seamless service to the end users through their workstation, then we must *integrate* them into the enterprise network, right? Well maybe!

When the term *integrate* is used in an information technology context, the term is frequently associated with at least three different implementations:

- The ability to access enterprise network systems (e.g., connect to a mainframe). This is the meaning when gateway software and hardware vendors advertise. There are many implementations of gateway solutions.

- The ability to share an enterprise network resource (e.g., the enterprise backbone network). This is the meaning when router and communications product vendors describe their products. There are many implementations of these, but they tend to require more attention than gateway solutions.

- The ability to share enterprise network data (e.g., client-server and distributed data base applications). This is what the information systems (IS) community thinks of most frequently. There are several implementations of this, but they tend to require the most planning, coordination, and support.

The same observations apply when considering support. Does integrating mean that all the networks must conform to a single network management technology and a single standard level of service?

Given this understanding of the various implications of the term integrate what does a headline like *ABC Company Integrates 1000 Workstations into the Enterprise Network with NetWare* mean?

Let's look at some of the implementations that could fit this headline.

• Installed NetWare for SAA (system application software) into each server to support the 3270 emulation programs that reside in each of the 1000 workstations. (see Fig. 10-1.)

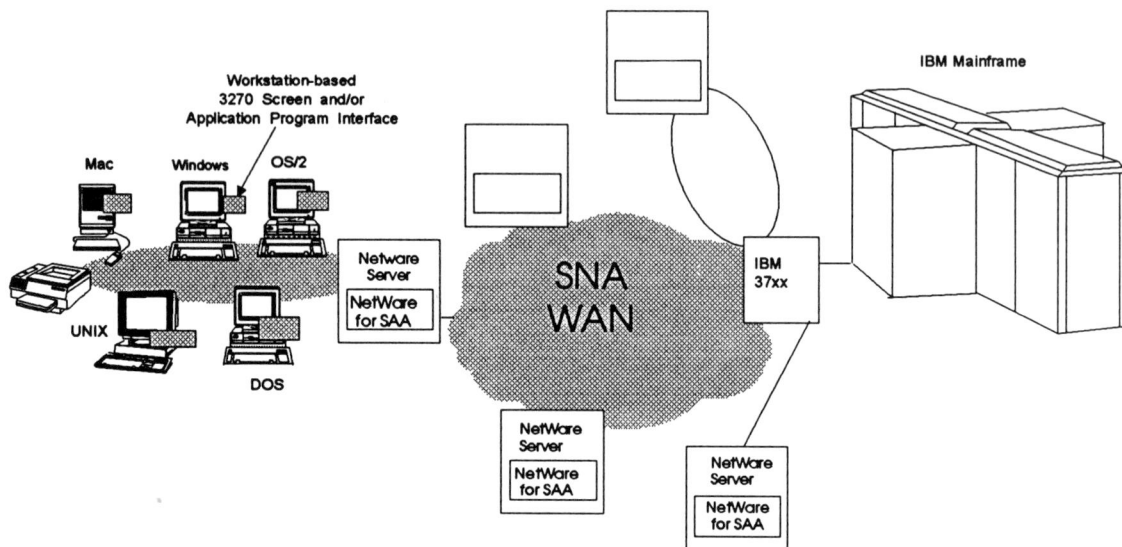

Figure 10-1   1000 Workstations Using 3270 Emulation

• Installed and channel attached two NetWare for SAA servers (we'll look at these in some detail later) to work with the 3270 emulation programs in each of the 1000 workstations. The servers are connected using NetWare's MultiProtocol Router Plus, which forms the routed backbone network. This scenario provides a NetWare backbone network for the 3270 users. (See Fig. 10-2.)

• Installed NetWare for SAA and NetWare SNA (system network architecture) Links on each enterprise wide-area-network-connected (WAN) server, allowing the local-area networks (LANs) to share the enterprise network SNA backbone. (See Fig. 10-3)

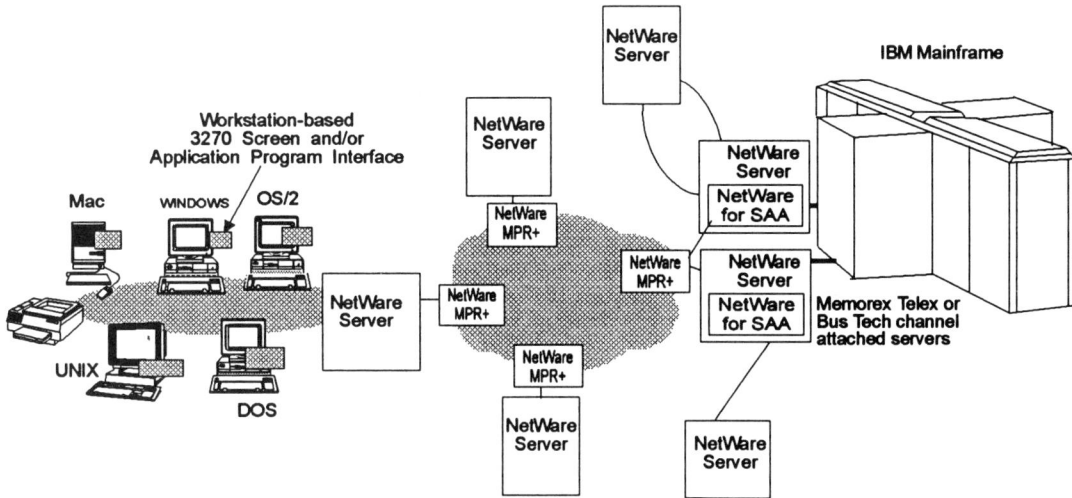

Figure 10-2   A NetWare Backbone to the Mainframe

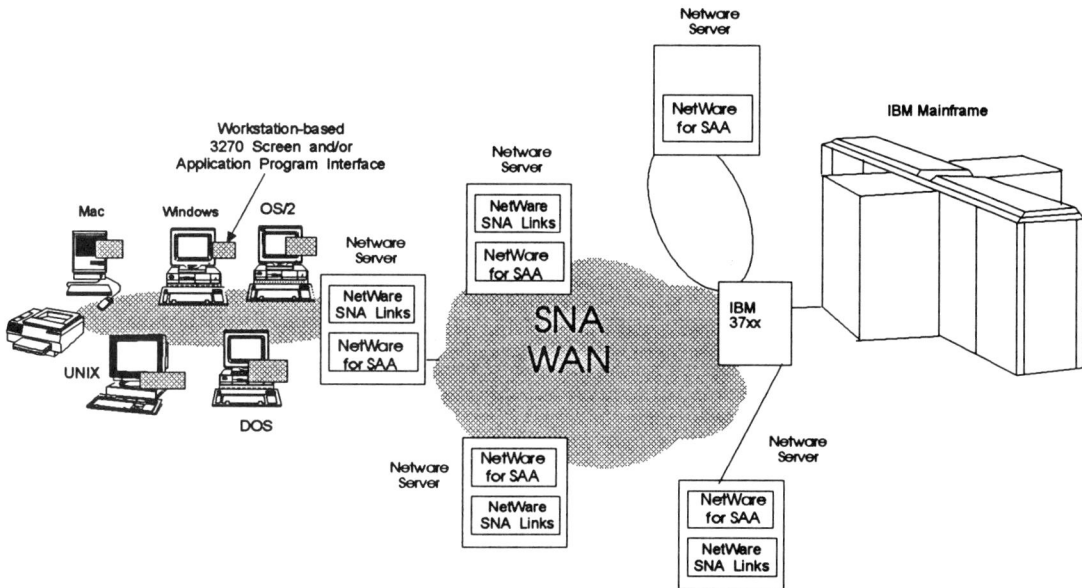

Figure 10-3   Sharing the SNA Backbone

• Installed a relational data base client on each workstation. This client in addition to the SNA emulation software in each workstation. NetWare for SAA is also in each server in order to allow communication across the SNA backbone to interface with the mainframe based data base server. (See Fig. 10-4.)

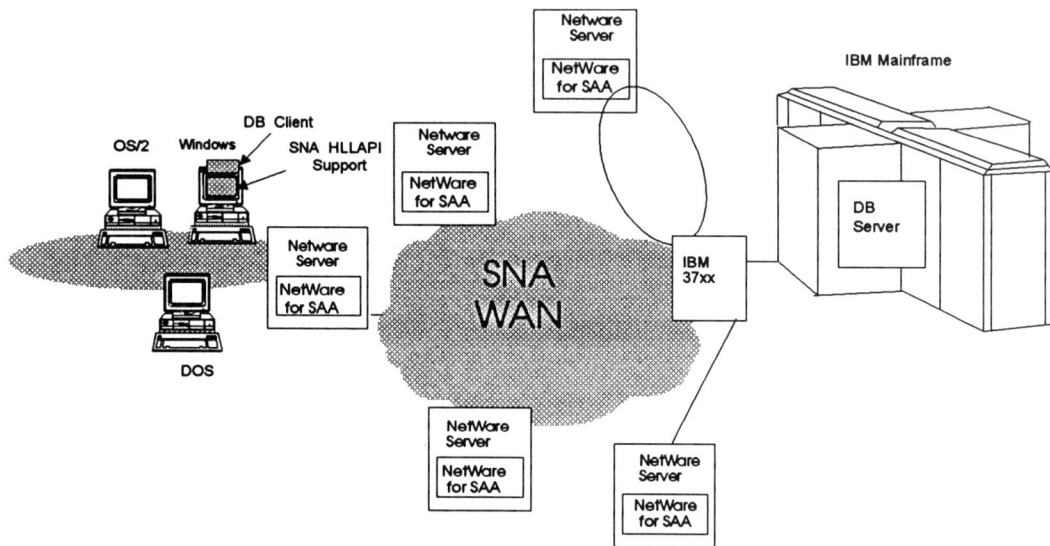

Figure 10-4   Workstation to Mainframe Data Base Access

• Provided the enterprise network organization with E-mail access to each of the workstations using NetWare's Message Handling System (MHS) as the server based message distribution system and the Global MHS components to interface with IBM mainframes, Transmission Control Protocol/Internet Protocol (TCP/IP) Simple Mail Transport Protocol (SMTP) services, and X.400 servers. The mainframe portrayed here uses the SNA Distributed Services (SNADS) for NetWare Global MHS. The IBM MVS operating system based-SNADS uses standard MVS JES to send the messages to the IBM VM operating system's RSCS which passed the data to IBM's PROFS or OfficeVision systems. (See Fig. 10-5.)

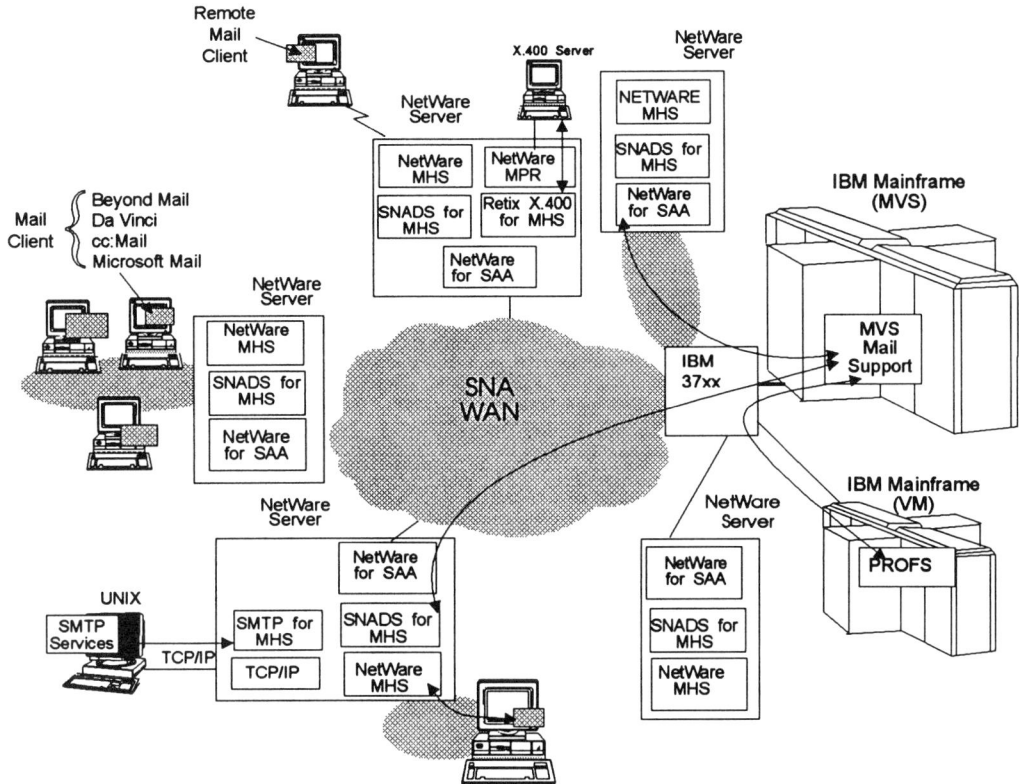

Figure 10-5   Enterprise-wide Electronic Mail Network

All of these are good examples of integration, however, without the specifics, the configuration, and more detail it is very hard to determine what level of integration was accomplished. This variation can significantly alter the complexity of the task at hand. It also significantly impacts our credibility with our management when our solution is compared with the trade press articles.

Use the easy and evolutionary definition of the word integrate whenever possible.

Now let's look at the elements of the enterprise network we may have to integrate.

10.3 Three Major Networks

Historically, most enterprise networks have included one or more mainframes and mini and midrange systems that have been installed over time to meet very specific business needs. IBM S/370- or S/390-based mainframes and AS/400-based midrange systems have a very significant presence in many of these enterprise networks. Other major enterprise network mainframe and mini systems vendors include include Digital, Unisys, and NCR. Additionally, the enterprise network is typically populated with thousands of terminals, workstations, and servers from various manufacturers using many different operating systems. While many networks and protocols abound in an enterprise, the three most dominant enterprise network technologies in the early 1990s are SNA-based, TCP/IP-based, and NetWare-based. DECnet also accounts for a large install base of DEC networks; however, it is typically limited to the existing DEC environments. The dominant networks of the 1990s are and will continue to be SNA,

Dominant networks:
- SNA
- TCP/IP
- NetWare

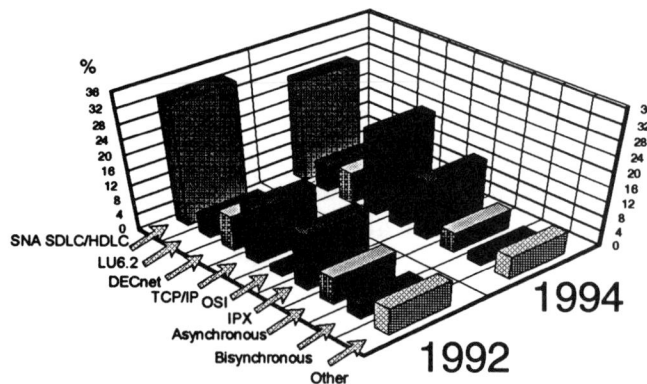

Percentage WAN Traffic by Protocol

Source: 1992 Survey of 400 Senior Network Planners
by Business Research Group, Newton, Mass.

Figure 10-6   Enterprise Network Protocols

TCP/IP, and NetWare, as shown in the 1992 survey results in Figure 10-6.

10.4 SNA Networks

The single common denominator among the mainframe and IBM mini-based (often referred to as midrange) operating environments is strong systems management. These systems were designed with control and management in mind. The ways this theme is evidenced ranges from the way reliability is managed to the way users are allowed to access resources and information. As part of this controlled and managed theme IBM introduced Systems Network Architecture (SNA) more than twenty years ago and has continued to grow and enhance it ever since. There are now more than 50,000 SNA networks.

SNA dominant with IBM mainframes

SNA provides the architectural basis for local and WAN managed connectivity that these enterprises needed to support the various user interconnection requirements. SNA also continues to evolve and become more open, as per the model in Figure 10-7 outlined by IBM in 1992. The central themes continue to be the

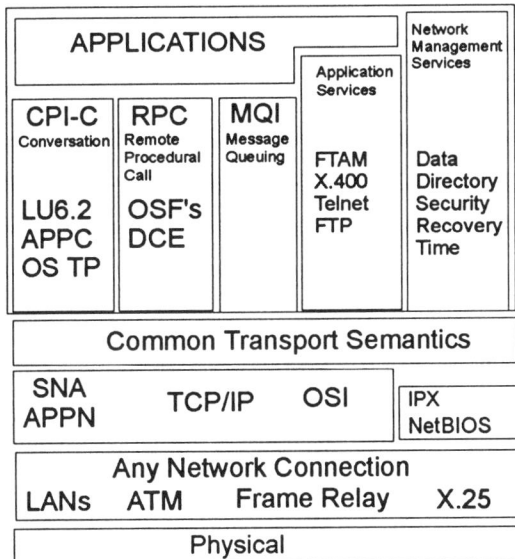

Figure 10-7   IBM's Open Systems Networking Model

protection of the customer's investments and management of the evolution as newer technologies are exploited.

One of the most frequently used SNA protocols in these SNA based networks continues to be the IBM 3270 terminal screen protocol, which conforms to IBM's SNA LU2 protocol. There are more than 20 million terminals using SNA's LU2 protocol today, additionally there are an estimated 8 million workstations that are emulating the 3270. The popularity of the this protocol for mainframe access becomes obvious when one realizes that most mainframe applications were written to the 3270 interface and that this interface can be front-ended with workstation software using various application program interfaces and screen-scraping technologies. (Screen scrapping allows the user to cut or paste to or from a screen that interfaces with the host.)

IBM 3270 protocol most dominant mainframe access

Terminal

Terminal is a generic term used to refer to the cathode-ray tube (CRT) display (also referred to as the monitor) and associated hardware that has the appropriate logic to send and receive characters or character streams between the display and a computer system .

Terminals are traditionally either totally self-contained units or they are optimized to share a control unit (also referred to as a communications controller) which manage the more sophisticated communications protocols.

Terminals for the most part are designed to work to very specific interfaces, and these device characteristics must be supported by the host system. For example, AS/400s do not support direct connections from an IBM 3270 terminal. Similarly the AS/400 5250 workstations cannot connect directly to an IBM mainframe. On the other hand, some hosts provide support for common terminals with special adapters and/or software. For example, the AS/400 can support DEC VT-100 and VT-220 ASCII Displays.

Workstations when provided with the appropriate communications software and adapter card or communications gateway connection can behave as terminals (emulate terminals). Because of technology price breaks and volume it is often possible to purchase PCs to emulate terminals for less than an actual terminal. In these cases, the primary consideration is frequently special keyboard layouts.

Workstations can be used as a terminal

Figure 10-8 depicts a classic 3270 terminal-controller-mainframe connection. The connection between the workstation and the controller (IBM 3174) in Figure 10-8 is a coax connection and the connection between the controller and the mainframe is via an IBM channel connection. This latter is referred to as a local connection.

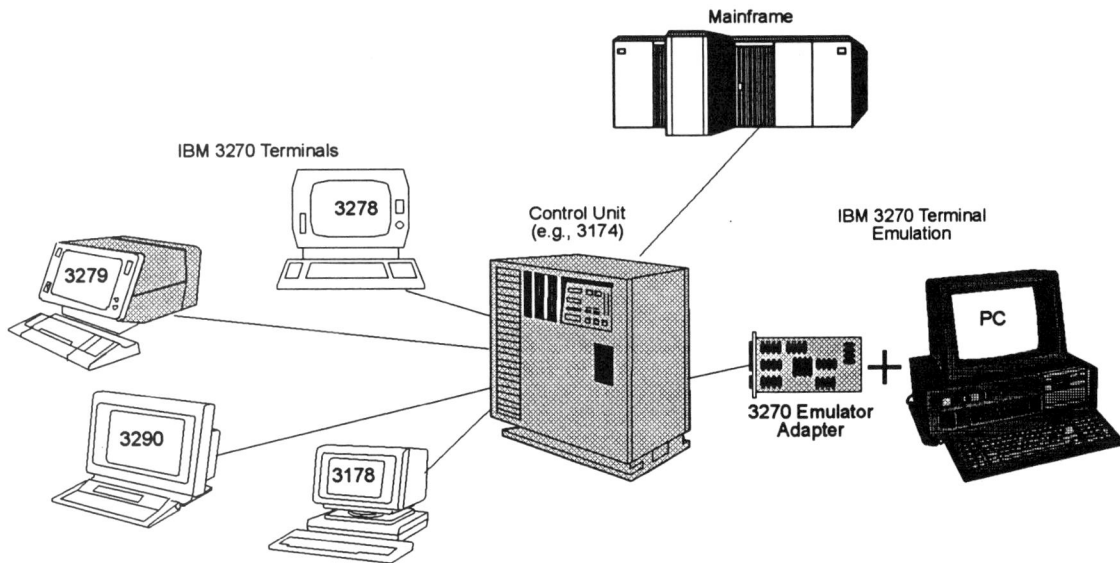

Figure 10-8   IBM 3270 Terminals and Control Unit

Another connection configuration between the communications controller and the front-end communications controller (e.g., IBM 3745) can be over telecommunications lines. This connection could be through modems over low speed analog lines to the front end (see Fig. 10-9) or through digital service unit/channel service units (DSU/CSUs) for digital connections through the front-end processor.

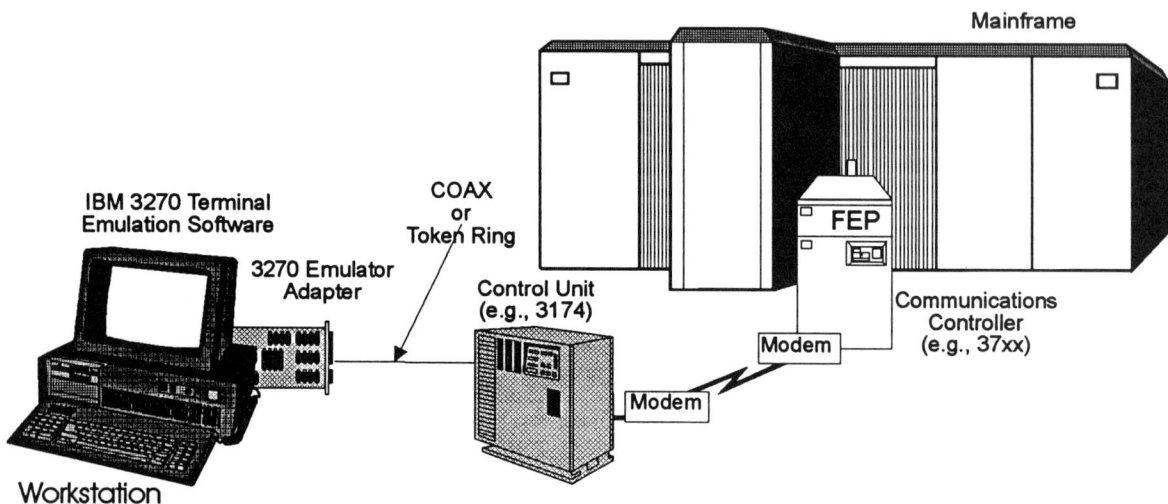

Figure 10-9 Low Speed Connection to Mainframe

For rack-mounted midrange systems the front-end communications processor and/or controller can be housed within the system. This is also typical for IBM AS/400 midrange systems and IBM rack-mounted S/390 systems.

The other systems use the terminal interface by emulator programs on their workstations or invisibly with workstation programs that use the terminal interface to communicate to mainframe applications. Enterprises with AS/400 systems installed are seeing a similar evolution with 5250 terminals.

Lots of folks are using 3270 interface

There are numerous 3270 screen emulation programs available for the various workstations. Some of these implementations include software programming interfaces that allow workstation utilities and applications to access mainframe applications.

Some of these products are hardware and software solutions that are entirely resident on the workstation, while others support splitting the emulation between the workstation and a dedicated gateway, or between the workstation and a server based communications subsystem such as NetWare for SAA (see Fig. 10-10).

Some vendors provide a 3270 application program interface

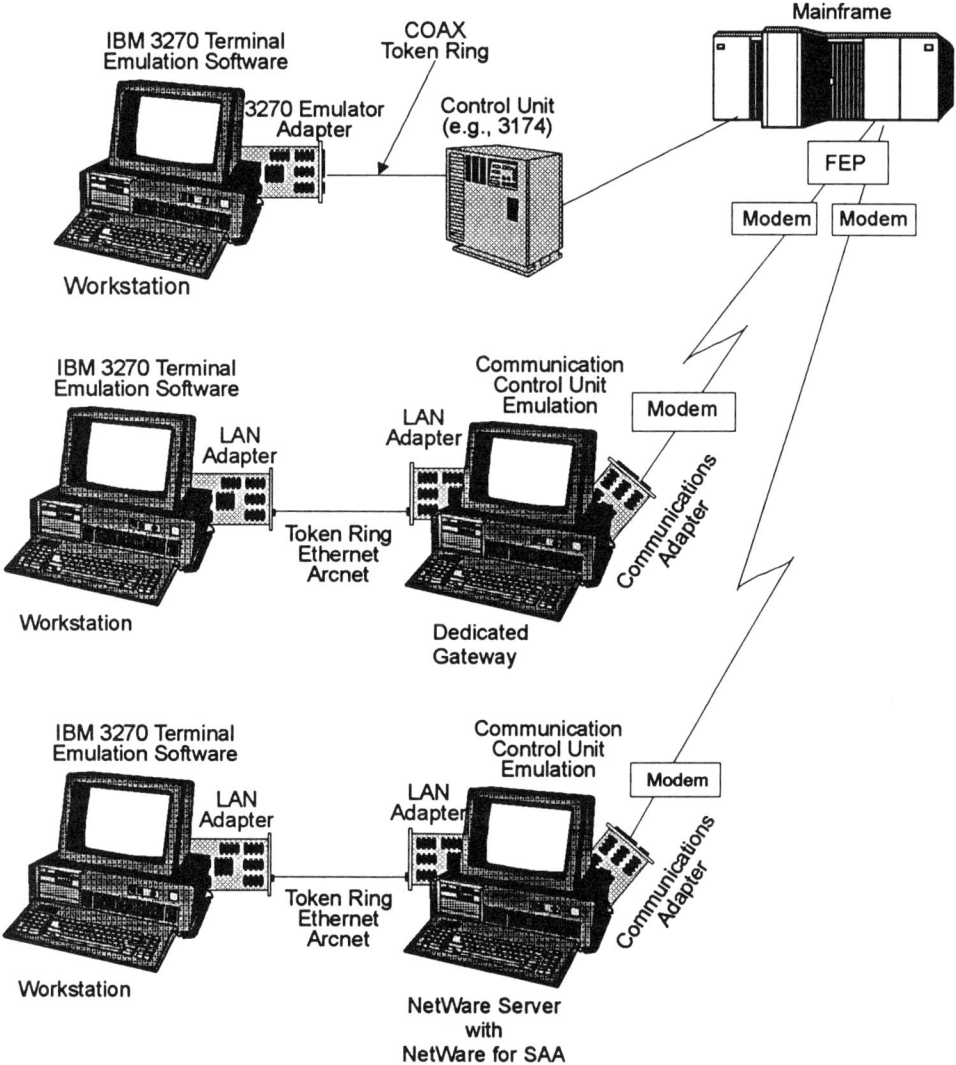

Figure 10-10   Terminal Emulation and Gateway Options

Mainframe connectivity provided:
- **On workstation**
- **In dedicated gateways**
- **As a server function**

NetWare for SAA could be labeled a gateway (controller emulator) in this context but, based on the services it provides, is more like an IBM host attachment subsystem.

Many of the newer applications and subsystems that were designed to use IBM's SNA communicate between the mainframe and the workstation or among systems using IBM's Advanced Program-to Program Communications (APPC) interface, which supports the SNA LU6.2 protocol for peer-to-peer communications across the SNA network. APPC provides highly sophisticated connectivity functionality and performance improvements over the 3270-based protocols.

IBM APPC and CPI-C used for sophisticated applications

IBM subsystems, such as CICS and DB2, make extensive use of APPC for distributed processing and client-server applications because of its peer-to-peer characteristics. The APPC interface has been enhanced with an SAA interface - the Common Programming Interface for Communication (CPI-C). CPI/C provides an SAA-compliant programming interface that lets software developers write programs that can communicate through any operating environment that supports the LU6.2 protocol. CPI-C also supports networks that use the Open Systems Interconnect Transaction Processing (OSI TP) protocol. It also includes developments from X/Open.

LU6.2/APPC/CPI-C

There is a lot of unnecessary confusion regarding LU6.2, APPC, and CPI-C. Think of LU6.2 as a sophisticated application-to- application protocol. APPC and CPI-C are programming interfaces that use the LU6.2. APPC was the programming interface that preceded the CPI-C specification and implementation. CPI-C uses APPC functions to provide the CPI-C services.

These interfaces are equally robust with systems and across local and wide-area networks.

APPC and CPI-C interfaces allow programs to communicate with peer workstations or systems. For example, an OS/2 workstation using the CPI-C interface can communicate with another OS/2 workstation on the Local-Area Network or across the SNA backbone. The same program could also communicate with an application on the mainframe. Without getting into the technical details, this peer-to-peer capability is provided by an SNA Advanced Peer-to-Peer Networking (APPN) component labeled a PU T2.1. PU2.1 allows conversations to be set up among peer systems without having to be a connection slave of the mainframe.

10.5 TCP/IP Networks

Transmission Control Protocol (TCP) and Internet Protocol (IP) were originally developed by the U.S. Department of Defense for use with the Advanced Research Projects Agency Network (ARPANet). This network has evolved into *the Internet*, a worldwide network consisting of more than thirty thousand registered institutions and more than ten million users. Although the original population consisted of mostly of government, educational, and scientific institution users, over the last several years the usage has taken on a significant commercial workload. TCP/IP and the Internet support a large variety of networks, which include satellite, radio packet, X.25, and Ethernet and Token Ring.

WANs:
- TCP/IP - partnership
- SNA - control

> **TCP/IP**
> - IP provides connectionless packet transmission across an internet
> - TCP makes sure the packets arrive or retransmits

Over the years TCP/IP, which is a public domain protocol, has become a very pervasive wide-area and local-area network internetworking base because of its relative ease of installation and design points. TCP/IP networks differ from the SNA networks in their management and control philosophy. For ease of description

I'll use the word *partnership* to describe the underlying TCP/IP network philosophy, whereas SNA networks might be characterized as *controlled*. As a result of these attributes TCP/IP is used extensively for interenterprise communications for universities, technical interest groups, and mixed workstation users around the world. TCP/IP protocols provide the necessary host-to-host transport and intermediate node protocols necessary for this type of networking. The primary controls are access authentication, bandwidth, and billing.

Novell provides extensive TCP/IP across its product lines. plus support in its:

- NetWare server as a transport protocol between the TCP/IP workstations and the server, for network routing, and as a vehicle by which UNIX workstations and systems can access the Network File System (NFS) services and share NetWare server-based files.

- LAN WorkPlace product line, which gives LAN-attached DOS, Windows, OS/2, and Macintosh workstations accessibility to both NetWare and TCP/IP network resources in a familiar way. LAN WorkPlace provides a familiar interface to TCP/IP capabilities, such as establishing terminal connections, executing programs remotely, and transferring or printing files on host computers.

- UNIX product line.

Novell has also introduced NetWare/IP which eliminates the need to run IPX as the transport protocol between the client and the NetWare server. NetWare/IP makes it possible for the client PCs to use TCP/IP as their transport to achieve all the services previously only available with IPX. NetWare/IP uses the same TCP/IP protocol stack as LAN WorkPlace.

TCP/IP capability is a rapidly increasing requirement to many NetWare users. This requirement is being driven by the increased need to interoperate with UNIX-based systems and the need to participate in the Internet for electronic mail.

TCP/IP popular in education, public sector, and interenterprise networks

TCP/IP is also integral on many VAX/VMS minicomputers and IBM mainframes, and as a result TCP/IP has become a single protocol that can be used to interoperate among a large number of heterogeneous operating system and business environments.

An increasingly popular IBM mainframe connection option is to connect workstations that have TCP/IP to the mainframe applications using 3270 emulation software supported as part of TCP/IP's TELNET service. Each workstation has a version of TN3270, which allows it to behave as if it were a 3270 connected to the mainframe. The primary commercial use of TN3270 to mainframes has traditionally been over private X.25 networks. Now with the general usage of multiprotocol routers many TCP/IP connections are through LANs that have a router backbone network (see Fig. 10-11).

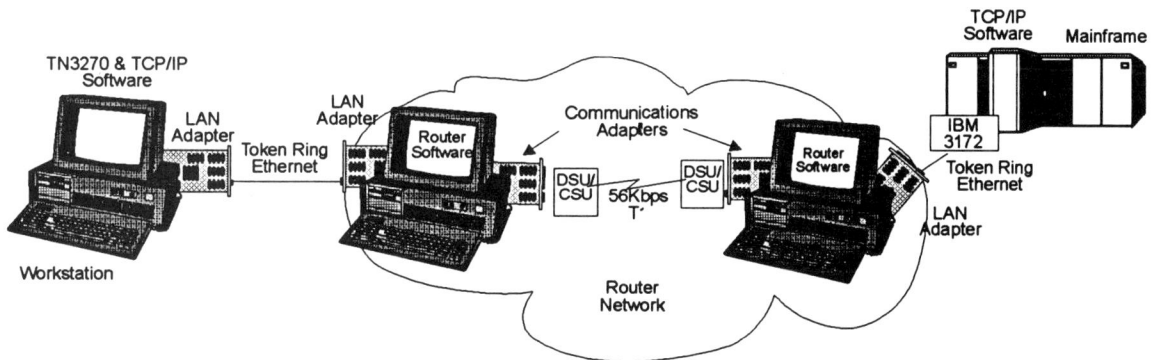

Figure 10-11   TCP/IP Mainframe Access

The primary considerations in using emulation is that care must be taken to support the keyboard mapping and that the TN3270 version supports the features the applications demand, for example, color graphic as provided by the IBM 3x79G terminal. Novell offers a TN3270 for the WorkPlace. NetWare for SAA will also include TN3270 support via a TN3270 NLM.

Additionally, IBM's new SNA model provides TCP/IP support using its new Multiprotocol Transport Network (MPTN) (see Fig. 10-12) which allows the separation of the APPC and CPI-C interface from the underlying network.

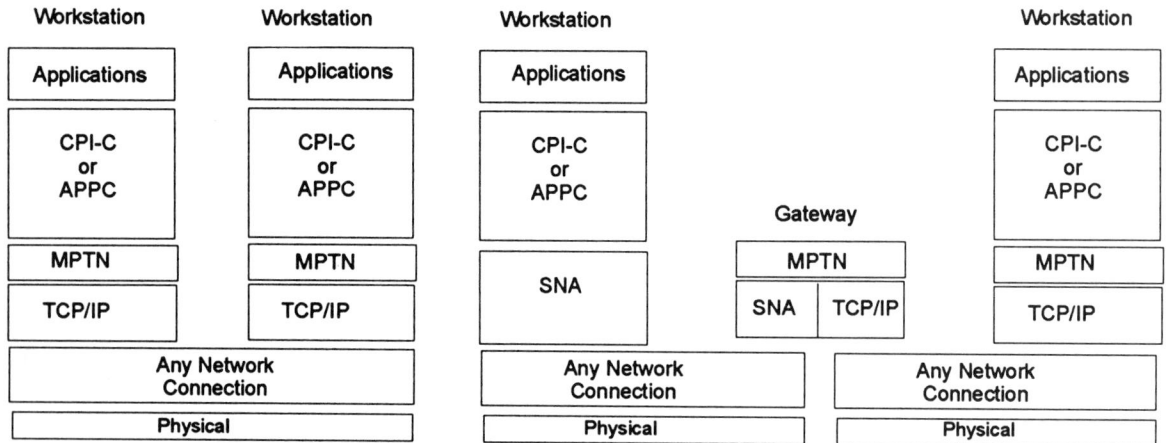

Workstation	Workstation	Workstation		Workstation
Applications	Applications	Applications		Applications
CPI-C or APPC	CPI-C or APPC	CPI-C or APPC	Gateway	CPI-C or APPC
MPTN	MPTN	SNA	MPTN	MPTN
TCP/IP	TCP/IP		SNA | TCP/IP	TCP/IP
Any Network Connection	Any Network Connection	Any Network Connection		Any Network Connection
Physical	Physical	Physical		Physical

Figure 10-12   TCP/IP and the New SNA

10.6 Local Area Networks

LAN protocols:
- **IPX/SPX**
- **Named Pipes**
- **NetBEUI**
- **NetBIOS**
- **TCP/IP**
- **APPC**

As local area networks (LANs) have evolved software vendors have introduced additional network protocols that were typically optimized to the characteristics of the connection media. For LANs the base assumption was very high bandwidth and high reliability when compared to WAN communication options. Now LAN protocols include Novell's IPX/SPX, IBM's NetBIOS, NetBEUI, and Named Pipes, as well as TCP/IP and APPC/CPI-C.

The key network and protocol challenge is interconnect networks with protocols whose design point is a single physical

LAN. Today bridges and routers extend these protocols with encapsulation techniques to extend the physical LAN to a logical conclusion and reach over intermediate networks not locally supported.

NetBIOS (Network Basic I/O System) is a protocol developed by IBM and Sytek for exchanging data between PCs. NetBIOS is used by IBM LAN Server and Artisoft's LANtastic network operating systems. (Does not support routing.)

NetBEUI is Microsoft's version of NetBIOS. (Does not support routing.)

IPX/SPX are Novell communication protocols. IPX (Internet Packet eXchange) is a connectionless service that sends packets to requested destinations. SPX (Sequenced Packet eXchange) provides a virtual circuit (connection-oriented) service.

TCP/IP (Transmission Control Protocol/Internet Protocol) is an industry standard suite of networking protocols enabling dissimilar systems to communicate with one another. TCP provides connection-oriented services. IP routes and sends packets. TCP/IP now supports the NetBIOS application programming interface.

Named Pipes provides two-way communication between unrelated processes on the same or different systems on a LAN. Supported on OS/2 LAN Manager.

Local Networks Aren't Local Anymore

While many networks are using LAN technology and LAN protocols, many of these networks extend across the wide-area network with bridges and router.

NetWare most pervasive networking operating system

10.7 NetWare Networks

As the LANs expanded, several networking operating systems also evolved to provide system services beyond communications. Novell's NetWare network operating system has become the most pervasive de facto standard within many enterprises.

For the most part NetWare networks integrate all DOS, Windows, OS/2, Mac, and UNIX workstations as well as numerous midrange and mainframe systems, including all UNIX systems, Digital's VAX/VMS, IBM's midrange and mainframe systems, and Unisys mainframes. To support these environments Novell, NetWare, and third-party vendors provide NetWare's very broad set of internetworking and networking protocols. These protocols include NetWare's native IPX/SPX, which has been extended to support Wide-Area Network needs. A typical NetWare network

---

IPX/SPX

Novell's Internetwork Packet Exchange (IPX) and Sequenced Packet Exchange (SPX) protocol is NetWare's native protocol. It was derived from the Xerox Network Systems (XNS) protocol stack, which was developed in the late 1970s at the Xerox Palo Alto Research Center (PARC).

IPX operates on the network layer and provides a packet delivery service. It supports addressing and routing between workstations and servers that support the protocol stack.

SPX operates on the transport layer, providing flow control, retransmission control, and guarantees packet delivery..

The Internet Engineering Task Force (IETF) has accepted IPXWAN as an alternative transport protocol on the Internet. The protocol stack is available and is documented under the IETF Request for Comment (RFC) 1362. This enables third-party developers to develop WAN products compatible with IPX.

supports IPX/SPX, TCP/IP, AppleTalk, SNA, Digital's LAT protocol, and OSI protocols. Additionally NetWare can be interconnected with IBM's mainframe using the IBM S/370 channel.

10.8 A Mixed Bag

The result is that enterprise network can be viewed as a big cloud (see Fig. 10-13) containing multiple networks, multiple protocols, various network management structures, such as SNA's NetView, TCP/IP's Simple Network Management Protocol (SNMP), and NetWare's NMS, and various performance and efficiency design points. But this no longer reflects the enterprise network. The enterprise network of the 1990s includes many more elements and considerations

Most enterprise network managers are still struggling to an-

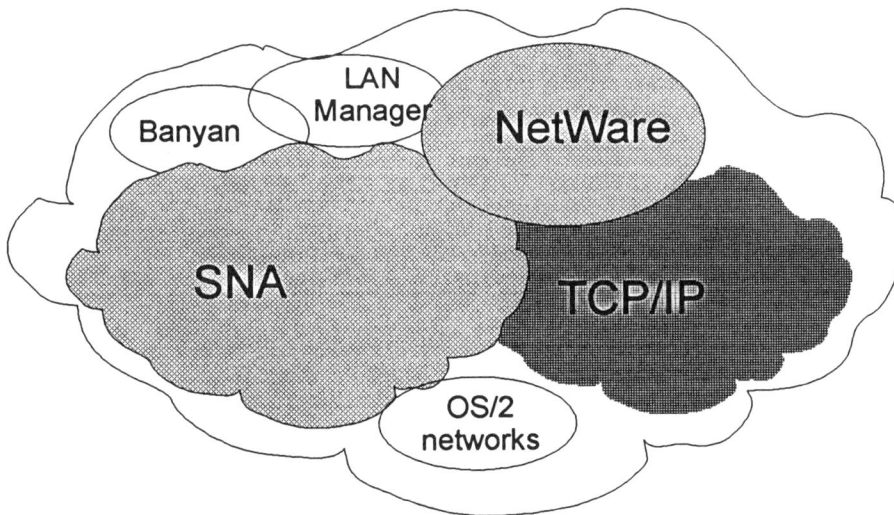

Figure 10-13   IS View of the Enterprise Network

swer the question of where the cloud ends for network support: does it end at the connection point, with the Local-Area Network, or with the end-user workstation? To the dismay of many IS executives this question has already been answered by many end

End user sees enterprise network as part of the workstation

users who expect quality end-to-end service! To these end users then enterprise network begins either in the desktop or from the desktop or laptop computer as depicted in Figure 10-14.

The end user's primary focus is on the equipment on their desk

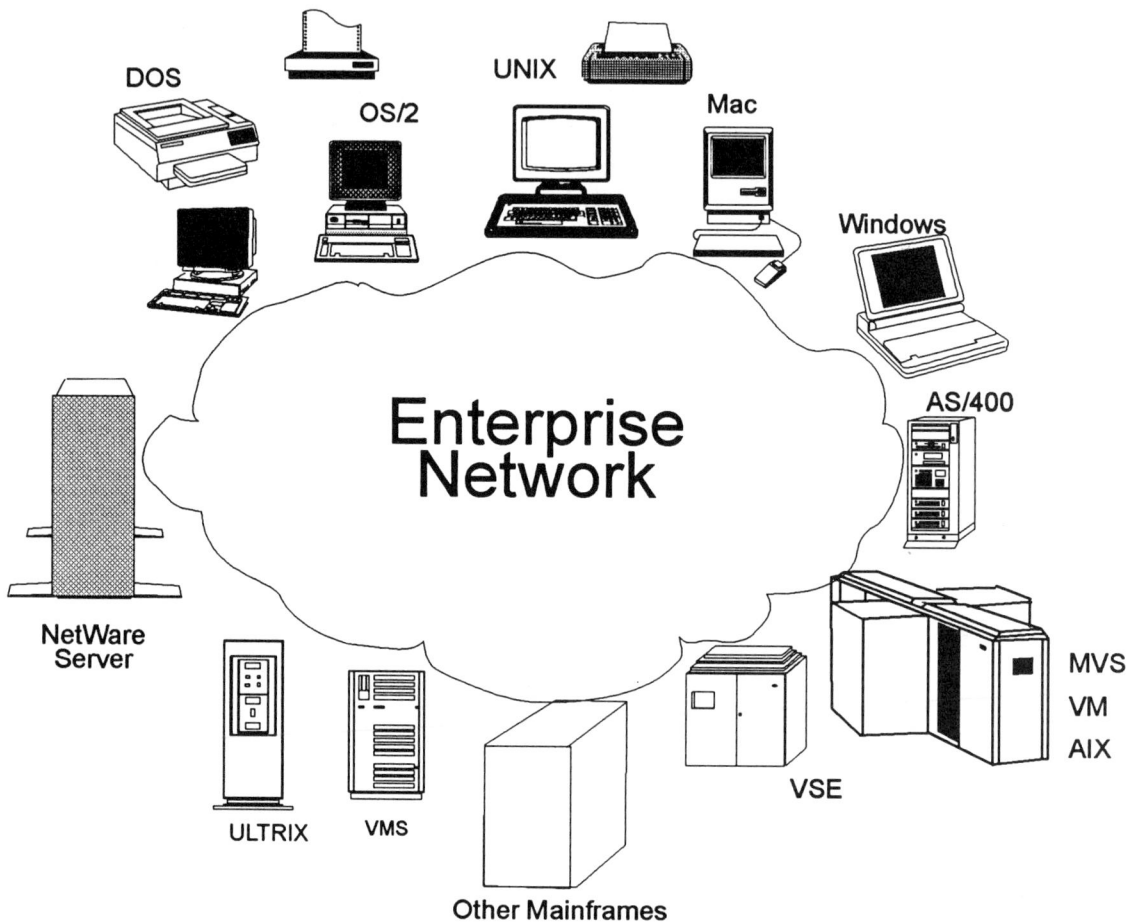

DOS

OS/2

UNIX

Mac

Windows

AS/400

Enterprise Network

NetWare Server

ULTRIX   VMS

VSE

MVS
VM
AIX

Other Mainframes

Figure 10-14   End User View of the Enterprise Network

The term enterprise network is ever-evolving for the user

and the data or computation services they need to accomplish their tasks. The end-user has no interest in the connectivity issues or topology. From an end user standpoint the enterprise network is expected to provide service between the user's terminal or workstation and the services they need. To these users the enterprise network typically provides access control, shared services, connections, and the support infrastructure associated with collecting and providing information and computational support to the enterprise's business users.

To the end user the term *enterprise network* is an ever evolving label that is continually augmented by newer and different technologies that for the most part continue to provide the same services from the end user viewpoint.

The enterprise network infrastructure challenge is to reconcile the various business and technical requirements and provide an industrial strength solution. Many of the issues facing the enterprise network organization are often more business and organizational issues than technical. The technical issues are associated with supporting a multiple protocols and a myriad of software and hardware environments. The business and organizational issues tend to center around the dollars and the staff available to support these workstation environments. The organizational issues tend to center around who decides which technology will be supported and funds purchase and support.

Integration issues:
- **Business**
- **Organizational**

> **User perspective:**
> - **The enterprise network extends from the desk to target**
> **IS perspective:**
> - **Still seeking a boundary**

If these issues are not understood from the onset, providing quality enterprise network support can become very difficult. Your understanding of these issues can directly influence the success in integrating a departmental, a networking operating system, and a network management into the existing enterprise.

The enterprise network supports the old and the new. The minimum IS responsibilities are for the WANs and host services, but these responsibilities are being extended to departmental LANs and can extend into the workstations.

As a result the LAN protocols will continue to have a growing impact on the enterprise network.

NetWare can provide some workstation, LAN and LAN to LAN, and mainframe access relief but clear business and organizational boundaries must be established to ensure customer satisfaction.

Chapter 11

LANs and Departmental WANs

11.1 Introduction

Despite the apparent nominal unit price of many of the workstation related components, the department and company must continually focus on the overall costs of the technology of the solutions in addition to the efficiency of each worker.

When scrutinized there are often significant cash flow, maintenance, training, and support expenses associated with these apparent inexpensive workstation solutions. These expenses are often hidden in relatively small purchases of personal computer peripherals, such as disk drives, communication adapters, printers, and software with multiple upgrades. There are other financial impacts that don't even show on the cash flow, only on the income statement. For example, in a service business the cost of being out of service because of a disk drive failure and no recently backed-up data can cost thousands of dollars of opportunity in an hour. (Figure 11-1 depicts some of the asset protection considerations that must be considered to support the user.)

Loss of data is probably the most common and frequent glitch for workstation users. Have you ever wondered why there are so many file backup, disk repair, data recovery, and undelete utilities? It is because there are many people who need them! The standard answer is "backup, backup, and backup!" This is important to the department since as the business units took control of the applications and the systems, they also took on the ongoing responsibilities associated with protecting the data and the business.

There are many hidden costs associated with workstation computing

Loss of data the number one problem

203

Figure 11-1 Data Backup Considerations

The LAN and a server can be an answer

The first step to backup usually entails the minimization of failure, which usually means the purchase of a reliable server hardware with large disk capacities, an uninterruptable power supply (UPS), and high-speed tape unit. The UPS systems offer battery-powered backup in case of electrical outages and spikes. Many of the data losses are associated with a power glitch and human error on the recovery.

The second step is to implement a rigorous way of moving critical data off the local disk and keeping it in a safe place. The first challenge is to assure that the backups are done on a regular basis and that you know that the data, if needed, can be restored in a reasonable amount of time. To assist this rigor process several hardware and software vendors offer automated backup systems. In fact, some of these systems run on their own processor in order to backup the server and all the workstations. Some of these systems even load their own tape cartridges.

To assist the vendors Novell has developed a NetWare Storage Management System (SMS) architecture and implementation that provides backup, recovery and archive product vendors with the necessary system services and application interfaces to support workstation and server backup and archive functions. It is intended that SMS protect the interface such that backed-up data can be restored even when the software release is changed.

SMS consists of the basic NetWare services necessary to access the required information and data on the server and the target workstations. This is accomplished with NetWare resident NLMs on the server and several target service agents (TSAs). The TSAs are NLMs and workstation executable programs that provide the data and information for their specific environments. For example, a backup and recovery product vendor might want to backup the server. Using SMS-provided Data Requester application programming interfaces, the backup software vendor's NLM would invoke the basic data and information access tasks from the server.

In Figure 11-2 a NetWare server with the SMS backup engine is backing up all the NetWare-network-connected workstations as well as the second NetWare server and the data of the server it is running on. The TSAs in each workstation allow the backup application to access the workstation data.

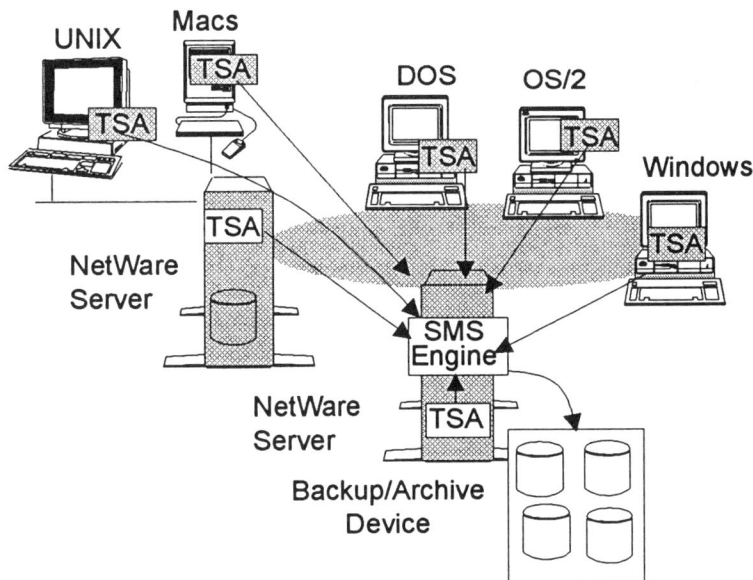

Figure 11-2   NetWare Storage Management System (SMS)

The SMS architecture provides an independent interface to all storage devices, including disk drives, tape drives, read-write optical media drives, and juke boxes. The SMS NetWare-based software supports all extended attributes and naming for Mac, UNIX, and OS/2 files.

The SMS capabilities also allow non-NetWare services to backup the NetWare server's data via the TSA. For example IBM's Data Facility Distributed Storage Manager (DFDSM) product can backup the NetWare server and any other workstation on the network as depicted in Figure 11-3.

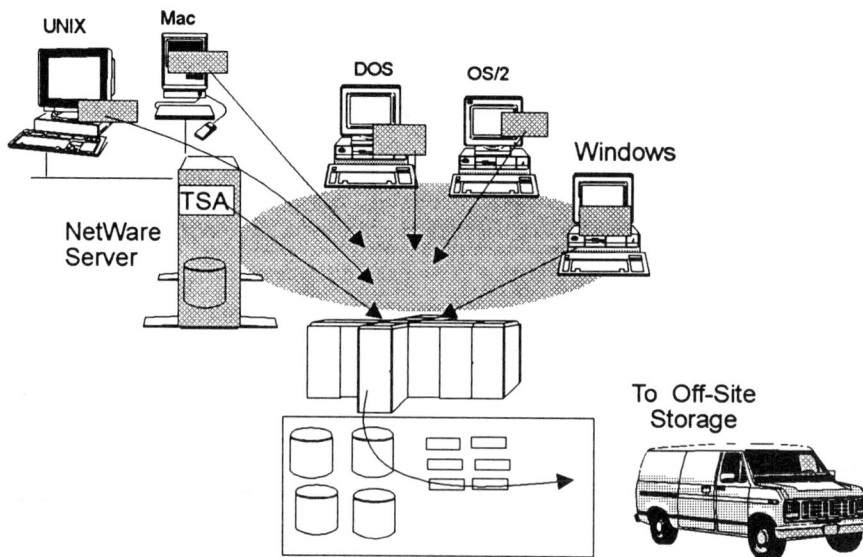

	AIX	DOS	MAC	NetWare	OS/2	Sun	Windows
MVS	TCP/IP	TCP/IP LU2	TCP/IP	TCP/IP APPC	TCP/IP APPC LU2	TCP/IP	TCP/IP
VM	TCP/IP CPI-C	TCP/IP CPI-C	TCP/IP	TCP/IP APPC CPI-C	TCP/IP APPC CPI-C	TCP/IP	TCP/IP CPI-C

Figure 11-3   IBM DFDSM

The second consideration is that of disaster recovery. Given the number of natural and other disaster s that have occurred over the last few years it should be hard to ignore disaster recovery. Recent disasters include:

- Severe winter storms
- New York's World Trade Center bombing
- Hurricane Andrew in 1992
- The Chicago flood
- New York nor'easter power outage
- Mid-west floods in 1993
- Earthquakes

Unfortunately many local area network managers still play the odds. It is really not that difficult to rebuild a LAN if the data is portable and the equipment is not unique; however, planning for a disaster should be part of the daily process of data backup and the technologies being used. Portability is key if you don't have a plan and alternate site. Figure 11-4 depicts the results of a survey reported by COMDISCO. The key message that can be gleaned from the results is that the information systems (IS) infrastructure (the data center in this case) is more rigorous in planning and testing disaster recovery plans than the LAN administrators.

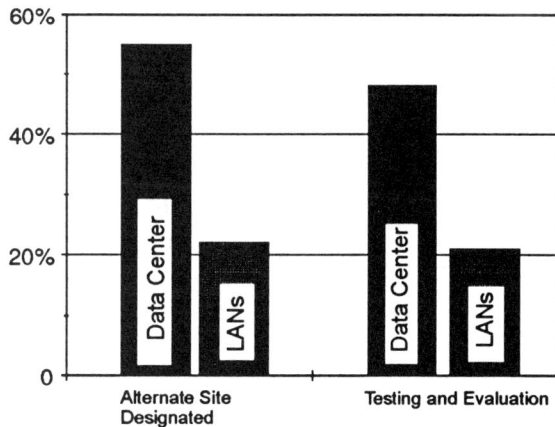

Source: COMDISCO /Information Week January 18, 1993 p 24

Figure 11-4   Who's Committed to Disaster Backup?

11.2 The Physical LAN

Let's look a the LAN a little closer. In the evolutionary sense the term LAN is the label used to collectively refer to the media, couplers, transceivers and adapter components that provide local (distance sensitive) connectivity among computer systems as shown in Figure 11-5.

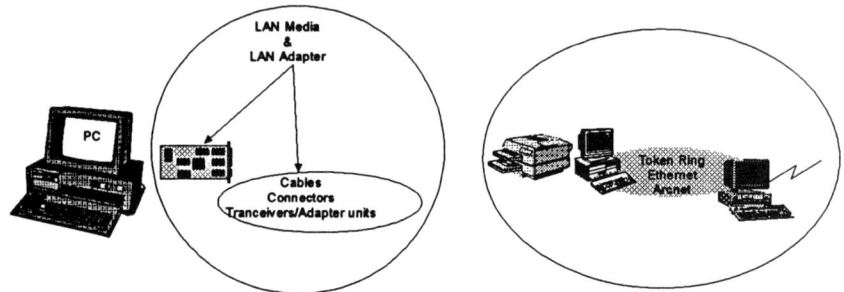

Figure 11-5   The Physical LAN

Token Ring
- **Easier to manage**
- **Provides predictable performance**
- **More expensive**

Ethernet
- **Easy to install**
- **Inexpensive**
- **Good performance with contention**
- **Hubs help contention**

The interconnection adapter type - Token Ring, Ethernet, or Arcnet - has traditionally been selected based on which organization made the purchase and whether any connectivity outside of the department was anticipated.

For example, if the IS organization provided the LANs, they are usually Token Ring since Token Ring configurations provide high reliability, high-speed and predictable performance. Another reason that Token Ring has been historically selected is because Ethernet was not supported by IBM SNA communication controllers until late 1990. Ethernet was frequently selected by departments and engineering organizations because Token Ring adapters were more expensive and some of their workstations wouldn't support Token Ring adapters. (Ethernet, in combination with one or more hubs, can show some of the positive management aspects of a Token Ring configuration, especially if only one workstation is connected to each drop from the hub.)

Once the LAN adapter card is attached to the media, special software designed to work with the LAN adapter card and card drivers allow specific LAN application software to intercommunicate using LAN protocols such as NetBIOS and IPX/SPX to communicate across the local wire. I will refer to these types of LANs as *physical LANs*. For example, typical physical LANs include Ethernet, ArcNet, Token Ring. This definition is still relevant for communications specialists and LAN hardware vendors and resellers.

Going back to the diagram on the right side of Figure 11-5, we see a physical LAN of one workstation and one microcomputer system dedicated as a gateway. This means that both systems have the same LAN adapter card, use the same LAN protocol to interconnect and communicate (e.g., NetBIOS or IPX/SPX) and that each system has resident software that uses these protocols to request and deliver data.

11.3 Peer-to-Peer LANs

Once the connectivity is in place specialized software can be placed in each workstation to allow resource sharing. For example a workstation may be provided with a file interception program that allows the specific workstation to access files on disks of other workstations and send printed output to a printer attached to another workstation. Figure 11-6 expands on the LAN in Figure 11-5 by adding a second workstation B with a printer attached to it. In this diagram workstation A and workstation B can both access the host system (e.g., a mainframe) because they each have a host presentation service software resident and this software is in communication with the dedicated gateway which communicates with the host. Additionally, in this configuration, workstation A if authorized by B can access files on B's workstation or print output to B's printer. The same could be true for B with regards to A's resources. Such implementations are referred to as peer networks, peer LANs, peer-to-peer networking or sometime just workgroup computing.

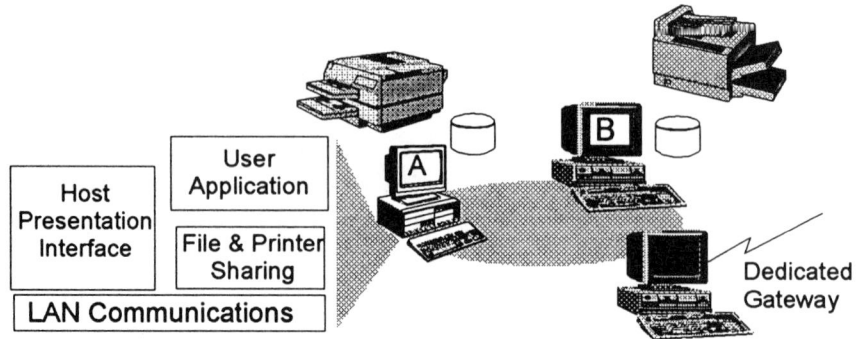

Figure 11-6   A Peer Networking Configuration

Peer networks have not been too common in the enterprise network environment. Microsoft has introduced workgroup computing among Windows users and provides a DOS interconnection. Novell provided NetWareLite, which has been superseded by Personal NetWare, a more comprehensive implementation that more easily fits into the overall NetWare structure as departmental solutions evolve. In general, workgroup computing really requires a multi-tasking operating system in the workstation in order to minimize the disruption of another user's workload impacting *peer-networked* workstation user's work. Novell DOS

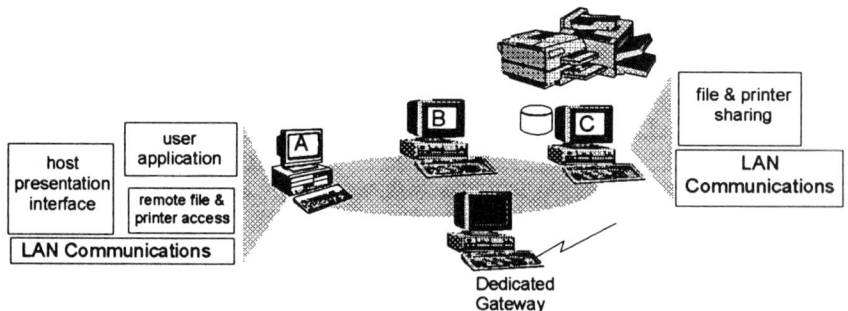

Figure 11-7   Creating a Server in a Peer Network

7, IBM's OS/2, Windows NT, and UNIX can provide the appropriate workload separation, thus leaving the next focus on the raw computing power of the workstation.

Peer networks and workgroup computing don't really help the data protection requirements, but they can be used to configure a server, as portrayed in Figure 11-7.

Once a workstation is configured to provide only sharing services, it is essentially a server. The primary concern about this implementation is that this peer network "server" should be based on an operating system that works effectively as a server and provides the necessary controls. NetWare is one such operating system. To facilitate interoperability Personal NetWare can transparently (seamlessly) connect to a NetWare server. Artisoft's LANtastic peer network is also being enhanced to connect to NetWare servers.

11.4 NetWare LAN

A typical network with a NetWare server provides file services and print services as depicted in Figure 11-8. The server in this diagram consolidates the gateway service, hosts the tape backup service, and provides file and print services. At the workstation a NetWare shell has been added that obviates the need for multiple

Figure 11-8   A Typical NetWare Server

interfaces for the various LAN-connected services. The host presentation services communicate through the shell to NetWare for SAA where they are passed on to the host. Unlike the peer network environment the files on each workstation are always private. However, NetWare print services can direct printed output to a workstation printer if this is requested.

The file services would also include the ability to mirror or duplex data. Mirroring data in the NetWare context means that two copies of the data are written and both copies are stored through the same disk controller. Duplexing data means that each copy is on media owned by different controllers. (Novell also provides a fault-tolerant server implementation that sends a second copy of the data to a second server dedicated to act as a hot backup should a failure in the primary server occur.)

11.5 A New Meaning for LAN

Over the last five years the common usage of the term LAN has grown in scope to refer to a more inclusive set of components. The general usage of LAN now frequently refers to the physical LAN and servers and workstation client software associated with communicating and providing services over the media. For the most part the de facto meaning of the term LAN is changed forever, based on the sheer number of people using it, to mean more than the connection media.

The description of a LAN on the insert on the adjacent page, taken from a trade journal, very nicely communicates how this sophisticated network operating system is presented to the departmental consumers.

The significance of this metamorphosis should not go by without recognizing the major marketing and technical breakthrough provided by the LAN software vendors that allowed them to present sophisticated network operating systems as unintimidating pieces of incidental software that slipped into the user's workstation almost transparently. For example, it is not uncommon to see the term NetWare LAN or LAN computing.

A LAN

A LAN turns a personal computer into a much more powerful multi-user machine because of added capabilities and shared resources. Information flow is improved when personal computers are connected and the PCs communicate with one another, sharing and exchanging various types of programs and data. In addition, devices connected to the LAN can also be shared. For example, disk drives, printers, and modems can be connected to the network and are then "shared" with the other computers. The key components of a LAN include the server(s),workstation(s), and shared devices. Servers provide services to each of the connected personal computers or workstations. (Understanding Local Area Networks ," by Nick Anis, *D/FW Computer Currents*, November 1992, pp. 50-52.

11.6 Bridged or Routed LAN

The term LAN has also taken on some additional attributes as the physical LANs have been extended (interconnected) with *bridges* and *routers* that extend the distance of the physical LANs both within a premise and to geographically distant locations. These are referred to as *bridged* and *routed* LANs (see Fig. 11-9).

For example, the billing department, which remote is from the sales department, would like to have ready access to the order data base located on the sales department LAN. A LAN solution is to interconnect the two department LANs with an interdepartmental network (two bridges or two routers and a line) and then access the data base as if it were local. The need to provide common access to a data base or just the physical need to interconnect workstations on the LAN beyond the physical limitations of the media have driven the need for bridged or routed LANs.

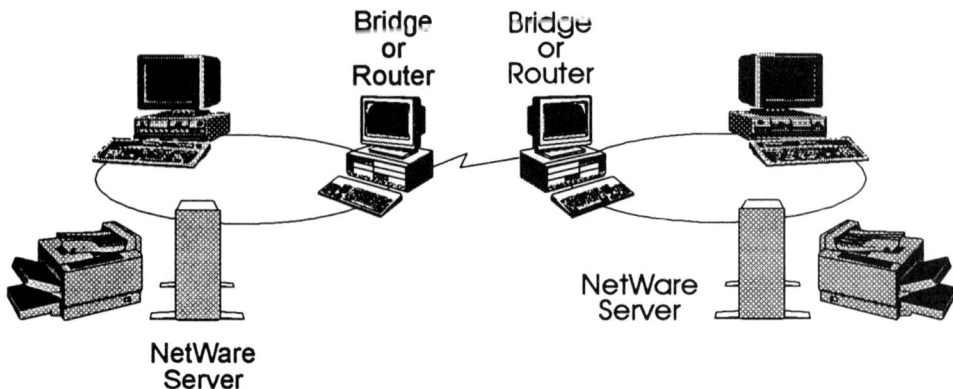

Figure 11-9   Bridged or Routed LAN

11.7 LAN Backbone

Another form of LAN, often referred to as a *backbone* LAN or *network backbone*, is created by interconnecting several physical LANs to a common LAN via routers or NetWare servers. This allows high-speed internetwork communications without any of the local traffic congestion.

Figure 11-10 depicts two NetWare servers that interconnect over a local physical LAN to create a physical backbone LAN. This configuration requires that each NetWare server is connected to both LANs and therefore must house 2 LAN adapter cards, also referred to as network interface cards (NICs). This configuration allows the workstations on either local LAN to exchange information without needing two adapter cards. The NetWare server provides the bridging function. You should also note that the printers are attached to the LAN rather than to the server or a workstation. This is possible if the printer is "network ready," which means that it has the LAN adapter built into the printer.

11.8 Wide Area Network

The term WAN refers to a wide area network, or more definitively, a network comprised of phones lines, microwave links, and satellite links. The wide in wide area network comes from the expectation that the connection is with some distant location,

2-LAN
Adapter Cards

Backbone

NetWare
Server

NetWare
Server

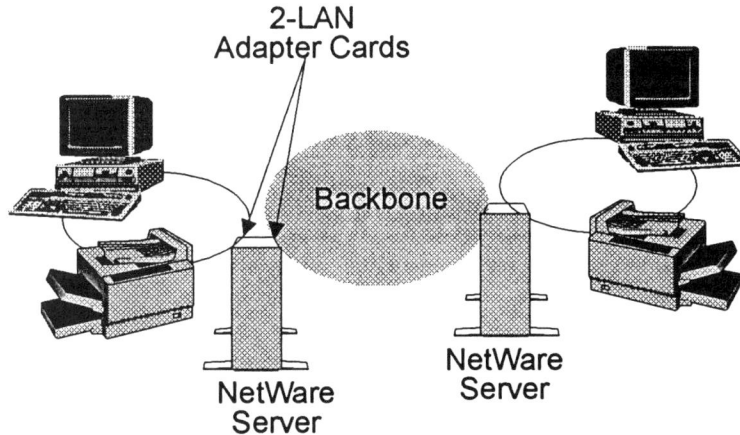

Figure 11-10   A LAN Backbone

but a phone line connection between adjacent buildings can also be referred to as a WAN connection because of the medium being used. WANs are fundamental to an enterprise network, since enterprise network implies multiple locations.

WANs are more expensive than physical LANs, they offer less bandwidth, and are frequently less reliable than physical LANs. The protocols for WANs tend to be more sophisticated (have more overhead) since retransmissions are much more costly in terms of elapsed time than retransmissions over a LAN. Because of the significant throughput and response time differences, WANs also introduce a significant challenge for IS managers who are trying to service LAN end-user expectation. To the typical LAN user *"a wide area network, more commonly known as a WAN, is a LAN which is more advanced. A WAN is a LAN that can be accessed over great distances from multiple locations."*

Many enterprises connect their NetWare LANs to their host using 9.6 Kbps phone lines. Others use 56 Kbps or 64 Kbps digital circuits, while those whose business applications demand it have installed T1 (1.544 Mbps) or E1 (2 Mbps) connections. Contrast these to 10 Mbps Ethernet or 16 Mbps Token Ring LAN connections. To reduce the cost of the higher bandwidth circuits many enterprises in Europe are using Integrated Service Digital Networks (ISDN) networks while U.S. enterprises are looking to Frame Relay and Asynchronous Transmission Mode (ATM) technologies. Other approaches include inverse multiplexer approaches that dialup additional bandwidths as the workload increases and give up lines as the workload subsides.

The future holds 100 Mbps to 155 Mbps LANs and DS3/E3 (45/34 Mbps) and SONET/SDH (155 Mbps) wide-area bandwidths for those who can afford them or are able to take advantage of them. While high bandwidths are becoming available for WANs, they are coming slowly and with newer technologies such as Frame Relay and ATM solutions in order to approach the price points many companies can afford for remote offices. The bottom line is that there is a big gap in the bandwidth taken for granted on the LAN and the bandwidth affordable for wide-area connection.

The biggest single challenge for an enterprise network provider when introducing the LAN user to WAN performance is managing the user's expectations. It is very hard to visualize the differences in orders of magnitude that the different media can provide until you see the number of zeros as I show in the following table:

media	char/s	bits/s
2400 baud dial-up line	300	2,400
9.6 Kbps	1200	9,600
56 Kbps leased or switched line	7,000	56,000
10 Mbps Ethernet	1,250,000	10,000,000
16 Mbps Token Ring	2,000,000	16,000,000
100 Mbps Switched Ethernet	19,375,00	100,000,000

This comparison doesn't even take into consideration the additional overheads current WAN protocols must incur in order to provide quality point-to-point delivery.

The most significant consideration to users of LANs when using WANs to interconnect is that the networking operating system provides additional communication protocol support for dealing with slower network pipes. For example, NetWare has implemented Packet Burst software that allows the sending of multiple packets before waiting and large packets that increase the payload per transmission.

Other WAN considerations include the effective throughput of the connections. WAN throughput enhancements usually include full-duplex communications and some form of compression. Compression can have a positive or negative effect on the network throughput because it takes time to compress the data. It makes more sense to use hardware compression than software compression. But even hardware compression can reduce the throughput above certain data rates. For example, a benchmark described in *LAN Times* (June 14, 1993) in an article describing Newport Systems' LAN²LAN Multiple Protocol Router (Newport Systems is a leading state-of-the-art NetWare router provider) shows that throughput was actually reduced at data rates exceeding 128 Kbps because the hardware couldn't compress the data and drive the line at maximum capacity. This means that while bandwidth will help performance, additional system considerations will be required in order to meet the demand.

11.9 Router Backbone

Despite the potential performance impacts many departmental LANs and enterprise networks are interconnecting their LAN networks out of sheer necessity. The departments are using 56 Kbps and T1 services with point-to-point routers, while many enterprise networks are using meshed router configurations to provide the perception of an enterprise-wide LAN. Figure 11-11 depicts a WAN network backbone comprised of routers that are connected to the NetWare servers via Ethernet connections. The physical LANs are Ethernet on the left and Token Ring on the right.

It is interesting to note that, in terms of throughput and sometimes even in terms of response time, the router solutions often out perform the traditional WAN connections using traditional end-to-end WAN protocols with the same bandwidth . This unexpected performance change is the result of a change in the underlying connection assumptions and the difference in the

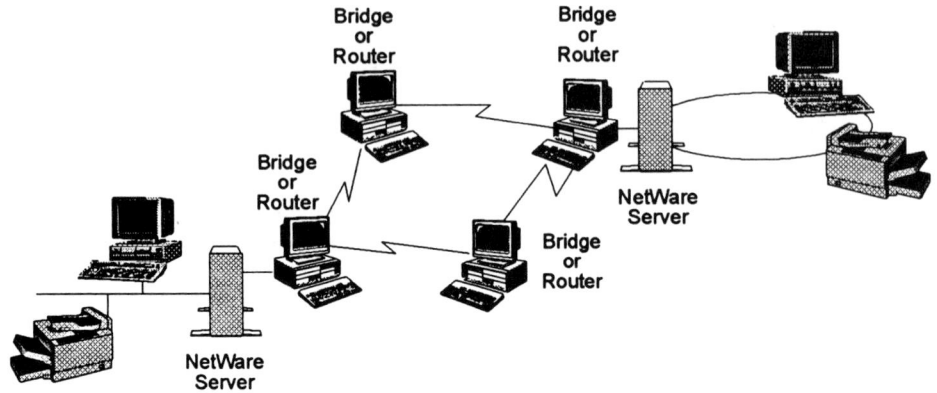

Figure 11-11   A Bridge or Router Backbone

LAN client-server protocols. Consider the following assumptions and note the consequences.

The underlying assumption for a traditional WAN connection are:

- The lines are unreliable lines and the network must protect against data loss with error checking
- There is little bandwidth and it must be managed
- The network is responsible for retransmissions
- The network must provide response time and throughput management

The consequence of these assumptions are connection-oriented protocols, error checking and correction codes in the data, packet tracking overheads and the reduction in response time and utilized bandwidth that are associated with these assumptions.

The assumptions for a LAN are that

- There is a lot of bandwidth

- Retransmissions don't take long
- The sender is responsible for checking data arrival
- All data can be treated alike.

The consequences of these assumptions are low overhead protocols at the network level, providing higher throughput and potentially better response time (albeit it is typically unpredictable). As long as the assumptions of the reliable network hold, the LAN protocols can potentially out perform the traditional WAN protocols. This is why many companies are using Token Ring connections to routers for their backbone network. The primary challenge is the current inability to manage response time, which can really only be accomplished with a connection-oriented protocol. I expect that we will see LAN protocol enhancements to provide connection oriented attributes over time. For example, IPXWAN already focuses on more quickly identifying a failure across the network.

Independent of these developments additional programming and application considerations come into play to over come some of the bandwidth limitations. Let's look at some of the other considerations.

11.10 Two Remote Server Data Base Scenarios

11.10.1 Centralizing a Local Data Base

The first scenario is characterized by a user who is used to accessing a data base file on a local server. The response to the end-user request is as if the data were on the disk on the user's workstation. A decision is made to move the database to a central location such that all remote locations can access the data directly with no intermediate node connections. (This is typically referred to as a star topology.) Figure 11-12 depicts the before and after data flows. Note that there are two possible network configurations to access the central server (Configuration R1 and Configuration R2); however, the more important differences are the data rate change and the number of messages that must cross the network to accomplish the same work that had been done before. The resulting response time was totally unacceptable to the end

Remote Server Database
Access Scenario

Remote
File
Server

Request First Sector
First Sector
Request Second Sector
Second Sector
Request Third Sector
Third Sector

Transfer Time
dependent on
9.6K-1.5Mbits/sec
connection

Application
on Local
Workstation

Response time
measured in
seconds

Remote Configuration (R1)

Remote
File
Server

Request First Sector
First Sector
Request Second Sector
Second Sector
Request Third Sector
Third Sector

Transfer Time
Dependent on
9.6K-1.5Mbits/sec
Connection

Application
on Local
Workstation

Response time
measured in
seconds

Remote Configuration (R2)

Local Server Database
Access Scenario

Local
File
Server

Request First Sector
First Sector
Request Second Sector
Second Sector
Request Third Sector
Third Sector

Transfer Time
Dependent on
10-16Mbit/sec
Connection

Application
on Local
Workstation

Response Time
Measured in
Milliseconds

Local
Configuration

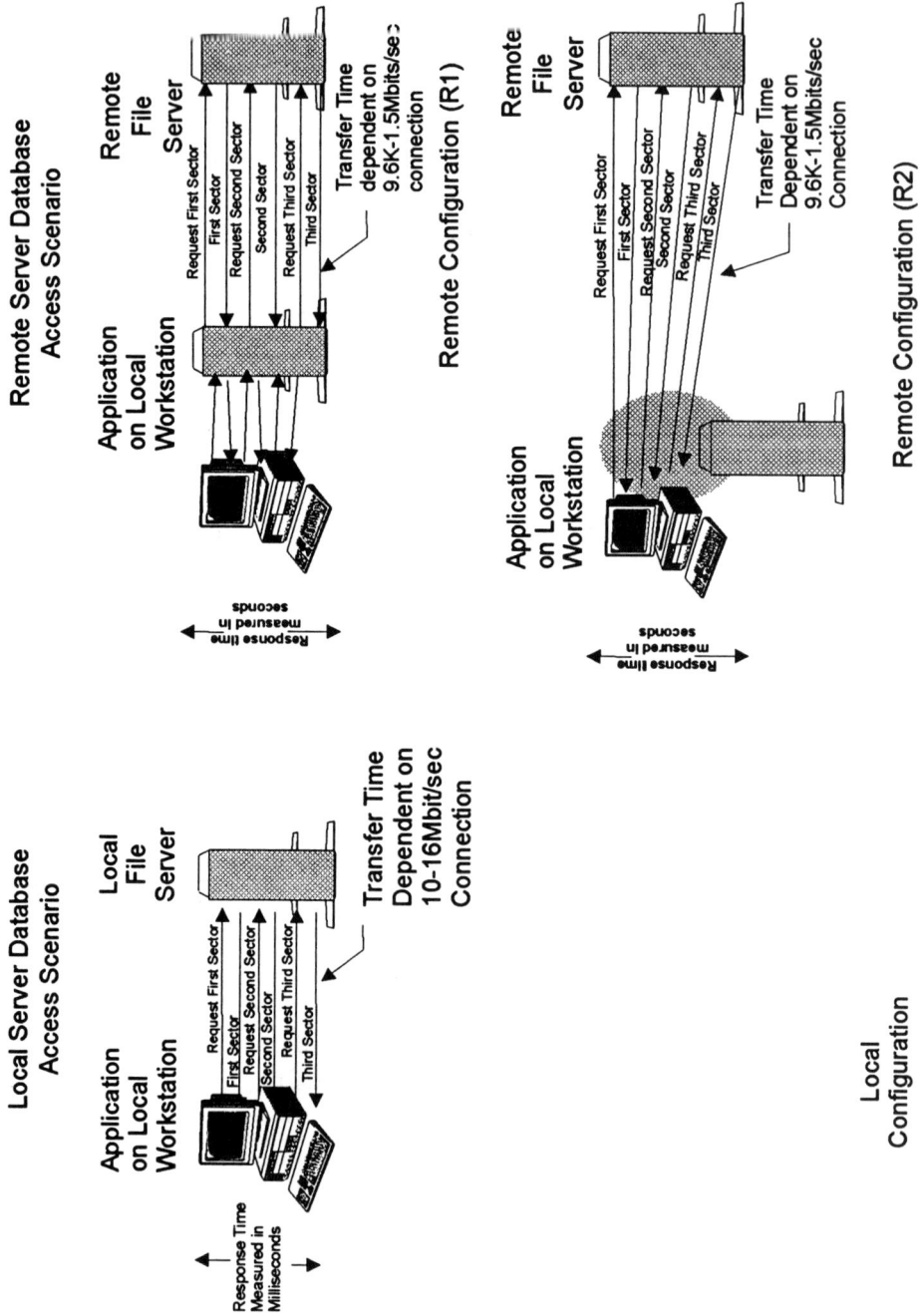

Figure 11-12   Remote Data Base Access

220

user, who resorted to a direct dial-in alternative even though it was more expensive.

11.10.2 Downsizing to a Centralized Server

The second scenario is characterized by an end user who has recently been moved off the company's mainframe as part of a downsizing effort. Prior to the downsizing the user accessed all the centralized applications through a 3270 screen emulation interface. The application ran entirely on the centralized host system. The application access was over a 9.6 Kbps connection and the user was seeing 1- to 2-second response times for the typical transaction.

The downsizing team had replaced the centrally located mainframe with a server and installed a workstation-oriented database since it was less expensive than a client-server data base. It was rationalized that this was adequate since the users only accessed the data in read mode. The idea was to use the existing 9.6 Kbps star network. The demos were all done at the central location over the existing Token Ring connection. The response time was super, applications that had delivered sub-second response time now delivered response times measured in the milliseconds . The test team even came in on the weekend to really *hammer* at the workstations to make sure that the application didn't deteriorate under load. It didn't, the success story was all but written.

The following Monday the application was cut-over to the new environment, and the problems began. The remote users saw response times measured in multiple seconds and sometimes minutes and for some users their gateway software hung because of time-outs. It was quickly determined that too much network traffic was the problem. The downsizing team initiated the fallback while they looked to resolve the problem. So far they only had a few hours worth of black eyes.

When it was determined that the lines were the problem, a quick fix was proposed — upgrade all the lines to 56 Kbps. Upon some investigation it was determined that this decision could easily cost $20,000 per month in phone line bills, which would be hard to sell to management. But all in all it was still cheaper than the ongoing software and hardware maintenance bill for the mainframe. One member of the downsizing team remembered that one 56 Kbps line was already installed, so they ran a benchmark. It helped, but response time was very sporadic even over this faster line. The next step was to determine why the WAN traffic varied. The analysis showed the same result as the remote server scenario just discussed.

The only solution was to regroup, select a client-server oriented data base product, and reprogram the applications for the new data base interface. The client-server-oriented data base optimizes the request for data such that minimal network traffic is required. This effort was completed within five months, after which the end-user response time was comparable to the mainframe solution. The IS team is now able to more quickly respond to application changes and 56 Kbps lines are on order.

The common elements for both of these scenarios are the desire to reduce cost while providing data access to all remote locations.

11.11 Some Remote Access Alternatives

Workstation to remote LAN environments usually require high-speed connections, data compression, or programming changes. However, there are some less expensive alternatives based on dialup technology that might meet the need. For the most part the bandwidth for these dial-up connections is 9.6 Kbps and under. Sometimes the effective data rate is increased with compression provided by the modem. The effective throughput is really a function of the protocols used between the client and the server. The effective response time is most significantly a function of which end of the line services are provided.

Two dial-up alternatives are depicted in Figure 11-13. The top example, the remote program scenario, is very similar to the previous scenarios, with the sole exception that this is a simple dialup to a dial-in server running software like NetWare Connect. Using a direct dialup to a dial-in server on the LAN with the data base server can significantly reduce the delays by providing a dedicated line to each user. For this configuration the workstation requires a modem connected to its communications port or to the local server and some dial-up client software. Since the user

Remote Program Scenario

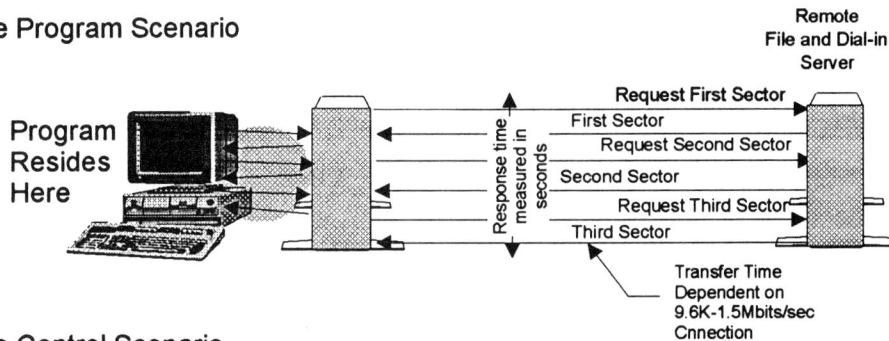

Remote
File and Dial-in
Server

Program
Resides
Here

Response time
measured in
seconds

Request First Sector
First Sector
Request Second Sector
Second Sector
Request Third Sector
Third Sector

Transfer Time
Dependent on
9.6K-1.5Mbits/sec
Cnnection

Remote Control Scenario

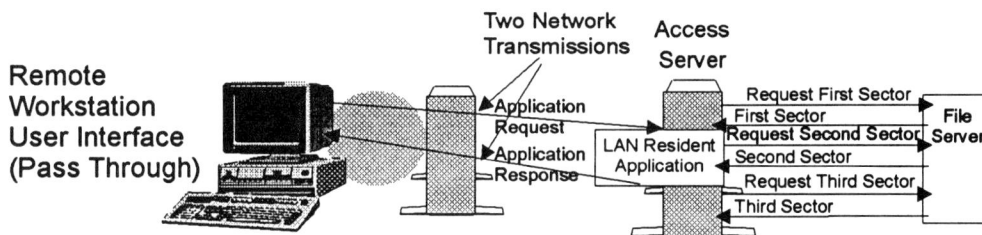

Two Network
Transmissions

Access
Server

Remote
Workstation
User Interface
(Pass Through)

Application
Request
Application
Response

LAN Resident
Application

Request First Sector
First Sector
Request Second Sector
Second Sector
Request Third Sector
Third Sector

File
Server

Figure 11-12   Remote Data Access Alternatives

initiates the dial-up, the only contention consideration is the port availability on the remote server LAN.

This approach only makes sense if access to the remote server is infrequent. Additionally, it does nothing to reduce the number of network transmissions required to access the data.

A more viable dial-up scenario is the remote-control scenario. The remote control scenario has a remarkable similarity to the traditional mainframe-based application scenario. The remote-control scenario makes the user's workstation a terminal and the application executes on an access server that is local to the data base server.

There are several common, commercially available products that support the remote control. Among the solutions are single-user solutions, such as: Timbuktu (Farallon Computing), Proxy (Funk Software), Carbon Copy (Microcom Systems, Inc.), pcANYWHERE (Symantec Corporation), and Co/Session (Triton Technologies).

These solutions require a workstation dedicated for the duration of the call on the LAN with the local server. Other software solutions include server-based approaches that allow multiple users to dial-in and access the local server, these include A+ for NetWare (Citrix), Novell-provided NetWare Access Services, UnixWare, and most recently NetWare Connect. There are also hardware solutions that use multiple processors to accommodate multiple users; these include LAN Central Station (Cubix), Flex-Com (Evergreen), Communique (IWI), and Chatterbox NRS (J&L Information Systems).

11.12 Summary

To try to distinguish between the physical LAN and the more inclusive meanings, the term *network* and *network computing* have been introduced by various users, vendors, and analysts. Unfortunately, these terms have also have other well established meanings in related areas, such as existing enterprise networks, public networks, and telecommunications networks. I will use the terms in LAN in the broader definition, which includes clients and servers. I specifically call out the medium if referring to the hardware (physical LAN) only. I will describe my usage of the terms *network* and *enterprise network* later in this section.

There are essentially three types of WAN attachment options:

• Dialup

• Leased line

• Public network leased or dial connection

To achieve anywhere close to the type of response that the local server provides new techniques for client-server technology approaches must be used. The other viable alternative is to use dial-in approaches to achieve dedicated lines and to off-load the network traffic by turning the workstation interface into a terminal. These remote-control technique can also be used for leased-lines connections if the application cannot be upgraded and the response time is unacceptable otherwise.

Chapter 12

Client-Server

12.1 Introduction

From implementers, integrators, vendors, and the media stand-point the term client-server has come to include a client-server computing model, C-language, relational data base, object oriented, local area networks (LANs), and network operating system. The term *client-server* is also being applied to technical solutions ranging from Windows workgroups through comprehensive distributed relational data base applications using networking operating systems.

The term client-server is applied to many solutions

The benefits of client-server are touted as providing:

- Long-term cost savings.
- Improved productivity at the workstations
- Reduced end-user learning curve with the graphical user interface (GUI)
- A less intimidating user interface
- More flexibility to adding required compute capacity on the server

There are also some less positive properties that are being voiced with regards to:

- Scalability
- Data synchronization
- Remote support management
- Staffing for round-the-clock support

While in the generic sense all these attributes and components are probably reasonable corequisites to a client-server computing model, the primary challenge faced by the reader or audience is to figure out which pieces of the client-server suite of tools the current article or discussion is covering. To assist in helping to keep this perspective I will focus on the term client-server computing as a technical term in order to differentiate it from other forms of distributed computing. This will allow you to read the rest of this book and trade journal articles with a better understanding of the issues and implications of the computing model independent of the other tools and facilities available.

A specific implementation of distributed computing

Client-server is a very specific implementation of distributed computing of which there are three popular applications:

- Peer- to-peer computing
- Master-slave *many-to-one and one-to-one*
- Client-server

12.2 Peer-to-Peer

Peer-to-peer computing allows all participating applications to exchange data with each other. In the peer-to-peer computing model either application can initiate requests. The connections can be *one-to-one*, *one-to-many*, *many-to-one*, and *many-to-many*. (see Fig. 12-1).

Most middleware software provides peer-to-peer services to applications that need to communicate with other applications. The middleware masks off the underlying data communication protocols and provides a level of connection management. This approach allows applications to communicate across networks using different protocols without any application programming changes beyond those required for the middleware interface. In a peer-to-peer environment the roles of each participating application are determined by the applications on both ends. This role negotiation can be quite burdensome because of the coordination required when negotiating the roles. The complexity also depends on the communications interface selected. Most peer-to-peer implementations are provided utilities, such as file-transfer programs or vendor-provided applications. Those companies that

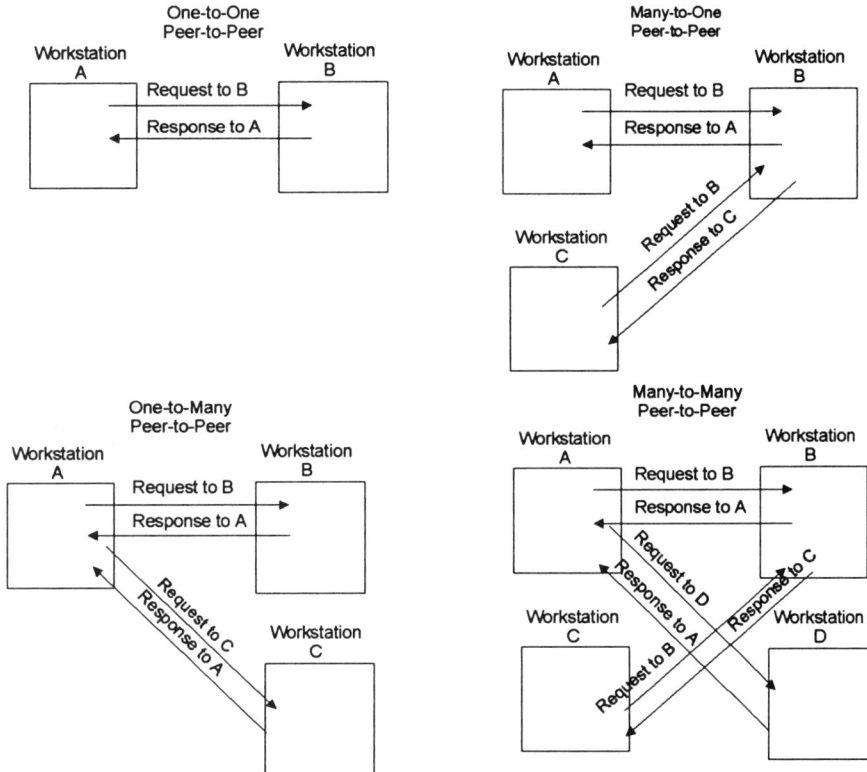

Figure 12-1   Peer-to-Peer Implementation Examples

need customized applications use middleware to mask the complexity from the application programs.

12.3 Master-Slave

The *master-slave* implementation looks very much like a many-to-one implementation of the peer-to-peer applications, however, only the roles are preestablished — there is a single master and the other workstations or systems are slaves (see Fig. 12-2). Because the roles are well established the slave applications and interfaces are significantly simpler. A classic *many-to-one* example of this model occurs when the 3270 terminal emulation software in multiple workstations connect to the mainframe. The emulator programs in each workstation are slaves to the main-

Master-Slave Many-to-One

Workstation
A

Enable for Input from A

Request to Subsystem

Response to A

Host

IBM CICS
Subsystem

Workstation
B

Enable for Input from B

Request to Subsystem

Response to B

Master-Slave One-to-One

Workstation
A

Enable for Input from A

Request to Subsystem

Response to A

Host

IBM TSO
Address Space

Workstation
B

Enable for Input from B

Request to Subsystem

Response to B

IBM TSO
Address Space

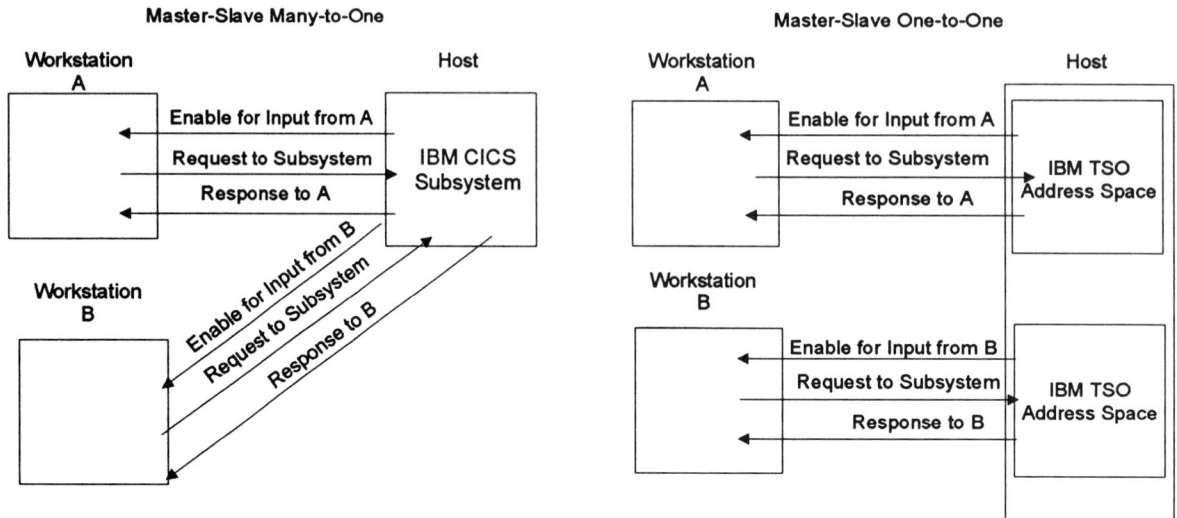

Figure 12-2   Master-Slave Examples

frame application. Most traditional transaction-oriented applications on mainframe or midrange systems are *many-to-one* master-slave applications, that is, the terminals all interact with a single subsystem at a specific time. The mainframe or midrange application controls the application environment. An analogy for the *many-to-one* model might be a public transportation bus. The bus can accommodate multiple passengers. Once a passenger is on the bus, however, the bus is the master since each passenger is a slave to the bus's route and stops until the passenger gets off.

Sometimes the master application only allows a *one-to-one* master-slave relationship between the workstation and the host. For example, most interactive implementations (different from transaction environments) set up a single unique environment for each connecting user or application in order to protect the system and other users. Examples include connections to IBM's MVS TSO and IBM's VM CMS interactive subsystems, which provide a user-dedicated master environment on the mainframe. IBM's transaction processing system, CICS, on the other hand, handles multiple users from a single environment. In the CICS example, the workstation user is in session with CICS and initiates transactions which are are processed by CICS which controls the users access and owns the transactions.

12.4 Client-Server

Client-server computing implementation is similar to the *many-to-one master-to-slave* computing model with the exception that roles are reversed — the *client is the master* and controls the actions, the host merely services the requests. Using the previous bus analogy, in this case the passenger (client) determines when to turn and when to stop.

The client-server model makes the client the master

The peer-to-peer technology can be used to implement a client-server application. For example peer-to-peer interfaces, such as Transmission Control Protocol/Internet Protocol's (TCP/IP's) Remote Procedural Calls (RPC), can be used to implement a client-server relationship, the network file system (NFS) is a specific example. Similarly, IBM's Advanced Program-to-Program Communications (APPC) peer-to-peer programming interface can be used to establish client-server relationships among both similar and different operating system environments. Novell's Sequenced Packet Exchange/Internetwork Packet Exchange (SPX/IPX) and IBM's NetBIOS peer-to-peer protocols also provide network-operating-system-specific peer-to-peer protocols upon which client-server applications can be built. In the NetWare context, NetWare uses two logical components to support the client-server environment. For example, NetWare provides a workstation NetWare shell that communicates with physically attached servers. The NetWare components typically communicate using Novell's IPX/SPX protocols. (Recently these components have been augmented with TCP/IP and AppleTalk protocols.)

The real key to determining whether this is a client-server application is to test the roles at each end of the communication.

Multiple Clients to Single Server

Workstation
A

Server

Request to Server #1

File Server
#1

Response to Client A

Workstation
B

Request to Server #1

Response to Client B

Multiple Clients to Multiple Server

Workstation
A

Server

Request to Server #1

File Server
#1

Response to Client A

Workstation
B

Request to Server #1

Response to Client A

Request to Server 2

File Server
#2

Response to Client B

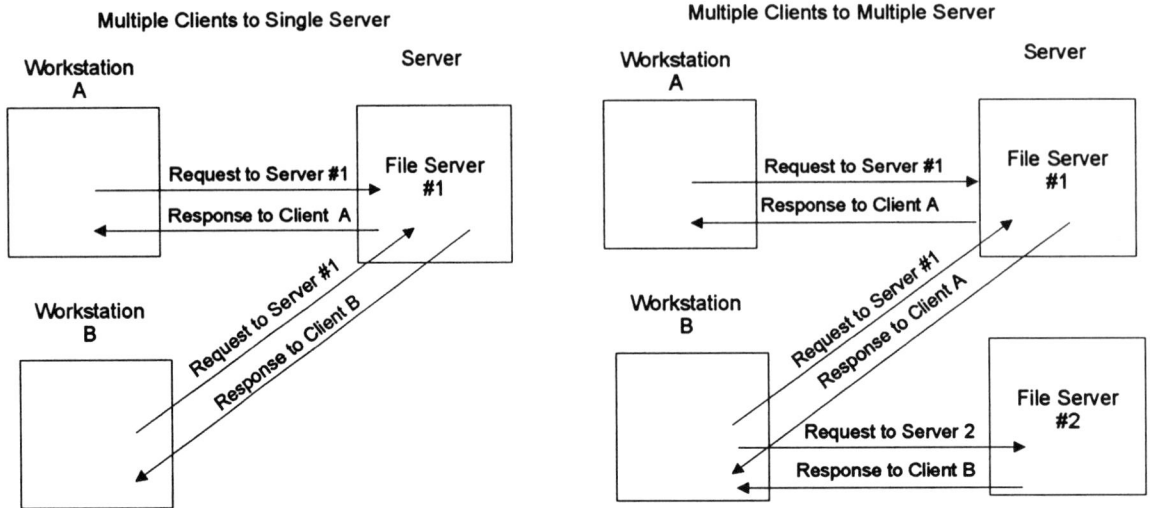

Figure 12-3   Client-server Example

Who is in charge makes the difference.

The client-server environment differs from the traditional mainframe subsystem and workstation environment with regards to control.

In the typical mainframe subsystem, the control is within the target subsystem. In the client-server model the control is with the client, that is, the application is not under the control of the server in a client-server environment.

This differs from the traditional mainframe subsystem environments, which achieved maximum performance and data synchronization by controlling the application.

Using the client-server model, the end-user application can request services from multiple servers at the same time (see Fig. 12-3). The simplest example is to copy a file on server A to server B. In this case, the workstation client established a service connection with both servers and moved the file from server A to the workstation (client) storage and then moved the data to server B.

The significance of this movement of control is that the workstation resident applications control the integrity of the server data when multiple servers are involved. (Special *two-phase commit protocols* were developed by various data base systems and communications vendors to allow applications to control the updates across multiple data base servers. Only the very sophisticated distributed data base management systems provide usable implementations of this capability.)

Client-Server Technology

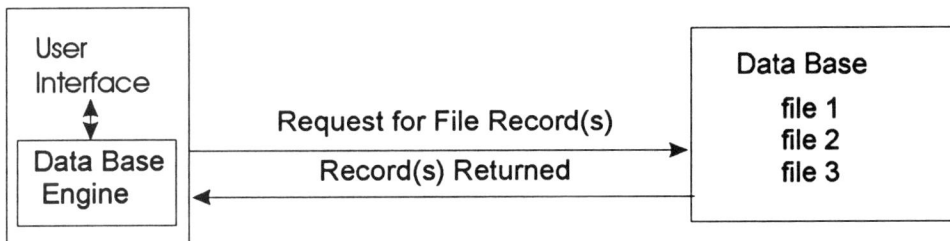

```
User
Interface
  ↕            Request for File Record(s) →      Data Base
Data Base      ← Record(s) Returned              file 1
Engine                                           file 2
                                                 file 3
```

Client-Server Application

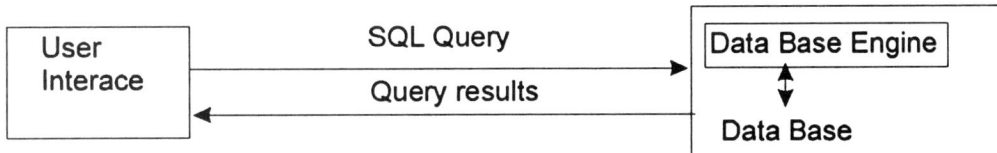

```
User            SQL Query →          Data Base Engine
Interace        ← Query results         ↕
                                      Data Base
```

Figure 12-4 Client-Server Technology and Application

By now you are probably asking yourself "What has peer-to-peer and master-slave got to do with client-server and NetWare?" It has been my experience that understanding which distributed computing model the application will use determines the performance, ease of management, and controls. For example, I have found that there is dramatic distinction between an application or service *using client-server technology* or a *client-server application* (see Fig. 12-4).

Important distinction between *client-server* technology and *client-server application*

Client-server technology is provided by most network operating systems such as NetWare. This technology is recognized as file and print services provided on servers. For the most part these services are provided transparently to the user and the workstation application. In this instance the workstation includes some NetWare client software that redirects the request for file sectors and print output. Therefore it can be said that NetWare provides a client-server implementation for these services.

These client-server technology solutions provide an inexpensive alternative to dedicating resources that can be shared. As long as the response time between the client and the server services is close to that achieved on a dedicated workstation, the client-server technology meets the users' needs. However, when the response time between the client and server does meet the performance demands (as described in the remote server scenarios in Chapter 11) more than the client-server technology is required.

The client-server application knows that there are delays between the client and the server.

The only sensible resolution is to make the application aware of the fact that its partner may be across a wide area network (WAN) or congested physical LAN. I refer to these applications as *client-server applications*.

NetWare is a client-server technology

The most frequently used client-server applications today are those that use client-server-oriented relational data base systems. The client-server application data base products can be purchased from such companies as ASK, IBM, Novell/Gupta, Oracle, and Sybase, to name a few. These data base systems tend to support many computing models, including client-server applications (see Fig. 12-5). This diagram depicts a NetWare LAN-based implementation or a relational data base with the data base engine residing on the server. This configuration leverages the client-

Client-Server Application Components

Relational
Data Base
Interface

NetWare
Client
Shell

Relational
Data Base
NLM

NetWare
File
Services

NetWare
Server

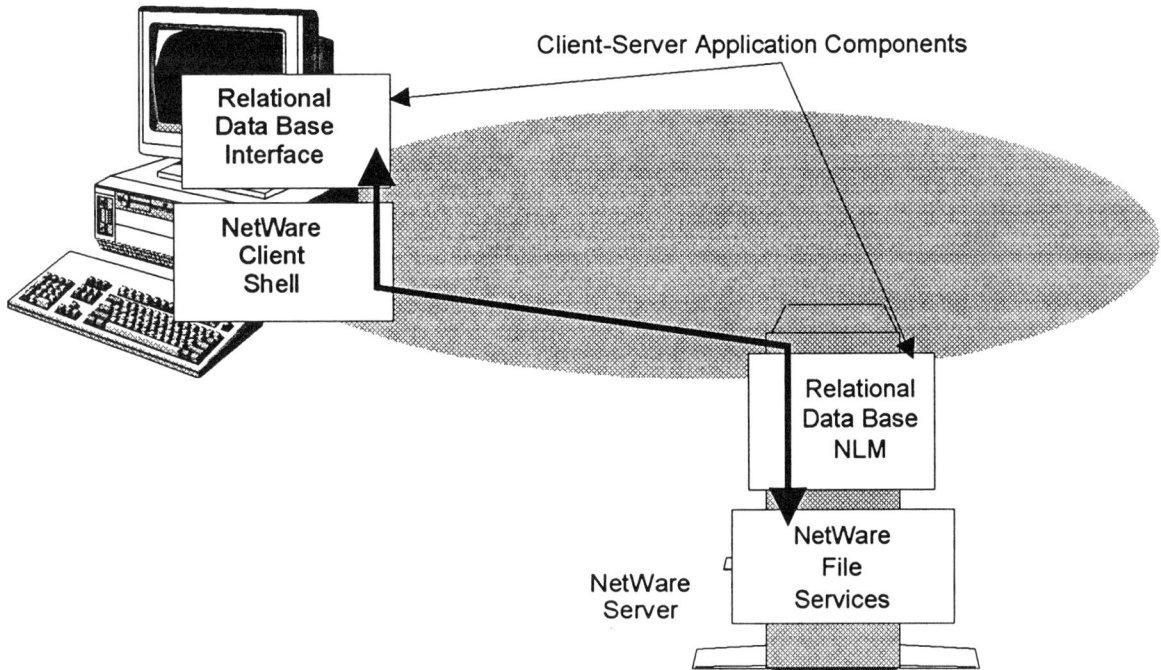

Figure 12-5   A Technology and Application Example

server technology provided by NetWare and the client-server application provided by the relational data base vendor.

Another client-server application example is depicted below. In this example a mainframe communications protocol interface must be resident on the workstation. These are most frequently 3270 or APPC emulation program interfaces as provided by such companies as Attachmate, DCA, Eicon, and Wall Data Systems. In this example these system-network-architecture (SNA) protocol interfaces use pass-through Novell's NetWare client shell software to Novell's NetWare for SAA. NetWare for SAA is being used as a gateway to the mainframe communications access method (VTAM) which interfaces to the relational data base engine, which in turn uses the mainframe's access methods to manage the physical data. This is probably the dominant configuration in the enterprise network context, since the corporate data bases still reside on the mainframe. Both the client-server implementations and the connectivity are discussed in much more detail later in the book.

Relational data bases are probably the easiest and most beneficial from a performance standpoint because the user or user application can pose a structured query that is passed to the target server, which executes the search and responds with an answer. The result is less data over the network and less impact on the underlying network and a reduction of network traffic. The primary considerations are that users structure their requests to minimize network traffic or that the application poses the query in such a manner that the client software can optimize it.

Chapter 13

Servers

13.1 Overview

Server is a generic term that is currently being used to refer to a service role that software on specific computer systems play. A network operating systems such as NetWare makes common local-area network (LAN) resources, such as files and printers, available to complement the workstation operating systems, such as DOS, Windows, Windows NT, OS/2, UNIX, and Mac.

Server is a generic term for a role a software service plays

Typical server configurations provide such services as:

- Disk space to off-load the workstation's disk storage requirements

- Shared file access and controls

- A common print service

- Communication gateway

- A network router

- A mailbox and distributor

- A shared data base service

In addition to the services, a server provides the necessary management capabilities including directories and security. By definition servers work together with some requesting intelligence within the same hardware and software configuration or on a workstation or other computer system. This intelligence (usually software) is referred to as a *requestor* or *client*, since this intelligence requests services from the server.

Figure 13-1 depicts the server and client software relationship. In the first example, the workstation uses the server for disk capacity. The server restricts access to the user who created the file (mine). In the second example, the workstation is sharing a file (Dept.) that is under the server's sharing control. In this case the server controls the access making the file accessible to those identified to access it.

The term *server* is frequently used to refer to a collective configuration of a computer (any technology) running any oper-

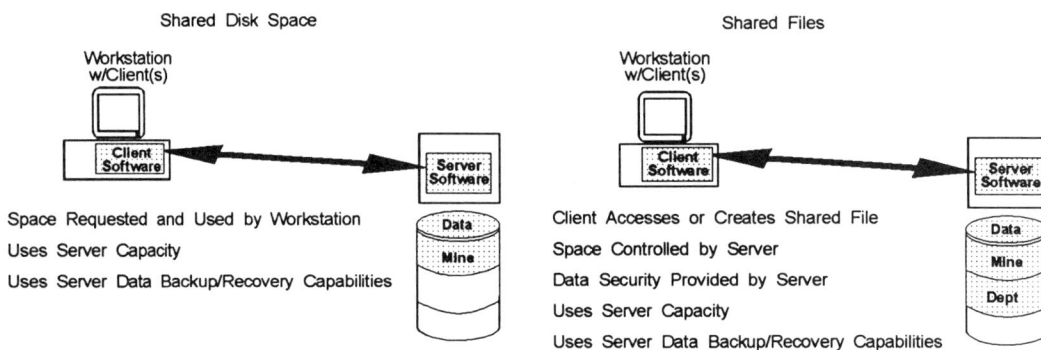

Shared Disk Space   Shared Files

Workstation
w/Client(s)

Client
Software

Server
Software

Space Requested and Used by Workstation

Uses Server Capacity

Uses Server Data Backup/Recovery Capabilities

Data

Mine

Workstation
w/Client(s)

Client
Software

Server
Software

Client Accesses or Creates Shared File

Space Controlled by Server

Data Security Provided by Server

Uses Server Capacity

Uses Server Data Backup/Recovery Capabilities

Data

Mine

Dept

Figure 13-1   Disk And File Sharing Servers

ating system or operating systems and applications that provide services to workstations. In the NetWare context a NetWare server is a software and hardware configuration running Net-Ware.

A NetWare server is a configuration that includes a sophisticated network operating system and server-oriented applications referred to as network loadable modules (NLMs). NetWare, runs in multiple environments. ranging from a dedicated operating system on a 286/386/486 Intel hardware base, as a cooperating system with OS/2, as a server service on UNIX and other platforms using NetWare for UNIX, and as a server service on Digital's virtual address extender (VAX) virtual memory system (VMS) using Interconnections Leverage for NetWare as depicted in Figure 13-2.

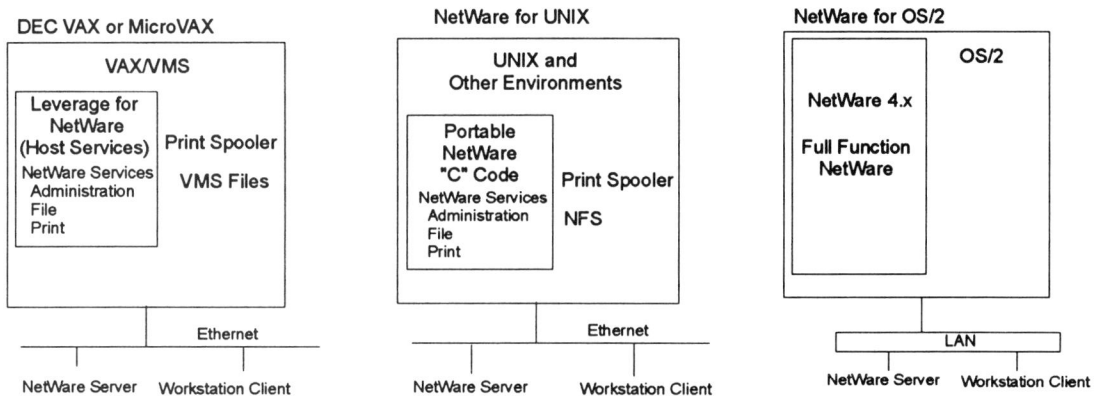

Figure 13-2   Various NetWare Server Environments

13.2 NetWare for UNIX

NetWare for UNIX is a set of applications that runs on several different operating systems, including UNIX. It provides a way that system vendors can offer their customers the capabilities of running their applications in their native environment as well as supporting their customers' NetWare-attached workstation base with NetWare file and print services. NetWare for UNIX supports UnixWare, DOS, OS/2, MS Windows, UNIX, or Macintosh systems workstations connected to the system. This implementation can take advantage of the capabilities of both the UNIX genera- purpose operating system and the specialized workstation

NetWare for UNIX is a a portable version of the NetWare operating system services

networking support using a single system with a single support staff.

Novell also provides the NetWare C Interface for UNIX to enable the development of applications that take advantage of the NetWare services.

NetWare for UNIX is available from Novell's NetWare for UNIX licensed partners, often under their own name. See Table 13-1 for a representative list of Vendors that offer NetWare UNIX-based capabilities.

Table 13-1

Acer/Altos	NEC
AT&T/NCR	Olivetti
Data General	Pyramid Technology Corporation
Digital Equipment Corporation	Rational Data Systems
Dolphin Server Tech.	Sequent
Fujitsu	SGI/MIPS Computer Systems
Hewlett-Packard	Sony
Hitachi	SunConnect
IBM Corporation	Stratus Computer, Inc.
ICL Corporation	Toshiba
Innovus	Unisys Corporation
Interactive Systems/SunSoft	Univel
Intergraph Corporation	

13.3 A NetWare for UNIX OEM Example

A good example of a vendor that has used the NetWare for UNIX approach for integrating NetWare into their environment is Unisys. Unisys offers an extensive product line that works with NetWare servers extending from standard NetWare workstation support through UnixWare and two NetWare for UNIX implementations: NetWare for U Series and NetWare for A Series.

NetWare for U Series is a NetWare for UNIX-based technology applied to the Unisys Intel-based U6000 Series platform. It allows standard NetWare clients to transparently access the U6000 Series-based NetWare server using Internet Packet Exchange/Sequenced Packet Exchange (IPX/SPX) protocols. The server supports DOS, Windows, Macintosh, and OS/2 clients.

NetWare for A Series allows computers supporting Unisys general-purpose operating systems, MCP/AS, to run NetWare. This implementation integrates hosts and workgroups into a NetWare network. NetWare for A Series supports DOS, OS/2, and Windows client workstations with print and files services as well as NetWare's administrative and security functions, such as resource accounting, password protection, and file backup. Most NetWare utilities are supported.

NetWare A-Series runs under the control of the MCP/AS operating system and uses the A Series file system, memory management, and other resources. This provides a scalable solution that allows the existing enterprise network applications and NetWare services to use the same system using the existing A Series utilities and file backup procedures to back up the NetWare volumes. Additionally, NetWare for A Series has system reliability similar to that found with system fault tolerant (SFT) NetWare by providing such capabilities as mirrored disk, multiple channels, and dual processors.

Unisys also provides a hardware/software product, the Host LAN Connection (HLCN), that allows an A Series system to connect directly to an 802.3 Ethernet LAN through a specialized integrated communications processor. Both IPX/SPX and NetBIOS protocols are supported.

13.4 Cross Platform NLMs

NetWare running in a dedicated environment currently provides the most comprehensive product support and has the most associated third party complimentary products.

Emerging developer cross platform tools for both client- and server-based software

Novell is focusing on this by providing tools that help developers build client-server-based applications that can be deployed across multiple platforms. Novell's AppWare provides a set of developer tools to assist the development of the workstation-based client portions of the client-server application. The second step is to provide similar enablers for the server services and applications NLMs. These NLMs can be deployed across Intel- and RISC-based servers and be accessible to developers of desktop applications using Novell's AppWare Foundation and AppWare loadable modules.

Network applications and services, such as messaging, data base, telephony, or imaging, will be delivered on Intel-and RISC-based NetWare platforms, including Digital's Alpha AXP, Hewlett-Packard's PA-RISC, and Sun Microsystems' SPARC, providing consistency and scalability as customers integrate new server platforms in their enterprise. Digital Equipment, Hewlett-Packard, and Sun Microsystems, all of whom have versions of NetWare for their RISC platforms, are working Cygnus Support (a Mountain View-based company) and Novell to enhance the GNU development tools for their platforms.. The objective is to enable the ability to cross-compile NLMs for Digital's Alpha AXP, Hewlett-Packard's PA RISC, and Sun's SPARC platforms in addition to the current Intel-based platforms.

The GNU development tools are a set of public domain tools and utilities that are used in most UNIX environments. Cygnus Support provides commercial releases and support for developers using these GNU tools. These development tools consist of C compilers, assembler, and debugger:

C and a C++ compilers called gcc and g++ respectively
An assembler called gas
A debugger called gdb
Development environment utilities
Binary utilities
An editor
Document formatting tools
A documentation browser
A patch installer

By using these GNU Cygnus Support tools the NetWare for UNIX licensed vendors will essentially have a processor-independent NetWare implementation.

13.5 NetWare for OS/2

NetWare for OS/2 is the closest implementation to having a native NetWare on a dedicated system. It runs all services and certified NetWare NLMs unmodified and provides comparable performance.

NetWare for OS/2 is NetWare 4.01 with some extensions that allow it to operate in a non-dedicated OS/2 environment. The OS/2 multitasking environment and NetWare for OS/2 allow a single computer to be any combination of an OS/2 workstation, an OS/2 server, an OS/2 NetWare workstation client, a DOS NetWare workstation client, a Windows NetWare workstation client, and/or a NetWare server at the same time.

NetWare for OS/2 is a full-function NetWare that shares the server hardware resources

NetWare for OS/2 runs as a parallel operating system to OS/2. It runs within its own protected contiguous block of memory and uses its own portion of the hard drive. Additionally, the proportion of CPU time available to OS/2 and to NetWare can be set either with parameters or dynamically via a NetWare-provided graphics monitor. NetWare can be set to get up to 92 percent of the system time. The additional 8 percent is used by OS/2 to support the NetWare environment. Anything under 92 percent is available to other OS/2 workload.

All of NetWare's services and NLMs are certified to run on NetWare 4.01, and device drivers will run unmodified in NetWare 4.01 for the OS/2 environment.

To achieve the coexistence of the two operating systems NetWare for OS/2 includes two device drivers that provide the interface between NetWare and the OS/2 operating system. These drivers provide NetWare the appearance of running in a dedicated system. The NetWare-provided virtual device driver (VNETWARE.SYS) is an OS/2 virtual device driver (VDD) that interfaces the NetWare server to the machine. The NetWare-provided physical device driver (PNETWARE.SYS) is an OS/2 physical device driver (PDD) that enables NetWare to communicate with and control physical devices. The various hardware features supported by these drivers are summarized in the Table 13-2.

Additionally, NetWare for OS/2 allows NetWare and OS/2 to

Table 13-2

VNETWARE.SYS	PNETWARE.SYS
Interrupt support	Registering/unregistering interrupts
Memory support	End of interrupts (EOIs)
Screen management	Memory allocation
Keyboard functionality	Screen foreground/background notification
Timer support	

dedicate or share hard drive and networks adapters.

For example, the system can be configured with disk drives dedicated to NetWare that OS/2 does not see and disks dedicated to OS/2 that NetWare does not see. However, the hard disk space can also be shared using a NetWare for OS/2-provided driver (DSKSHARE.DSK) that provides disk sharing for contiguous portions on command hard drives. The NetWare partition of the shared disk is formatted and managed solely by NetWare. The OS/2 and NetWare disk partitions are "fire-walled" such that only the owning environment can access the space.

NetWare for OS/2 can share a network board with other protocols, such as those that use NDIS. For NetWare-supported protocols NetWare for OS/2 includes two drivers that allow the NetWare server and an OS/2 workstation client to share a network adapter board. NetWare LANSHARE.LAN is used to support the NetWare server path, and LANSHARE.SYS is used as the driver for the NetWare client for OS/2.

13.6 NetWare for Macintosh 4.0

Another variation of server is characterized by NetWare for Macintosh and NetWare NFS. In these cases Novell has only implemented the server portion and uses the native client support provided by Apple or UNIX software vendors. No NetWare client software required other than comparable native client software in each workstation. NetWare for Macintosh 4.x is a full function Macintosh server with client software coresident on the NetWare server as depicted in Figure 13-3.

NetWare for Macintosh provides NetWare services to connected MAC s

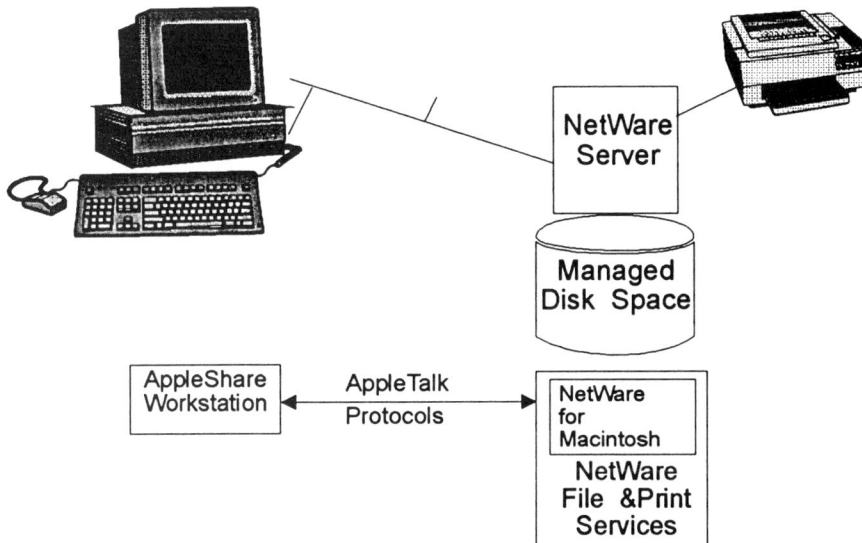

Figure 13-3   NetWare for Macintosh

This Macintosh server supports the full line of Macintosh workstations, including the Classic, Quadra, and PowerBook. These workstations must have AppleShare Workstation and System 6 or later. The NetWare for Macintosh server provides file services, print services, administrative utilities, and AppleTalk routing for Macintosh users on a NetWare network. Macintosh users are able to improve their overall system fault tolerance, resource accounting, and enhance security.

The server supports Macintosh Standards and is compatible with Apple Computer's AppleTalk Filing Protocol (AFP) 2.0 standard, thus ensuring that all Macintosh applications run on a NetWare server. It supports both AppleTalk Phase I and Phase II to provide an open platform on which to build network applications. With the AppleTalk router in NetWare for Macintosh, any Macintosh user can access file and print services and other Macintosh networks connected to the same internetwork.

Additionally this server provides the user with the ability to quickly retrieve commonly used CD-ROM, taking advantage of the way NetWare caches files.

NetWare for Macintosh provides print services to Macintosh, DOS, Microsoft Windows, and UNIX machines. Its support includes an AppleTalk Extended Remote Printer NLM that lets the NetWare Print Server service printers on an AppleTalk network. Additionally, AppleTalk Print Services can be dynamically reconfigured via a menu-driven support.

These print services support PostScript, Diablo 630, and Post-Text mode printing to Apple LaserWriter and compatible printers. NetWare for Macintosh also supports text printing to a number of Apple ImageWriter printers. TrueType fonts and PostScript Level II are supported if the application, printer driver, and output printer support them. PostScript printers can be attached through serial, parallel, or AppleTalk connections.

NetWare for Macintosh includes optional AppleTalk routing services that support LocalTalk, ARCnet, Ethernet, Token Ring, and fiber distributed data interface (FDDI) cabling media, and simple network management protocol (SNMP). This NLM enables a network supervisor to activate, deactivate, and configure the AppleTalk router, and to designate the NetWare server to act as an AppleTalk router.

Macintosh users can send print jobs to printers connected to AppleTalk networks, to the serial or parallel port of a NetWare server, to a NetWare print server, or to a specially configured DOS workstation. Applications can print through the NetWare print queues to any PostScript printer using PostScript or Diablo 630 emulation.

13.7 NetWare NFS

NetWare NFS is a set of NLMs that works in conjunction with the TCP/IP NLMs (see Fig. 13-4) to gives UNIX workstations the ability to use the NetWare server for:

- File space and sharing (NFS)

- NetWare printer sharing (Line Printer daemon)
- UNIX printer sharing (Line Printer Gateway)
- File transfer (File Transfer Protocol daemon)
- Remote NetWare server management (XCONSOLE)

NetWare NFS server provides NFS to NFS clients

UNIX workstation simply requires the NFS client software. (There are more than 150 vendors that have licensed rights from Sun to sell NFS.) Once the NFS client is installed, the UNIX workstations have transparent entry to the NetWare network and can access network resources such as directories, printers, or local UNIX resources.

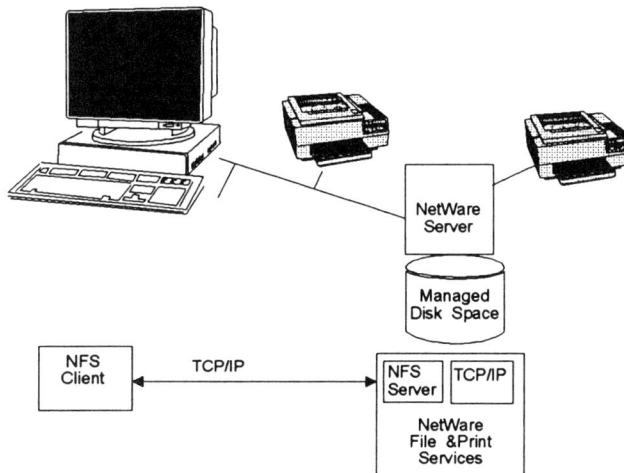

Figure 13-4   NetWare Space and Print for UNIX

13.8 Superservers

While the software determines whether the computer is a server or not, some manufacturers recognizing that the computers used in a server capacity need special capabilities have customized or built very specific hardware systems to provide the server function.

These servers, often referred to as superservers, might be customized Intel-based, RISC-based, or proprietary hardware processors. In general, these superservers focus on extra levels of capacity, higher performance, and high reliability. There are

Superserver is a label used to describe a hardware platform that is suited for server software, capacity and reliability

additional server configurations that support multiple systems, multiple CPUs, and multiple workstations. Multiple CPUs are often desirable to provide fault tolerance and/or additional capacity.

Superservers are sold by companies such as Advance Logic Research, AST Research, Auspex, Compaq, Everex Systems, NCR Corporation, Netframe, Parallan, and Tricord.

13.9 High Availability

13.9.1 NetWare SFT III

SFT III provides high availability to NetWare clients by providing server and data redundancy

To support server high availability Novell provides NetWare System Fault Tolerance III (SFT III), which is a hardware and software configuration that supports two loosely connected servers that are connected to each other via special mirrored server link connections. These servers can be placed up to 100 feet apart using a coax adapter card or up to 4 Km with a fiber adapter at data rates of up to 1.2 Gbits/s. From a user standpoint, only a single server is seen, the second server maintaining the same memory and disk content image, which are kept synchronized via the mirrored server link as depicted in Figure 13-5.

The SFT III configuration protects the user availability by masking server memory failures, server hard disk failures, and potentially unavailability due to a catastrophe, if the second server is sufficiently far away not to be involved in the catastrophe. It does not protect failures caused by the system or NLM software.

For many businesses that use their servers for critical business services, unscheduled downtime can easily cost $1000 to $100,000 per hour loss productivity based on idle workers, loss of business, or greater business exposure. The SFT III configuration addresses one aspect of this by providing a mirrored drive. However, once the failure has occurred, there is no more redundancy. Depending on the disk, a disk failure, replacement, and rebuild cycle can take from 24 to 48 hours. To address this need several hardware vendors now provide hardware disk solutions that include soft-fail disk subsystems and techniques to hot-swap new drives even without a screwdriver. There are, however,

NetWare Mirrored
Server Link
Cards

NetWare
Server

NetWare
Server

Mirrored
Server
Engine

Mirrored
Server
Engine

I/O
Engine

Mirrored
Server Link

I/O
Engine

Workstation

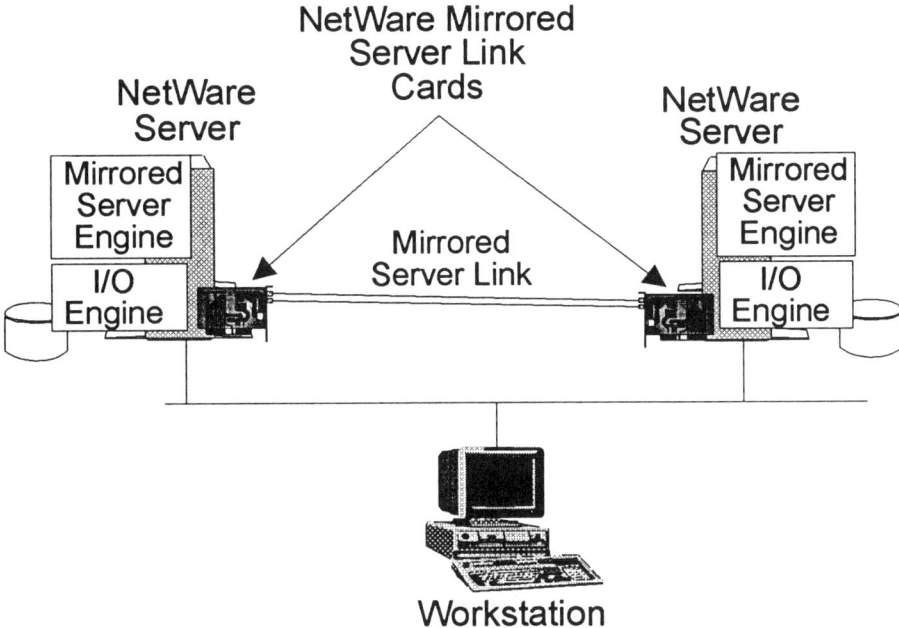

Figure 13-5   Fault Tolerant NetWare Configuration

multiple soft-fail options with trade-offs that range from price to performance. SFT III provides CPU and disk storage redundancy using special NetWare software. There are, however, other approaches that provide high availability storage that can be used in a standard NetWare configuration or with SFT III.

13.9.2 High Availability Disk Storage

High availability disk approaches included a combination of software and hardware that is configured such that if a disk failure is encountered the system keeps on running with no impact to the quality of the data or performance. A second configuration consideration is to enable the replacement of the failed device as soon as possible without disruption in performance since there is no redundancy until the new unit is in place. This is addressed with

Specially designed hardware and good backup and recovery procedures protect the data

special hardware that supports hot-swap drives and storage sub-systems that have spare drives swapped in failure situations.

In addition to hot swaps there is frequently a requirement to dynamically expand the capacity of expansion because of the potential outage time associated with a shutdown and reorganization. I'll spend some time here because the hard disk is the heart of most server systems and the considerations should be understood. This area of high data availability is one that the mainframe infrastructure has finely honed for the last 30 years causing some LAN users to look to ways of leveraging this IS support by using the mainframe for storing mission-critical data and providing the necessary availability with the appropriate backup.

User error biggest cause of data loss

Before we look at the options and considerations let's look at the causes of data loss as reported from a survey of 800 U.S. storage administrators and (MIS) managers of LANs, minicomputers, mainframes and super-computers (see Fig. 13-6). The categories really break into two major categories: user error (71 percent) and hardware failure (25 percent). SFT III and the RAID technologies minimize the impact of the system component fail-

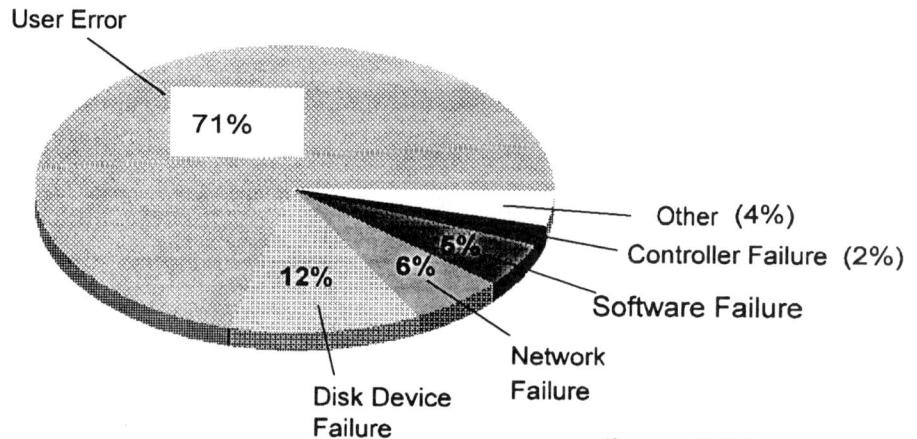

User Error

71%

Other (4%)

Controller Failure (2%)

Software Failure

Network Failure

Disk Device Failure

12%

6%

5%

(Source: IDC Survey, *LAN Times*, May 25, 1992.)

Figure 13-6   Causes of Data Loss

ures reducing the number and duration of outages. Robust backup and recovery software with rigorous and thoroughly tested procedures to gracefully and quickly recover the data are required to minimize the impact data loss for 71 percent of the problems. Now let's look at techniques to avoid any user impact due to disk or controller hardware failures.

Soft-fail disk drive configurations and data-writing algorithms are currently identified using the *RAID* nomenclature. *RAID* is the acronym for redundant array of inexpensive drives. *RAID* is a method of spreading your data over multiple drives and providing redundancy in the subsystem to improve reliability. The number designators represent the way the data and parity information is stored across the disks in your disk drives. The various algorithms are differentiated by numbers (e.g., 0 through 5). The numbers do not connote more or less capability, the merely identify the algorithm.

RAID technologies address disk hardware failure

Tables 13-3 and 13-4 provide a brief overview of what the various RAID types are and some of the considerations. The bottom line, however, is that the most prevalent approach in the LAN community is some variation of RAID 1 because of its ease of implementation and understanding by the consumer. All the variations of RAID implementations are supported in a NetWare environment with the exception of RAID 3. This support is either a NetWare option or is provided by the storage subsystem vendor.

When all is said and done, the following represents a checklist of the key considerations when selecting a storage base:

- *Usable disk space.* RAID 1 provides 50 percent usable capacity. High RAID levels can achieve up to 90 percent usable space

- *Cost.* Cost is a function of the breadth of support required for each installation. The key tradeoffs are a function of the technology used, the manual intervention and skill required to operate and react, and the number of LANs that need the RAID-level support. Another alternative is to use a central server with the appropriate features to support the mission critical data backup.

Table 13-3

RAID	Description	Considerations
Raid 0 **Data striping** **(performance)**	Evenly distributes the records across spanned disks. Reduces time required for the desired sector to pass underneath the read/write heads	High performance. No data redundancy if one drive fails all data is gone!
Raid 1 **Disk mirroring** **(safety)**	Output written to 2 drives connected to a single controller. NetWare has a native option	If media failure keeps on running If controller failure data is unavailable 100% data redundancy
Raid 1 **Disk duplexing** **(safety)**	A disk mirroring extension. Mirrors to parallel disks and on independent controllers	Fault tolerant 100% data redundancy
RAID 0 & RAID 1 **(safety & performance)**	Combined mirror stripped offers improved read performance because the data can be read from either drive. Writes take longer because double writes. Supported by NetWare	Fault tolerant 100% data redundancy High performance
RAID 2 **(safety & performance)**	Distributes data and interleaving check information. Data integrity is achieved by using the Hamming error correction code	Fault tolerant Less than 100% redundancy Performance degradation Requires multiple drives for error checking. Usable disk space ranges from 50% in a 4 drive system to 73% in an 11-drive system

Table 13-3 (Continued)

RAID 3 **(safety & performance)**	The controller stripes the block of data across the drives in the array. Stores only information necessary to reconstruct the data on the failed drive. The correction or parity information is stored on a dedicated drive. When a drive fails, there is a bit-by-bit reconstruction of the lost information. Using bits on drives 1, 2, 4, it can determine the data for drive 3	Fault tolerant Less than 100% redundancy Every 4 drives of data require an additional drive for parity information Must access every drive in the array for each disk request. It can only process one input/output (I/O) at a time, which makes it very good for large data transfers and very poor for data base application
RAID 4 **(safety & performance)**	Data striped across all but one of the available drives -- the first block is written to drive 1, the second to drive two, and so on. Increases disk read performance, since most transactions involve a single drive. Independent disk transactions allow drives in the array to service concurrent read requests. Every transaction involves a write to the parity drive	Fault tolerant Less than 100% Improves throughput by using the array's entire bandwidth, especially as the read-to-write ratio increases
RAID 5 **(safety & performance)**	Data and parity striped across all drives. By interleaving, the parity not limited by the single file write restriction of RAIDs 3 and 4. Because data are written a segment at a time disk transactions are independent	Fault tolerant Less than 100% If a drive fails, the controller rebuilds the data from the parity on the remaining good drives Suited for file server applications with a high small block I/O rate

Table 13-4

ID Level	Disk Spanning	RAID 0	RAID 1	RAID 2	RAID 3	RAID 4	RAID 5
Usable space	100%	100%	50%	73%	90%	90%	90%
Parity & redundancy	None	None	Duplicated	Parity drives	Parity drives	Parity drives	Parity interleaved on all drives
Parity type	None	None	None	Bit-interleaved	Bit-interleaved	Block/sector	Block/sector
Minimum# of drives in array	2	2	2	4	3	3	3
Advantages	Extends volume size beyond single unit	Improved performance due to concurrent writes	Easily integrated Redundancy Duplicate data lets system continue even though a drive has failed Performance is enhanced by the availability of multiple spindles	More usable space Great for super computers and sequential I/O	Parallel data Paths uses fewer disks for error checking Good throughput on large data transfers	Ability to process multiple simultaneous reads	Multiple simultaneous reads and writes handle high volume of small block transactions
Disadvantages	No performance or fault tolerance advantages Increases likelihood of the array failing	If one fails, the whole subsystem fails	Twice the expense of a nonmirrored system	Performance Error checking scheme requires multiple drives Single reads or writes must access every disk in array	Performance suffers with small data random disk accesses	Can only process a single write transaction at a time	Generally slower than 3 on large file transfers Suffers a performance hit when writing to the disk

- Performance/throughput. Each RAID level offers different variation of performance design points. For example, Raid 3 offers good sequential I/O access, but has high overhead for transaction oriented data base calls because of their randomness. On the other hand, RAID 5 handles transactional data very well, but slows down with large file transfers.

- *Second failure exposures.* Most RAID levels provide fault tolerance (except RAID 0), but the redundancy may be lost for some period of time after a failure. To minimize or all but eliminate this this exposure some vendors offer the ability to hot-swap disk drives. This hot-swap can be a manual effort requiring human intervention or might entail a hot spare feature that provides automatic swapping.

- *Disk addition or reconstruction.* The physical introduction of a spare drive must be done smoothly and non-disruptively. It is important to assure that the hardware subsystem or the software subsystem effectively uses rebuilds the new disk without extending or introducing an outage. For example some mirror systems require you to reinitialize software to add the new drive or add an additional drive.

- *Single points of failure.* A high availability storage system must include elimination of single points of failure. It is usually the simple things such as cable or power supply failure that miss the normal checklist items.

- *Problem alert and determination.* A robust solution includes a mechanism to recognize that a failure has occurred, that there is a mechanism to communicate the occurrence and the appropriate diagnostic information to a responsible person. The need for this capability is especially true in fault tolerant systems where the user only sees the problem when there is a hard failure.

In summary there are several technologies available for NetWare fault tolerant applications that are ideal for local networks. However, in the enterprise network context, the key features include appropriate controls to protect the data from the 71 percent of the user error failures and to provide the remote notification and diagnosis to the operations organization in a timely manner.

High Availability vs. Fault Tolerance

Many information systems professionals have been working with the terms *fault tolerance* and *high availability* for many years. In a systems context, high availability refers to the ability of the user to access to computational and data resources when they are needed. Availability is typically reported as a percentage where 100 percent would indicate the required resources were available when requested for the period measured.

Similarly in a systems context, the term fault tolerance has been associated with the identification of a fault (failure) and correction with assured data integrity. Fault tolerance in a data systems context requires a technology to identify that a failure has occurred and the wherewithal to make that the correct data is provided. For example, most enterprise network fault-tolerant systems include a mechanism to compare whether the data received is correct. This requires three sources of data of which two must compare or the data is flagged. Such fault-tolerant systems tend to be very sophisticated and expensive.

The SFT and RAID technologies are best characterized as high-availability solutions when business transactions with data update are involved.

This is not a major concern for most commercial applications when considering that the failure is logged and the transaction can be scrutinized later. However, for those companies that require fault tolerance, these capabilities can be added with some application- or system-level software that

---

SFT and RAID provide high availability Fault tolerance for update data transactions is provided with additional software using SFT and RAID

13.10 Multiprocessing Servers

To address scaling, Novell is introducing NetWare multiprocessing (NetWare MP).support which will support what I refer to as loosely-coupled multiprocessing, as depicted in Figure 13-7. This multiprocessing supports systems with the ability to house multiple CPUs (systems) connected to the same systems bus or let the customer configure a multiprocessing configuration among different servers connected via a physical LAN or even run an NLM in an idle workstation. UNIX users can scale by taking advantage of UNIX-symmetric multiprocessing support (referred to as SMP), a tightly-coupled configuration. The UNIX operating system SMP support allows the NetWare for UNIX implementations to use multiple CPUs that are transparent to NetWare.

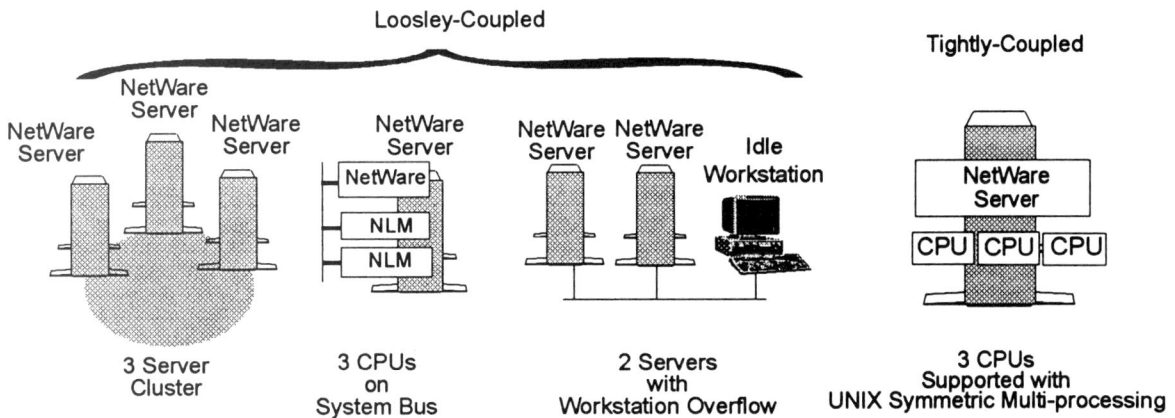

Figure 13-7 NetWare Multiprocessing Configurations

Loosely-coupled processors means that there are multiple operating systems (one on each processor) involved and they communicate and pass data among each other to complete a job.

Tightly-coupled means that a single operating system uses multiple CPUs using common memory to complete a job.

13.11 IBM Mainframe Servers

Mainframe servers are referred to as subsystems

Sometimes IBM mainframes and midrange systems are used in a server capacity. That is, some applications on the mainframe provide services to local and remote requesters or clients. Services include file transfer, file access, print serving, data collection and distribution, communication serving, data base serving, data archive, and data backup. Typically mainframe services that can be viewed as servers are often referred to as *subsystems*.

There are several vendors that provide file servers on the mainframe. Several server applications and variations are supported for IBM MVS operating-system-based implementations. These include IBM's NFS and Andrew File System (AFS) for TCP/IP clients, and Syzygy's Extended Access Method /Network (XAM/NET) for SNA-connected DOS and Windows workstation, and IBM's LAN Resource Extension and Services (LAN-RES) which extends the NetWare server's disk capacity. These implementations allow distributed workstations to access centrally located data files in a native format using native access methods. Typical commercial applications of these mainframe-based servers are report and file distribution, operational data collection, report distribution, and data backup.

13.11.1 MVS-based NFS

Mainframe NFS server supports workstation files

Figure 13-8 depicts an MVS-based NFS server. The NFS server software resides on the MVS mainframe and NFS client software resides on each of the workstations that wish to access the

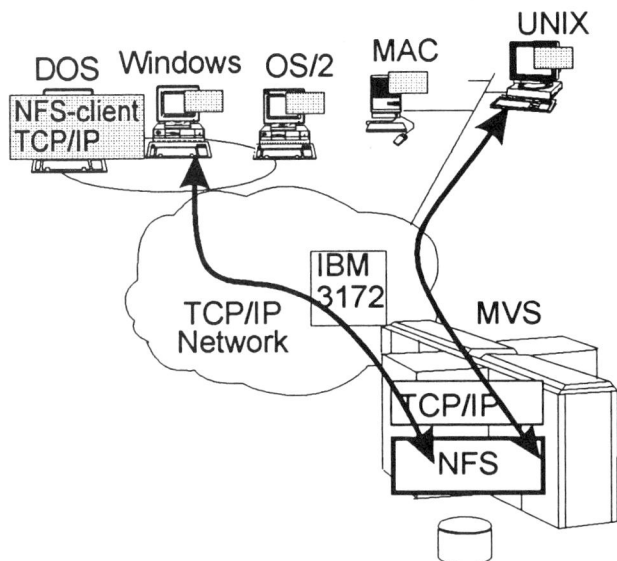

Figure 13-8   MVS-based NFS Server

centrally located files. TCP/IP is used as the network protocol. The NFS files are typically in a format that only the workstations can read. A mainframe NFS client that can read and translate ASCII-data would be required for the mainframe-based applications to read the NFS-based files.

File transfer between mainframe and NFS server:
- **MVS NFS client**
  or
- **Data must travel to the workstation and back to the mainframe.**

13.11.2 An MVS-based Disk Server - XAM/NET

Figure 13-9 depicts another mainframe-based server implementation that supports DOS and Windows files on mainframe-based virtual disk volumes. XAM/NET redirector software resides in each workstation. This redirector software provides the workstation with one or more virtual disk drives. Accesses to these virtual disk drives are forwarded to the mainframe resident XAM/NET software which, in turn, provides access to the virtual disk files resident at the mainframe. Other PC-based services include print services and bi-directional file transfers between the mainframe and the PC and between the mainframe and the virtual DOS drive, the latter transfer can be accomplished without the data traversing the network. XAM/NET also allows mainframe applications to access the mainframe-based virtual files through a mainframe-

An SNA network-based mainframe disk server

File transfer between mainframe and mainframe-DOS file without network traffic

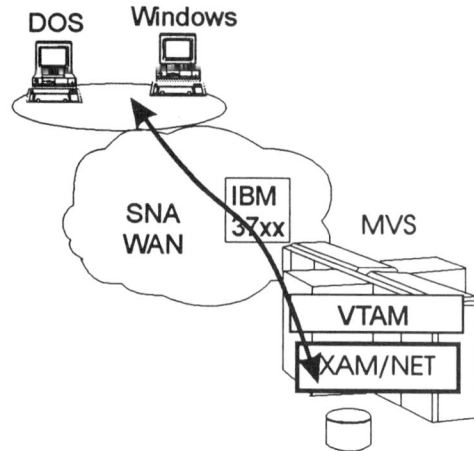

Figure 13-9   A Mainframe-based File Server

Mainframe applications can access mainframe-based DOS files

based software interface. This product makes the mainframe a file server, very much like NetWare makes an Intel processor a file and print server.

This type of solution supports direct workstation access as well as access from workstations on NetWare LANs. In both instances the user and programming interfaces are unchanged for local or remote data access.

For example,assume that a workstation user in San Francisco needs the inventory status of a particular product line for an executive status report due that day.

The user enters a spreadsheet application (e.g., Lotus 1-2-3), loads the E:PRODUCTX.WK3 file, scrutinizes the results on the workstation screen, customizes a report, and creates a graph of the trend. In this scenario the file was on the mainframe accessible to all authorized users; however, the user did not know or care where the file really was. To the user the data were on disk drive E; in reality the file was stored on a shared virtual volume on the mainframe because it is a convenient place for the information services (IS) organization to store the data and have them accessible to the entire enterprise. This on-demand approach eliminates the need to send data to locations that don't need it as well as reducing the network traffic and eliminating the unwieldy distri-

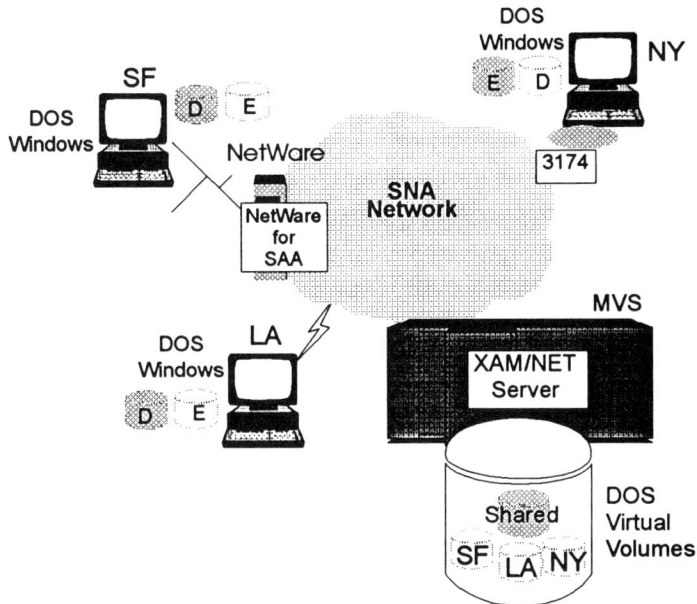

Figure 13-10   Using a Mainframe File Server

bution procedures. Figure 13-10 depicts the configuration of the previous scenario. It also shows that each location has a private virtual volume and access to a shared virtual volume. Note that D: or E: workstation volume designations are only relevant to each workstation. The volumes are mapped to each users configuration. Also note that the DOS and Windows workstations are connected either directly to the MVS mainframe or through NetWare for SAA.

Another example using XAM/NET at the same company as the previous scenario has another user needing to have a report generated before the analysis can be done. The user selects a Windows icon, enters two dates, a from date and a to date and an eight character label for the report. The user then depresses the enter key. The user then looks on the E: drive for the report label. This report is imported into the user's spreadsheet and manipulated. This user had submitted an MVS batch job and had the output routed to the appropriate disk file on the mainframe. This file was then reviewed as if it were on the workstation

13.11.3 A Mainframe-based Server Extension -LANRES

**A mainframe-based
NetWare server
extension**

IBM's LANRES product is representative of another variation of a mainframe-based server. This variation extends the disk capacity of the NetWare server rather than the individual user. It differs from the NFS and XAM/NET implementations in that no client software, beyond the standard NetWare file server software is required in each workstation. (Remember both NFS and XAM/NET use client software, NFS client and XAM/NET redirectors.) Using the LANRES variation the NetWare server attached workstations are totally unaware that their files might be stored on an IBM mainframe. (See Fig. 13-11.) In addition to being a virtual disk server, LANRES extends printer support to the mainframe and to the LAN, includes file transfer capabilities between the LANRES virtual disks and the mainframe, and provides some mainframe-centric administration.

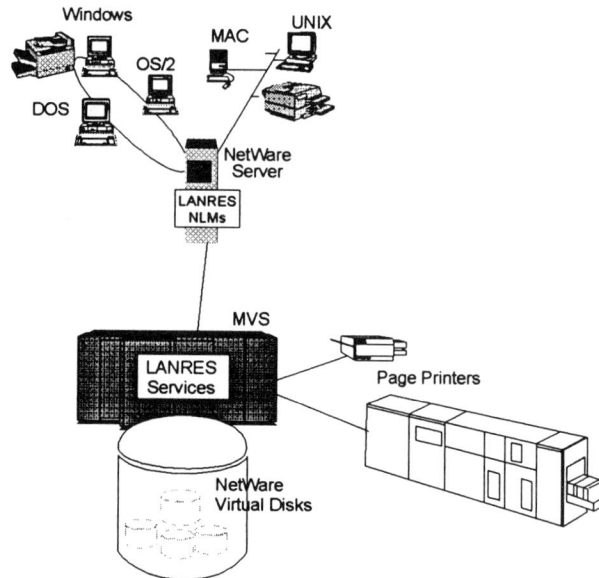

Figure 13-11   IBM LANRES a NetWare Extension

LANRES has multiple connection options which include IBM's S/370 channel connection (4.5 M-Bytes per second), IBM ESCON connection (10 M-Bytes per second), Token Ring, Ethernet, and remote connections. These connections are supported by proprietary channel communications support, TCP, and SNA protocols. (See Fig. 13-12.)

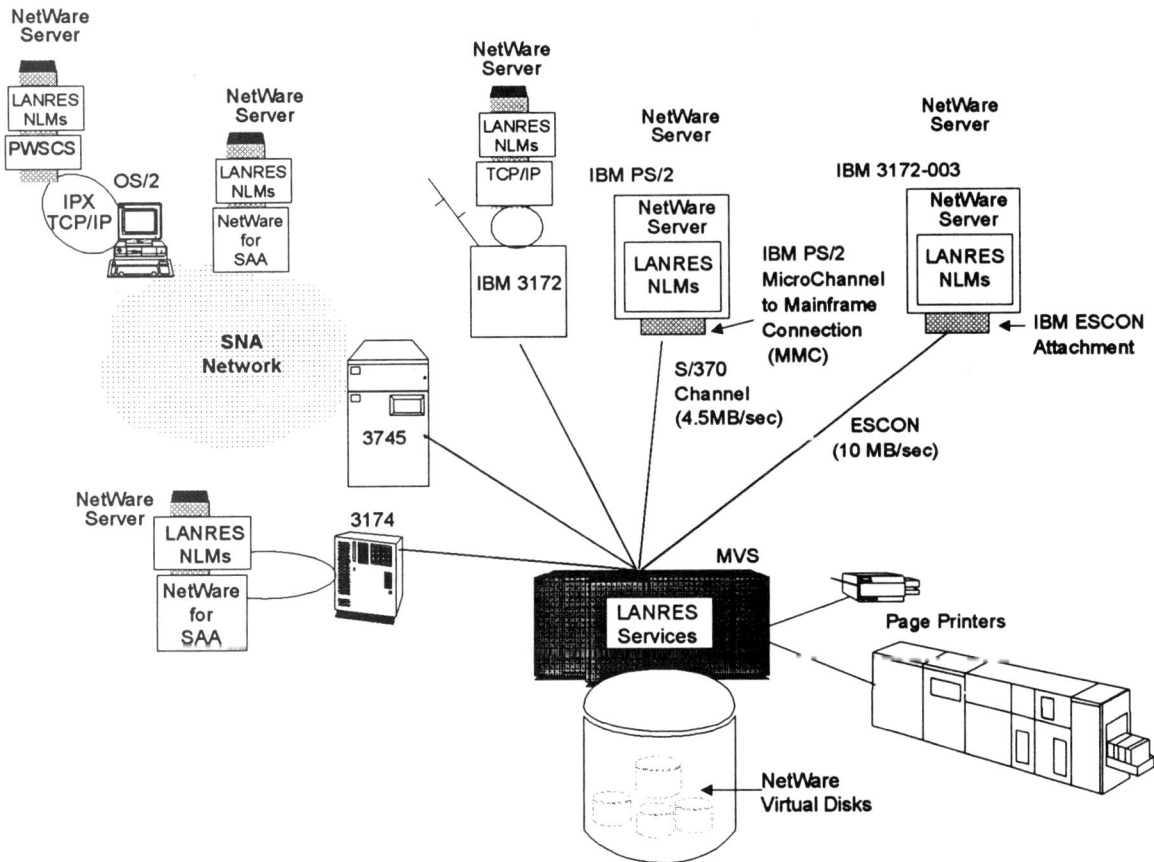

Figure 13-12   LANRES Connection Flexibility

Figure 13-12 depicts a variety of connectivity options available with LANRES/MVS. (IBM also offers a LANRES/VM product with the same connectivity plus an additional channel

LANRES enables use of standard mainframe based back and recovery infrastructure

connectivity software option using VM Programmable Workstation Communication Services (VM PWSCS).

LANRES-type disk server functions can significantly improve the data management of an enterprise network for mission critical data backup and as an on-demand data distribution vehicle.

For example, a large insurance company division's users needed to distribute and collect mainframe data to and from the NetWare file server, they also want to have their mission-critical NetWare-based files backed up with the same confidence they had with backup and recovery procedures, and they were looking for a way to free-up a significant amount NetWare disk space that was being used for on-line documentation and reports. This online documentation and reports were replicated across multiple servers in the company.

Before selecting LANRES the company explored many LAN-centric options including setting up a superserver in the "glasshouse." This superserver was to be connected to a large hierarchical storage management system (often generically referred to as an HSM system), include a very sophisticated tape cartridge stacking system, and an expansive array of read-write optical storage devices and juke boxes. The team analyzing this did a very thorough job and developed a bill of material that easily approached $200,000 dollars without any consideration for the skills and administration involved. During one of the review sessions, one of the line-of-business executives asked the team how their proposal differed from the services that she was currently getting from the IS organization for her mainframe-based applications. When the team answered that the solution would essentially provide comparable support, they were asked why they couldn't use the existing capabilities.

During a review of many software and data distribution, file transfer, and data backup products, the team was introduced to a mainframe server approach using LANRES at the NetWorld trade show. After several weeks of study and many discussions between the NetWare administrators and the mainframe programming and operations staff, a pilot was scheduled. The pilot entailed the purchase of an IBM PS/2 MicroChannel to Mainframe Connection (MMC) adapter that was placed in a Micro-Channel-based NetWare server, together with the LANRES NLMs, and the LANRES/MVS software was installed on the mainframe. Initially, the new virtual disks were set up for test purposes only. No one was really comfortable about the what might happen. The mainframe operations organization was concerned that the channel attachment or the mainframe-based LANRES software might somehow impact the MVS system and the LAN administrators expected very slow delivery of data.

Neither happened! There were no outages caused by the addition of LANRES and even the LAN administrators couldn't tell the difference in performance between the the real and the virtual drives. The LAN administrator commented that adding capacity was significantly less risky now because it could be done without any hardware changes on the server and he didn't feel that any control had been given up.

LANRES supports the your, mine and ours model

The NetWare server was configured with the mainframe volumes, which included a mirror copy . The users were given a new volume, the G: drive, to access all the on-line documentation and daily company-wide reports eliminating these from 15 servers.

All the users were satisfied with satisfied and the IS operations organization backed-up the virtual drives just as they would any VSAM file as part of their normal nightly and weekly cycles. The entire project was completed in five months and the price tag was significantly less than $200,000 without any of the risk the initial LAN-centric model introduced. An additional benefit was discovered as user began to use the print capabilities which allowed mainframe generated reports to be printed from their NetWare attached printers.

LANRES connects through various media with the appropriate performance considerations. It is therefore important to note that the NetWare file access method for LANRES and similar implementations is in the NetWare server and the data resides on the mainframe direct access storage devices (DASD). This means that all file transfers from the LANRES virtual disks to the mainframe actually travel from the mainframe to the server and back to the mainframe. Given that very high bandwidth options such as the S/370 Channel Attachment and ESCON serial optical

connections are available, this overhead is not a major consideration., however, as remote line connections come into play care
should be taken to manage the expectations.

13.11.4 Not All Mainframe Subsystems Are Servers

Several relational data base implementations, including IBM's
DB2, can also make the mainframe a data base server. Similarly
DISOSS on MVS can provide a mainframe-based centralized
message server.

While NFS, XAM/NET, LANRES, DB2, and DISOSS are
servers and subsystems, however not all subsystems are server
even though from an external viewpoint the differences might not
be obvious. When assessing mainframe-based client-server implementations it is important to recognize the differences since
these differences can dramatically impact the cost, the flexibility,
and the overall viability of the solution.

For example, in Figure 13-13 a user logged into an IBM IMS
or CICS subsystem entering a transaction is not really using the
mainframe subsystem(s) as a server. In this case the mainframe
subsystem supports the communication, and houses and controls
the application. The application is not independent of the server
environment. (This implementation fits the *master-slave model*.)

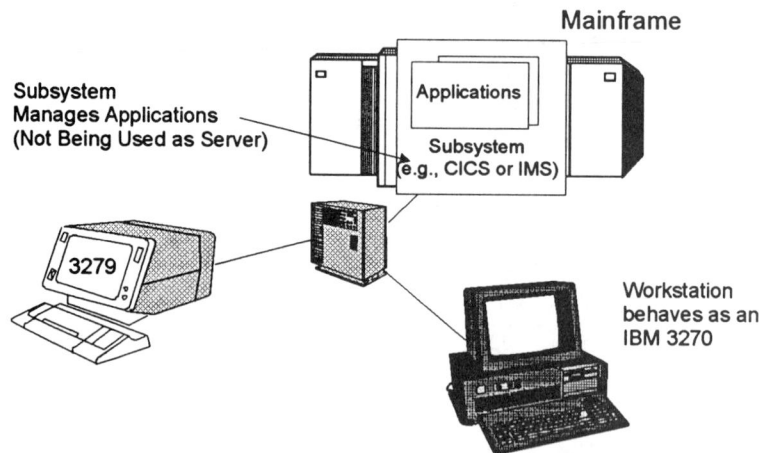

Figure 13-13   A Mainframe Subsystem

Some vendors might call the mainframe an application server in this instance, especially if they are selling a multiuser subsystem that supports dumb terminal connections. The distinction that I suggest is very important is the application control: *Servers serve they do not control. It is this distinction that provides the openness to new and different applications.*

IBM's relational data base system, DB2, on the other hand, is always a server. It is a server to any application that uses it whether the application is on the same mainframe, on some other system, or on any workstation (see Fig. 13-14).

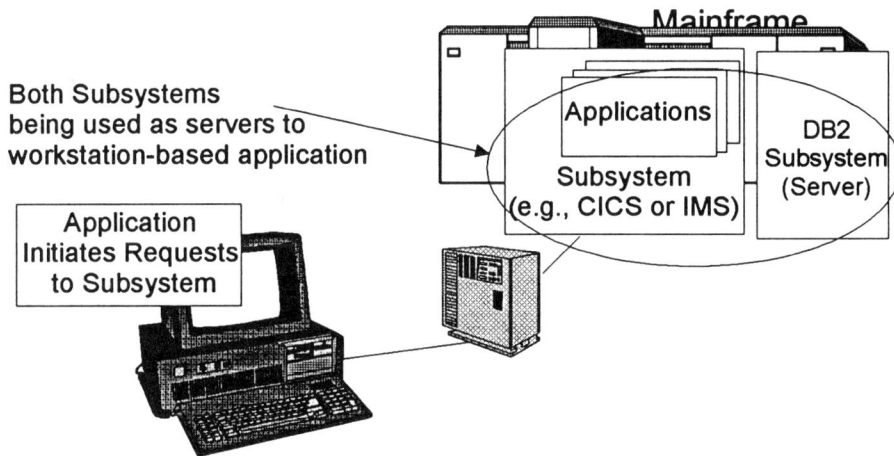

Figure 13-14 IBM's DB2 Subsystem is a Server

At this point let's also differentiate two very different mainframe server implementations.

The first server implementation, configuration A in Figure 13-15, portrays the mainframe as a subsystem that handles multiple requests from multiple users.

The second implementation, configuration B in Figure 13-15, is a single-user server implementation. The single-user server model is very pervasive because it is very easy to market and implement. This implementation has the workstation user log into a private address space of MVS/TSO or VM/CMS and then uses the provided PC terminal emulation software logic to send or receive files. The single-user server implementation uses standard 3270 emulation software and hardware on the workstation or workstation and LAN. It uses standard mainframe software rather than a subsystem (each user has their own environment). The workstation software typically uses an IBM 3270 application programming interface to communicate with a standard file transfer interface on the mainframe.

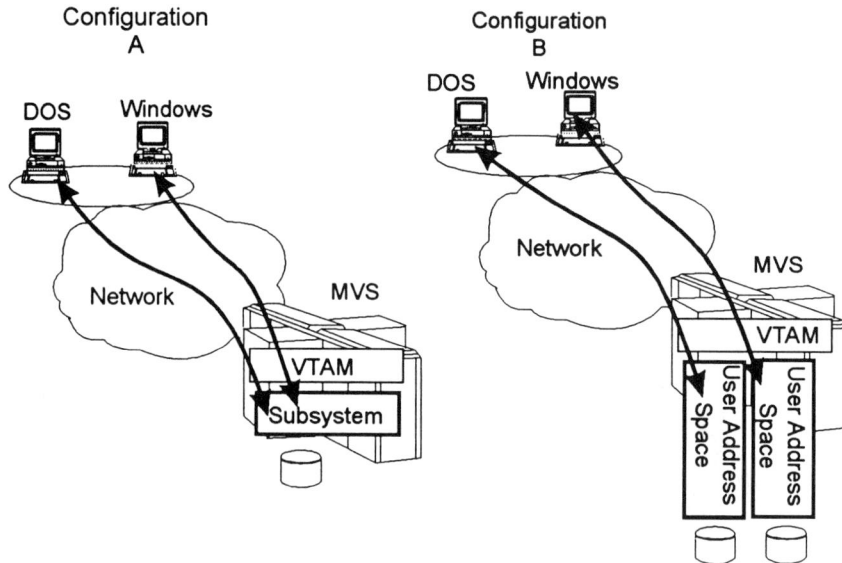

Figure 13-15   Multiple- and Single-user Server

The key distinction between the subsystem and the single-user server model is the amount of overhead required to support each. The subsystem approach needs the least overhead and optimum network utilization, while the single user implementation typically requires significant overhead, which is associated with establishing the session and logging in and out of the TSO or CMS address space. The data network traffic is usually limited to 3270 emulation protocols.

In summary not all subsystems on a host are servers and not all subsystems on the host are designed to be efficient servers.

The server test for mainframe-based subsystems is to determine whether the application or the subsystem is in control. If the application is controlled by the subsystem, the subsystem is not a server. This is not uncommon, since in mainframe architectures some subsystems need to be in control to provide the robustness and data integrity. If the application can request services of one or more subsystems, the subsystem is typically in the server role. In short, the requesting software is the client and it initiates all requests for service. The server software can provide access controls based on authorized information.

If a subsystem like DB2, NFS, XAM/NET, or LANRES is not being used, the user is probably connecting into TSO or CMS as a single-user server.

Avoid Reinventing the Mainframe

Understanding the difference between a server and subsystem role is important because it helps determine where the application and the subsystem should run. The benefits of client-server technology can be derived independent of the underlying hardware platform if these differences are understood.

Most of the conversations today are on downsizing - it is important that if a company has selected a client-server model for downsizing that it not pursue a avenue of moving subsystems that do not operate as servers to a different platform thinking they are implementing a client-server solution. The idea is to provide new and better services using the client-server model not convert one mainframe subsystem to a different mainframe (new technology) subsystem.

13.12 Summary

The key point in this chapter discussing the the various server configurations and attributes was to point out that a server is a software configuration that can use any number of hardware platforms and features. Probably the most important attributes are the ability of the software/hardware to scale and the reliability of the server software and hardware. Server hardware configurations (see Fig. 13-16) include mainframes, midrange systems, Intel-based, or RISC-based PCs. These systems can operate as dedicated servers to client applications, or they can host server software in addition to their normal applications. There are many software vendors that provide software to enablethesehardware platforms to provide server services to NetWare networks.

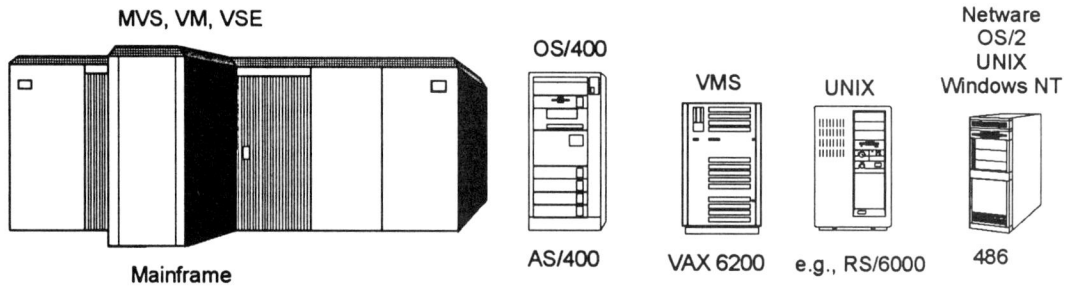

Figure 13-16 General Purpose Server Platforms

Chapter 14

The Personal Workplace

14.1 Introduction

Let's look at a representative user that the enterprise network supports. To this user the desktop (or laptop or handheld) computer is a workplace extension, the key considerations being that the computer and the required applications are available to do what needs to be done when it needs to be done.

The user tends to differentiate function and data based on ownership, accessibility, and control. For example, there are functions and user data that support the user's personal business needs (personal data related to the tasks at hand, likened to a note pad and calculator), there are department functions/applications and data (which could include office memos, location-specific tables, and that associated with unique local applications), and there are also company applications and data that are typically managed and controlled by some remote organization.

The primary considerations users have are that they will not run out of space to do the job and that the data and applications are safe (see Fig. 14-1).

The users are constantly being barraged with productivity carrots by telemarketing, by exciting ads and articles in professional journals, and even in travel magazines on airplanes. These products tend to be targeted to provide increased personal or departmental

Figure 14-1 Typical Enterprise Network User

Users decide what they need

productivity. Unfortunately, in today's pressure cooker business environment most executives, managers, business professionals, and even the very qualified technical professionals working closely with some of these technologies are constantly challenged and frequently confounded when it comes to making any recommendation or even assessing potential difficulties. (A frequent casualty of the end-user technology consumer market is detailed and thorough documentation.)

No single tool seems to do the job

This means that the only folks who are really able to assess and exploit many of these technologies are those individuals who are directly affected by the technologies or products. For example, to write this book I was very interested in new writing tools that would improve my productivity. (I currently use Word for Windows, WordPerfect, Pagemaker, several on-line dictionaries, and numerous graphics tools, including CorelDraw, Freelance, PicturePublisher, and Photoshop, just to name a few tools.) I use this many tools because no single tool seems to provide exactly what I need to gain the anticipated productivity. To make matters worse I have even lost function or flexibility when upgrading to a newer level of the product.

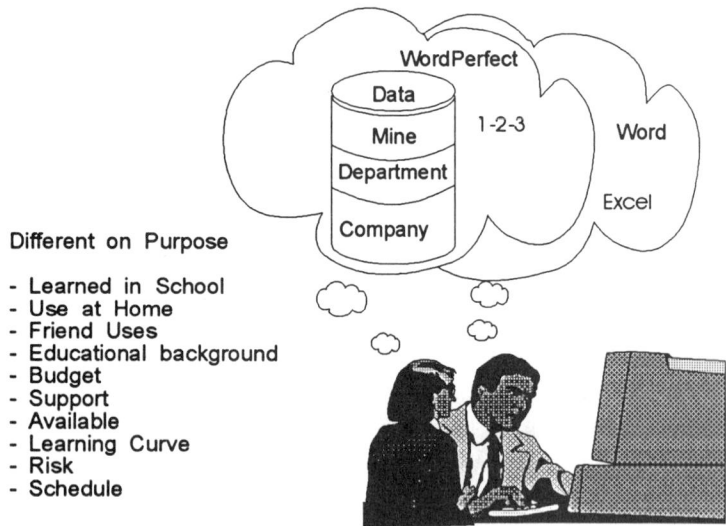

Different on Purpose

- Learned in School
- Use at Home
- Friend Uses
- Educational background
- Budget
- Support
- Available
- Learning Curve
- Risk
- Schedule

WordPerfect

Data
Mine
Department
Company

1-2-3   Word

Excel

Figure 14-2 Different Tools

The long and the short of this is that users and departments want or are using different tools (see Fig. 14-2), making it very difficult for the enterprise network organization to support them all. One fleeting thought might be to standardize, but this is only viable in a very controlled environment. For example, one company I worked with standardized on a Windows operating system and tools. The publications department users, however, wanted to use Macintosh systems since that was what they knew best. Because the company didn't falter on their resolve for a corporate standard, the publications personnel brought their own Macs to work.

Corporatewide standards are easily bypassed

But even if the company had purchased the Macs, the issues wouldn't have changed, since the corporate applications were not targeted to run on the Macs. This scenario has some even more obvious considerations. For example, consider Figure 14-3, which depicts a user surrounded with the technology of his trade:

- Enterprise network technology is characterized by the 3270 terminal and the 3270 printer

- A personal computer is used for some desktop letters and spreadsheets, which are printed on the personal laser printer

- A fax machine is required to receive and send urgent mail

- The everpresent copier in the background is required to make copies of the faxes, which could become a fire hazard if fax paper is not discarded

- The everpresent file cabinets and bookshelves to house the user's manuals and other business-related material.

Old and new technologies can represent a productivity challenge

If Figure 14-3 depicts a clutter on and around the desktop, it should be noted that I left out the wires and power strips required to support the various components. (Note that books and hardcopy play a major role in this desktop environment.)

Figure 14-3 portrays the enterprise network challenge - that of providing applications that coexist with the personal and departmental productivity tools and facilities. The vision is that a need for manuals and file cabinets and so forth. Ideally, the enterprise network technologies make the tasks of coordinating between the various business applications much easier, for example, the user depicted in Figure 14-4.

Figure 14-3   Typical Multi-technology Workdesk

Figure 14-4   Idealized Workstation

The implementation of this idealized work environment model (Fig. 14-4) can be approached from two directions:

- The single-system model, in which all of the applications are written to a common interface using a common operating environment

or

- A coexistence approach, whereby new and old applications are integrated with technologies (interfaces) that allow a given single-work environment to access and participate with the other applications in the environments.

Two approaches, but one works much better than the other

While neither is trivial at an enterprise level, which typically includes thousands of users with various interface and application requirements, the coexistence approach is more readily achievable and is certainly more timely. The exposure is usually quality of support. The more environments supported, the greater the probability that problem resolution for some subset will become slower based on the availability of the skills available in the traditional information services (IS) organization. In short the more you support, the greater the need to change the traditional support infrastructure. For example, a different support approach might be to buy a 7-day-with-24-hour 800 number support hotline service for specific environments.

In order to meaningfully discuss the integration considerations associated with NetWare, it is important to sort through what the users are working with (see Fig. 14-5). For example, what are personal computers, workstations and terminals? How do they relate to operating systems, the applications and the connectivity?

The term *personal computer,* or PC, is used in a generic sense to refer to a single-user desktop computer, ergo the term personal. PC is typically applied to Intel-based, microcomputer-based systems, but is appropriately used to include non-Intel-based systems such as the Macintosh desktop computers. These systems come in a shape that fits on your desk; as tower systems, which typically stand on the floor; and laptop systems, which you can put on almost any flat surface, including desks, airplane trays, your knees, and phone booth surfaces.

Personal computer:
- **Single user**
- **Various technologies**

Figure 14-5   Workstation Terminology

Typical operating systems include DOS (Microsoft DOS, IBM DOS, and Novell DOS), Windows, OS/2, Mac System/7, and UNIX (e.g., SCO UNIX and IBM AIX). A representation of personal computers is shown in Figure 14-6 and these icons are used throughout this book.

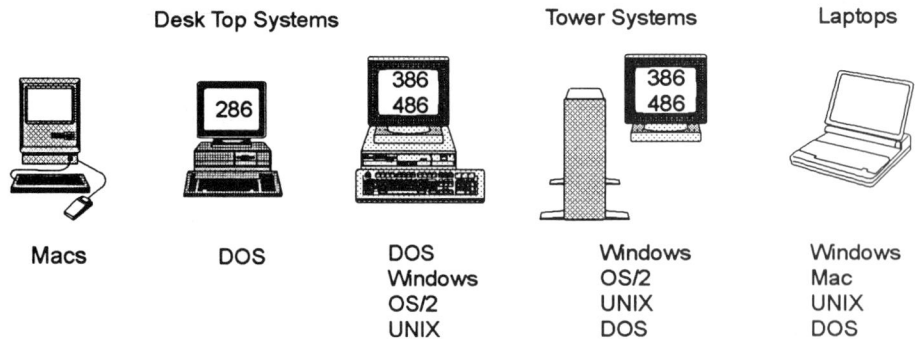

Desk Top Systems			Tower Systems	Laptops
Macs	DOS	DOS Windows OS/2 UNIX	Windows OS/2 UNIX DOS	Windows Mac UNIX DOS

Figure 14-6   Personal Computers

The term *workstation* is usually used in the context of a computer system:

- RISC-based computer with a UNIX operating system. In this context it is used to differentiate it from a PC and a UNIX server.

- Hardware and software configurations that initially provided more power than PCs, had more peripherals, and a had a much higher price tag than a PC. Technological hardware and software advances have blurred the distinctions over the past few years.

- Any personal computer and RISC UNIX computer system that is not being used as a server or host system.

I use the term *workstation* in this broader context (see Fig. 14-7), and I use the term *UNIX-workstations* whenever I refer to UNIX workstations specifically. The two significant criteria needed to qualify as a workstation are that it is a computer (versus a terminal) and that it is attached to some host service.

Workstation means single-user-connected computer

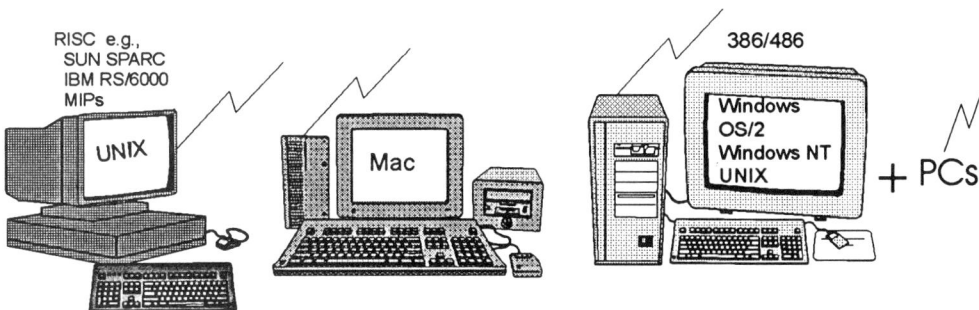

Figure 14-7   Workstations

Workstations can use single-user operating systems that process one transaction at a time, such as DOS, or they can use operating systems that support multiple tasks running at the same time. IBM's OS/2, UNIX, and Microsoft's Windows NT operating systems provide these workstations with the ability to run multiple tasks at the same time.

The UNIX operating system originated as a multi-user operating system and several vendors provide their workstation UNIX versions with the ability to support multiple users on the same system when the appropriate communication hardware adapters are present. This configuration is sometimes referred to this as a *multiuser workstation*. To my way of thinking, however, the term *multiuser workstation* is really a characterization to connote low price. Based on the hardware and software usage, this configuration is more analogous to a mainframe or midrange system (a host) with terminals connected or a server with clients connected than a workstation. I therefore use *workstation* to connote a *single-user* hardware and software configuration.

The term multi-user workstation means host

14.2 NetWare and the Workstation

The easiest way to discuss NetWare's role in the enterprise network is to put the services in a workstation context. This approach shows not only how NetWare provides services, but also how it can participate in reducing the complexity associated with:

- Multiple mixed workstation environments
- Multiple mixed services access from a single workstation
- Compound (or intermediate) services

The easiest benefit to describe is the multiple mixed workstation environment. This is often applicable in organizations where several different workstation operating systems are used. The primary objective of NetWare in these configurations is to provide disk space, more rigorous backup and recovery management, printer sharing, and communication gateway sharing. Additionally, certain files need to be exchanged among specific users, and last but not least, mail and attachments can be exchanged. The configuration in Figure 14-8 represents this environment. The challenge is for each workstation to be able to any or all servers.

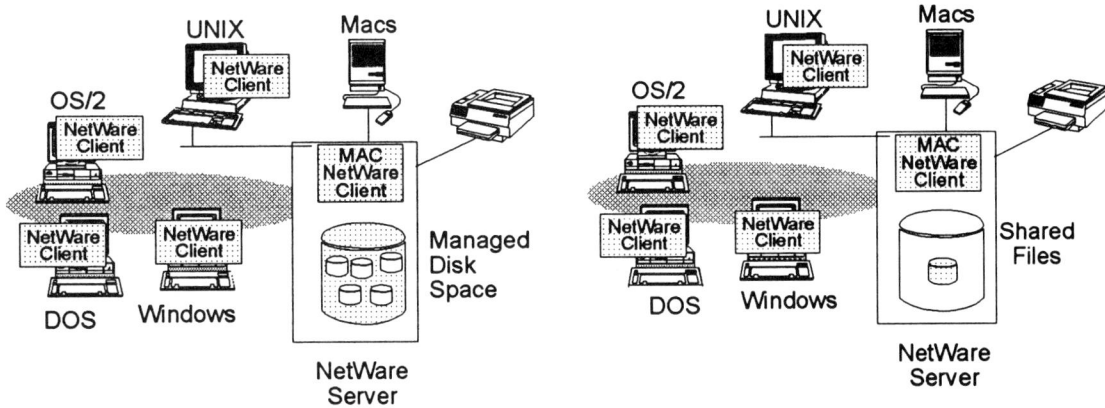

Figure 14-8   NetWare Space and File Sharing Services

While this mix appear to be a representative environment, I am going to go through the various environments from a workstation-user standpoint in within a NetWare context in order to avoid descriptions that get so complex they defy English descriptions. Figure 14-9 depicts the workstations we will look at with some specific environments.

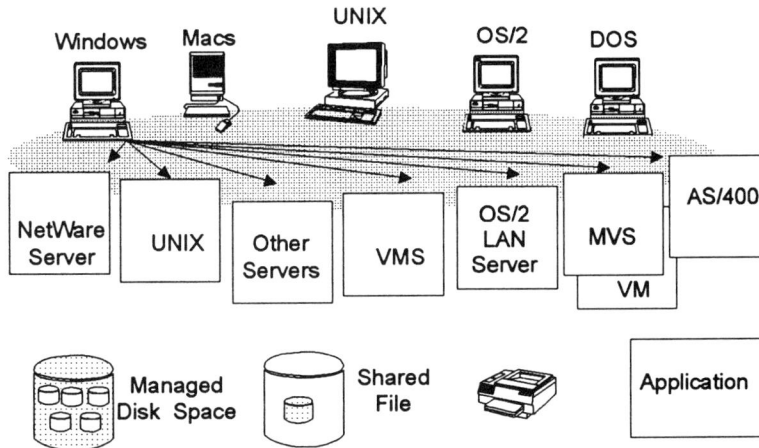

Figure 14-9   Workstation Access to Multiple Servers

To keep the discussion simple, in the rest of this chapter we will only look at representative services such as managed disk space, file sharing, and application access.

14.3 DOS and Windows Workstations

The DOS or Windows-based workstation can access the various services and applications depicted in Figure 14-10.

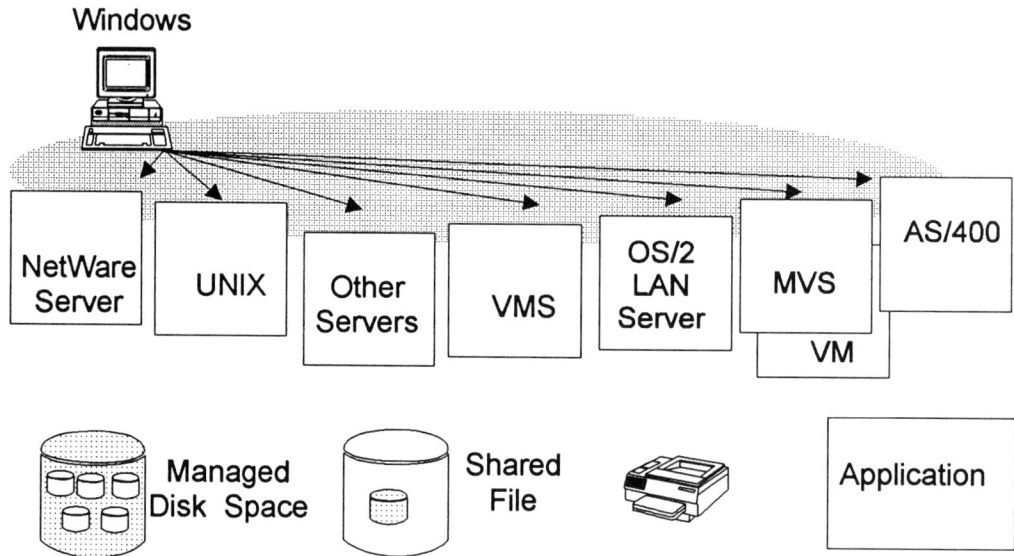

Figure 14-10   Windows Access to Multiple Platforms

Now let's look at some of the DOS or Windows workstation access and service options to access other than just the NetWare servers. Since all these different options and subtitles can become confusing, I'm going to start with Figure 14-11 which depicts the different products and configurations that a workstation user might need. The specific descriptions for each of these follow.

14.3.1 NetWare LAN Print and File Support

Let's begin with the DOS workstation. (The workstation could be an IBM PC, XT, AT, or compatible, IBM PS/2; or Compaq 386/486 or compatible.) In our example the DOS workstation might be configured with a Token Ring adapter for LAN attach-

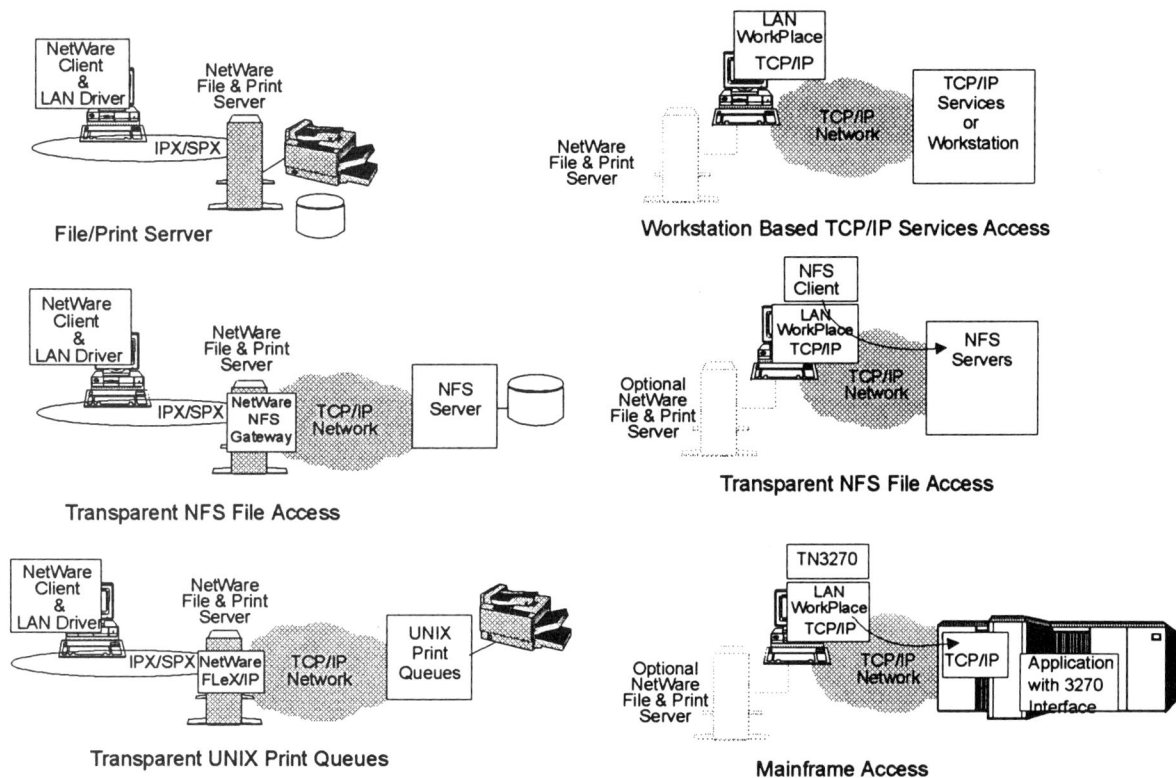

Figure 14-11   DOS and Windows Platform Access

ment. The workstation startup procedures have been set up to bring up a NetWare workstation shell with the Token Ring and the appropriate drivers.

The startup procedure establishes network connectivity for the workstation. When the user logs in the appropriate NetWare server, the Netware profile associated with that authenticated user's ID determines the user's virtual configuration and enables the appropriate disk and printer redirectors. One could compare this log in with a mainframe TSO or CMS log-on and the user profile that is set up for the logged on user.

For example, the workstation (see Fig. 14-12) could have a C-drive and a local printer (LPT1). After the appropriate network log in the user profile might provide access to several additional drives, such as D, E, and F. Additionally, the user might have a logical printer port LPT2 for output that is to be directed to the NetWare printer. All access to the NetWare resources is transparent to the workstation software, which sees the NetWare managed resources as local devices. They are really virtual devices in that the disks are NetWare managed disk space that they can spread across physical drives.

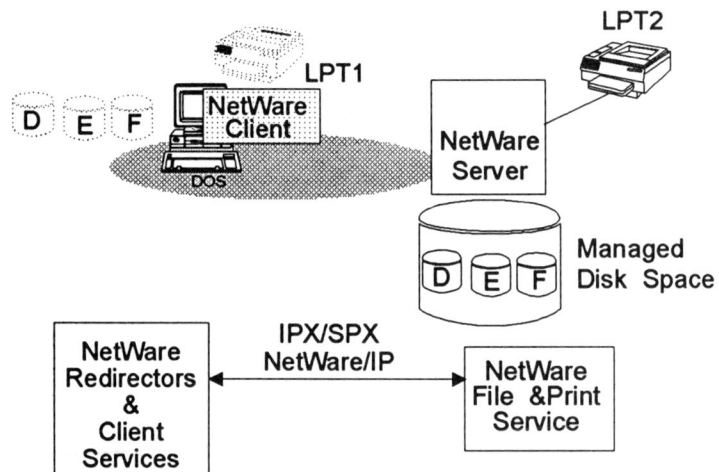

Figure 14-12   DOS and Windows File Server Support

In our example scenario the NetWare Client for DOS enables the user to access all resources available on the network that the user is authorized to access. The basic shell services have been provided by NetWare for several years, however, with the introduction of NetWare 4.0 additional memory management and memory usage capabilities, some built-in diagnostic and automatic recovery from disconnect capabilities, and some optional security and performance enhancements were added. These additions are discussed separately.

The NetWare Client for DOS is based on NetWare's modular universal client architecture. This universal client architecture provides a common technology for access to all NetWare services and resources available from any NetWare 2.x, NetWare 3.x, NetWare 4.x, or NetWare for UNIX server. NetWare 4.0's Directory Services provides the ability to access multiple servers with a single log in.

NetWare's client architecture provides access to a consistent set of network services for all desktop platforms supported by NetWare. These platforms include:

- DOS
- Macintosh
- Microsoft Windows
- Microsoft Windows NT
- UNIX

One of the primary consideration in the DOS environment is effective memory management, since 640 K becomes awfully small considering the number of programs and services that need to run in it. To provide some relief here, the universal client provides a memory-size optimized set of selectable loadable modules (referred to as VLMs). The appropriate VLMs are selected for the specific workstation service requirements, such as automatic reconnect. Additionally, the VLMs can be swapped in and out of expanded or extended memory automatically. This leaves more of the 640 K available for user applications.

To minimize the disruption of an unwanted disconnection with the server the client supports an autoreconnect service. Once the client software is reloaded, autoreconnect automatically reconnects the client to the server and rebuilds the client's environment to match what its state was before the interruption.

As a remote support tool the NetWare Client for DOS includes a network management responder (NMR.VLM). This responder module provides network performance and configuration information that is displayed by the NetWare Management System (NMS) and for troubleshooting and tuning the network.

The NetWare Client provides an optional VLM, SECU-RITY.VLM, to address enterprise network security requirements. This is part of Netware 4.x's enhanced security that provides the appropriate packet signature that makes it very difficult for a would-be intruder to forge packets.

The Windows workstation scenario is identical to the DOS scenario from a usage standpoint: all Windows utilities see the NetWare managed resources as virtual devices. Additionally, NetWare's unique facilities are accessible from icons on the Windows screen. The primary exception in the Windows environment is that NetWare can be loaded either prior to loading Windows or from Windows as a DOS box. The primary difference here is that if the NetWare Client is loaded prior to Windows, the NetWare services apply to all Windows activity, if loaded from a DOS box, the access to NetWare is limited to requests from within the DOS box.

From a memory requirements standpoint, the DOS or Windows workstation has a LAN driver, the IPX/SPX stack or NetWare/IP stack, and some NetWare shell functions.

14.3.2 DOS Workstation Shares UNIX Network Files

Let's say that the DOS/Windows user needs to access and/or share files with a remote UNIX system. The UNIX system currently stores the specific files by using NFS.

This can be accomplished by a NetWare-network-connected workstation user without any additional software on the client DOS or the UNIX target by using the NetWare NFS Gateway capability. The NetWare NFS Gateway is NetWare server-based software that transparently extends DOS and MS Windows users' access to files to any NFS server using the existing IPX/SPX protocol stack for communications between the DOS/Windows workstation and the the NetWare NFS Gateway NLMs. The NFS Gateway uses NetWare's TCP/IP NLMs to communicate with the target NFS (see Fig. 14-13).

The NFS Gateway is configured during initialization when the NLM uses the information in the configuration file and creates the NetWare volumes that are then mounted on the specified NFS server.

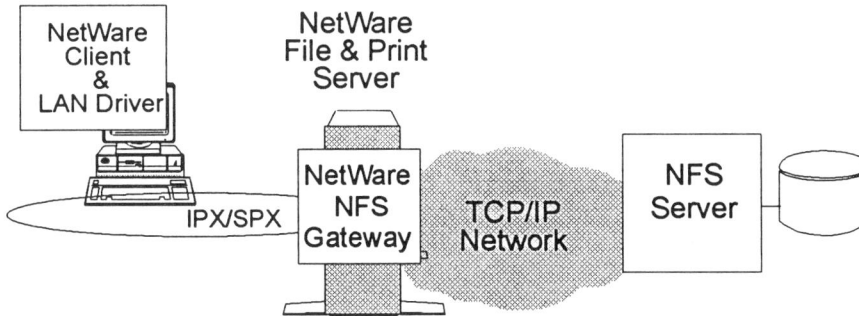

Figure 14-13 Transparent NFS File Access

The NFS servers being accessed must have the Version 1 mount protocol, the Version 2 NFS protocols, and the Version 3 network lock manager and status monitor protocols installed. The only installation requirement outside of the NetWare server is the modification of the export data base on the remote NFS server.

Services supported:

- Sun Microsystems, Inc., Network File System (NFS) Protocol, Version 2

- Sun Microsystems, Inc., Mount Protocol

- Sun Microsystems, Inc., External Data Representation Protocol (XDR)

- Sun Microsystems, Inc., Remote Procedure Call (RPC)

- Sun Microsystems, Inc., Portmapper Protocol

- MIT, X Window System-X11/R4

- VT100/220 Terminal emulation access to XCONSOLE

• RFC 854 Telnet used as an initiation and transport mechanism

The NFS Netware gateway provides a solution for accessing the NFS-based data without any additional workstation overhead.

14.3.3 Routing Print Output to UNIX Print Queues

If the DOS/Windows workstation user wants to direct print output to a remote UNIX system print queue, it can do so if the NetWare FLeX/IP NLM and TCP/IP NLMs are loaded on the Netware server. NetWare FLeX/IP provides the DOS or Windows user with a transparent redirection capability that routes the output to the designated UNIX print queue and designated printers (see Fig. 14-14).

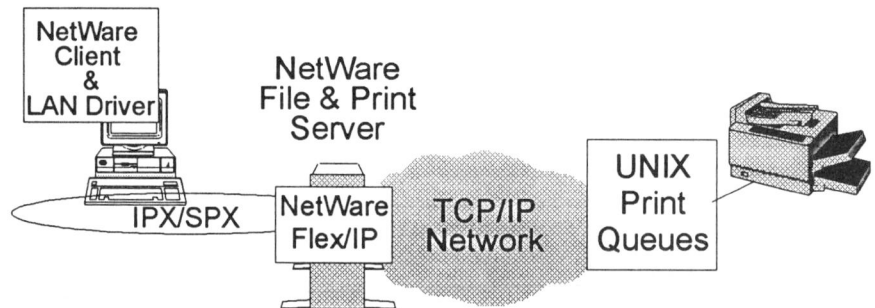

Figure 14-14   Transparent UNIX Print Queues

This is achieved totally transparently to the workstation user and the workstation, since it is all done in the server.

14.3.4 DOS Workstation with TCP/IP Interoperability

Another DOS/Windows workstation connection option provided by Novell allows each workstation to participate in their company's or public TCP/IP network. The workstation can be connected to the NetWare network; however, this is totally optional.

The business requirement is for the DOS/Windows user to access TCP/IP services across the company's internet. It is decided that TCP/IP provides the most flexible network and cross-platform services since the target systems include UNIX workstations, UNIX servers, several Digital VAX systems, and an IBM mainframe. For now let's assume that there is no NetWare network.

Novell's LAN WorkPlace for DOS is selected for the DOS/Windows workstations because it provides DOS and Windows with interoperability with all TCP/IP interconnected systems and services in a familiar way and exploits Windows' graphical user interface. Since LAN WorkPlace for DOS is a workstation-based software package, the user's workstation now contains the communications adapter drivers, TCP/IP protocol stack, and the LAN WorkPlace functional services. Using these services, DOS/Windows has the following feature's:

- Remote system log in via various terminal emulation software, such as:

  DEC VT100 and VT220 terminal emulation
  Windows TN3270 terminal emulation
  DOS 3270 terminal emulation (this is an option)
  TelAPI support for third-party terminal emulation
  A DOS X Windows client (XPC) and Telnet server

- File transfer capabilities

  Windows-based FTP client, Rapid Filer
  FTP Client for DOS users
  FTP servers for DOS and Windows users
  Directory copy support
  Automatic file type determination

- Printing services

  RPR, LPR, LPQ, and LPRM for remote and local printing
  L-utilities enable printing on UNIX- and VMS-printers

- UNIX-style services

  R-utilities for remote command execution, file, and print

services
Finger and Talk to communicate with other network users

- Remote connection support

  Serial Line Internet Protocol (SLIP)
  Point-to-Point Protocol (PPP)
  Application Programming Interfaces (APIs)
  Support for Windows Socket APIs

- Supports applications from other companies, such as:

  Quarterdeck's DESQview/X
  VisionWare's X-Vision
  Oracle's SQL Net TCP/IP for MS-DOS
  The Sybase PC Net-Library for DOS

Access to these features provide the DOS/Windows user with the ability to log into remote TCP/IP systems, transfer and accept files being transferred, and direct output to local and remote printers (see Fig. 14-15).

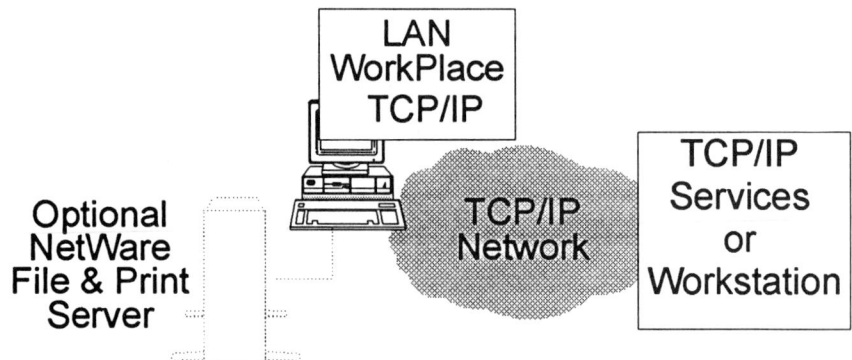

Figure 14-15   Workstation Based TCP/IP Services

LAN WorkPlace supports the following U.S. Department of Defense Internet Protocol standards:

- IP (Internet Protocol) RFC 791
- IP Subnet Extension RFC 950
- IP Broadcast Datagrams RFC 919

- IP Broadcast Datagrams with Subnets RFC 922
- IP on Ethernet RFC 894
- IP on ARCnet RFC 1201
- IPX or IP Tunneling RFC 1234
- TCP (Transmission Control Protocol, 0-64 sockets) RFC 793
- UDP (User Datagram Protocol, 0-32 sockets) RFC 768
- IP-IEEE (Internet Protocol on IEEE 802) RFC 1042
- NetBIOS (NetBIOS Service Protocol on TCP/IP) RFCs 1001, 1002
- ARP (Address Resolution Protocol) RFC 826
- RARP (Reverse Address Resolution Protocol) RFC 903
- ICMP (Internet Control Message Protocol) RFC 792
- DNS (Domain Name System) Resolver RFCs 1034, 1035
- TELNET (Telnet) Protocol RFC 854

VT-series emulation for both DOS and MS Windows

- FTP (File Transfer Protocol) RFCs 949, 959
- TFTP (Trivial File Transfer Protocol) RFC 783

Both client and server for DOS

- BOOTP (Bootstrap Protocol) RFCs 951, 1084
- IP over ARCnet Networks RFC 1201
- IPX over IP Tunneling RFC 1234
- LPD (Line Printer Daemon Protocol) RFC 1179
- RPC (Remote Procedure Call) RDC 1057
- PPP (Point-to-Point Protocol) RFCs 1171, 1172
- SLIP (Serial Line Internet Protocol) RFCs 1055, 1144
- SNMP (Simple Network Management Protocol) RFC 1157
- MIB (Management Information Base) RFCs 1156, 1213

If the DOS/Windows user needs the ability to access remote files, NFS Client for LAN WorkPlace product is installed in the workstation to augment the LAN WorkPlace product. This allows the user to transparently access files on remote NFS servers using standard DOS and Windows interfaces (see Fig. 14-16).

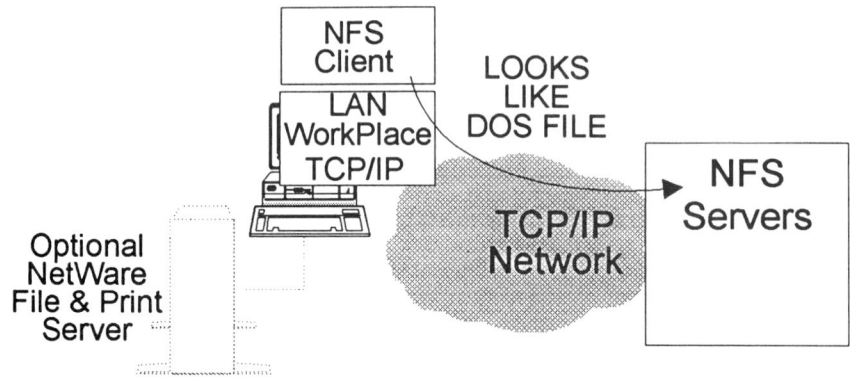

Figure 14-16   Transparent NFS File Access

To connect to the IBM mainframe (MVS in our scenario) the DOS/Windows workstation must include the TN3270 for LAN WorkPlace software. This software enables the user to log in to the IBM mainframes running MVS or VM (see Fig. 14-17), at which point the MVS system sees the user as a logged-in IBM 3278 display terminal (models 2 through 5 are supported). The user can even log into several different applications and different mainframe systems at the same time. The DOS/Windows work-station user can now access the 3270 application and capture the screen content, transfer files between the mainframe environ-ment, if the mainframe application is using TSO, CMS, or a CICS application, as well as print to disk. The product also supports mainframe-based applications that use extended attributes, such as blinking, highlighting, and reverse video.

For the corporate application developer, TN3270 for LAN WorkPlace also includes an Application Programming Interface (API) that can be used to write workstation applications that access the system as a 3270 and send or receive files or execute transactions.

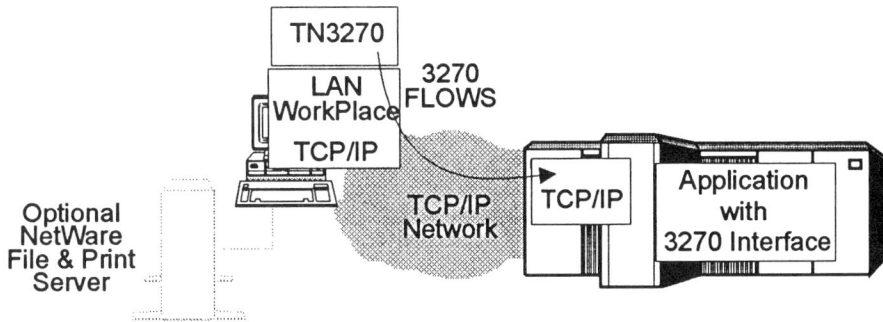

Figure 14-17   Mainframe Access with TN3270

So far the workstation contains the communications adapter driver, TCP/IP, and potentially three services: the base LAN WorkPlace software, the NFS Client for LAN WorkPlace, and TN3270. (The access to remote TCP/IP systems via other terminal emulators such as the VT100 is part of the base, but third-party emulators may also be used.)

LAN WorkPlace for DOS supports Novell's Open Data Link Interface (ODI) technology such that the TCP/IP and NetWare IPX/SPX protocols can concurrently share common network adapters (see Fig. 14-18) to connect to Ethernet, Token Ring, FDDI, and ARCnet networks.

LAN WorkPlace also provides an IP Tunnel ODI Driver that encapsulates IPX/SPX in user datagram protocol/internet protocol (UDP/IP) for connection to remote NetWare servers, allowing the workstation user to access NetWare IPX resources over a TCP/IP internet (see Fig. 14-19).

If the workstation is also connected to NetWare or uses the encapsulation feature, the NetWare IPX/SPX stack is loaded in addition to the TCP/IP stack. With the recent addition of Net-Ware/IP, only the LAN WorkPlace TCP/IP and NetWare/IP stacks are required to access the NetWare file server.

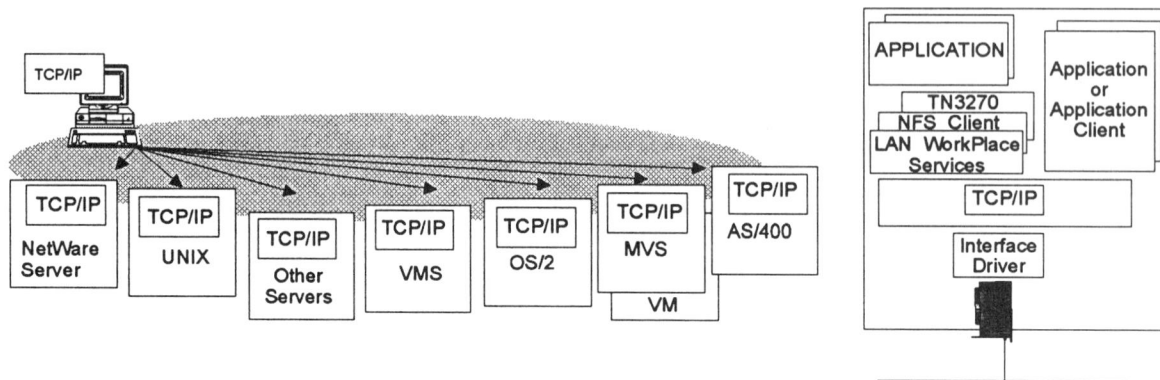

Figure 14-18   Workstations Using TCP/IP

LAN WorkPlace for DOS is delivered as a single workstation product and each participating DOS/Windows workstation has a copy of it. The user or network supervisor must install LAN WorkPlace for DOS software in each workstation one at a time.

To use NetWare/IP the DOS and Windows workstations require:
- Netware/IP client software
- LAN WorkPlaceTCP/IP transport
- Windows Socket Library
- An ODI driver
- VLM programs and utilities
- Transport support utilities
- NetWare Tools for DOS and Windows

in addition to the NetWare/IP module in the NetWare server

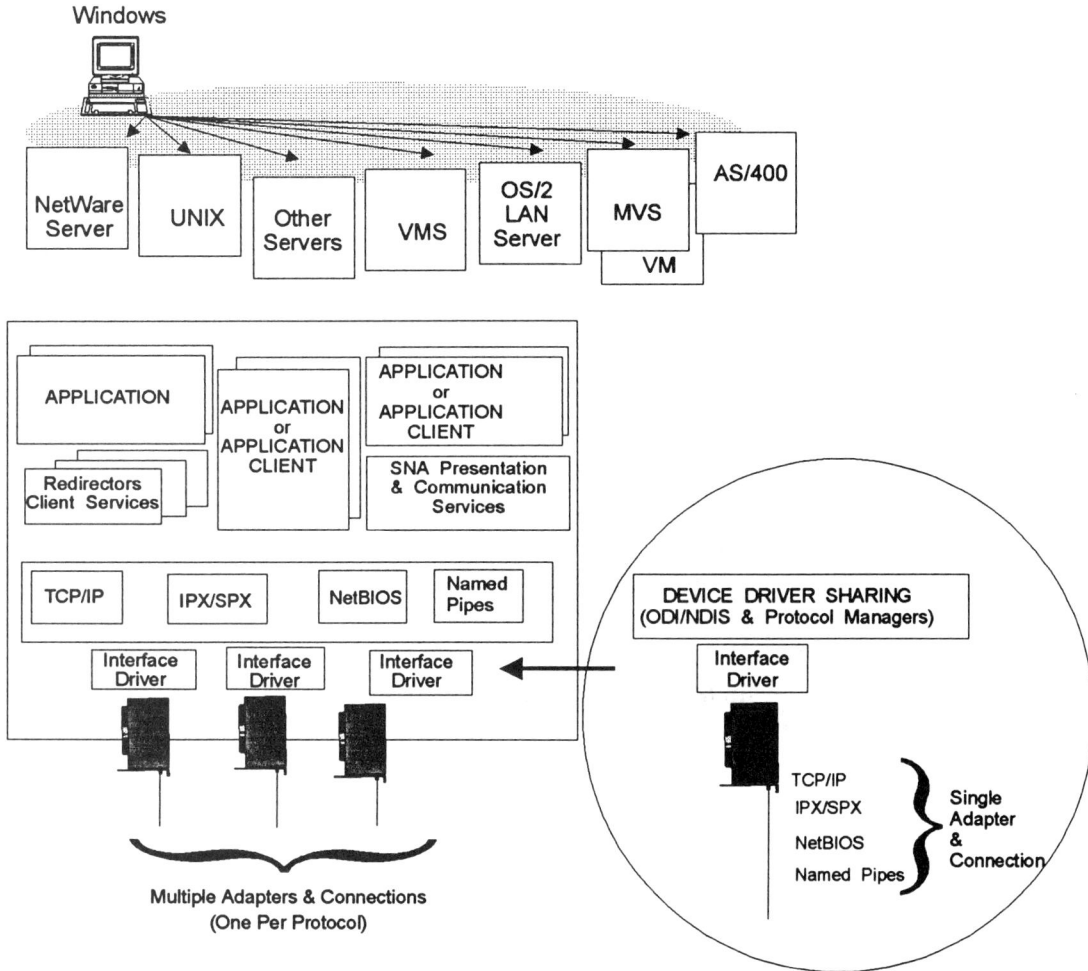

Figure 14-19   ODI Adapter Sharing

As an alternative to the multiple copies and multiple points of installation and administration Novell can provide LAN Work-Group. LAN WorkGroup is a workgroup package of LAN Work-Place for DOS that uses the NetWare server to store a single copy of the software, and provides central setup and administration of the TCP/IP configurations and internet addresses and services. LAN WorkGroup enables a workgroup administrator to perform a single installation of the product onto a NetWare server, enabling all server users to share the copy. It also provides a platform from which administrators can perform global updates, configure workstations, and monitor use. Administration of the workgroup is centralized on the NetWare server, freeing users from these tasks.

14.3.5 DOS and Windows Users Access the IBM AS/400

DOS and Windows workstation users often find that they must access their organization's or the enterprise's AS/400 system. To accomplish this the workstation must have 5250 terminal emulation software or have IBM's AS/400 PC Support (PCS) program installed. The PC Support program provides the workstation user with the ability to access the AS/400 resident applications as a terminal, to transfer files, to use the AS/400 printers (referred to as Virtual Printer), to store and share workstation information using the AS/400 Shared Folders function, to send and receive messages to and from the AS/400, and to submit AS/400 commands from the workstation.

The most pervasive approach to sharing AS/400 data with the workstation user is for the user to use the data on the AS/400 directly. This is accomplished with terminal emulation. Typically terminal emulation software supports the IBM 5250, 3196, 3197C, 3197D, and 3477 displays and 3812 printers. Terminal emulation software connection options usually include providing a direct connection from the workstation to a communications line, a direct connection to the AS/400 local controllers, or to connect directly to an integrated communications adapter via leased or dial-up connections. Alternatively, a LAN-connected workstations terminal emulators can connect to communications gateway or they may connect through Novell's NetWare for SAA. Most AS/400 terminal software packages support the NetWare for SAA (see Fig. 14-20).

From the workstation user's standpoint the terminal emulation software packages provide the same features independently of the connection. However, if the user's workstation is directly connected via a communications line or LAN, it is likely that a significant portion of the worksation's memory space is consumed by the emulation and communications software. This

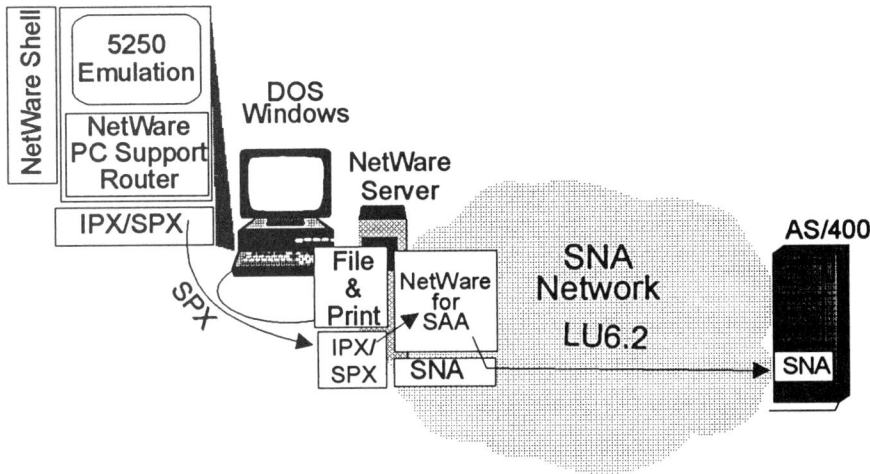

Figure 14-20   IBM 5250 Emulation with NetWare for SAA

usually leads to more expensive communications adapters or to using a LAN-connected gateway that supports the communications end of the emulation.

Let's look at a few DOS and Windows workstation user scenarios. A finance company that has several AS/400s and has installed multiple NetWare LANs to support the PCs with disk space, local DOS file sharing, and print sharing. As part of a new business application process the user must access several AS/400 applications in order to make the correct choices in processing a loan application. In the past this check was made by someone else who stacked up the requests and processed them in batches.

The user's workstation is attached to a Token Ring LAN that is connected to the NetWare server and the AS/400. Having determined that a terminal emulation program can run in the workstation and use the same Token Ring adapter as is being used by the NetWare connection, a terminal emulation software purchase is made based on its presentation capabilities and flexibility. This technical solution also appeared to be the least expensive since no additional hardware was needed.

After loading the workstation with the emulator and the appropriate communications software there wasn't enough of the 640K memory left to run the application concurrently. The application, which was really a DOS application running in a DOS window, began to hang and Windows frequently sent messages that it was waiting for memory to free up.

After some research the user discovered that more than a third of the workstation memory overhead and some of the communications workload could be eliminated with an outboard communications gateway. With the communications portions of the protocol stack off-loaded to the gateway, only the presentation portion of the emulation software must run in the workstation. Having determined this the user reviewed the gateway options and found that most of the gateway products available tended to be matched with that vendor's terminal emulation software and that the gateway would require a dedicated PC to serve as the gateway.

The user ended up selecting Netware for SAA as the solution base because it allowed the user to use the selected terminal emulation software without the communications portion and to install the "gateway" function on the existing NetWare server. The user also installed the HostPrint NLM, which directed AS/400 output to the appropriate NetWare-managed printer using standard NetWare Print Services.

Another company with a NetWare server that provided file and print services had a similar requirement, that is, to access key decision data from the AS/400 system. However, this company wanted to have a more integrated implementation. The IS manager had recommended that the users install IBM's PC support on their workstations to provide the users with access to the AS/400 applications using the 5250 emulation provided in the PCS package. This access would give the users the ability to automate transfer files between the AS/400 and the workstation and more importantly, it allowed the AS/400 to act as a central shared data repository using the Shared Folder function (see Fig. 14-21).

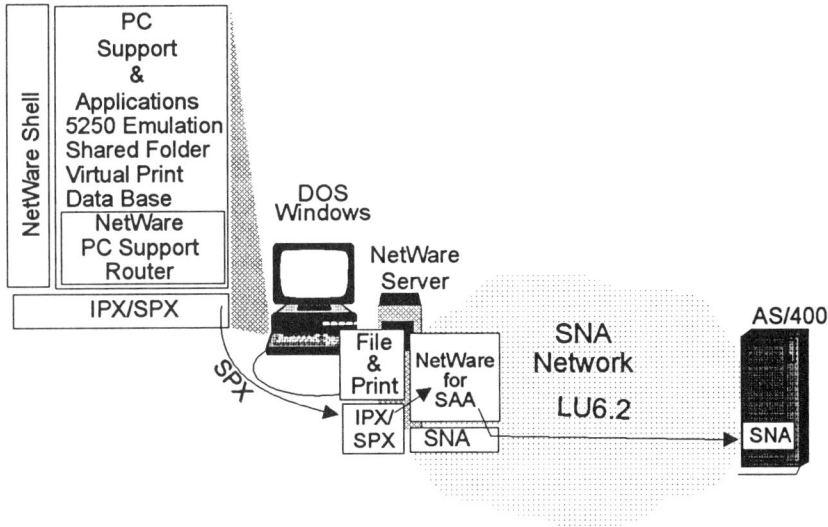

Figure 14-21   IBM PCS Support with NetWare for SAA

The implementation of PCS again exposed some significant overheads in a workstation requiring the IBM LAN Support Program in each workstation in addition to the IPX/SPX protocol stack and network driver. The total overhead on a workstation ranges from 60 K to 300 KBytes, depending on the specific configuration. By installing NetWare for SAA in the server and a NetWare PC Support Router in the workstation, only a 5-KBytes memory overhead would be introduced. The NetWare-supplied router encapsulates the PC Support data within IPX/SPX packets and ships the data to Netware for SAA, which in turn sends it to the AS/400 using advanced program-to-program communications (APPC) sessions. NetWare for SAA supports up to 253 PC Support sessions. However, care must be taken to count correctly. For example, if PC Support uses a session for each function that the workstation invokes, a workstation user using the virtual printer function, the shared folder, terminal access, and sending a file is essentially using 4 sessions. Four such users would therefore use up a 16-user version of NetWare.

There are several data base packages available that build on IBM's PC Support and NetWare for SAA to aid in the development of reports, graphical displays, and decision support information based on AS/400 stored data. For example, Gupta's SQLRouter, as depicted in Figure 14-22 provides report generation and application tools to access remote data-based systems, such as are found on the AS/400. In the figure Gupta's SQLWindows sits on Gupta's SQLRouter to AS/400, which uses IBM PC Support facilities and takes advantage of NetWare's PC Support Router.

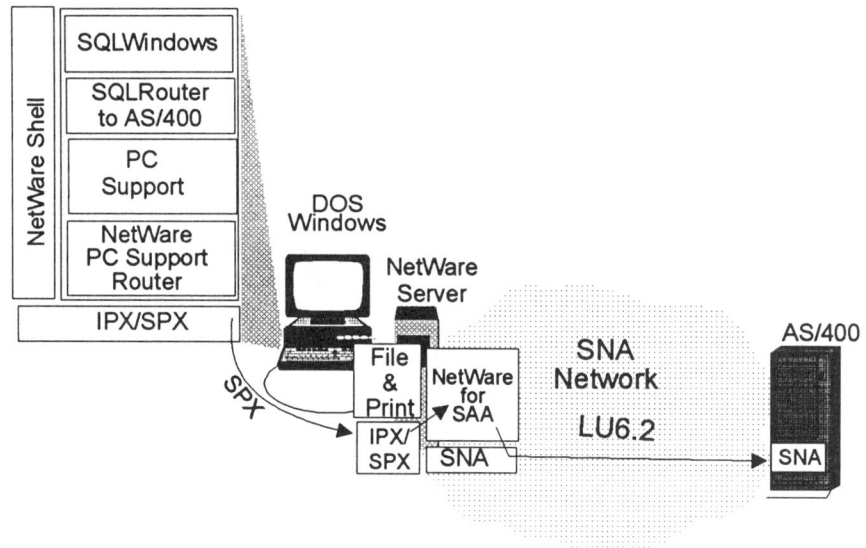

Figure 14-22   Gupta's SQL to AS/400

Figure 14-23 graphically depicts the DOS or Windows workstation to AS/400 capabilities. Note that the flow for the most part is from the workstation to the AS/400. Only the print output from the AS/400 to NetWare HostPrint flows in the opposite direction. The printer output can be the result of an AS/400 logged-on application or initiated from an AS/400 application. The workstation user can also cause print to be directed to the AS/400 printer.

Now having seen the options for sharing resources with an AS/400, it is also important to note that the AS/400 or multiple AS/400s can provide a network for accessing remote NetWare servers. The AS/400 and its communication lines can be used as network hub and multiple AS/400s can be used to provide a backbone network by using NetWare for SAA and NetWare SNA Links.

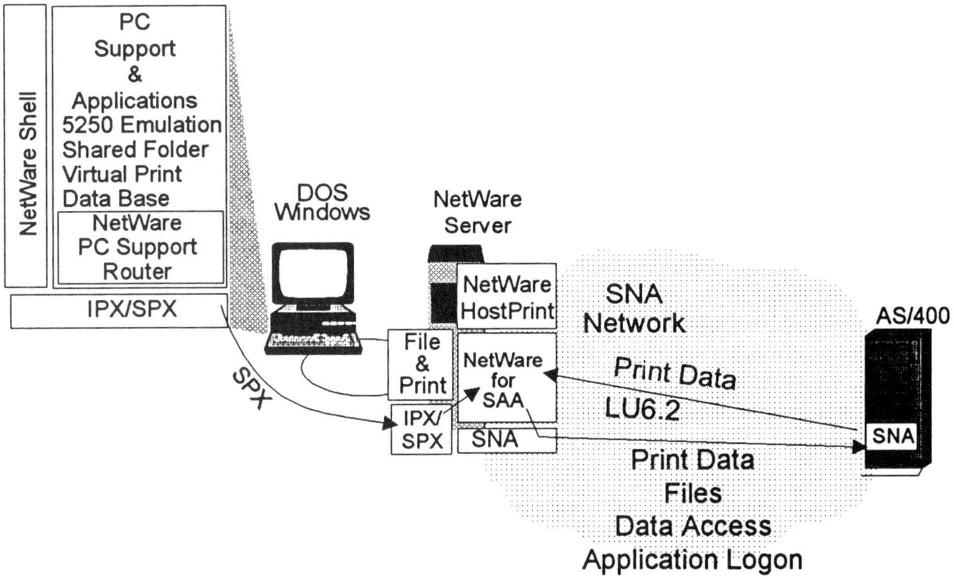

Figure 14-23 PC Support and NetWare HostPrint

Figure 14-24 shows three NetWare LANs connected to an AS/400, which transfers encapsulated IPX/SPX traffic to the target servers. For example, the workstation on LAN A can access the file server on LAN C and send printed output to LAN B just as if these networks were on the same NetWare network. NetWare SNA Links receives traffic targeted to cross the SNA network, it encapsulates the IPX/SPX or TCP/IP traffic, and passes it across to NetWare for SAA, which has a session established with the destination NetWare for SAA and SNA Links through the AS/400. It is important to note that the session is through the AS/400 because of its APPN support. There is no store and forward application required on the AS/400. From an SNA session standpoint the session is from SNA Links in Server

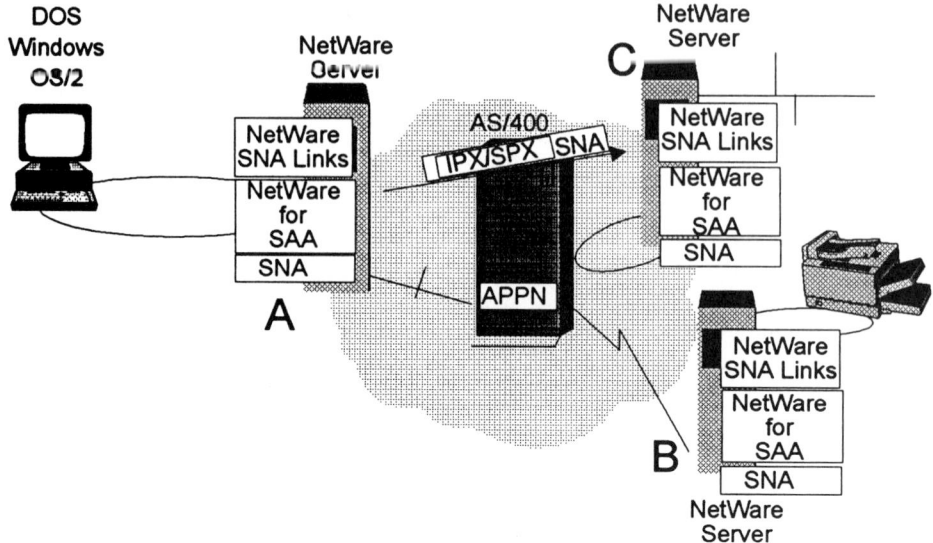

Figure 14-24   Workstation to Remote NetWare

A to SNA Links in Server C, and so forth. In this configuration the SNA backbone network is the AS/400.

Figure 14-25 depicts three AS/400s that form an SNA backbone. The three NetWare LANs are connected to the nearest AS/400 using various connectivity technology. The SNA Links sessions are still point-to-point, that is, the SNA Links software in server A is in session with the SNA Links in server C and probably has another session with server B. The AS/400s are essentially intermediate nodes.

Having looked at Windows and DOS workstation users capabilities with NetWare, UNIX services, TCP/IP services, and AS/400 services, let's look at how these users would access an IBM mainframe.

14.3.6 Accessing the IBM Mainframe over SNA

The easiest mainframe access is via a terminal emulator, just as it was for UNIX, TCP/IP, and AS/400 systems. There are also multiple ways to access the mainframe. The most frequent access is via an SNA network through an SNA front-end processor that provides the communication controls and protects the mainframe

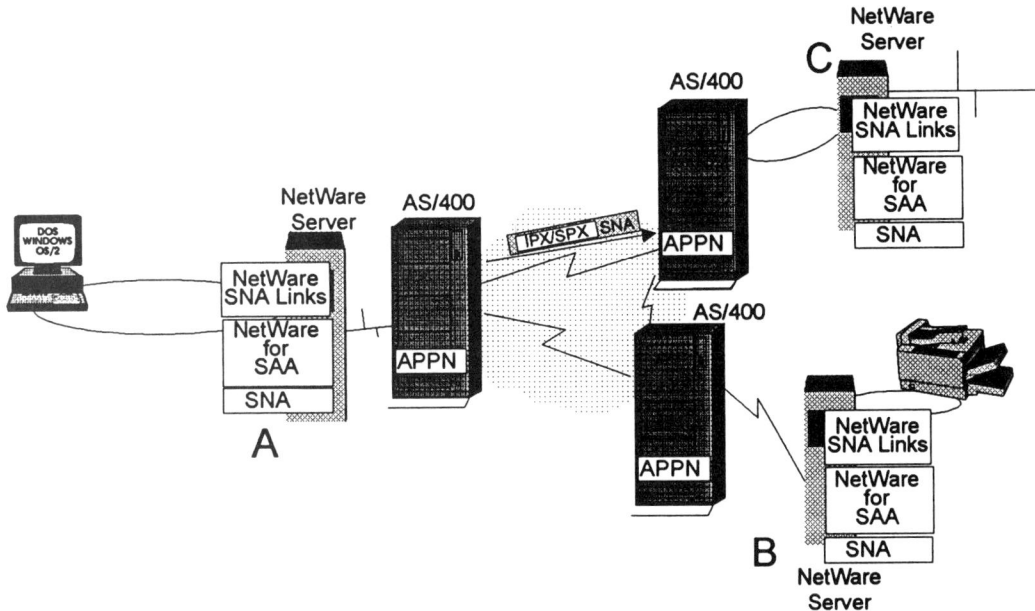

Figure 14-25   Workstation using SNA Links Backbone

from handling the communications interrupts. The data are passed from the front end to the mainframe in an orderly and effective manner.

We have already discussed how a workstation using TCP/IP and TN3270 can access the mainframe's 3270 applications if the mainframe has TCP/IP support. Some vendors even provide TN3270 gateways that sit in front of the mainframe and convert the TCP/IP flows into standard SNA 3270 flows such that TCP/IP doesn't have to run on the mainframe.

Although TCP/IP is gaining popularity most mainframe connections are still through SNA. The DOS and Windows workstations use 3270 emulators to access the mainframe, just as the AS/400 users did; however, there are many more choices for mainframe terminal emulation than AS/400 terminal emulation.

NetWare for SAA provides a very solid base as a communications subsystem to support the workstation access and assure reasonable performance and availability.

Before we look at the connection options let's look at what services the workstation users are accessing and how. The most prevalent workstation to mainframe access is to the mainframe's on-line transaction processing systems. The typical scenario is that the workstation user has 3270 emulation software in the workstation together with the other nonmainframe applications. In a DOS workstation the emulator software is typically set up to be hot-keyed to when needed. (Hot-keying may involve depressing two keys, such as the ALT key and the Esc key, at the same time.) In a Windows environment the emulator is usually run as a window or minimized to an icon until needed. When needed the terminal screen is presented and the users enter data into the fields as they have done for the last 25 years. The mainframe sees all interactions as if they were from a supported 3270 terminal. This approach allows users to access VM, MVS, and VSE systems with little regard to mainframe software levels, and the mainframe applications are unaffected by the attributes of the workstation (see Fig. 14-26).

There are many 3270 emulators available, but care must be taken to select one that meets your applications needs. Keyboard mapping and national language support are often bothersome.

Using the dumb terminal screen, however, has lost a lot of its appeal since the workstation tools provide more sophisticated services and "eye candy." By eye-candy I mean the use of colorful icons and data presentations , which are much more appealing to the eye than green, gray, or white characters on a screen. To assist this, several masking techniques have emerged.

Historically, some companies wrote workstation application programs that masked the user from the actual screen and helped automate the input process. These programs typically used display protocol emulation application programming interfaces. These application programming interfaces (APIs) include LLAPI, HLLAPI, and EHLAPI. The interfaces often dealt with very low-level aspects of the communications, which made them prone to emulator implementation changes as the technology and approach to emulation improved. The lower level 3270 emulation APIs are being phased out, with the emulator high-level language application programming interface (EHLAPI) the apparent sur-

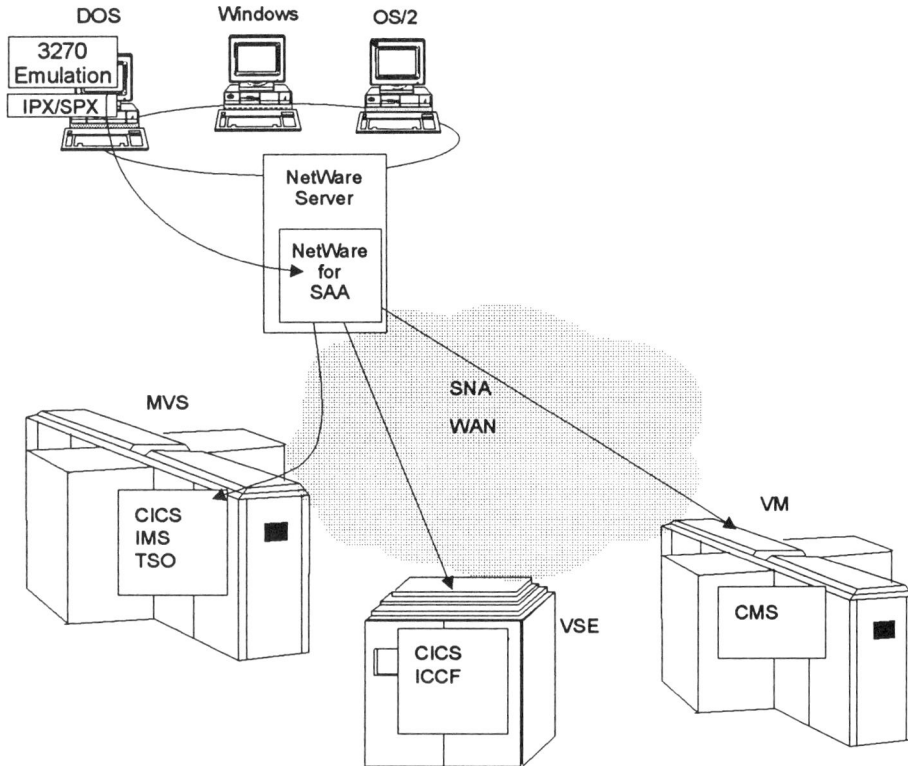

Figure 14-26   IBM 3270 Emulation from a NetWare LAN

vivor. There are a number of application development products that enhance programmer productivity as the applications are written. These tools use the 3270 emulation program's application program interface and enable functions to be coded without intimate communications knowledge.

Although the 3270 display was essentially a dumb terminal, IBM designed some basic file transfer protocols into the communication protocol and provided these functions in the IBM mainframe communications products. These products are recognizable by their name — IND$FILE. This file transfer utility is supported by MVS/TSO, VM/CMS, and CICS. It is initiated at the workstation that invokes a file transfer program on the workstation (part of the emulator) and invokes a TSO, CMS, or CICS service on the mainframe. This utility provides for file-to-file transfer by pushing or pulling data streams between the workstation and the mainframe. IND$FILE supports ASCII-to-EBCDIC, EBCIDIC-to-ASCII, and binary transmissions. This utility can also be invoked by a program.

As the 3270 data stream capabilities began limiting the transfer rates and the peer-to-peer flexibility, most terminal emulators added LU6.2 protocol support by providing an APPC programming interface. The more sophisticated file transfer programs now use these interfaces; however, their use usually requires software at both the workstation end and the mainframe end. One such architected interface is IBM's DISOSS file transfer interface. Unfortunately, the mainframe operating systems and subsystems have been slow to provide mainframe services that use an open client-server model. As a result the 3270 interface remains the de facto king, since the workstation user can add value to the end-use application without having to deal with the infrastructure as long as the data that are needed are painted on the screen or available to IND$FILE.

So what mainframe services can the user get from the DOS or Windows workstation? Excluding the remote log in, IND$FILE service, and the screen scrapping techniques the primary services available are sophisticated batch file transfer programs, print out redirectors, client-server and master slave data base services, corporate mail boxes, and shared virtual files and virtual disks that can be accessed by the entire company. The OSI-based File Transfer, Access and Management (FTAM) promises to provide a generic file access and transfer interface, but it has been slow to take off.

I have already described one virtual volume implementation using XAM/NET as the example. The bottom line is that most of the newer application frontends will be built from the outside in, that is, more of the applications will be removed from the mainframe and moved into one of two locations: the workstation or the server.

Both approaches continue to emerge. Let's look at the implementations. In Figure 14-27 we see two evolution scenarios, one or the other of which is being pursued by some companies and vendors. The current momentum is on getting the application into

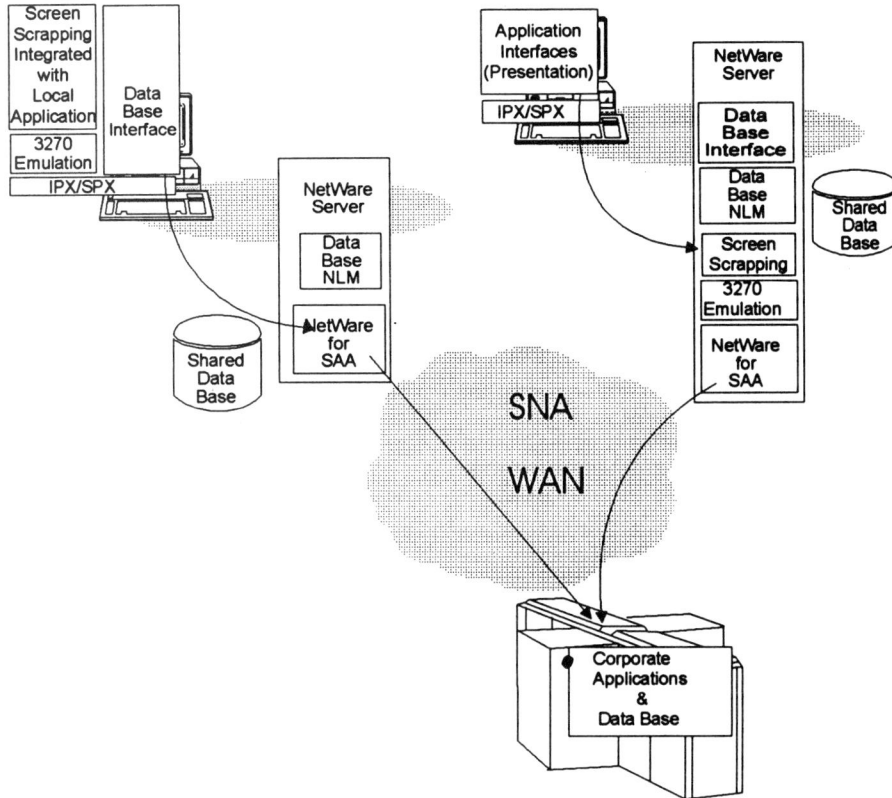

Figure 14-27   Evolving Application Placement

the workstation and sharing the data via a server. However, several recent product introductions show more network middleware and emulation functions being pulled out of the workstation. What has this trend to do with NetWare and access to mainframe services? Everything. If the gateway functions move to the server, many of the support and development issues that make workstation to mainframe applications difficult will disappear. Additionally, if these functions are on the server, it focuses the attention to robust solutions that will more suitably interface with the mainframe. For example, it would be much easier to implement FTAM or a new relational data base if only changes that were required occurred on the server and the external interfaces to the clients were preserved.

14.4 OS/2 Workstations

14.4.1 OS/2 Workstations Access NetWare Servers

NetWare Client for OS/2 gives users transparent access to such NetWare resources as file, print, database, and communication services. The OS/2 workstation user can access NetWare managed services just as any DOS or Windows user, can; however, because OS/2 supports multitasking, several OS/2 sessions can run on a workstation at a time. The workstation can even be emulating DOS and Windows environments. These sessions are run as private connections to NetWare. For example, a single OS/2 workstation could have three concurrent sessions with a DOS connection, a Windows connection, and an OS/2 connection. These concurrent connections can share the same physical and logical network connection, but each is treated as a unique session by NetWare. (see Fig. 14-28). This means one OS/2 workstation can concurrently access multiple servers.

For example, the workstation might be configured to use information from a NetWare file server and simultaneously query

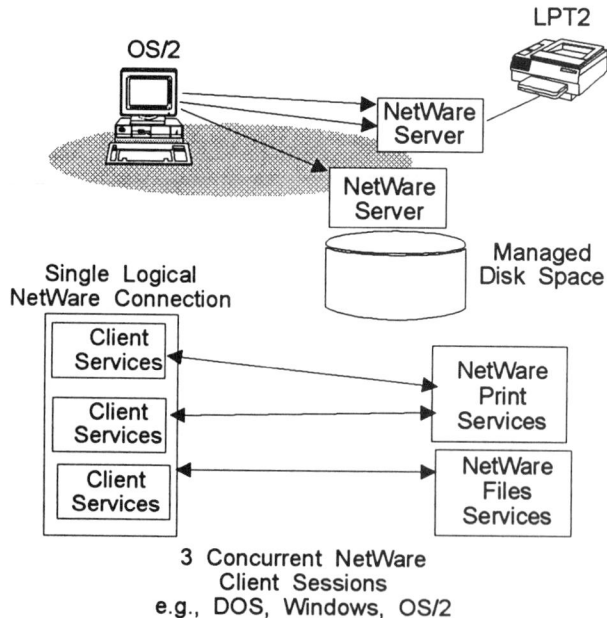

Figure 14-28 NetWare Print and File Server for OS/2

a data base on an application server. The NetWare Client for OS/2 is required if you want to run OS/2-distributed application servers on NetWare networks. It supplies the network connection protocols and IPC mechanisms -Named Pipes, NetBIOS, and Novell's SPX/IPX- needed to run the OS/2-distributed application.

The NetWare Client for OS/2 coexists with IBM's Communication Manager, Remote Data Services, 3270 and 5250 connectivity, PC Support for the AS/400, and IBM LAN Services, which connects the workstation to IBM's LAN servers. It supports both LANSUP and ODINSUP. LANSUP can be configured using the NDIS driver or ODINSUP with an ODI driver.

The NetWare Client for OS/2 also includes built-in diagnostic capabilities that automatically capture diagnostic information and pass it to the NetWare Management System (NMS). This information is used to build a graphic of the network and help the network supervisors to troubleshoot and fine-tune the networks.

The NetWare Client for OS/2 is distributed as a companywide license; network supervisors can install it on an unlimited number of workstations in a single company.

14.4.2 OS/2 Workstations with TCP/IP Interoperability

LAN WorkPlace for OS/2 provides all of the features of LAN WorkPlace for DOS (see DOS workstation with TCP/IP interoperability). In addition LAN WorkPlace for OS/2 allows the user to exploit OS/2 multitasking capabilities by supporting multiple concurrent sessions through TCP/IP communication protocols.

LAN WorkPlace for OS/2 supports the following U.S. Department of Defense Internet Protocol standards:

- IP (Internet Protocol) RFC 791
- IP Subnet Extension RFC 950
- IP Broadcast Datagrams RFC 919
- IP Broadcast Datagrams with Subnets RFC 922
- IP on Ethernet RFC 894
- IP on ARCnet RFC 1201
- IPX or IP Tunneling RFC 1234

- TCP (Transmission Control Protocol, 0-64 sockets) RFC 793
- UDP (User Datagram Protocol, 0-32 sockets) RFC 768
- IP-IEEE (Internet Protocol on IEEE 802) RFC 1042
- NetBIOS (NetBIOS Service Protocol on TCP/IP) RFCs 1001, 1002
- ARP (Address Resolution Protocol) RFC 826
- RARP (Reverse Address Resolution Protocol) RFC 903
- ICMP (Internet Control Message Protocol) RFC 792
- DNS (Domain Name System) Resolver RFCs 1034, 1035
- TELNET (Telnet) Protocol RFC 854

VT-series emulation for both DOS and MS Windows

- FTP (File Transfer Protocol) RFCs 949, 959
- TFTP (Trivial File Transfer Protocol) RFC 783

Both client and server for DOS

- BOOTP (Bootstrap Protocol) RFCs 951, 1084
- IP over ARCnet Networks RFC 1201
- IPX over IP Tunneling RFC 1234
- LPD (Line Printer Daemon) Protocol RFC 1179
- RPC (Remote Procedure Call) RDC 1057
- PPP (Point-to-Point Protocol) RFCs 1171, 1172
- SLIP (Serial Line Internet Protocol) RFCs 1055, 1144
- SNMP (Simple Network Management Protocol) RFC 1157
- MIB (Management Information Base) RFCs 1156, 1213

A combination of 128 TCP/IP and UDP sockets are supported.

14.5 Macintosh Workstations

14.5.1 Mac Workstations Access NetWare Servers

Any Apple workstation user with any Macintosh computer, including the Classic, Quadra, and PowerBook with System 6.0.5

or later operating environment and AppleShare Workstation 7.1 or later software that is connected to a LocalTalk, Ethernet, and Token Ring LAN can use the same NetWare services that DOS, MS Windows, and OS/2 users can.

The Macintosh user logs in to the NetWare network to share files and access print services through the Macintosh Chooser. From the workstation standpoint all interfaces are familiar and NetWare functions do show though. Macintosh users view a file stored on the NetWare server as a familiar graphical icon. The NetWare for Macintosh services interfaces on the NetWare server provide file services, print services, administrative utilities, and AppleTalk routing for Macintosh users on the NetWare network.

Mac users can also share files on a CD-ROM. Because NetWare caches files, users can quickly retrieve commonly accessed CD-ROM files. In addition, administrators can maintain control of network information by applying NetWare security to specific files on the CD-ROM drive.

Macintosh users and administrators can map DOS file extensions to a specific Macintosh application, so that Macintosh users immediately recognize DOS files as icons of the corresponding Macintosh application. Double-clicking on such icons automatically launches the corresponding Macintosh application.

14.5.2 Mac Workstations with TCP/IP Interoperability

LAN WorkPlace for Macintosh provides Apple Macintosh System 6 and 7 users with transparent access to PCs, VAX minicomputers, IBM mainframes, UNIX workstations, and host-connected peripherals, such as printers and plotters, that are connected on an industry-standard TCP/IP network with the look and feel of the Macintosh desktop operating system.

LAN WorkPlace for Macintosh consists of the Novell TCP/IP transport, HostAccess network application software, and the NetStat desk accessory. HostAccess provides industry-standard network communications utilities, including terminal emulation and file transfer capabilities. HostAccess can use Novell's TCP/IP transport or Apple Computer's MacTCP.

LAN WorkPlace for Macintosh lets the user have TCP/IP, NetWare for Macintosh, and AppleShare active at the same time.

To access to NetWare servers the workstation must have AppleShare software and NetWare for Macintosh must be loaded on the NetWare server.

LAN WorkPlace for Macintosh provides:

- Full-featured terminal emulation capabilities to support concurrent sessions to multiple hosts using VT100 terminal emulation. The screens can be painted and the sessions can be recorded.

- File transfer capabilities using FTP file transfer through command-line and mouse-driven interfaces. These transfers support ASCII, binary, and MacBinary transfer modes.

- UNIX-style services including the Whois/Finger utility.

- Support for Apple Computer's MultiFinder software.

LAN WorkPlace for Macintosh runs on the Macintosh SE, SE/30, Plus, or Macintosh II, and it must be connected through any Macintosh Ethernet adapter card, as well as the built-in Ethernet interface in the Macintosh Quadra and the SCSI-based Ethernet adapter in the Macintosh PowerBook, or it can connect through a gateway such as the Shiva FastPath 4 or Token Ring.

14.6 UNIX Workstations

UNIX users can transparently access the NetWare environment from their native operating system environment if the NetWare NFS NLMs are loaded on the NetWare server. This allows UNIX users to share files and other network resources with NetWare clients, such as DOS, Macintosh, and OS/2 computers, in a fully integrated, seamless manner.

NFS, which was developed and licensed by Sun Microsystems, Inc., is the most commonly used distributed file system in the UNIX community. Sun licenses NFS technology to more than 250 vendors.

With this Netware NFS on the NetWare server UNIX clients can access NetWare volumes using the standard UNIX/NFS MOUNT command with UNIX file attributes and naming conventions. User authentication, file locking, record locking, and permissions mapping are provided transparently.

The File Transfer Protocol daemon (FTPSERV) is also supported to provide the UNIX users with the ability to connect to any authorized NetWare server and initiate file transfers to and from any NetWare volume or directory. Additionally, the UNIX user can submit print jobs to standard NetWare printer queues, and NetWare users can send output to the UNIX attached printers.

XCONSOLE can be used to access the NetWare server console to manage the NFS performance and security.

Supported services:

- Sun Microsystems, Inc., Network File System (NFS) Protocol, Version 2

- Sun Microsystems, Inc., Mount Protocol

- Sun Microsystems, Inc., External Data Representation Protocol (XDR)

- Sun Microsystems, Inc., Remote Procedure Call (RPC)

- Sun Microsystems, Inc., Portmapper Protocol

- Sun Microsystems, Inc., Lockd and Statd

- DARPA (RFC 959) File Transfer Protocol (FTP)

- Berkeley UNIX Line Printer Daemon Protocol (LPD) RFC 1179

- MIT, X Window System-X11/R4

- VT100/220 Terminal emulation access to XCONSOLE

- RFC 854 Telnet used as an initiation and transport mechanism

UNIX users who do not have NFS can still access NetWare resources transparently from within their native UNIX environment if they have TCP/IP, FTP, LPD, or the X Window System, and if NetWare FLeX/IP NLMs are loaded on the NetWare server. UNIX users can share NetWare managed printers and files.

NetWare FLeX/IP provides a bidirectional print gateway that allows UNIX TCP/IP users to submit print jobs to NetWare print queues and lets NetWare users spool print jobs to UNIX attached printers.

Using the native FTP commands, the UNIX user can transfer files to and from any NetWare volume or directory that the user is authorized to access across the NetWare network. Only the gateway NetWare server need support NetWare FLeX/IP or TCP/IP.

NetWare FLeX/IP provides XCONSOLE, an X Windows application, which converts NetWare console screens to X Window System screens. This lets any authorized X Window System user manage NetWare servers remotely.

The UNIX system specifications include:

- Sun Microsystems, Inc., Portmapper Protocol

- DARPA (RFC 959) File Transfer Protocol (FTP)

- Berkeley UNIX Line Printer Daemon Protocol (LPD) RFC 1179

- MIT, X Window System-X11/R4

- VT100/220 Terminal emulation access to XCONSOLE

- RFC 854 Telnet is used for initiation and the transport mechanism

Novell also provides a desktop UNIX operating system, UNIXWare. UnixWare Personal Edition is a 32-bit, single-user NetWare UNIX Client. It is full implementation of UNIX System V Release 4.2 (SVR4.2) that seamlessly accesses to NetWare File and Print services using IPX/SPX.

Chapter 15

Managing the Enterprise Network

The enterprise network's management team challenge is to determine where the enterprise network infrastructure responsibilities end and how to effectively manage the area inside the cloud. Since a very significant piece of the decision is the tools that are available to manage the enterprise network, the evaluation is based on how each network management system fits into or with the other. Again the comparison is very difficult since the tools do not line side by side.

15.1 Managing from NetView

NetView is probably the most comprehensive management system to support automated operations and high volume and highly controlled networks. IBM's NetView, however, does not manage beyond the SNA-conforming elements such as network controllers, modems, and mainframe operating system interfaces without help. Once the SNA network boundaries have been reached, other management tools must be employed. These tools can be used as part of NetView or independently. For example, the TCP/IP-based simple network management protocol (SNMP) and NetWare management tools can interface to NetView in order to extend its reach. NetView applications (command list scripts (CLISTs)) can be written to automate the gathering of statistical data and the presentation of the status from these tools.

Figure 15-1 depicts NetView managing multiple NetWare servers through a common collection point provided by Novell's NetWare Management System (NMS) and NetWare for SAA.

Managed Resource Events:
Logical Links to Mainframe
(Ethernet, Token Ring, SDLC, QLLC/X.25)

NetView Alerts
server resources thresholds
server running out disk space
server connection capacity exceeded
directory and file warnings
unathorized access attempts
token ring beaconing
SDLC and LLC failures
etc.

NetView Query Commands
server information and parameters
volume/file/directory information
user volume usage and status
vesion number of cummunication service
status of the Transaction Tracking ServiceTTS)
etc.

NetView Control Commands
enable/disable server login
shut down a server
broadcast to users
set date/time/control parameters
volume and file management
directory management
load and unload NLMs
enable/disable TTS
etc.

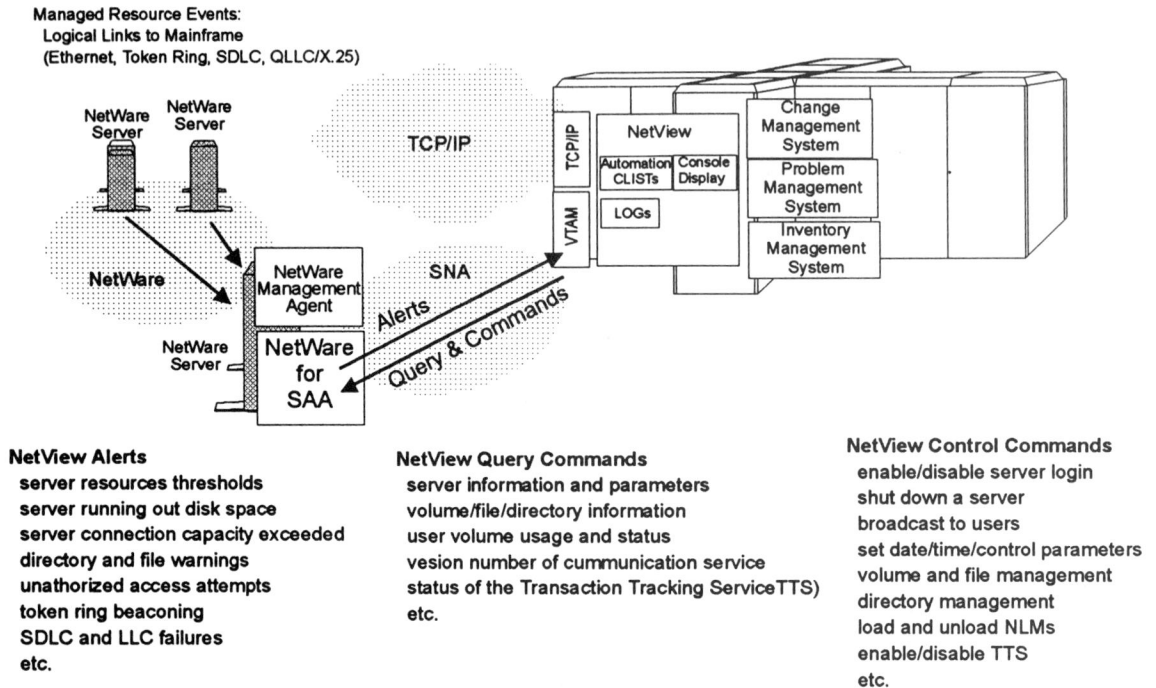

Figure 15-1   Netware Network and NetView

NetWare for SAA provides a NetView Entry Point. It collects the appropriate information using a NetWare Management Agent (NMA). The Netware Management Agent is a NetWare management system component that is installed in each NetWare server to allow remote monitoring and error detection. (As an aside the NMA is architected to communicate with NMS and SNMP management services as well as NetView via NetWare for SAA.)

The NetWare Management Agent for NetView uses NetWare for SAA to send alerts to NetView and allows NetView operators to cause NetWare queries and control commands to be executed from a NetView console. The gathering of information (queries), operational commands, and exception condition (alert) handling can be automated using standard NetView CLISTs. Unlike the NetView SNMP and open systems interconnection (OSI) implementation, no special interfaces or mainframe software is required for Netware to communicate with NetView. NetWare Code Points are included in NetView (V2.1). Figure 15-1 depicts a single collection point, however, each Netware for SAA occurrence can directly connect to NetView.

Another way to manage a heterogeneous network from NetView is via TCP/IP with SNMP. TCP/IP's SNMP is a pervasive voluntary reporting and command tool that can be used to collect information about a resource and has a limited number of proactive facilities. Unlike NetView, SNMP extends beyond the physical network and can participate in any environment that can run TCP/IP. As a result SNMP can be used to "manage" any object that wants to participate. For example, SNMP agents can reside in routers, bridges, servers, and workstations. Participation

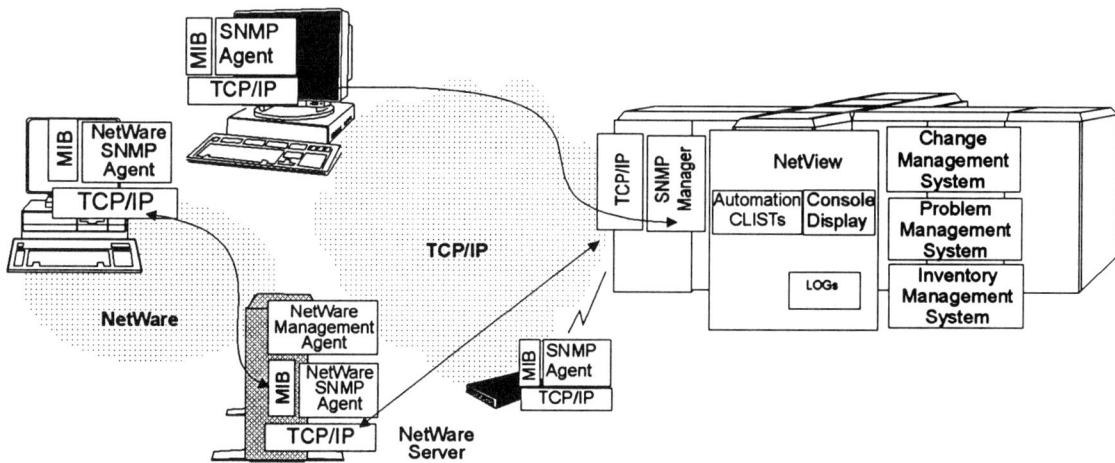

Figure 15-2   Managing a TCP Network with NetView

requires an agent and that the component have a management information base (MIB), which describes the object(s) being managed. A network management station (NMS) is required to provide the displays, administer, and control the objects being managed. (Watch out for the acronyms here. NMS can now be Netware Management System and an SNMP Network Management Station.)

Figure 15-2 depicts NetView managing four objects (two workstations, a NetWare server, and a modem) through the SNMP manager on the mainframe. The NMA in the NetWare server can be configured to send server SNMP alarms to any SNMP console.

NetView seems to provide the best option for managing an entire network from a single point since it interfaces with the SNA- managed objects as well as the TCP/IP- and NetWare-managed objects via the appropriate interfaces. NetView, however, was not intended to manage and control some of the new boundaries of the enterprise network, although there is nothing that would preclude NetView from doing so with the help of various vendors and evolving interfaces. IBM has already introduced NetView/6000 and LAN/NetView as part of its evolution to embrace the new boundaries.

Novell provides a NetWare Services Manager for LAN NetView, an OS/2-based NetWare management application that snaps into IBM's LAN NetView product that is consistent with IBM's enterprise network management strategy. The NetWare Services Manager for LAN NetView allows administrators to manage NetWare and LAN Server networks from a single management console. The NetWare Services Manager for LAN NetView has distributed NetWare Management Agents, which reside in each NetWare server. The following servers and workstations are supported:

- NetWare 2.x (no agents)
- NetWare 3.x
- NetWare 4.x
- NetWare Access Server
- NetWare SNA Gateway

- NetWare Communication Server
- NetWare Print Server
- NetWare Remote Print Server
- NetWare Data Base Server

Figure 15-3 graphically depicts the NetView boundaries in the environments we have just covered. The intent is that each circle connotes all the elements of a NetWare, TCP/IP, or SNA network within an enterprise. The unlabeled circle represents the other networks that somehow intersect with the internet. It would appear that NetView can manage the combination of SNA and TCP/IP objects and NetWare servers. The NetWare network could be more comprehensively covered by NetView if all the elements participated in TCP/IP SNMP, which is an available option.

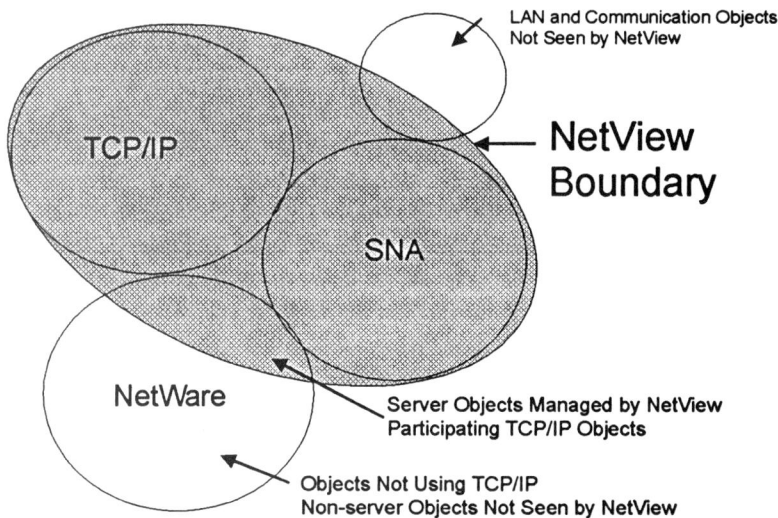

Figure 15-3   NetView Management Boundary

15.2 Managing from TCP/IP

An alternative to managing the entire enterprise network with NetView is to use TCP/IP and NetView. NetView is still the best vehicle to manage SNA networks and mainframes. While TCP/IP has found its way into the mainframe for communications and as a base for managing objects with SNMP, the SNA and mainframe resources do not participate with TCP/IP SNMP. Several vendors including Novell are offering SNMP Management Station solutions.

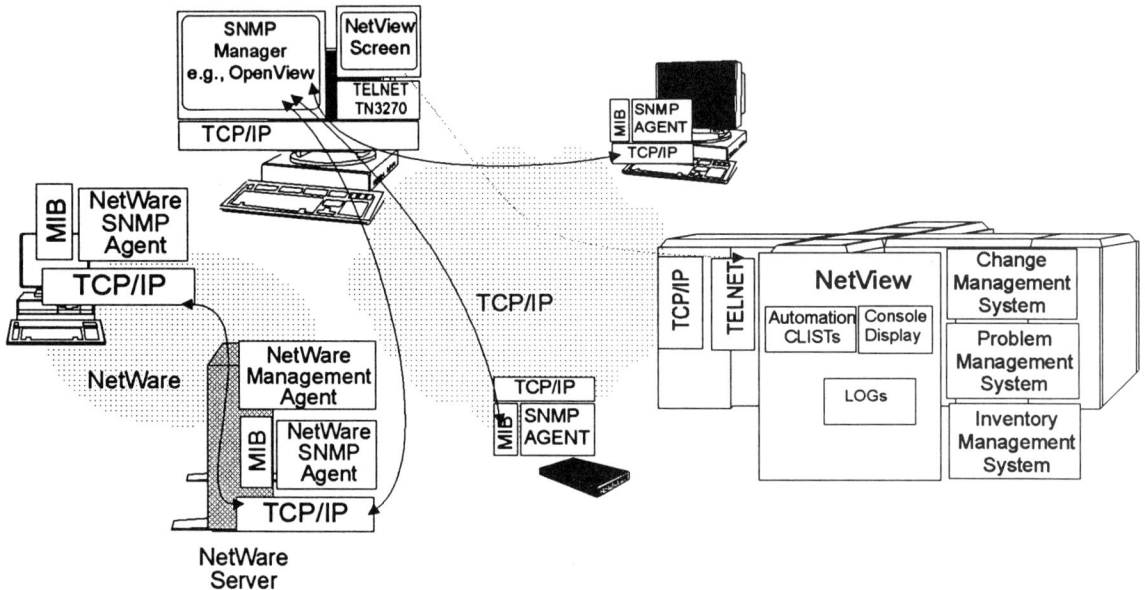

Figure 15-4   Managing a TCP/IP Network with NetView

For example, Hewlett-Packard provides an OpenView product that can be used to manage the enterprise network objects that interact with TCP/IP and SNMP. NetWare servers can participate in this management structure since it supports TCP/IP, and its NetWare Management Agent provides the SNMP agent.

Figure 15-4 depicts a two network management system that uses TCP/IP SNMP to manage all possible items and NetView to

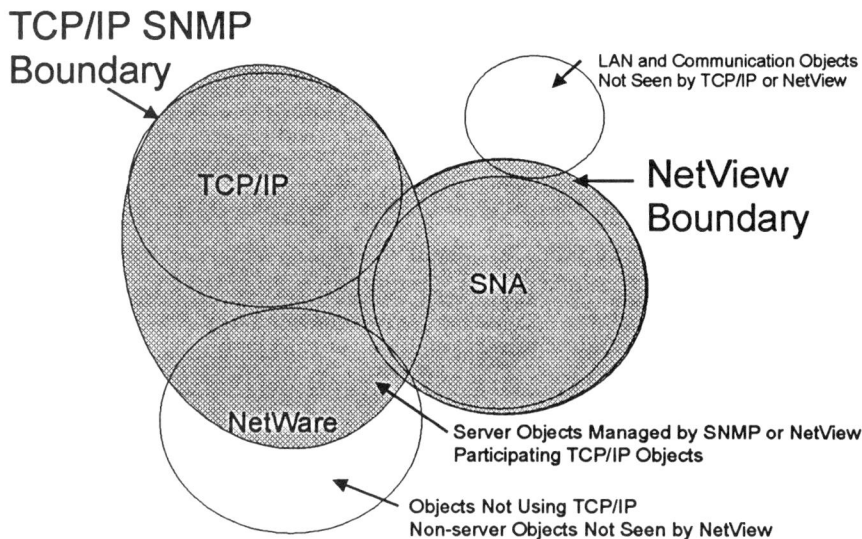

Figure 15-5   Managing the Network with TCP/IP SNMP

manage those that it does natively.

In other words, the boundaries could be depicted as in Figure 15-5 Remember there are two windows into the resulting enterprise network: a TCP/IP SNMP and NetView . I should also point out that although many vendors have embraced SNMP for their device management, there are many variations when it comes to how the important data is presented. It will take more than just installing the SNMP management software to make this work effectively. But this is a very good start and more and more vendors are supporting this approach.

15.3 Managing from NetWare

15.3.1 Managing NetWare and TCP/IP

Novell's Network Management System can also be used to manage the TCP/IP internet and NetWare server objects as well as network interconnectivity if the LANalyzer agent is added at

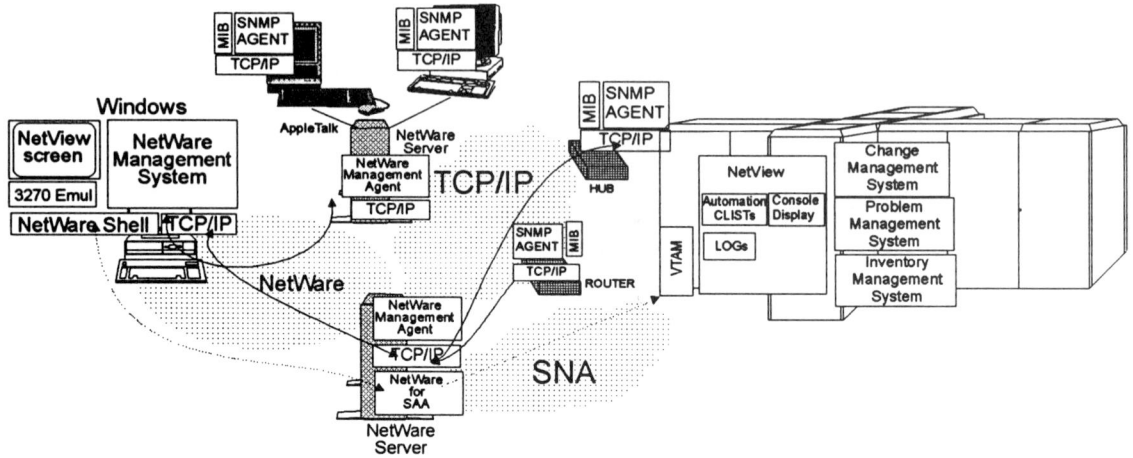

Figure 15-6   Managing a TCP/IP Internet

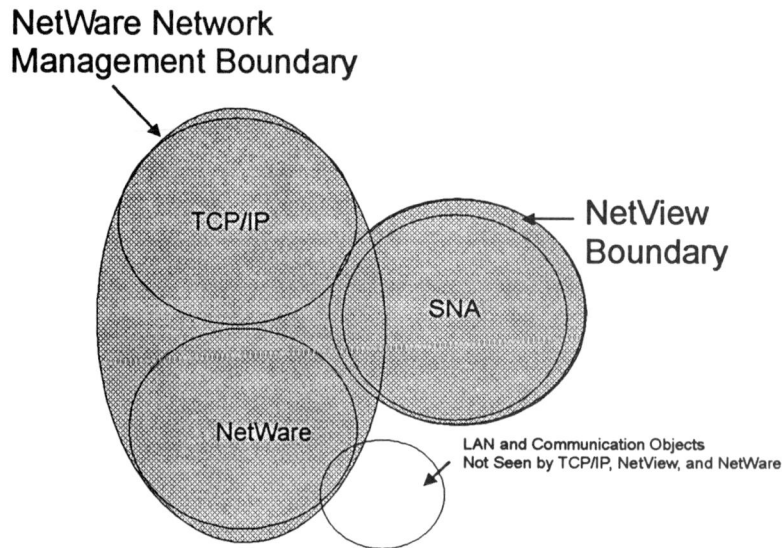

Figure 15-7   NetWare Network Management Boundary

the appropriate points, as portrayed in Figure 15-5 (Figure 15-6 does not include the LANalyzer agents).

Using the same models as before, NetWare and NetView appear to provide the most comprehensive management solution. In Figure 15-7 NetWare network management includes not only the network management products provided by Novell but also the myriad of workstation management products that are supported using a NetWare base. In fact, some of these products support not only NetWare but also networks and components not supported by NetView, NetWare, or TCP/IP SNMP.

15.3.2 Managing the SNA Network

Another approach to managing the network is provided by Net-Ware. This is a NetWare-based approach that allows the network management to be run from a network management workstation(s) and supports all the NetWare managed resources and

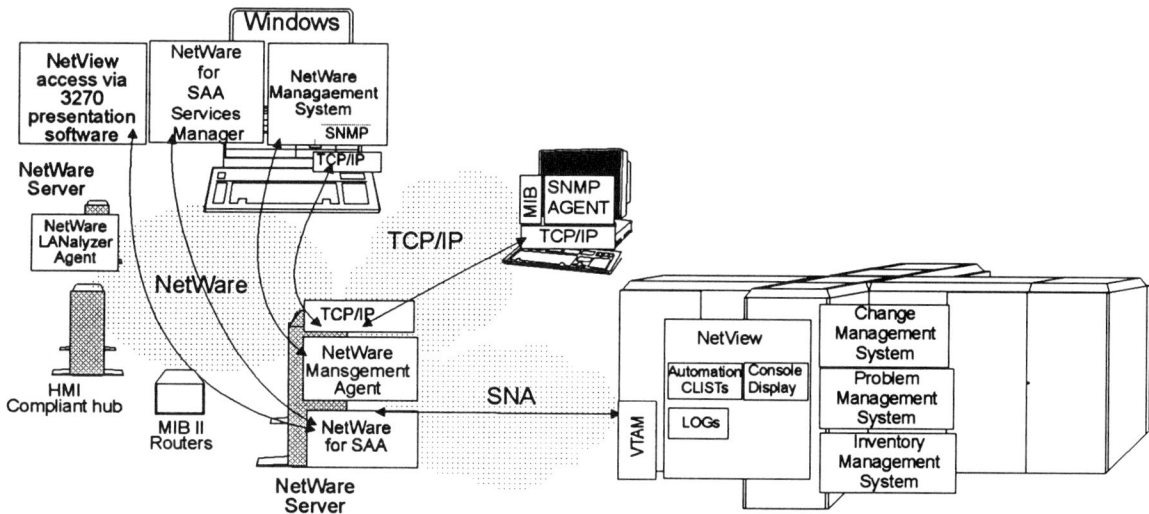

Figure 15-8   Managing the Enterprise Network from NMS

TCP/IP network resources while providing a window into NetView which allows it to manage those resources outside of NetWare's access.

The NetWare for SAA Services Manager 2.0, formerly NetWare Communication Services Manager, (see Fig. 15-8) is an MS Windows-based software application that provides extensive network management capabilities for configuring, monitoring, and maintaining multiple NetWare for SAA servers anywhere on a network - even over wide area links. It offers a comprehensive set of network management tools for fault, performance, and configuration management. The maximum number of servers that can be managed depends on the amount of network management data being collected and the bandwidth of the network links involved, the memory in the workstation, and the CPU speed of the workstation.

The NetWare for SAA Services Manager is a client-server application that communicates with the designated network management agents and other software modules on each NetWare server being managed using the IPX/SPX protocol. The NetWare for SAA Services manager user operates at supervisor- or operator-equivalent rights on the managed NetWare server. Using this facility the network supervisors can identify problem situations and quickly respond. The supervisors can view configuration information, see communication services on the network, and dynamically control services down to the session level. The NetWare for SAA Services Manager displays session status, including network address, user ID, logical unit (LU) pool, and other useful information about SNA connections. Real-time controls that can be performed from the NetWare for SAA Services Manager include:

- Loading and unloading NLMs
- Restarting a server
- Reloading a communication service
- Initiating a trace
- Resetting a host session.

The NetWare for SAA Services Manager also allows network supervisors to set up specific management domains to monitor specific events. Network supervisors can view configuration information, see communication services on the network, and dynamically control services down to the session level. The NetWare for SAA Services Manager displays session status, including network address, user ID, LU pool, and other useful information about SNA connections. To assist in the managing the performance of the SNA network seen by NetWare, NetWare for SAA Services Manager enables the collection and graphically displaying statistical information for critical resources such as SNA host data links, LAN connections and communication services. The data can be displayed with Novell's NMS graphing capabilities or the data can also be analyzed with other Microsoft Windows applications such as Microsoft Excel, using a Windows Dynamic Data Exchange (DDE) link.

NetWare for SAA Services Manager provides audit trail logs of NetWare for SAA service usage. A log file can include all host connection usage including the NetWare user name, the physical network address, the host application, and the duration of the connection. This information can be used for security, billing or usage tracking purposes. The NetWare for SAA Services Manager's Event Monitor can also be configured to receive instant notification of potential security violations, such as "User Login Failed-Invalid Password" or "Communication Service Unloaded."

15.4 Summary

NetWare offers a variety of avenues to manage the the enterprise network (LAN-centric) or to be managed by the enterprise network existing infrastructure (mainframe-centric). The management tools include the ability to manage a NetWare-based SNA network comprised of multiple servers running NetWare for SAA and managing these from a single or selected control points with the NetWare for SAA Services Manager. Additionally, TCP/IP connected network objects can be managed through the SNMP interfaces available with Novell's NetWare Management System. Additionally, NetWare provides a NetWare-based network resource management infrastructure which includes dispersed Net-Ware Management Agents in the appropriate servers and network elements and these together with Novell's LANalyzer enables the network management staff to be alerted to problems, do problem determination and in many cases make appropriate software adjustments from a remote location.

For those organizations wanting to manage the NetWare elements from NetView, Netware for SAA has incorporated some key alerts and enables NetView actions. The NetWare servers can be monitored and managed from the NetView console or via from automated operations using pre-programmed scripts.

Chapter 16

Managing the Personal Workplace

16.1 Overview

From an enterprise network standpoint the workstation is the user's domain until it uses the enterprise network's resources. The user's and the enterprise network provider's realities are that the users generally have very similar requirements when it comes to service. The communality disappears when it comes down to the specific workstation, tools, and services. To compound this, the specific requirements for bandwidth, data access, data exchange, and printer support tend to change very rapidly, as do the tools

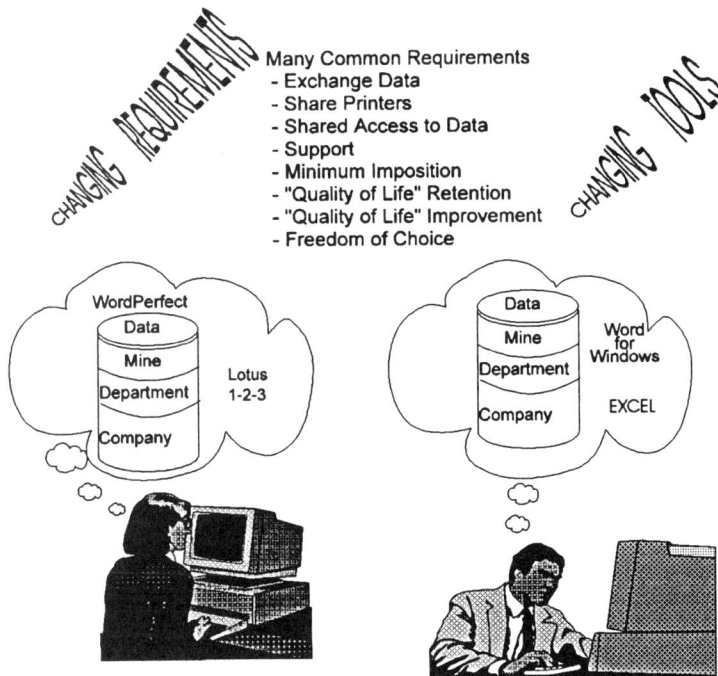

CHANGING REQUIREMENTS

CHANGING TOOLS

Many Common Requirements
- Exchange Data
- Share Printers
- Shared Access to Data
- Support
- Minimum Imposition
- "Quality of Life" Retention
- "Quality of Life" Improvement
- Freedom of Choice

WordPerfect

Data
Mine
Department
Company

Lotus 1-2-3

Data
Mine
Department
Company

Word for Windows

EXCEL

Figure 16-1   Common and Diverse User Requirements

that the users select for their productivity (as depicted in Figure 16-1). The enterprise network team's challenge is to support these environments in a responsive, efficient, and cost effective manner without imposing undue restrictions on the users.

In short, someone either in the enterprise network organization or someone working closely with that organization is constantly focusing on the quality of service and how this service can be delivered.

Often the responsible person or person(s), frequently referred to as local-area network (LAN) administrators (see Fig. 16-2), are tied to the specific departments and they focus on the *tools and services* necessary for the productive execution of the department's mission. This mission differs somewhat from the traditional (IS) organization member whose focus is typically on the *management of the company's core business applications and*

Figure 16-2 LAN Administrator's Considerations

technology and provide the administrative rigors that protect the company's information assets, provide quality companywide application, and data access at consistent service levels at minimal costs.

In many companies the LAN administrators were on their own because of the state of the technology available to provide these services from a remote location. Therefore in the early 1990s supporting the workstation from a remote location was almost impossible. While there were scattered tools that allowed for software distribution, license metering, and remote workstation access for problem determination, they tended be relatively fragmented in support and access capabilities.

By 1993 the entire industry had become much more aware of the issue of volumes. For example, it became relatively easy to install a new version of software on a workstation albeit time consuming. However, even with all the dynamic installation help the vendors provide, installing this same software on several workstations can easily become a nightmare when one considers the different configurations and software levels, not to mention the time and idiosyncrasies that require attention.

The quick-fix answer for software distribution that one might get from the uninitiated is to use the server as a program library. In other words, store one copy of the software on the server. This is a super solution for data-distribution or data-collection applications. For software it can also solve several problems, such as reduced disk space consumption and software metering. But it is an incomplete solution for software unless the software is constructed to allow user-specific control data to be separated from the program data, and it does not address how to update the associated workstation operating system and application invocation files.

More comprehensive solutions are emerging, however. These enterprise-ready software distribution and change systems provide notification of the change, the scheduling of the change, the removal of the old controls, the addition of the new controls, the ability to remove the new changes, and restore the old environment. These notifications are fundamental to a successful software change management system. The system does all of them based on rules that test the workstations hardware capabilities, operational environment for sufficient working storage, if there's sufficient disk space, and the appropriate software pre- and corequisites. Additionally, the tools should provide audit trails to identify if and when the changes occurred.

The industry terms for tools that provide these workstation services are:

- Hardware and software inventory
- Software metering
- Software applications management
- Asset management
- Software control

The implementation of these capabilities may involve more than one product, but the controls are fundamental to not only the workstation directories, but also the LAN's directory services. (We discuss how NetWare supports NetWare managed file controls with the Netware Directory service in Section 5.)

There are currently many vendors that provide various degrees of support for remote change management of multiple workstations. As a note of caution be sure to look for the ability to apply changes to multiple workstations simultaneously and synchronously, as there are products available that are one-at-a-time change tools. These tools are not enterprise network ready for change support, but they may be applicable for specific remote repair actions.

Let's look at two areas that demand enterprise network attention when supporting workstations. First we'll look at Novell's software distribution and installation tool — the NetWare Navigator and then we'll look at some developments in providing help with remote workstation hardware information gathering and problem isolation.

16.2 Remote Software Installation

As the enterprise network boundary continues to extend deeper into the desktop many new desktop-specific services are expected to be provided by the network operating system. Workstation operating systems, data, end-user applications, and other software administration and control usually head the list.

In general the associated administrative tasks include:

- Distribute and collect widely used data
- Distribute and install custom in-house applications
- Distribute and install software products
- Distribute and install operating systems
- Running automated virus scans, backups, and archives
- Conducting automated software and hardware inventories at each workstation

To address this need Novell acquired and extended a technology that relieves the administrative tasks by automating the distribution and software upgrade functions. Novell now provides three NetWare Navigator products: the Network Navigator, the DOS LAN Distributor, and the OS/2 Client Support product. They are based on a proven Electronic Software Distribution (ESD) technology that has been on the market since 1986 and has been implemented in networks of more than 10,000 nodes. As of this writing Novell is developing Electronic Software Licensing (ESL) software that will provide a simple means of controlling the acquisition and use of desktop software.

In general these products work in network environments that support server based files that can be accessed by the participating workstations. The concept behind these products is that there are two players required, an administrator and a client. The administer packages the software, distributes the software, and schedules the software, in addition to checking the status of updates scheduled. The "client" in turn is software that receives the update requests from the server, initiates the auto install, returns status, and optionally return inventory status.

In other words the knowledgeable administrator writes a script to install the appropriate software. This scripts are tailored to specific target environments. Conceptually when the workstation logs into the network, a hook is placed in the workstation that brings in a "robot" (my words) service. This robot service takes over the workstation, locks the workstations keyboard, and logs into the network with an encrypted user ID and password. It then applies the scripts that the administrator prepared. This might include downloading data and software, installing some software, installing or upgrading a new operating system or Windows, and returning that status. Upon completion the robot will either log off or log off and reboot the system. The reboot is required for operating system and Windows updates.

The software distribution can be pulled by the client workstation or pushed to the target workstation if the workstation is powered on and the Netware Navigator Scheduler TSR is loaded. In the push mode all events run automatically and unattended. This mode is most frequently used with the optional scheduling feature that schedules tasks to occur automatically on a daily, weekly, or monthly basis. If the workstation is being used when the package is scheduled, the NetWare Navigator warns users that a scheduled function is about to occur. Users can then choose either to quit their applications or to delay the scheduled function.

NetWare Navigator is implemented as a set of NLMs that allow administrators to install and distribute software, data, applications, workstation operating systems and network operating systems, from a central location, without user intervention. In addition, NetWare Navigator uses a distribution/staging server design to provide full-fledged, multitiered software distribution to NetWare, non-NetWare, and host environments, without requiring additional servers.

The NetWare Navigator is NetWare specific and uses NetWare protocols, security, and directory capabilities. NetWare Navigator also provides built-in support for an automated upgrade to NetWare 4.01.

The NetWare Navigator supports DOS, Windows, and OS/2 workstation environments, applying user transparent changes. The NetWare Navigator also interfaces to and supports non-NetWare LAN environments by using Novell's DOS LAN Distributor. Additionally Novell offers other versions that support other environments, such as:

- An MVS/VTAM (virtual telecommunications access method) Dispatcher product that provides distribution support from the MVS-based IBM mainframe

- A VM Dispatcher product that provides distribution support from the VM-based IBM mainframe
- Tandem Dispatcher product that provides distribution support from Tandem systems running the Guardian 90 operating system
- A DOS product that runs on host connected DOS clients
- An OS/2 product that runs on host-connected OS/2 clients

The Navigator product uses a distributor workstation and makes extensive use of the graphical user interface (GUI). From this console the administrator can develop scripts, create distribution packages, schedule distributions, check the status of scheduled tasks to determine where in the process they are, and whether the installation or data distribution was successful. NetWare Navigator logs the package status.

The graphical user interface also provides the interface used to generate installation scripts, verify conditions on a workstation, back up existing software, install new software, run keystroke files, collect audit information, and modify AUTOEXEC.BAT, CONFIG.SYS, and other files. The scripting interface also includes a keystroke record/playback feature to set up automated installation scripts for menu-driven software on client workstations. The keystrokes can be recorded and automatically played as part of the installation script on the target (client) workstations.

The Network Navigator DOS LAN Distributor is a non-NetWare implementation of the Navigator Electronic Software Distribution (ESD) product that supports DOS, Windows, and OS/2 environments. It provides comparable functions for any network operating system (NOS) that provides file sharing. The key distinction is that it cannot take advantage of the NetWare-specific features, such as enhanced security and directory awareness.

Network Navigator OS/2 Client Support enables OS/2 workstations to receive software distributions through the Network Navigator DOS LAN Distributor product. OS/2 Client Support provides commands and utilities to address issues unique to OS/2, such as the STARTUP.CMD file, OS/2 icon management, and the OS/2 initialization (*.INI) files. In addition, installation scripting for OS/2 clients uses OS/2 command (*.cmd) files or REXX files. The Network Navigator OS/2 Client Support provides the administrator and OS/2 users the same capabilities as DOS users connected to the DOS LAN Distributor have with some additional features:

- Easy-to-use, Presentation Manager-based graphical interface with icons and menus dedicated to specific tasks. For example, administrators and users can employ this interface to schedule events, create keystroke files, test keystroke files, and create software installation scripts

- Icons and menus dedicated to specific tasks

- Commands and utilities to address issues unique to OS/2

Because OS/2 is a multitasking environment, it supports background updates to software and data.

In summary the NetWare Navigator family of products is worth looking at as you look to extend the boundaries of your enterprise network. Its initial appeal is that it supports both NetWare and mainframe environments.

Probably the biggest challenge to managing the workstations in the enterprise comes form the workstation operating system environment coverage. For example, tool A only supports DOS and Windows, tool B only supports Windows, tool C only supports Mac, and so on. A comprehensive solution for the enterprise network provides continuity across workstation platforms. This is especially true as more cross platform client-server applications emerge. The Netware Navigator is representative of a class of products required for the next step in supporting the enterprise network.

16.3 Remote Workstation Hardware Management

Another key enterprise network management consideration is the ability to remotely access the workstation and operate on it as if it were local in order to do problem determination and make changes. Dealing with hardware problems on remote workstations is still a major challenge, although there are an increasing number of programs that allow the user to see the underlying CMOS and system settings. To do this more effectively requires hardware enhancements from the system hardware, hardware adapter, and peripheral vendors. These enhancements will come in the form of self describing devices with pre-specified information bases that will allow a remote software agent to query the device, establish its attributes and settings, determine the health of the components of the device and be prepared to accept setting changes or execute diagnostics. The Desktop Management Task Force (DMTF) is working on making this vision a reality. The task force has already enrolled key industry computer system and component manufacturers to work on a standard that will be built into their hardware in the near term.

The DMTF has proposed a layered Desktop Management Interface (DMI). This desktop management interface will provide an interfaces to diagnostic and management tools and interfaces to the actual hardware and underlying software componentry.

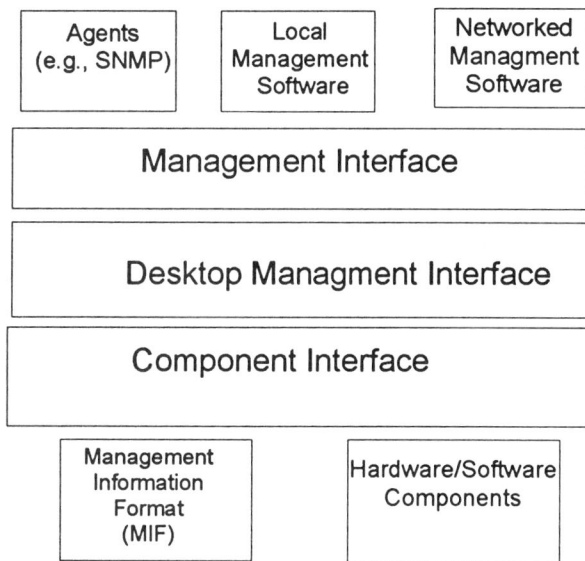

Figure 16-3   The Desktop Management Interface (DMI)

The desktop interface will interface with local diagnostic software as well as remote management software agents that can interact with the DMTF's proposed management interface. (See Fig. 16-3.)   Similarly there will be a component interface that interfaces with the hardware drivers and components such as modems, communication adapter cards, network interface adapters, disk controllers, printers, as well as the actual mother boards.

To affect this, a management information format (MIF) is being defined that enables a component to describe the manageable aspects of the components and drivers. This MIF would be queried by a remote agent in preparation of monitoring for status, initiating diagnostics, and identifying what actions can be taken to reset the component, correct conflicting settings, and perhaps invoke a backup component or memory. The possibilities abound, however, this effort is moving very rapidly and the networking operating system client software is probably the first place these "dials" will be operated from. I expect that we will see this type of technology before the end of 1994.

To this point in the book we have covered the the NetWare components and how they fit together with each other and interoperate in the enterprise network context. we have also explored how NetWare continues to play an increasing role in the facilitating of the workstation and its management. Now we will look at the how to protect the personal, departmental and corporate assets.

Section 5

NetWare Network Security

This section focuses on security breaches that might be introduced by integrating local-area networks (LANs) into the enterprise network and how these exposures can be managed.

Chapter 17

Security Considerations

17.1 Introduction

Enterprise network security is usually a corporate asset audit item. The information systems (IS) organization in turn must focus on minimizing their networks' vulnerability to unauthorized access to confidential information or of impeding the normal network operations. Security often overlaps system management (reliability and availability of services), recovery management (ranging from lost files to disaster site recovery), and data management (including but not limited to data integrity) and asset management.

Although it might not be as apparent as departmental network security, focus for the most part closely maps to the enterprise network IS management goals. After making a conscious or de facto risk assessment, the ease-of-use and flexibility option is frequently pursued instead of the more expensive and obtrusive rigorous control option. The decision is service level over control, a decision that often makes sense considering the relatively low risk. Unfortunately, as these departmental networks connect into the enterprise network and use enterprise data, the overall risk increases dramatically. This integration demands more controls at the workstation and in the departmental network.

This section describes the challenges of integrating departmental networking into the enterprise network. It then describes how NetWare, NetWare-based third-party utilities (NetWare Loadable Modules (NLMs)) and Novell's new Netware Directory Services (NDS) can be used to meet the security challenge. The combination of Novell- and third-party-provided NetWare facilities may, in fact, provide even more flexibility with less obtrusive control than some of the well entrenched enterprise network implementations. To bring this point home Novell and several partners are in the process of being evaluated for C2 Orange Book Security Classification compliance in the United States and E2 security classification compliance in Europe.

The emphasis in this section is on exploring techniques to minimize the exposures to *malicious security compromises* which can surface when remote access to enterprise network resources, data, and services are not protected.

17.2 Background

Security has always been a primary responsibility and concern for the IS organization. Extreme care is taken to protect the "family jewels" (the corporate data and services) from loss, compromise, theft,or disruption. Most large company departmental workgroups are given limited access to the enterprise network and host systems. But the increased sophistication of the departmental network user, the need to access and share corporate data, and the economics of sharing communications links are changing this.. Two computing cultures from entirely different ends of the security spectrum are coming together.

The mature enterprise network IS organization has focused on security with:

- Well-defined security goals
- Appropriate protection with facilities, mechanisms, and processes
- Monitoring the achievement of these goals
- Continuous risk assessment and trade-off processes
- Constant review, reassessment, and actions

The workgroup organization's typical IS focus is on availability of resources, ease-of-access, ease-of-use, high productivity, and business goals, all at minimal technical expense. Many departmental users still don't even use passwords and others that do rarely change them. Programs are frequently downloaded from bulletin boards and diskettes are frequently swapped with

Dichotomy:
- **Ease of access**
- **Access control**

Enterprise Network Established:
- **Security awareness**
- **Process**

Departmental Network focus:
- **Productivity**
- **Cost**

installation procedures even among various companies. The biggest security focus came from the Michael Angelo virus scare in 1992, and each group went out and bought a virus scanning product to be secure.

Now the two different groups are coming together and the management and technical challenge is to increase the security on the workstation and departmental network without frustrating the workstation user and without significantly increasing the LAN administrator's or the enterprise network support organization's workload?

Solution Requires::
- **No more work**
- **Flexible**
- **More secure**

17. 3 The World that Was?

Providing security for a mainframe is not easy despite favorable environmental controls, some very sophisticated tools, layered operating systems, and a security policy and infrastructure.. For example, most mainframes and minis, especially the large ones, are typically walled-off together with their associated storage devices and communication equipment. These systems are rarely seen by unauthorized personnel. These systems are operated by employees who are trained in the security aspects of running the systems and protecting the area. The approach is simple: if you secure the area, the physical asset is protected.

Security principal #1:
  Secure the area

To provide authorized user access to the data and the computational power of the host systems, controlled local and remote communication links were installed often using fiber technology for local attachments, that while more expensive, has very good resistance to tapping. These links together with the network and systems software were usually configured to allow access only to specific applications. The remote connections were typically via leased lines connected to a remote communication controller with known terminals attached. These facilities and the technologies provided the IS organization with a set of tools to limit the access points to controlled locations. To further eliminate "leaving the door ajar" many networks were set up to disconnect the terminal from the application after a prespecified period of user inactivity. This essentially closes the door that the user might have inadvertently left open by logging on and leaving the terminal area unattended.

Security principal #2:
  Limit the access points

As a further control, network access was finely configured to assure only authorized access by limiting the terminal access to specific application based on the terminal location, the user ID, and password. For terminals that were enabled to access several applications on the network, the user would typically have to enter a valid network user ID and password, followed by an application password. In this case the network provides a very specific path to a specific system and a specific transaction processing control program, which in turn enables the user to a specific set of transactions based on the user ID and perhaps a second password. In some cases the actual terminal identification and the location of the terminal determines the accessibility to certain transactions and data. The transaction itself also controls the visibility of the data and whether the data can be updated, deleted, or read.

In the case of some mainframe environments, the operating system, transaction processing control program, and application architecture also limit the possibility of compromise from outside in that the program flow cannot be changed by any user accessing the application. In fact, many IS shops have very rigorous program change procedures that include code walk-throughs before a change is applied. The change is applied to a library that can only be updated by an authorized systems programmer with the approval of the security administrator. Since the on-line applications could only be accessed by using their externals, they were essentially *execute only*, which protects the applications from theft and increases the difficulty associated with trying to compromise them.

Probably the only ways that a mainframe using a secure operating system, such as IBM's MVS, could be compromised are by a person inside the authorized area with knowledge of the system programmer's password(s) or by "jamming" the system by creating a workload overload situation that might open a systems integrity window to crash the system or open it up long enough to compromise the system. For the most part, however, on-line transaction processing systems guard against such jamming.

Security principal #3:
• Limit access to authorized users

Security principal #4:
• Secure the sources for compromise from within

Exposures:
• Inside and password breech
• Jamming

As a result of the recognition of the exposures, the IS primary security focus has traditionally been in the areas of user password management and penetration detection. With the understanding that change introduces exposure, most mainframe systems have comprehensive change management programs that track data changes, program changes, and any situation that could affect availability or security. These logs are reviewed for anomalies to detect problems or exposures. Additionally, most systems track invalid user ID log on attempts and generate alerts, track password retries, and invalidate the password after three retries and send an alert, report log on attempts from unauthorized locations, and keep extensive audit trails for logged on users,.

While it is understood that data can be copied from the communications lines, most IS organizations have examined the cost of encryption and the associated complexities of key management and have decided to take the risk and focus on limiting the access authority of any remote user. For the most part encryption is used almost exclusively by defense and intelligence agencies, military contractors, the financial services industry for applications such as electronic funds transfer, and unique applications such as those that use the airwaves to communicate between two points.

Are these enterprise network environments secure? Probably not as secure as they could be, but they are protected, monitored, and managed. If asked, most IS executives are focused on providing service to their customers in terms of availability and data integrity, with security coming in somewhere down the list. The inclusion of the departmental LANs in the enterprise network, however, has caused much reexamination.

The systems are protected and monitored

17.4 A New World

LANs and workstations have dramatically altered the security picture from the dumb terminal accessing a controlled mainframe. The powerful new technologies, the ready availability of data analyzers, the ease with which a LAN can be tapped into, and the ease of accessibility to the relatively powerful yet unprotected workstations by unauthorized personnel can really present a security challenge. It certainly challenges the first security principal of securing the area.

When trying to protect the corporate assets and allowing workstations to access the enterprise network and applications, the enterprise network organization finds itself in a situation similar to that of the Secret Service protecting the President of the United States. The Secret Service have a similar challenge whenever the president goes into a crowd and wants to meet people. The Secret Service officers mumble under their breath and manage the situation as they have been trained to do. But these agents have an advantage that IS organizations don't have, they are present to assess the situation! The IS organization may be thousands of miles away or asleep when a perpetrator penetrates the workstation. Or worse yet, the perpetrator may be using an unwary or unsuspecting user as his or her surrogate.

The introduction of small or notso small, programmable, and open workstations makes it increasingly difficult to protect against equipment theft, software theft, data theft, and malicious compromise of a system or assuring data integrity. As long as these exposures can be localized to a workstation or department, the user or department can be expected to manage the risks. However, when one department connects to another department the exposure becomes a shared risk. When the user-managed network connects to the enterprise network or an IS managed system the risk belongs to the IS organization. The exposure then becomes an enterprise network problem to be solved. From an enterprise network standpoint, personal computers and departmental networks have significantly increased the number of entry points into the enterprise network and there is little infrastructure in place to control the access. This challenges the second security principal of limiting the access points.

Why does adding departmental networks to the enterprise network alter the security picture? It doesn't really alter security exposures, the exposures have existed within the departmental networks and with workstations in general all along. The enterprise network connection merely introduces an organization that is much more keenly aware of the exposures, the requirements, and that the stakes have been increased.

Challenges the first two principles of security:
- **secure the area**
- **limit the access**

New Security Issues :
- **NO!**
- **More Focus -YES!**
- **More risk -MAYBE**

Exposures
- **Many more open points of entry**
- **Dial-in**
- **Dial-out BBS, Compuserve, etc.**
- **Diskettes**
- **Network resident protocol analyzers**
- **Shared files on server**

To protect the corporate assets some companies have physically isolated workstations and LANs that have mission-critical applications from other departmental LANs. Others have limited some access to very specific applications that can only be read via IBM 3270 application interfaces. Some organizations limit enterprise network access with file transfer mechanisms to data exchange between the enterprise managed systems and the departmentally managed systems. Unfortunately, these are restrictive approaches and fly in the face of increased demand for corporate data and real-time operational data access. The new client-server technologies also introduce one level of indirection between the user and the system when it comes to security since neither can really be sure that the client software is only doing what it was intended to do.

Traditional security guidelines for LAN and wide area network (WAN) communication protection include:

- Locking up wiring boxes and junction closets
- Establishing a security policy for sensitive data
- Restricting the transmission of sensitive data
- Compressing data to make it difficult to read and alter, and improving transmission time
- Encrypting all data
- Monitoring for tapping with electrical characteristic change-detection devices

Unfortunately protecting the data is only a small part of the job of securing a network. While some of the measures on the list are common sense and are appropriate, others are overkill when one considers the exposure at the workstation and departmental network levels. Some of these security controls can be likened to securing the windows while forgetting to close the doors when one considers that the workstation is often left unattended and connected and logged into key applications.

17.5 How is this Security Delivered?

Whose responsibility is workstation security? From a product standpoint, which layer of software should be accountable to control access? Should it be the target applications? The network? The network operating system? The workstation operating system? The workstation application? A workstation utility? The only viable answer to all these questions is probably yes!

Each layer of the path must be responsible for its portion of the security, but the ultimate accountability must be with the user and the workstation software since it is virtually impossible to see if the entity at the other end of the wire is a person or a computer program.

Can the networking operating system and network operating systems help? You bet!

Can it do everything required? Possibly, but not probably. Let's look at the enterprise network in the context of multiple different operating systems that are glued together by a network operating system for specific services. It is important to note that it is unlikely that NetWare will control mainframe-based data sets, but it is feasible that NetWare may control access to a workstation's files since NetWare already has resident client software on the workstation. Part of the strength in a networking operating system is its ability to graft disparate operating environments together without impacting any of the environments. Its transparency and value are the key. Should the networking operating systems help protect the enterprise network security? Absolutely, if the networking operating systems don't, and there is a business demand, someone else will, but the NetWare is well positioned.

A networking operating system can play a major role in workstation security

NetWare already provides extensive access and visibility controls to resources on the Netware server, now the question is can and will these mechanisms be applied to workstation resident files. (I am referring to files that are associated with accessing and interacting directly with enterprise network resources.)

The networking operating system can directly support:

- Enforce network password rules
- Control access to the network
- Lock access after service access connection idle
- Assure network log in passwords are encrypted
- Assure that the source of the data is from the authorized user (authentication)
- Control access to network managed resources (e.g., directories, files, E-mail, printers, routers, gateways)
- Log activity against network managed workstation resources (e.g., directories, files, printers, gateways, routers)
- Provide hooks to guard against viruses on network managed volumes
- Provide productivity tools to manage groups and large volumes of users
- Operate with data encryption

Working together with the vendors for the workstation specific environments and tools, the network operating system can provide an environment from which workstation client-server utilities can operate. Representative workstation-specific services that can operate out of a server include:

- Guarding against viruses
- Recording the addition or removal of hardware
- Monitoring software inventory changes
- Workstation program registration

17.6 Why the Concern?

Why is enterprise network management concerned about into grating workstations and LANs into their network? Because they perceive a greater exposure to theft of valuable assets, malicious damage, data damage, and service damage.

Corporate spies have stolen trade secret data from companies such as Texas Instruments and Corning Glass Works and sold these to competitors costing these companies billions of dollars. The key is that the top three security breaches are from:

- Unauthorized computer access
- Tapping data communications
- Physical access to a network

Workstations with corporate network and data access increase the exposures because there are many ways a workstation can be compromised, ranging from no password protection to broadcasting sensitive data across an unsecure LAN. These exposures to theft can result in millions of dollars of lost opportunity, but an equally and potentially more frightening exposure is that of computer viruses that can mindlessly down an entire enterprise network.

For example, a workstation could spawn E-mail messages that overload the mail server and stress the network capacity causing unpredictable results. These types of occurrences are not limited to LANs, for example, on November 2, 1988, a Cornell graduate student created an Internet worm that was designed to travel from one computer to another using known UNIX loopholes. However, a programming error caused it to replicate uncontrollably, clogging the infected computers until the internet was shut down. IBM's internal internet (VNET) had a similar experience when a student in Europe created a mail-spawning program that clogged the network until it was shut down.

On the workstation end probably the most visible malicious penetration was 1992's focus on the Michael Angelo virus, which was a date triggered virus that executed on March 6, Michael Angelo's birthday. This virus overwrites the hard disk with random information found in memory. It wrote over the disks file allocation table and master boot record, rendering the hard disk useless. To make matters worse it was unwittingly shipped on several company's demo and product disks. This was a deliberate, mindless prank that caught many users, including one of the workstations in my organization. Luckily we were able to reconstruct the data and programs from the backup, but not without a lot of work. While this was by no means the worst virus of even the most common virus, it received enough attention to help the users focus on security.

The common denominator for these incidents is the ability to transfer execrable code to another environment and to find a mechanism to allow this code to execute. Most production on-line systems using robust operating systems such as IBM's MVS and on-line transaction processing subsystems like IBM's IMS and CICS do not have a direct connection between data and execrable code. Therefore these on-line systems are far less susceptible to such compromises without inside help.

On the other hand, interactive systems, such as these provided with DOS, Windows, OS/2, UNIX, and Mac workstations as well as mainframes, such as IBM's VM and TSO, allow users or user programs to control program execution. In these interactive environments, extra care must be taken to firewall the users with these capabilities from the general production system software or application software. Without a fire-walling technology the only recourse is to educate the users, limit access to the workstations, install detection tools, install correction tools, monitor activity for anomalies, and constantly review and tune the security based on experience.

The steps to solve these problems are usually: network passwords, network audit trail, and limited access to networking equipment, but this is really only the beginning since workstations introduce many opportunities to bypass these protection mechanisms.

Now let us look at some of the workstation specific controls.

Chapter 18

Workstation Security

18.1 The First Line of Defense

The first security hurdle to overcome when implementing a network operating system is establishing the respective security responsibilities among the users and the enterprise network organization. These responsibilities must be based on the principles that are consistent with the user's desires and abilities in order not to be ignored or by-passed. The technical challenge is that the user workstation is a very powerful system that can introduce security risks because of its flexibility and computing capabilities. For example, a user can easily create network log in scripts that contain stored log-on IDs and passwords. These IDs and passwords might not, and probably aren't encrypted so that if the workstation disk storage were searched the authorized user IDs and passwords could be found and used from other workstations by an unauthorized person.

A workstation is really a very sophisticated system that when connected to the enterprise network essentially becomes a key enterprise network resource, at least for the user and the owning department. It might also be viewed as part of the enterprise network. Unfortunately in many instances these workstations are treated more like a typewriter or calculator with an eye into the mainframe than a system. The problem is that while many of the security facilities that could protect the enterprise network and the user workstation are available to the user, most are not invoked.

For example; How many of your company's workstations are locked with the key lock when not in use? How many are password protected in the CMOS? How many are left on all the time (including over night) without a keyboard lock? Without this level of protection the workstations represent a major security risk.

Even with a password, it is surprising how easy it is for perpetrators to guess the password when they know something about the user or are in the user's office. This is because most passwords are selected from something the user can remember, and because most of us are passworded to death with PIN numbers, phone card numbers, and numerous different system and network passwords. As a result, if given the choice, we typically use something that we won't forget, like our name, a spouse's first name, a child's name, or an important date. If forced to change the password on a regular basis, the passwords we choose are often repetitive.

The only solution is to implement a password structure that forces some rigor or has a secondary authentication. Secondary authentication mechanisms can involve fingerprint scanners, retina scanners, smart card readers, tokens, and signature verification. Unfortunately, while they greatly improve log-in security, these secondary authentication techniques tend to introduce expense and inconvenience. This leaves a good password control tool and password encryption with a solid security policy in force as the most probable solutions.

If the workstation is not secure, then all the best network log in schemes are at risk, in spite of whether the connection is to a local network server or a host system across the enterprise network. I've lost count of the number of workstation users I know who have their network operating system log in as part of their startup procedure (e.g., their AUTOEXEC.BAT). Not only is the log in process included in this procedure but quite frequently so is the password, if a password is required. This approach makes the log in very easy. In fact, there is really nothing wrong with this approach to ease of use if the workstation is truly secured with a key, CMOS password, and/or keyboard lock such that no one other than the intended user has access to this important information.. But if these workstation locking controls are not being used, anyone can gain access the the log in information.

For those users who have been educated and conscientious enough to manually input their password at network log in time there are other risks. One such exposure is a relatively easy to implement spoofing technique in which case the perpetrator alters the startup procedure and installs a program in an unattended workstation. From the user standpoint the log in procedure behaves the same, and sometimes some erratic unexplained characters fly across the screen but go away. When the user responds to the request for password, the spoofing program stores the password in a special file, which is then passed on over the network. Alternatively, if less sophisticated, the spoofing program causes a hang condition, and the user re-boots (not an unusual event) and logs in as normal. At some later point the perpetrator returns and reads the file with the passwords.

In a local-area network (LAN) situation the perpetrator does not even have to touch the user's workstation. The perpetrator can create a Trojan Horse program, so named because it is brought in by the users who believe it to something else. This Trojan Horse program is usually made available in a public network library and typically provides some desired service that the user would like to use. In addition to the services that the program purportedly provides, it can update the user's log in procedure to accomplish the same password theft as the previous scenario, in this case the passwords could be written to a shared file on the server. Without the appropriate auditing and monitoring mechanisms, this program can easily go undetected and be untraceable. On the other hand, in a well monitored environment the perpetrator could quickly be detected.

Right about now some of you are thinking that "this Trojan Horse stuff is academically interesting, but it couldn't happen to me." Well it happened to me in 1985. While managing a large IS organization my security officer found a "neat little Christmas card program" in a shared library on one of our IBM VM systems. This Christmas card program would paint a Christmas tree on my terminal screen to the tune of "Jingle Bells." He prodded me to try it out. When I typed in XMAS as requested, the image of a Christmas tree started to move up my screen to the tune of "Jingle Bells." Suddenly, before it was finished painting the message "your files are being deleted" flashed on the screen and my file names in each of my directories flashed by. I could do nothing to stop it. All sort of crazy thoughts ran through my mind — When was the last backup? Where was my security officer going to be employed tomorrow? He smiled, "I just wanted you to experience a Trojan Horse. I found this one and declawed it yesterday." Hence I have a deep respect for this type of penetration.

Since an intruder needs both a valid user and a matching valid password, the first hurdle is a valid user ID. User ID lists should not be readily available, since easy accessibility makes it easier to penetrate network. Once your user ID is known, the perpetrators only need to guess the password.

> **The first line of defense is to secure the workstation such that it cannot be used to penetrate the enterprise network.**

18.2 The Single Sign On

Most multiserver and multisystem network users have some sort of single sign-on procedure to improve ease of access. This ease-of-use technique may result in an increased security risk, because a single successful log on gives a perpetrator access to many servers and systems. The single sign on is especially risky if log on scripts are stored in easy-to-access .BAT files that anyone could read if the workstation was left unattended without a keyboard lock security mechanism activated.

The more sophisticated single-log-on implementations may adequately protect the scripts, but often send new passwords to all the systems and servers that the user accesses, to keep them synchronized. To capture the user's password the perpetrator simply causes the user's password to be invalidated by exceeding the valid number retries. When the user resets the password, the perpetrator monitors the data exchange for the new repetitive passwords as they flow over the LAN. All this can be done with a relatively inexpensive LAN protocol analyzer that record all the traffic and frequently provide all sorts of data analysis capabilities to reduce the search and analysis time. To further the exposure some passwords are even sent in the clear (unencrypted) across the LAN or wide-area network (WAN).

A more appropriate solution is for password synchronization to be done by a service on the server, which significantly reduces the risk of identification being made by a protocol analyzer. Additionally, Token Ring LANs and Ethernet Hubs can reduce the ease with which the perpetrator can insert the protocol analyzer into the network without detection. Traditional Ethernet LANs offer no such comfort.

An even more sophisticated way for authentication to be made is implemented as part of the Distributed Computing Environment Kerberos system. Kerberos uses an on-line key-distribution service that the client accesses to obtain a ticket for a designated service. This ticket contains an encrypted key (using the Data Encryption Standard (DES) encryption algorithm) that is generated for that one session. This encryption includes such information as the identity of the client and the time of the request. The service also returns the session key encrypted under the client's master key. On the workstation the client key is obtained as a function of the user's password. This key is then used as an electronic signature that authenticates the client when accessing a remote system. This type of solution solves the LAN monitoring problem and the password coordination problem.

18.3 Password Protection

Once users have been identified, their passwords and IDs move along with them from file server to file server rather than requiring that they reenter them. Each time an ID and password are entered, there is a possibility that someone else will pick them off the network. To protect the user from this exposure an *object reuse facility* is often used. When the *object reuse facility is* used the user only enters an ID and password once and therefore tightens security holes. (An object reuse facility is a requirement for a C2 rating.)

All current network operating systems use encryption or a hash value when transmitting the log in password. The most common approach is a *one-way encryption*. This technique encrypts or hashes the initial password and stores it in that form. Subsequent log in passwords are encrypted or hashed using the same algorithm and compared with the encrypted or hashed stored password.

These encrypted or hashed passwords are stored on the server in the network operating system files where they cannot be accessed by the users. The only access to these files is via authorized backup utilities or physical access. While this technique was adequate for many departmental applications for a while, it is no longer sufficient because of the sophistication of inexpensive network (LAN) analysis tools.

Password pluckers are a new type of over-the-counter, password cracking program being marketed to users and network administrators who forget their passwords. In the wrong hands, these programs can be used to compromise otherwise secure systems. These powerful, double-edged cracking products can pull out passwords from a variety of computer platforms, including IBM PC-compatibles, Apple Computer, Inc., Macintoshes, and even Novell, Inc.'s, NetWare.

18.4 Virus Protection

One of the primary responsibilities of an enterprise network manager is to protect the network so that it is available for use by all its users and that the network does not become an unguarded doorway to allow theft of information, compromised data, or general disruption of service. For the most part, there is some logic associated with the theft of information and the compromising of data. I use the word logic here in the context that the perpetrator has an intent and is focused on not being detected and apprehended. This logic allows a good security officer who has a sense of the business assets and business pressures the ability to identify risky areas, set traps, and force a trail to be left.

Unfortunately these thoughtful approaches do not really help when it comes to dealing with the mindless characteristics of viruses. The sole purpose of a virus is disruption. In most cases victims are random and often those least able to recover from the virus without an impact to their business. A Dataquest/National

Computer Security Association virus study in late 1991 concluded that over 60 percent of American companies and government agencies are hit by viruses each quarter.

Some representative viruses include: Stoned, Michael, No-Int, Casc1701, Casc1704, Green Caterpillar, Jerusalem, Yankee Doodle, Frodo, Darkavenger, Hilton, Twin, Groove, Mummy, and Dedicated. These viruses are typically introduced by insiders and rather innocently by workstation users from floppy diskettes or from programs that are imported from bulletin boards. Once a virus has infected a workstation, it can move through the network from computer to computer and create havoc.

The first defense is to keep viruses off workstations and the second is to have mechanisms to detect its presence if a virus get by the first defense. Numerous virus-filter and -detection software and hardware products have been developed to assist the workstation users and the network managers in protecting the network and the user. Antivirus tools are now included with operating systems, by workstation utilities, plus platforms are provided by network operating systems, such as NetWare. These virus-detection mechanisms come in multiple forms for a workstation, server, or domain of servers:

- Manually invoked scans

- Automatically invoked scans

- Scheduled scans (specified times or random)

- Real-time monitoring (periodically, e.g., scans in the early morning hours)

These detection mechanisms are usually accompanied by various notification options that include a:

- Pop-up to the workstation user

- Broadcast to a designated group of users

- Message to an E-mail address through the message handling system

- Message to the pager of a duty manager

In the enterprise network context, the detection of viruses cannot be left up to the individual workstation user, since the protection against a virus infecting the network is as good as the least secure workstation. This means that a server, group of servers, minis, and mainframes need to be configured to provide the appropriate coverage and fast response system. It is also probably unlikely that a single detection tool from a single vendor meets the enterprise network's needs because of the large mix of hardware and software platforms and connectivity options.

As such each network operating system must provide hooks and a platform for the various tools and facilitate mechanisms to communicate the alerts and logs to that (those) appropriate collection point(s) while being protected itself. There are multiple NetWare Loadable Modules (NLMs) that provide a variety of virus scanning and action tools. Some of these NLMs not only scan the workstation's hard disk but also the server volumes for viruses or virus tracks (changes) before the program files are installed on the server. NetWare 4.0 provides software vendors an application programming interfaces (API) to link antivirus software to NetWare, making it easier to access anti virus software. Additionally, the network operating system and the anti-virus product need to be secure from the penetration such that the NLMs are not unloaded or the alarms disabled. This demands solid, authorized user identification and password protection.

Since enterprise networks by definition include many workstations, servers, minis, and mainframes, virus-detection accuracy is probably the single most important attribute for the detection tools. Since the volume of potential viruses in a large enterprise network can easily approach the thousands, it is important to select detection products that carefully screen those situations flagged before turning on the alert (alarm). If the screening is not done, the network managers will expend a lot of unproductive time or worse, start viewing the tool with a "cry wolf" attitude.

The enterprise network antivirus tool(s) should have selectable options for the necessary types of scans. Typical scans include file types, such as .exe, .com, and .bat, as well as compressed and archived files, workstation and NLM memory, and boot record on the physical storage media. Probably the most comprehensive file scan is one that is activated when the file is opened or copied. While this potentially doubles the load time, the duration is typically so small (a 10- to 20 second time frame) that it is not a problem.

Again, volume is important, so the antivirus tool should be able to handle exception lists and support groups, plus check files copied to the server, files copied from the server to another server or workstation, and files executed on the server. At a minimum an antivirus scan should be included as an integral part of the backup procedures in order to be sure that compromised data or a virus aren't being backed up.

Once detected the antivirus tool(s) must be able to delete the virus, move the virus, disinfect the file, or correct the boot record. It should also maintain an audit log of all activity for a given domain. This audit log should report files skipped and the reason they were skipped (e.g., it was open or locked at the time of the scan). The log should also include all the results from the scans and the actions taken,. Which lets you check the status of all servers from a central location.

Representative products include:

- CPANET (Central Point Software, Beaverton, Oregon)
- UNTOUCHABLE NLM (Fifth Generation, Baton Rouge Louisiana)
- INOCULAN (Cheyenne Software, Roslyn Heights, New York)
- LANPROTECT (Intel PCED, Hillsboro, Oregon)
- SITELOCK (Brightwork Development, Tinton Falls, New Jersey)

18.5 How Safe is Your Connection?

Because LANs are built around the concept of sharing the wire, the secure network operating system must have a method to authenticate the identity of the requester on every packet. Without this protection intruders might be able to forge packets to gain access to the server.

In a worst case scenario the intruder could become the supervisor long enough to create an authorized log in ID with supervisor authority.

In 1992, some students and professors at Leiden University in the Netherlands demonstrated this threat by penetrating a NetWare server and taking over a logged-in user's ID and using that user's privileges long enough to increase their own privileges. This was accomplished by determining the user's network address and connection number (both readily available to anyone on the LAN) and request sequence number (a number that ranges from 0 to 255). The intruders simply tried different sequence numbers until they matched. (The server simply throws away the out-of-sequence traffic.)

To close this hole Novell implemented a *packet signature* that would validate the client-server communications. A *session key* is assigned to each client requesting a Packet signature during the log in process. Every time the client makes a request, it signs the request with an encrypted signature based on the session key, the last packet's signature, and a fingerprint algorithm. This signature is then appended to the packet and sent to the server.

The server receives the request makes its calculations, and compares the results. If the packet signature doesn't match, the packet is thrown away and a message is sent to the network console.

The packet signature uses an encryption scheme licensed by RSA Data Security, Inc., based in Redwood City, California. The fix, which was added shortly after the demonstration in NetWare 4.0, includes a digital signature technique that encrypts each packet of data before it flows over a network. Previously, NetWare only encrypted the ID and password information.

Data encryption techniques not only make it expensive to read the stolen data, it also provides a level of integrity protection in that most encryption techniques use chained messages constructed such that any alteration of a previous message invalidates the rest.

Although encryption techniques are being used more frequently for a variety of applications, including password protection, masking data on credit cards, and encrypting files on workstation disk drives and floppies, protecting data traversing LANs and WANs is still in the future for the average enterprise network, albeit the near future. In fact, as the number of LANs with sensitive data increase and the technology required to support the encryption continues to plummet in cost and improve in terms of reduction in complexity, the price and interest portions of the product acceptance algorithm are tipping in favor of encryption. Most companies will look to the carriers to provide economical, secure data transmissions, but are continually reexamining the option for their in-house LANs.

RSA Public-key Crypto

RSA, developed by Ron Rivest, Adi Shamir, and Leonard Adleman while they were at MIT in 1978, is a public-key cryptographic algorithm used for both encryption and authentication. It is modeled around an algorithm of factoring very large numbers. The key size determines the potential time to break the code.

The RSA algorithm is patented in the United States by RSA Data Security, Inc., of Redwood City, California, a company formed to market the RSA algorithm. Outside the United States, the RSA algorithm is in the public domain.

Encryption technologies have been use by government agencies and many financial institutions especially for funds transfer applications, now these technologies are being explored for lower price points and supporting the various workstations and protocols of today's enterprise network. For example an enterprise network solution must support DOS, UNIX, OS/2 and Macs. It must support TCP/IP, ISO IP, Novell IPX, DECnet Phase IV, and other popular protocols to be comprehensive. More over this solution must be transparent to the network and the protocols.

One such implementation is being marketed by Semaphore Communications Corp., a Xerox Company. Semaphore offers the Network Security System (NSS) which is a set of products that secure data transmission and provide access control for an enterprise network. The product includes single node and workgroup encryption units. These units are interconnected with hub encryption units and site encryption units that can be placed at the routers to protect data that will be sent across a wide area network.

The primary technical consideration with encryption is the question of whether it can be implemented in the software, on a board that is inserted in the workstation, attaches to an outboard unit. Software encryption can be very CPU intensive, boards take up valuable workstation real estate unless the capability is integrated in the network attachment adapter such as an Ethernet adapter or Token Ring adapter. I would expect to see variations of these emerging in the next year and half.

18.6 Inventory Tools Increase Security

The primary objective of a LAN inventory package is to identify the hardware and software components for each workstation attached to the LAN. These programs catalog the CPU, memory, coprocessors, video adapters, hard drives, and network cards, as well as operating system and version numbers. As a result LAN inventory packages can be very helpful in addressing any enterprise network security risks that are associated with physical equipment tracking.

LAN inventory packages can scan for all the information during the network log on, or they can be memory resident in the workstation to monitor changes at regular time intervals. Some packages notify network managers about changes as they occur. These alerts can frequently be tailored to certain types of changes, while others provide change reports reporting the before and after change configurations.

Recently some of these inventory packages have been extended to track software components beyond the operating system. This extension significantly improves the time it takes to identify the presence of a new program or a change to a program on a workstation. For this reason it can become an excellent change management tool for monitoring the workstation configuration and software. Additionally, this software tracking significantly reduces the time necessary for damage control should a virus or other intruder appear.

Some network managers see the inventory tools as a way of tracking all the software on each workstation, while some companies with very sensitive data would prefer diskless workstations to control the software on the workstation. Others who need more flexibility would prefer software registration tools to control the software at the workstation.

Many security conscious network managers also want these programs to identify who is connected to the server. With Ethernet LANs there is always a chance that a phantom user is on the network. (An alternative to monitoring for this is to provide electronic packet signatures such that only valid users can participate.)

In summary, most there are multiple separate software products and packages that are required to support security, software-metering, inventory, software registration, virus protection, and so on, but most network managers would like these functions into a single package or provided by the networking operating system.

Chapter 19

NetWare Security

19.1 Introduction

Large and small corporations are moving mission-critical data, such as payroll and reservation systems, from mainframes and other systems to local area networks. NetWare 4.01 enables them to choose whether to retain centralized control of the network or to delegate some administrative responsibilities to other network users. At the same time strict control is retained over who has access to supervisory privileges:

- Public-key data encryption

- New auditing functions

- An Application Programming Interface (API) that will allow software suppliers to more easily design antivirus programs that run on NetWare local area networks

NetWare security can be made as simple or as comprehensive as the installation requires. Access rights can be set to limit a user's access to specific files, within designated directories, to a specified workstation, or during specific hours of the day. Similarly, access rights can be assigned to the properties of every object, including items such as a phone number or a password.

NetWare 4 includes a new directory that, together with some packet signature capabilities and sophisticated password handling, provides a very robust security platform.

The LOGIN command controls the workstation access to the NetWare network. The LOGIN processing assures that access is granted to only those with valid user IDs (also referred to as *name-of-user object*) and matching valid passwords. A person must know both in order to access a secured network. While NetWare does not require a password to be entered, participation in an enterprise network demands that passwords be mandatory. With the level of intruder detection selected, the administrator can set retry thresholds; select retention time for accruing reject log in tries in terms of minutes, hours, or days; and to select the length of password lockout.

NetWarealso provided to:

- Log in time control restricts the hours during which a user can LOGIN. This interval is set by a 7 day 24-hour time map
- Limit the number of concurrent server connections that this user can have
- Limit the amount of disk space for each user
- Controls access for accounts based on expiration date
- Controls the users log in address (NetAddress Restrictions)

NetWare also logs LOGIN activity and LOGIN attempts. These attemptscan be monitored to keep track such as information as how many times an incorrect ID and password are entered. These audit reports can be used to identify when unauthorized accesses are being attempted.

NetWare currently encrypts passwords and authentication certificates. It has has committed to providing packet data encryption in a future release.

19.2 Log In Security

NetWare provides all the password controls found on well-established enterprise network systems. For example:

- Passwords are never displayed on the monitor or transmitted across the network.

- Minimum password length controls can be used to eliminatethe use of trival passwords. The default is five characters. Although passwords can be much longer if the minimum password length is set to 11 or more, Macintosh users will not be able to log in. (Since the maximum length of the password for a Macintosh user is 10 characters.).

- Periodic password change controls are available, the defaults is to require a password change every 90 days.

- Unique password usage controls. NetWare "remembers" the last eight previous passwords that have been used for at least one day.

From a user standpoint the authentication and access control processes are totally transparent. The NetWare log in consists of entering a user name (ID) and a password. NetWare does the rest. However, behind the scenes NetWare uses some very sophisticated techniques to *authenticate* the user, control the visibility and access of NetWare managed resources, and *authenticate* every action of a user. Let's walk-through a scenario, obviously not somnething that the user sees!

The local-area network (LAN) administrator (network supervisor) creates a user ID and assigns values and access authorizations for each. The log in security is established by creating a user password. Each time a password is created or changed, NetWare invokes the RSA public-key crypto algorithm to generate a user's public and private key. The user's private key is then stored on the server encrypted under the user's password.

After the user enters LOGIN and the user name, the authentication process begins. The NetWare shell program sends the log in request and user name to the server directory. The server interrogates the object directory to determine the user's access to the network, which includes validating that the user can log in at this time of day and week, whether this user can access the network from this workstation, whether the account is still current, and whether a password is required. Since this is an enterprise network example, the answer is yes.

Once it is determined that a password is required, the server begins the user authentication process. The server retrieves the encrypted user's private key and encrypted password and sends the private key and a random key in a message that is encrypted under the user's encrypted password.

The NetWare shell then asks the user for the password. The shell software then uses the user's password to decrypt the random key in the message in order to obtain the private key.

In the next exchange with the server the client applies the digital signature (private key) to the request and responds to the server. The server compares this digital signature (private key) and the user's public key stored in the server's directory to verify that a valid password was entered. The user's password never passes over the network wire, thus avoiding interception. This technique is referred to as *zero-knowledge proof.*

Once the user has the appropriate encrypted signature, which authenticates the user ID, passwords must not be reentered to access other servers to which this user has access authorization. Authentication is done as a background. This includes scanning an access control list to ensure that the user has been granted rights to the resource by an authorized administrator.

Each time a user logs in to the network, the security algorithm generates a new encrypted private key.

The authentication process uses a Kerberos-like handshake technique that employs an encrypted password and a server-provided encrypted key to establish a digital signature that is used to authenticate all communications with NetWare. To ensure security, critical authentication data for a particular user (including the password) is never transmitted across the network. The data that provides the basis of authentication is valid only for the duration of the current log in session. The authentication guarantees that:

- Only the purported sender built the message
- The message came from the workstation where the authentication data was created
- The message pertains to the current session.

- The message contains no information counterfeited from another session
- The message has not been tampered with or corrupted

NetWare also provides security by controlling the visibility to resources and the operations and access authorities of each user. The scope of visibility and authority is tied to the user ID. The user ID is set up by assignments that grant access to one or more directories, files, or objects with associated rights. (Novell refers to the user ID as *trustee* of the assigned objects.) As a productivity tool a group can be formed for user IDs and other objects. For example, a name (*group object*) can be created listing all of the user IDs. All the user IDs in that group are granted access with one trustee assignment. Similarly, if the trustee assignment is itself a group object, then every user in the group is granted access to all objects in that group.

NetWare Directory and Security Terminology

- **Log In Security (controls which users can access the network)**
- **Trustees (are users with access to directories, files, and objects)**
- **Rights (determine the level of access for each trustee)**
- **Inheritance (passes rights from higher to lower levels)**
- **Attributes (describe characteristics of directories and files)**
- **Effective Rights (a user's actual calculated rights to a directory, file, or object)**
- **Objects (a label for the NetWare Directory Services entry to correspond with people, computers, services, countries, organizations, and so on.**

In other words, the administration is accomplished through relationships coming from the resource to which the access and *rights* are granted or from the user ID (*object trustee*) that is accessing the objects. Therefore each directory, file, and object has a list of trustee assignments called a *trustees list*. This list tells who can access that directory, file, or object. Each user ID also has a list of what it can access and how. This is all managed through the directory services via selections from lists, thus eliminating rekeying and minimizing errors.

Each object is also assigned rights as part of the authorization process. For example, an assignment could grant a trustee the right to create files in a directory.

Because directories, files, and objects contain such different information, the rights that control access to each are different. For example, there are five kinds of rights in NetWare v4.0:

- Directory rights control what a trustee can do with the directory
- File rights control what a trustee can do with the file
- *Object* rights control what a trustee can do with the object
- *Property* rights control access to information stored within the object
- *Access Control right* is required to grant directory or file rights to other users

To get a feel for the comprehensives of the NetWare security I am including several tables that will provide a sense of the capabilities and the types of items that are tracked and controlled. Table 19-1 lists the controls available to lockout intruder, Table 19-2 lists the key directory attributes to protect and control how the contents are treated, Table 19-3 lists the attributes to protect and control how files are treated.

Beyond lockout and control audit trails are extreamly important. Table 19-4 provides a checklist of some representative controls that are desireable for audit purposes. Any changes in status and the tracking mechanism should have the flexibility to flag specific events and take action. Action might include sending a message to a pager or sending an E-mail message.

Table 19-1 Intruder Lockout Options

NETADMIN Option	NetWare Administrator Option	Usage
Detect Intruders	Detect intruders	NetWare keeps track of incorrect log in attempts
Log in Intruder Limit	Incorrect log in attempts	Limits incorrect password on log in attempts. When exceeded the account is locked
Interval for Intruder Attempt reset (D/H/M)	Intruder attempt reset interval (Days/Hours/Minutes)	The time NetWare waits before resetting the incorrect log in attempt count
Lockout after detection	Lock account after detection	Denies network access to any user who exceeds the incorrect log in attempt or log in intruder limit number
Interval for Intruder lockout reset (D/H/M)	Intruder lockout reset interval (Days/Hours/Minutes)	The time after a user has been locked out before NetWare allows the user to log in again

Table 19-2 Directory Attributes

Attribute	Description
Normal (N)	Sets the directory to no attributes
Delete Inhibit (Dl)	Prevents any user from erasing the directory
Hidden (H)	Hides the directory from the DOS or OS/2 DIR command and prevents it from being deleted or copied.
Purge (P)	Tells NetWare to purge the directory and any file in the directory when deleted.
Rename Inhibit (RI)	Prevents any user from renaming the directory
Immediate Compress (Ic)	Marks the directory so that all files in it are compressed
Don't Compare (Dc)	Marks the directory so files in it are never compared.
Don't Migrate (Dm)	Mark the directory so that files in it are never migrated to a secondary storage device (like a tape drive or optical disk)
System (Sy)	The directory is hidden from the DOS or OS/2 DIR command and cannot be deleted or copied.

Table 19-3   File Attributes

Attribute	Description
Archive Needed (A)	Indicates that the file has been changed since the last back up. Set when file is modified. Backup programs clears.
Can't Compress (Cc)	A status flag set by NetWare to indicate that the file cannot be compressed because of limited space savings.
Compressed (Co)	A status flag set by NetWare to indicate that the file is compressed.
Copy Inhibit (Ci)	(Only valid on Macintosh workstations.) Prevents user from copying the file.
Delete Inhibit (Di)	Prevents any user from erasing the file.
Don't Compress (Dc)	Marks the file so that it is never compressed.
Don't Migrate (Dm)	Marks the file so that it will never be migrated to a secondary storage device (like a tape drive or optical disk).
Execute Only (X)	Prevents a file from being copied. Backup utilities do not backup the file.
Hidden (H)	Hides the file from the DOS or OS/2 DIR command and prevents it from being deleted or copied. The NetWare NDIR command shows the file if the user has the right to see it.
Immediate Compress (Ic)	Marks the file so that it is compressed on disk as soon as the operating system is able to.
Indexed (Q)	A status flag set by NetWare when a file exceeds a set size. Indicates that the file is indexed for fast access.
Migrated (M)	A status flag set by NetWare to indicates that the file is migrated.
Purge (P)	Tells NetWare to purge the file when it is deleted. The file cannot be salvaged with the FILER utility.
Read Only (Ro)	Indicates that no one can write to this file.
Rename Inhibit (R)	Prevents a user from renaming a file.
Shareable (S)	Allows the file to be accessed by more than one user at a time. It is usually used in combination with the Read Only attribute.
System (Sy)	A DOS and OS/2 attribute. The NetWare NDIR command shows the file, if the user has the right to see it.
Transactional (T)	Indicates that the file is protected by TTS (transaction tracking system). TTS prevents data corruption by ensuring that either all changes are made or no changes are made when a file is being modified.

Table 19-4   Audit Logs

Control	Features
Tracking	Registered files Scanned file with viruses
Scanning controls	Scheduled On demand Periodic After event(s)
Events	Any files activity on all files File activity on selected files Inbound writes Outbound writes Outbound reads Deletes Moves Renames Data base updates
Actions	Notification • User • Contact • Groups • E-mail • Pager Lock access Repair Move Rename File registration
Recognition methods	Habit checking Virus database Physical scans Memory scans File monitor

NetWare provides many of these capabilities, but includes a way of controlling the authority and visibility to certain data of the auditors. Using the AUDITCON utility, auditors can audit Directory Services transactions as well as those specific to a volume, file, system, or server. These include:

- Log ins and log outs
- Trustee modifications
- File creations, deletions, reads, and writes
- Directory creations, deletions, reads, and writes
- Requests to manipulate queues
- Events directly related to Directory Services objects
- Events directly related to users

The designated auditors can track events and activities on the network, but they do not have rights to open or modify network files unless they are granted rights by the network supervisor. The auditing is enabled at the volume level for file system auditing. (See Tables 19-5 and 19-6.)

You can view the report to see all its contents or apply a filter. Multiple filters can be created for variety of reports.

- Auditing reports
- Edit report filters
- Report by date and time
- Report by event
- Report excludes paths/files
- Report excludes users
- Report includes paths/files
- Close old audit file
- Copy old audit file
- Delete old audit file
- Display audit
- Reset audit data file

Table 19-5   Auditing Volumes and Servers

Option		Explanation
Audit by Event		Events are dependent on the files/directories and users audited. This is either set for specific users and events or done globally.
	File Events *Events recorded:*	Directory create or delete File open, close, read, and write Globally for all files/directories By user or file By user and file
	QMS Events	QMS (Queue Management Service) activities affecting queues, such as requests to create or destroy a queue
	Server Events	Events that affect a specific server, such as mounting a volume, creating or deleting a bindery object, or bringing down a server all the server events are recorded
	User Events	include log ins and log outs, and creating or deleting users
Audit by File		The user select from a list of all files and directories. Each event is recorded for the file or directory selected
Audit by User		The user identifications to be audited are selected from a list. Each event is recorded
Audit Options Configuration		Audit file parameters to specify what will be done when audit file reaches specified size
Change Audit Password		Change the auditor password for the volume
Disable Volume		Disables auditing for this volume
Display Audit		Displays volume's Audit Data file information

Table 19-6   Directory Services Events:

Option	Explanation
Audit by DS Event	Select the events you want to audit
Audit Options	Audit file parameters to specify what will be done when specified size is reached
Change Audit Password	Change the Auditor password for the container
Disable Container Auditing	Disables auditing for this container
Display Audit Information	Displays general information about the Audit Data file for the volume or container

NetWare 4.0 also provides security controls for NetWare log ins from Apple Macintosh clients using its integrated support of AppleTalk protocols. The Mac network addresses can be limited, audited, and excluded.

19.3 Orange Book Compliance

The Trusted Computer System Evaluation Criteria, which is better known as *The Orange Book* because of its bright cover, published by the Department of Defense Computer Center (part of the National Security Agency) on August 15, 1983, established a standard to describe the overall confidence one can place on the system's ability to protect sensitive information. Each rating class specifies the required functional abilities of such features as user identification and authentication, auditing, and data labeling; it also defines the level of assurance required to ensure that the product's security mechanisms are properly implemented and cannot be circumvented.

For example:

A1 Verified Design
B3 Security Domains
B2 Structured Protection
B1 Labeled Security Protection
C2 Controlled Access Protection
C1 Discretionary Security Protection
D   Minimal Protection

The criteria for each class of security controls are cumulative; for example, whereas class C products incorporate discretionary security controls, class B products include mandatory controls and other requirements in addition to discretionary controls.

Many users have accepted the C2 rating as the minimum level of security for data base and other systems processing sensitive business data. At a C2 security level, users are individually accountable for their actions through the use of log on procedures, audit trails of security-related events, and resource isolation.

Novell and several partners (chief among these are Gordant, Inc., Mergent International, Inc., AT&T's Secure Communications Systems business unit, and Datamedia Corp.) recently announced plans to seek C2 (in the United States) and E2 (in

Europe) security evaluations. E2 classification differs from that the Orange Book classification in the ITSEC addresses assurance-related criteria separately from the criteria for evaluating system functional abilities. The E2 criteria also go beyond protecting the confidentiality of information to include the integrity and availability of information.

The significance of Novell's effort and the government's agreement is that this is the first time that the federal government has agreed to undertake the evaluation of a multivendor offering.

Many currently available relational data base products that run on NetWare provide a subset of class C2 features, and these vendors are developing products to meet the complete range of C2 requirements.

Novell's declaration has moved much more focus to security and has caused some previously disinterested customers to take a closer look at NetWare in their enterprise context.

19.4 Security Summary

In summary with the introduction of NetWare provides a variety of access control options and security features. NetWare 4 and its new directory significantly increases the options and expands the scope to an enterprise view of the servers from a single workstation. With the new directory a the user no longer has to log on to each server, the network will provide the user with the access to all authorized servers based on the logon ID.

With the ongoing security, control, and audit enhancements Novell has positioned Netware as a viable enterprise network force in the eyes of many information security professionals. These advances, in conjunction with other third party products which track hardware and software inventory, provide software metering and even provide copy protection with execute only capabilities compare to the state of the art in even the more sophisticated enterprise network organizations. The biggest caveat is that these capabilities must be activated before they can be effective an this will take some planning time for most organizations.

Chapter 20

Summary

20.1 The Highlights

To this point, if you have read this book the way that I had intended, you have:

- touched upon the distinctions between an enterprise network versus multiple networks interconnected in an enterprise and how NetWare can perform in both roles,

  Enterprise network means managed

- reviewed the variations of downsizing, rightsizing, reengineering and upsizing and NetWare can be applied in each approach

  NetWare independent of management approach

- noted that the enterprise network boundary is extending into the workstation and as NetWare is

  Network boundary is in the workstation

- noted that new techniques and technologies are required to support end users and their workstations and NetWare provides leverage here

  NetWare supports end users

- identified where in the S-curve your company and specific organizations are, and recognizing that NetWare departmental networks are moving into the integration stage

  Many departments in entering third stage

- noted mixed environments is an opportunity that can be harnessed using networking operating systems such as NetWare to mask or provide a focal point

  NetWare supports mixed workstations

- noted that network operating systems, specifically NetWare are well positioned to support the extension of the enterprise boundary to support the departmental user

  NetWare extends support to the workstation

NetWare comprehensive NOS

- looked at NetWare more as a comprehensive network operating system and integration vehicle rather than a LAN-based file server with add-on features

Supports multiple network protocols

- explored how the various user workstations interconnect with network servers, minis and mainframes and how NetWare supports IPX/SPX, TCP/IP, SNA, and mainframe channel connectivity

Client-server building block

- explored the significance of client-server technology as a vehicle for future flexibility and growth and identified that NetWare provides the building-blocks for client-server applications

NetWare for SAA supports IS

- noted the role of NetWare for SAA has evolved the concept of an SNA gateway to an enterprise network subsystem that supports IS infrastructure and bridges LAN-centric and mainframe-centric network management and services

Three network management approaches - mix or match

- explored the enterprise network management options including Novell's NetWare Network Management, TCP/IP SNMP interfaces, and IBM's NetView, identifying that NetWare servers can be managed from NetView

Focus on security

- assured yourself that Netware and NetWare-based tools can provide the appropriate security required to protect the enterprise assets.

Overall you have identified how NetWare can be applied to support many of your enterprise network needs and that NetWare can be effectively managed using the co-operative your, mine and our model support model.

Focus on integration

In short this book has focused more on the integration concerns, issues, and technologies required to provide more effective end-user workstation support using NetWare than the specific operational details of NetWare.

20.2 Different Roots Converging

The first step to understanding NetWare is that its roots are in departmental LANs and supporting mixed workstation environments. As a result many of the interfaces and tools are oriented toward departmental approaches. As part of the evolution of NetWare 3.11 and the introduction of NetWare 4 many of the issues that the IS organization is familiar is are surfacing. This is most noticeable in the richness of controls as listed in Chapter 9 of the Security section.

The evolving LAN-centric and mainframe-centric management models are best highlighted by the way problems are approached and resolved. For example traditional IS enterprise network infrastructure approaches installation planning with an extensive bill of material, clearly identified steps, a documented plan, in depth logistics and a pilot. This approach has evolved from the mindset that the solutions will be "fully cooked" before they are rolled out and that they will have to live with these solutions for a long time.

In contrast LAN-centric projects tend to be more focused on the here and now with the expectation that technology will keep up with their needs. It is not uncommon for the department solution to be designed by an integrator or consultant, the software and hardware is ordered and the solution is installed and made to work. One solution typically arrives before the other and one tends to last longer than the other. The trouble is that the Network Administrator's responsibilities (see Fig. 20-1) aren't getting any easier and the LAN Administrator's responsibilities (see Fig. 20-2) may soon look very similar. The best of both worlds would be to use the strengths of both. I have referred to

Departmental Approach

> **What you don't know can't hurt you ...**
> **but if it does it can be fixed.**

Enterprise Network Infrastructure approach

> **Avoid problems whenever you can ...**
> **but if you can't you will have to fix them.**

Figure 20-1 Enterprise Network Administrator

Figure 20-2 LAN Administrator

this a s "judo" in this book. NetWare can provide a source of of convergence using the yours, mine, ours model.

In addition to the differences in approach, the enterprise network staff's responsiveness is often hampered by the sheer complexity of interfacing and managing multiapplication, mutliplatform, multi-department applications and systems that are currently implemented, even without the introduction of departmental networks. Unfortunately, the environment is not going to get any easier. The departmental approach takes the diversity head on and solves it with various protocols and vendor pressure. Those that use NetWare are able to support a broad base of workstation, mini and mainframe interoperabilty using many of the technologies and approaches described in this book.

The enterprise network management team is challenged by having to meet service-level agreements and their commitment not to expose the network users to availability, performance, security, and data integrity risks. The LANs frequently implemented with technologies often unknown to the information systems (IS) infrastructure, and many evolved without any attention to remote support, problem management, security, and controls, since they were relatively isolated to a specific group of users. The differences in systems management rigors and accountability between the departmental LANs and the enterprise network, however, are reconcilable given the right change agents and using a technology that meets both organization's requirements. I have tried to focus on the security and network, LAN, and workstation management tools to help close the knowledge gap.

Independent of the risks, businesses are pushing for the integration of workstations into the enterprise network. Pragmatic workstation, LAN, and IS integration solutions are evolving in many companies despite the complexity, but often with some unnecessary pain due to misunderstanding the difference in approaches to solutions. The pressure to integrate the workstations into the network is getting so intense that even IS executives who are not normally interested in "pioneering" untested technology are getting far more comfortable in making short term technology decisions. These executives now feel that if they pick an evolutionary technology, there is sufficient hardware and software innovation and price pressure that they will be able to buy their way out should they pick the wrong horse(s).

Some of the IS executives are using judo by picking NetWare as their enterprise network integration vehicle, leveraging the user momentum. They also view this as a relatively safe solution. The perception of safety comes from the sheer number of organizations that have NetWare installed, the number of vendors that support it, the pay-as-you-go approach to buying the functions, and the number of skills available to fix a problem. Another compelling reason is that it is already installed and just needs a little tweaking.

> **NetWare is often the safest choice for integrating your enterprise network independent of what level of integration you have selected.**

It was intended that this book provide some insights, information, and considerations so that readers can effectively and efficiently meet their corporate tactical and strategic goals of integrating the workstations into the enterprise network using NetWare.

To this end, I have identified many of the current management challenges that IS faces; I have introduced the breadth of management options and capabilities that NetWare brings; and then I focused on some of the key areas that require attention and some technical understanding as to how NetWare applies.

The material was presented in a blended manner that mixes concepts and reality. The emphasis was on those areas that I have heard were of most concern or where there was least understanding.

My premise throughout the book is that the overall management objective is to maximize business responsiveness and minimize short-term and longer-term risk. The more detailed sections are intended to provide some specifics in order to fill any gaps.

Experience to date indicates that:

- It is important to define the boundaries of an enterprise network and then put a strategy in place that allows success while still being responsive to the customer base

- Novell's NetWare fills many of the gaps, but using it doesn't require a strategic decision

- Lots of folks are looking at how to integrate workstations into the enterprise network, and NetWare appears to be providing solutions

- NetWare and NetWare-associated products are being used to unobtrusively integrate workstations into the enterprise network, and can reduce the risk in the integration process

  A winning strategy:
  Invests in leveraging the workers (users)
  Is based on mass consumer base
  Provides support where it fits best
  Sets the pace for transparent transition
  Uses *Judo*
  Values the worker momentum and adjusts to it

- The CIO focus is on the business and how to orchestrate and *apply technology* to make and keep the company competitive. At the very least the CIO is focused on balancing the strategic with the tactical

- The IS organization is focused on the operational aspects of balancing the existing with the new

- The user support organizations are focused on pragmatically supporting the department's day-to-day needs, specifically services that are under their control

- In general the IS business goals of the early to mid 1990s are:

  Responsiveness to the customer requests
  Customer satisfaction levels
  Flexibility

These goals can be relatively simple or very difficult, depending on the enterprise network boundaries supported and the services and management tools used

- The yours, mine, and ours model works best

  Most companies are using it either formally or informally
  Using workstations, physical LANs, routers, and NetWare
  Users and the LAN supervisors in charge of their destiny
  The user departments are paying their way

- Departments need and want help with audit readiness, data backup/recovery, and security

- Technology and standards trends

  TCP/IP appears to be general interoperability interface
  IPX/SPX appears to be the dominant LANs protocol
  SNA networks are not going away
  Extensive use of multiprotocol routers for networks
  Ethernet and Token Ring distinctions are disappearing
  Windows is the dominant user workstation environment
  OS/2 is the platform of choice for commercial applications
  Both central and distributed support tools will be required

- NetWare technologies are pervasive

  Provide departmental and enterprise network tools

- IS should invest in:

  Flexible and transparent interfaces
  Transparent remote support services
  Data backup/archive and recovery
  Network accounting and security
  Industry-driven tools and knowledge

20.3 Conclusion

NetWare qualifies as a major component of the workstation and enterprise network integration. The NetWare product line and the many associated third party products provide a solid and responsive base to effectively support a yours, mine, and ours enterprise network infrastructure. This infrastructure allows the enterprise network to be more responsive to the business needs, while becoming more influential in the overall enterprise network area.

Based on what I have seen in the industry and learned from numerous LAN and enterprise executives and technicians, a winning integration strategy:

- Invests in leveraging the workers (users)
- Is based on mass consumer base
- Follows the money
- Provides support where it fits best
- Sets the pace for transparent transition
- Uses *Judo*
- Values the worker momentum and adjusts
- Includes NetWare as a lever to integrate workstations into the enterprise network (see Fig. 20-3)

Figure 20-3 NetWare Supports Many Directions

Bibliography

Anderson, Robert E., PCS, NetWare, and Ethernet: Getting It Together: News 3x/400, For AS/400 and S/3x Professionals, November, 1993 pp. 165-172.

Baker, Steven, Serving Up NetWare: LAN, The Local Area Network Magazine, December, 1992 pp. 65-70.

Bochenski, Barbara, Implementing Production Quality Client/Server Systems: John Wiley & Sons, Inc., Somerset, N.J., 1994.

Bolles, Gary, A., NetWare Global Messaging: Where the Message Is NetWare: Network Computing, a CMP Publication, Computing in a Network Environment, May 1992 p. 20.

Burgard, Mike, Unixware Links Unix with NetWare: UnixWorld, McGraw-Hill's Magazine of Open Computing, August, 1993 pp. 99-102.

Carr, Jim, Network Operating Systems Novell Upgrades Netware for the Enterprise: Data Communications, McGraw-Hill's Networking Technology Magazine, June 1992 p. 64.

Clarke, David James IV, The Complete NetWare Construction Kit: John Wiley & Sons, Inc., Somerset, N.J., 1993.

Cohen, Frederick B., A Short Course on Computer Viruses, Second Edition: John Wiley & Sons, Inc., Somerset, N.J., 1994.

Conrad, James W., Handbook of Communications Systems Management, Second Edition: Auerbach Publications, A Division of Warren Gorham Lamont, Boston, Mass., 1991.

Conrad, James W., Handbook of Communications Systems Management, 1992-93 Yearbook: Auerbach Publications, A Division of Warren Gorham Lamont, Boston, Mass., 1992.

Conrad, James W., Handbook of Communicatons Systems Management, 1993-94 Yearbook: Auerbach Publications, A Division of Warren Gorham Lamont, Boston, Mass., 1993.

Connectivity Solutions, InterConnections: Computer, September, 1993 p. 98.

Currid, Cheryl, Networking with Personal NetWare: John Wiley & Sons, Inc., Somerset, N.J., 1993.

Cypser, R. J., Communications for Cooperating Systems OSI, SNA, and TCP/IP: Addison Wesley Publishing Co., Reading, Mass., 1991.

Day, Michael, Enterprise Series Downsizing to NetWare: New Riders Publishing, Carmel, Ind., 1992.

Dion, Kim, IBS AS/400 Connectivity Using NetWare for SAA: Novell Research, NetWare Application Notes, January 1993, Version 1.3.

Freed, Les and Derfler, Frank J., Jr., PC Magazine Guide to Using NetWare: Ziff-Davis Press, Emeryville, Calif., 1991.

Goglia, Patricia A., Testing Client/Server Applications: John Wiley & Sons, Inc., Somerset, N.J., 1993.

Grant, David and Robinson, Jim, Test Drive NetWare 4.0: LAN, The The Network Solutions Magazine, July 1993, pp. 138-150.

Greenfield, David, Novell Hub Management: How Big a Boost?: Data Communications, McGraw-Hill's Networking Technology Magazine, January 1992, pp. 39-42.

Guruge, Anura, Adding SNA Congnizance to Bridge/Routers: Enterprise Systems Journal, November 1992, pp. 30-37.

Hall, Eric, Cutting SNA Infrastructures with NetWare SNA v1.3: Network Computing, a CMP Publication, April 1993, pp. 148-151.

Herron, John and Ruiz, Ben, Lan Systems Inc, Netware 4.0: The Work Behind the Network: Data Communications, McGraw-Hill's Networking Technology Magazine, September 1993, pp. 85-92.

Heywood, Drew, et al., Enterprise Series Connectivity: Local Area Networks: New Riders Publishing, Carmel, Ind. 1992.

Heywood, Peter, Bringing SNMP to End-Node Management: Data Communications, McGraw-Hill's Networking Technology Magazine, July 1992, pp. 47-48.

Hoskins, Jim, IBM RISC System/6000 A Business Perspective: John Wiley & Sons, Inc., N.Y. 1991.

Hurwicz, Mike, All Roads Lead to NetWare: LAN, The Network Solutions Magazine, May 1993, pp. 67-73.

International Business Machines Corporation, DFDSM: General Information, Release 1, Tucson, Ariz., October 1992.

International Business Machines Corporation, IBM International Technical Support Centers DFDSM Presentation Guide: San Jose, Calif., August 1992.

Introducing NetWare Global MHS 2.0: Inside NetWare, A Publication of The Cobb Group, Tips & Techniques for Novell NetWare, Versions 2.2, 3.11, & 4.0., October 1993, Vol. 2, No. 10, pp. 12-13.

Jamar, Scott, Product Line Manager, Internetworking Products Division, NetWare Integrated Communications Interface, Novell, Inc. San Jose, Calif., April 29, 1993, Marketing Requirement Document Version.1.0.

Jander, Mary, Netware's SNMP Debut: Something to Grow On: Data Communications, Lan Interconnect, McGraw-Hill's Networking Technology Magazine, March 1992 pp. 89-90.

Krochmal, Jim and Morris, Larry, Enterprise Series LAN Applications - Client/Server Databases: New Riders Publishing , Carmel, Ind., 1993.

Lamb, Jason, Securing NetWare: LAN The Networking Solutions Magazine, October 1993, pp. 91-98.

LAN Resource Extension and service/MVS, IBM Corp, 1993, Document No. GC24-5625.

LAN Resource Extension and service/VM, IBM Corp, 1993, Document No. GC24-5618.

Martin, James, Local Area Networks Architectures and Implementations: Prentice-Hall, Englewood Cliffs, N.J., 1989.

Molta, Dave, Novell's Burst Mode IPX: Tuning Up the Old Train: Network Computing, A CMP Publication, June 1993, pp. 162-168.

NetWare 4.01 Security Enhancement: Inside NetWare, A Publication of The Cobb Group, Tips & Techniques for Novell NetWare Versions 2.2, 3.11, & 4.0, November 1993, Vo. 2, No. 11, p. 16.

NetWare 3270 Host Printer Services Administration Guide: Novell, Inc. July 9, 1992, Part No. 100-001390-001.

NetWare Buyer's Guide, Novell, Inc., 1994, Part No. 482-000020.

NetWare Communication Services Manager Guide, Novell, Inc., April 14, 1992, Part No. 100-000733-001.

NetWare Concepts: Novell, Inc., August 22, 1992, Part No. 100-001417-001.

NetWare Hub Technology Overview: Novell, Inc., October 1991.

NetWare Lite, NetWare Peer to Peer Operating System: Novell, Inc., For NetWare Lite V1.1, Part No. 100-001003-002.

NetWare MultiProtocol Router Configuring for Performance: Novell, Inc., July 1992, Part No. 462-000308-001.

NetWare Print Services: Novell, Inc., August 24, 1992, Part No. 100-001419-001.

NetWare Reference Guide for NetView Operators: Novell, Inc., December 1992, Part No. 100-001242-002.

NetWare for SAA Installation and Troubleshooting Update: Novell, Inc., Instructors Guide, Course 720, Revision 1.01, Part No. 100-001283-002.

NetWare for SAA Services Manager Guide, Novell, Inc., 1992., Part No. 100-001667-001.

Nye, R. Lynn, Jr., An Internetworking Chat: IBM Internet Journal, September, 1993, pp. 20-26.

Palley, Karyn, NetWare Security: NetWare Connection, November/December 1993, pp. 28-31.

Protecting Your NetWare 4.0 Investment: Inside NetWare, A Publication of The Cobb Group, Tips & Techniques for Novell NetWare Versions 2.2, 3.11, & 4.0, September 1993, Vol. 2, No. 9, p. 12.

Renaud, Paul E., Introduction to Client/Server Systems, A Practical Guide for Systems Professionals: John Wiley & Sons, Inc., Somerset, N.J., 1993.

Rosenfeld, David, Token-Ring Source Routing with Novell NetWare: Network Computing, A CMP Publication, October 1991. pp. 96-98.

Rothfeder, Jeffrey, Holes in the Net: Corporate Computing, May 1993, pp. 114-120.

Ruley, John D., et al, Networking Windows NT: John Wiley & Sons, Inc., Somerset N.J., 1993.

Salamone, Salvatore, A Magic Bullet for Netware Viruses: Data Communications, McGraw-Hill's Technology Magazine, December,1992, pp. 45-46.

Salamone, Salvatore, DEC and Netware Share and Share Alike: Data Communications, Lan Interconnect, McGraw-Hill's Networking Technology Magazine, November 21, 1993, pp. 41-43.

Salamone, Salvatore, WAN Links for Netware? No Problem: Data Communications, McGraw-Hill's Technology Magazine, October 1993, pp. 41-42.

Schneier, Bruce, Applied Cryptography, Protocols, Algorithms, and Source Code in C: John Wiley & Sons, Inc., Somerset, N.J., 1993.

Sheldon, Tom, Novell NetWare 4, The Complete Reference: Osborne, McGraw-Hill, Berkeley, Calif., 1993.

Sheldon, Tom, Novell NetWare 386, The Complete Reference: Osborne McGraw-Hill, Berkeley, Calif., 1990.

Siyan, Karanjit, NETWARE The Professional Reference: New Riders Publishing, Carmel, Ind., 1992.

Slone, John P. and Drinan, Ann, Handbook of Local Area Networks: Auerbauch Publications, A division of Warren Gorham Lamont, Boston, Mass., 1991.

Slone, John P. and Drinan, Ann, Handbook of Local Area Networks, 1992-93 Yearbook: Auerbach Publications, A Division of Warren Gorham Lamont, Boston, Mass., 1992.

Slone, John P. and Drinan, Ann, Handbook of Local Area Networks, 1993-94 Yearbook, Auerbach Publications, A Division of Warren Gorham Lamont, Boston, Mass., 1993.

Smith, Patrick and BSG, Professional Reference Series Client/Server Computing, All-in-One Reference for Total Systems Development!: Sams Publishing, Carmel, Ind., 1992.

St. Clair, Melanie, Routers Become Platform Independent: Lan Times, McGraw-Hill, An Industry Update Written Independently of the Lan Times Editorial Staff and Sponsored by Novell, Inc., San Mateo, Calif..

The Host as Data Server Using LANRES and Novell NetWare: IBM Corp., July 1993, Document No. GG24-4069.

The NetWare Global Network: Novell, Inc., 1992, Part No. 461-000221-001.

Thomas, Richard, RMT Connections, Ltd., Burst Mode Boosts Netware's Wide-Area Acumen: Data Communications, Lan Interconnect, McGraw-Hill's Networking Technology Magazine, September 21, 1992, pp. 63-70.

Tolly, Kevin and Roque, Nito, Interlab, Netware and Mainframes: A More Perfect Union: Data Communications, Lan Interconnect, McGraw-

Hill's Networking Technology Magazine, September 21, 1992, pp. 73-76.

Ziegler, Kurt, Jr., A Distributed Information System Study, IBM Systems Journal: International Business Machines Corporation, Volume 18/Number 3, Armonk, N.Y., 1979.

Ziegler, Kurt, Jr., Distributed Computing and the Mainframe Leveraging Your Investments: Wiley -Interscience, N.Y., 1991.

Index

O

software encryption, 357
software inventory, 371
software levels, 325
software maintenance, 16
software metering, 30, 326
software packaging, 327
software registration, 358
software theft, 340
software tracking, 357
spoofing, 348
Sprint, 6
SPX, *see* IPX/SPX
SQL, 59, 148
SQL Net TCP/IP, 286
SQL Router, 296
SQL Windows, 171, 296
SQLBase, 170
SQLServer for NetWare, 175
SQLServer for NetWare, 170
Standard Message Format (SMF), 165
star topology, 219
strategic weapons, 49
Stoned, 352
strategic decision, 379
subsystems, 256, 267
Sun Solaris, 43
SunOS, 43
superservers, 245, 268
superstructure, 99
support boundaries, 68
    see also enterprise network
    boundaries
support infrastructure, 201
support staffs, 94
switched networks, 115, 174
Sybase, 232
Sybase Net-Library, 286
SynOptics, 39
systems management, 187
Systems Network Architecture (SNA), 24

T

T1 link, 35, 174, 215

TCP/IP, xii, 8, 24, 45, 59, 102, 104,
    126, 152, 159 - 160, 163 - 164, 166,
    169, 174, 184, 186 - 187, 193 - 197,
    199, 229, 244, 256 - 257, 261,
    285 - 286, 289 - 291, 297 - 299, 305,
    307, 309 - 311, 313 - 316, 320 - 321,
    356, 374, 380
TCP/IP Interoperability, 284
TCP/IP networks, 193, 195
TCP/IP NLM, 284
TCP/IP WAN services, 174
technical support, 51
TelAPI, 285
telephony, 40
Telnet, 195, 287
    see also TCP/IP
terminal, 120 - 121, 188 - 189
terminal emulation, 8 - 10, 80, 121, 128,
    138 - 139, 189, 266, 292, 294
terminal identification, 338
terminal location, 338
terminal server, 125
terminology, xv - xvi, 27, 61, 277
third-party programs, 23
Timbuktu, 117, 223
    see also remote control
TN3270, 195 - 196, 285, 288 - 289, 299
Token Ring, 25, 32, 132, 137, 149, 159,
    174, 193, 208 - 209, 215, 217, 221,
    244, 261, 278 - 279, 289, 293, 307,
    380
Token Ring Adapter, 105
tools, 240, 270 - 271, 323, 326, 343
traces, 320
trade-offs, xiii
training, 59
Trojan Horse, 348 - 349
trouble shooting, 30
Trustees, 363
TSA, 205 - 206
TSO, *see* IBM MVS TSO
Twin, 352